OUR NATION BETRAYED

From Impeachment to Infinite War

By
Garland Favorito

BLACK FOREST PRESS
San Diego, California
July, 2002
First Revised Edition

OUR NATION BETRAYED

From Impeachment
to
Infinite War

By
Garland Favorito

PUBLISHED IN THE UNITED STATES OF AMERICA
BY
BLACK FOREST PRESS
P.O.Box 6342
Chula Vista, CA 91909-6342

DEDICATION

For Linda Ives, who has valiantly fought the mutually assured destruction political policy, in hopes that she will one day attain justice for those who murdered her son, Kevin, and his friend, Don Henry;

For the family of Larry McDonald (D, 7th-GA), my former Congressman, who gave his life on KAL 007 for our freedom before I even understood what it meant to be free;

And, for the many American patriots who spent their personal time and money attempting to ensure that equal justice applies to all Americans, including the President of the United States.

And, for the few brave American souls willing to risk ridicule and shame to expose the war on terror for what it really is.

Disclaimer

This document is an original work of the author. It may include reference to information commonly known or freely available to the general public. Any resemblance to other published information is purely coincidental. The author has in no way attempted to use material not of his own origination, and has signed a personal Confidentiality Agreement stating that all of his statements and claims have been accurately authenticated and substantiated as truth. Black Forest Press disclaims any association with or responsibility for the ideas, opinions or facts as expressed by the author of this book.

Printed in the United States of America
Library of Congress
Cataloging-in-Publication

ISBN:1-58275-100-5

Copyright © May 2000, July 2002 by Garland Favorito

CONTENTS

The final three chapters are epilogues to the original book version

FOREWORD

It has been my privilege to know Garland Favorito for nearly six years and I have found him to be an American patriot in the purest sense. He has worked timelessly at his own expense researching and studying to decipher essential facts often overlooked or excluded by the establishment media.

Garland is a citizen activist, that is, he works as a computer analyst or programmer during the day and in his spare time organizes rallies, networks with other patriots and writes articles. He is also a frequent guest on talk shows; lobbies for righteous causes and gives his time and personal funds to those causes he believes are worthy.

Garland cares not about political correctness. His sole purpose in writing this book is not to please the political bosses, but instead hold them accountable for their numerous criminal and treasonous acts.

Garland provides a fresh and insightful look (much from first hand experience) at how a relatively small group of dedicated Americans fighting for truth impeached the most powerful leader in the world all the while their real motives were withheld from the American public.

We must never forget that the freedoms, we as Americans take for granted, were bought with the sacrifice, blood and courage of our forefathers.

This book hopefully will inspire you to continue the noble fight to keep America free.

Pat Matrisciana

ACKNOWLEDGMENTS

The following are resources, nearly all of whom I have met, who deserve special thanks for their work:

- Pat Matrisciana who courageously filmed government corruption of a magnitude never before seen by Americans;

- Bill Triplett, Ed Timperlake and other Congressional investigators who refused to remain silent while the politicians sold our country to the Communist Chinese military;

- Willis Carto, who survived attacks by the CIA, FBI, IRS and ATF to expose the war on terror and publish American Free Press articles that other media outlets would not dare to print;

- Phylis and Victoria Collier who are carrying on the legacy of Votescam authors, Jim and Ken Collier, in exposing the most corrupt bi-partisan scandal in America;

- Daniel Hopsicker who provided photographs, documents and witnesses proving that drug trafficker Barry Seal, was actually a CIA operative working for George H.W. Bush;

- Jayna Davis, the former KFOR-TV reporter who amassed undisputed facts identifying potential Middle Eastern acoomplices in the Oklahoma City bombing

- Chris Ruddy who made dedicated efforts to report the evidence that indicated Vince Foster was murdered;

- Michael Ruppert, From the Wilderness publisher and former LAPD narcotics officer who confronted CIA Director Deutch during an L.A. town hall meeting about agency involvement in drug trafficking;

- Col. Bo Gritz, whose dedication to the Prisoner of War recovery effort led him to discover one of America's darkest and best kept secrets: CIA drug trafficking;

- Paul Weyrich, founder of many valuable organizations, who produced real investigative reporting with *"American Investigator"* for America's Voice TV;

- Sara Flounders, Brian Becker and the International Action Center authors, who reported from around the world, the evidence of NATO atrocities committed against Yugoslavia;

- John McManus and all the wonderful people at the John Birch Society, who endure constant character assassination for exposing the traitors in our government;

- Will Grigg and all the intriguing journalists at *The New American* magazine, who exposed fascinating information not available to the general American public;

- Ramsey Clark, who persisted in attempting to hold accountable those within the American government responsible for the slaughters in Waco and Yugoslavia;

- Joe and Elizabeth Farah who opened a gateway of previously unavailable information with *World Net Daily*;

- Dr Gene Shroder and his associates, whose research work into the origin and history of unconstitutional executive orders has helped prevent tyranny on America;

- Jim Robinson and all Free Republic members who exchange vital information through their web site;

- Larry Klayman and Judicial Watch, who exposed Chinese Communist infiltration of Clinton / Gore campaigns and the DNC;

- Jerry Seper and the dedicated columnists at the *Washington Times*, who were proven factually correct time and time again, one Congressional investigation after another;

- Jim Agresti of *JustFacts.com* and the talented people of *Black Forest Press* who turned a pipe dream into reality.

- My mother, Dorothy Hudson, whose wealth of historical information gave me the initial incentive to write this book.

PREFACE

During the decade of the 90s I underwent a transformation from complete political naïveté to a state of learning things that sometimes I wish I did not know. As the depth and breadth of corruption in the Clinton administration became evident, I decided to join the impeachment movement.

However, I was surprised when opposing House Republican leaders kept serious evidence of the crimes that originated the impeachment movement out of the Articles of Impeachment. I was further stunned when Senate Republican leaders set up trial procedures to ensure that hostile witnesses and damaging evidence against the President would not be heard at his trial.

At that time, I knew something was rotten in the American government and I decided to find out what it was. It didn't take long before I had uncovered plenty of existing research for what had corrupted and compromised the Republican leaders. This détente of mutually assured destruction that paralyzes the American form of government is so threatening to our future that I knew I had to write this book to tell the story.

The intent of the book is:

- To document the astounding evidence of Clinton administration corruption collected in many Congressional investigations and other sources but not readily available to the public;

- To explain how major media organizations distorted political news to protect Bill Clinton and manipulate public opinion to implement their own agenda;

- To detail the incredible cover-up that the Republican leadership established to keep Bill Clinton in office and explain the real reasons behind it.

- To illustrate how citizens like me can awaken, get involved and make a real difference in protecting their freedom and preserving the American form of government that made us the most powerful nation on the face of the earth.

As a citizen author, I have assembled evidence from many different researchers who, I believe, provide accurate factual assessments. If you find the level of current government corruption too hard to fathom, I simply ask that you consider the evidence, verify it for accuracy and then reach your own conclusion. But please hurry because we are running out of time. The Bush Administration and Republican oriented Congress have implemented specific legislation and executive orders that will soon negate our right to vote and remove many of our rights as U.S. citizens. The two Epilogue chapters will explain the new threats we face.

INTRODUCTION

This book presents overwhelming evidence that President Bill Clinton and his circle of power were involved in criminal activity in Arkansas, treason and bribery with the Communist Chinese government, and abuse of government agencies like the IRS and FBI, which were used to persecute political adversaries. Much of the evidence presented was actually collected in Congressional investigations but not used in the Articles of Impeachment by "opposition" Republican leaders who were shackled with their own corruption, including specific involvment in CIA drug trafficking.

Many people made personal sacrifices in an attempt to hold Bill Clinton accountable to the same standards of justice that apply to other American citizens, including:

- Pat Matrisciana, who produced unprecedented videos that documented government corruption and awoke the American citizens;

- Howard Phillips, who assembled the Coalition for a Congressional Impeachment Inquiry and remained determined to fight for our Constitutional principles during five long years;

- Bill Dannemeyer, the former Congressman who used his experience, contacts and knowledge to pursue impeachment doggedly on his own time and at his own expense;

- Bob Barr (R, 7th-GA), who mustered enough courage to confront the Washington, D.C. power structure by introducing H. Res. 304, the Presidential Impeachment Inquiry;

- Larry Klayman, the Judicial Watch founder, who took on the U.S. Department of Justice and became the only real independent counsel in Washington;

- Jim Robinson, the Free Republic founder, who circumvented a corrupted national media by proving he could rally thousands of people to a critical cause through the Internet.

Despite sincere, dedicated efforts of these individuals and thousands of others, the Republican Congressional leaders decided to protect Bill Clinton. Instead of presenting the serious evidence and conducting a standard impeachment trial, which would have surely resulted in conviction, House Republican leaders suppressed that evidence, and Senate Republican leaders sabotaged the trial so that most of the facts would never be heard by the American public.

Immediately after the trial, Yugoslavia became the fourth country to fall victim to impeccably timed bombs ordered by Bill Clinton during the peak of one his scandals. The bombing killed 2000 innocent Yugoslavian civilians and displaced hundreds of thousands of Kosovars who we were allegedly trying to help. It completely diverted national attention from the release of the Cox Report, which documented devastating treasonous administration policies. The report detailed how the administration allowed the Communist Chinese military access to prohibited dual use military technology and precious nuclear secrets. Previous congressional investigations determined that the Communist Chinese military paid for that access by funneling millions of dollars in illegal campaign contributions to the Clinton / Gore campaigns and the Democrat National Committee.

Despite these offenses, the Republican leadership was ultimately paralyzed during the impeachment by the need to conceal several worldwide CIA drug trafficking operations controlled by former President George Bush. Bill Clinton took beginning steps to reveal this dark secret immediately after the House Judiciary Committee voted to begin the impeachment inquiry. Had Republicans seriously attempted to remove him, President Bill Clinton was capable of revealing as much of this secret as necessary to devastate the year 2000 Republican presidential candidacy of the former President's son, George W. Bush. Upon election, George W. Bush quickly moved to increase worldwide CIA drug operations dramatically by implementing a massive, misdirected war on terror that threatens the very foundation of our freedom. This book tells the incredible story. Buckle your seat belt and dig in.

I
The Real Impeachment Movement

CHAPTER ONE
MY AWAKENING

THE PLAYERS EMERGE

It was the summer of 1988 and the Democrats had come to my hometown of Atlanta to hold their national convention and select nominees for the upcoming Presidential elections. Their eventual candidate, Massachusetts Governor, Michael Dukakis, would take on then Vice President George Bush, who was completing two terms under President Ronald Reagan, the most popular president in my lifetime.

The individual who gave the nomination speech was a governor from Arkansas named Bill Clinton. His speech, which was supposed to be about 15 minutes, lasted approximately 52 minutes. Some of the crowd waved white handkerchiefs of surrender while he was talking, and many cheered when he said "In conclusion...". That was the first time most of America got to see Bill Clinton. Little did I or anyone else outside of Arkansas know the about the evidence trail of money laundering, drug trafficking, embezzlement, extortion and illicit sex that Bill Clinton had already left in his state.

At the convention, Dukakis presented his running mate for Vice President, Texan Lloyd Bentsen. Although the Dukakis / Bentzen ticket was unsuccessful, Bentzen was appointed as Secretary of the Treasury by Bill Clinton when he became President. On February 28, 1993, the month after Bill Clinton was sworn in, the Treasury Department's Bureau of Alcohol Tobacco and Firearms (ATF) attacked the Branch Davidian church near Waco, Texas, killing six Davidians and four ATF agents.

A letter from Assistant Treasury Secretary of Enforcement, Christopher Cuyler to Michael Langan indicated that the ATF knew the Davidians were "Seventh Day Adventists" and that the raid would be conducted by the "...ATF, assisted by state local and military authorities..." in conflict with the Posse Comitatus act. The attack eventually led to the deaths of 80 more Davidians when the entire complex was destroyed by the FBI and military personnel on April 19, 1993.

In an attempt to investigate the initial event, Bentzen selected former Philadephia Police Commissioner, Willie Williams, former Justice Department attorney Henry Ruth and former Philadephia Inquirer editor Edward Guthman. All were involved in the tactical operation, investigation, cover-up or reporting for the 1985 Philadelphia city sponsored firebombing of a MOVE house that resulted in the destruction of nearly full city block.

One historically significant occurrence of that 1988 convention was a stirring speech by John F. Kennedy Jr., son of President John F. Kennedy, who was assassinated on Nov. 22, 1963, in an event still cloaked in the secrecy of sealed government files. John Kennedy JR's life would also conclude in an unusual death 36 years after his father's when his plane crashed neared Martha's Vineyard with his wife, Carolyn, and sister-in-law, Lauren Bessette, aboard.

The national news media would repeatedly imply that Kennedy was a somewhat reckless, inexperienced pilot, who was flying in a dark haze without an instrument rating certification. In reality, good visibility allowed visual flight rules to be in effect, Kennedy was within sight of the island, he had sterling references from his flight instructors and he had flown over 300 hours when only 40 were needed for an instrumentation license. By the time of his death, I would realize that this reporting was just one more example in a stream of false and distorted politically related information generated by the national news media.

Like most Americans, I had little or no interest in politics or the inner workings of the American government. When I moved to Georgia, I entered the Marietta district of Larry McDonald, a Democrat whom I quickly grew to admire because he kept in touch with the citizens. I remember receiving a flyer from him explaining how he had voted on ten key issues. Since I agreed with most of his positions, it gave me a level of comfort that my interests were being taken care of in Washington without my being involved.

We lost Larry on the ill-fated flight, KAL 007, that was supposedly shot down by the Soviet Union in September of 1983. Almost 15 years later, I began to learn the unusual details behind the downing of that plane described in *Incident at*

Sakhalin and other books. I started to realize how valuable Larry McDonald had been to us as citizens, and I invited his widow, Cathy McDonald, to be a co-host of the first National Town Hall on Impeachment in Marietta, Georgia, on March 17, 1998. By then, I discovered that all Congressmen are not like Larry McDonald and that citizens must become involved in their government to protect their own freedom.

Before the KAL 007 plane crash, I got married and moved to Stone Mountain, Georgia. During this time my civic involvement was basically limited to occasional editorials that I would send to the *Atlanta Journal Constitution*. I usually refuted statements from a previous editorial since I had little motivation to originate my own viewpoint. I kept my letters concise and logical while trying to make a good counterpoint. I achieved about an 80 percent success rate at getting my letters published. I was even invited to several *Atlanta Journal* editorial dinners for letter writers and met the editor, Durwood McCallister, whom I admired. However, much later after he retired, my editorials turned to issues of honest government, and my success ratio dropped to about 20 percent.

At Stone Mountain we were represented by another Democrat named Elliot Levitas. I met him and my future Congressman at my first *Atlanta Journal* editorial dinner. I attended several annual editorial dinners, but this one was particularly interesting because the other Congressman in attendance was Newt Gingrich, who had been recently elected to represent a western area of Georgia. A few years later we moved into what is now the 6th District of Georgia, and Newt Gingrich became my Congressman when he also moved into that district and won the seat. Gingrich moved after his original district was gerrymandered under the leadership of the nation's longest running State House Speaker, Tom Murphy, who apparently did not relish the thought of Newt as his Congressman. Gingrich would go on to be elected Speaker of the U.S. House and hold that position when the House impeached President Bill Clinton.

Before we moved from Stone Mountain, Elliott Levitas was defeated by Republican, Pat Swindall. Ironically, Pat Swindall was indicted three weeks before the 1988 elections on charges of perjury, the same charge passed in the Articles of Impeachment against Bill Clinton by the House of

Representatives. He was later convicted after being forced to resign from Congress. The case centered around an IRS sting operation that could have easily been considered entrapment. The perjury charge resulted from his statements involving his lack of knowledge about the source of a mortgage loan for his home. Compared with the standards subsequently set by President Bill Clinton, it was relatively trivial, but it proved to be historically significant. The prosecutor was a U.S. attorney who later won the Congressional district represented by my former Congressman, Larry McDonald. I would come to know him as Bob Barr, the Congressman who filed the H. Res. 304 Presidential Impeachment Inquiry and went on to be a House manager in the Senate impeachment trial of President Bill Clinton.

THE 1992 ELECTION

Bill Clinton left Atlanta in 1988 with many believing he was the buffoon of the Democrat National Convention. He redeemed himself somewhat with an appearance on *The Johnny Carson Show,* where he seemed to be a likable guy who may simply be a little long winded. I did not expect him to play a major role in politics again, but much to my amazement, he was nominated for President in 1992 by my own governor, Zell Miller. Miller was a successful governor of Georgia who also mentored his successor, current governor, Roy Barnes. I would later find out that Barnes, while in the Georgia House in 1996, actually opposed an exact duplicate of his own amendment to pass a Georgia fingerprint law. The law supported a national ID scheme to standardize all state drivers' licenses biometrically. The scheme was apparently based on a clause inserted by Senator Dianne Feinstein into the 1996 Illegal Immigration and Reform Act, a part of the overall Defense bill.

Zell Miller was able to make the successful nomination after Bill Clinton received some unusual help, unbeknownst to me and the rest of America. His public perception was improved by a *60 Minutes* broadcast designed to doctor his negative image from an affair with Gennifer Flowers. His financial saving grace came in the form of a $3,000,000 loan from the Worthen Bank. Worthen Bank was co-owned by a heavy financial supporter of both political parties named

Jackson Stephens and the soon to be famous, Lippo Group. It would be years before intelligence reports revealed that the Lippo Group also had a banking partnership with China Resources, "an agent of political, military and economic espionage" for the Communist Chinese government according to DIA and Senate Governmental Affairs investigators.

Although a presidential nominee usually tries to balance the ticket, geographically and politically, Bill Clinton chose former Tennessee Senator, Al Gore, as his Vice Presidential running mate. It was a strange choice since they were from adjoining southern states. Six years later congressional investigation evidence would show that both independently received significant illegal financing from the Communist Chinese Government.

After he was nominated, Bill Clinton was speaking on television once as I watched with some good friends from Vietnam who did not have the privilege of being raised here. They mentioned how deceptive Bill Clinton acted when he spoke. I had noticed how everything he said was carefully planned and rehearsed, even as he was saying it. He never spoke from the heart. I wondered why my friends could see that clearly, and other people who were born and raised in America could not. Perhaps his biggest deception of all came during his candidacy when Bill Clinton promised "the most ethical administration in the history of the Republic".

Former Vice President Bush won the Presidency in 1988 and became popular, even with opposition party leaders, after the Gulf War, which started when Iraqi troops moved into Kuwait. An alliance of nations using a plan named Desert Storm, drove the Iraqi army out of Kuwait with a minimum loss of life, despite severe threats of chemical and biological warfare. Much later, I learned that before the invasion by Saddam Hussein, American Ambassador, April Glaspie, told the Iraqis that "We have no interest in your border dispute with Kuwait".

Years later, after meeting Capt. Joyce Riley and Dr. Len Horowitz, I also would learn that the war against Iraq was not as successful as we were led to believe. The death toll continued to climb after the war was over while the Defense Department denied the existence of Gulf War Syndrome. The United Nations started chemical and biological weapons inspections in Iraq after the war, and they continued for years.

These inspections would eventually play a surprising part in the impeachment process.

By 1992, the economy was tight, and President Bush's popularity was slipping because he lacked no clear domestic economic policy. Democrats were complaining that unemployment was around seven percent even though inflation and interest rates were around five percent or less. I remembered when Reagan and Bush took office inflation peaked around 13 percent, interest rates had zoomed to 19 percent and unemployment was over 10 percent. The unemployment, inflation and interest rates combined into what was called the "financial misery index", which was at an all time high.

Despite these facts, Bush only mentioned their success in reducing the financial misery index once in the very last debate. In fact, he totally distanced himself from former President Ronald Reagan and rarely mentioned his name throughout the campaign. I found this unbelievably strange since Reagan was immensely popular. I would not understand until years later of the conflict and potential reasons for their distance and the unpopularity of George Bush even within his own party.

During this time, former IBM salesman and EDS founder, Ross Perot, formed a group named United We Stand. He developed a specific agenda, communicated the precise problems that America was facing and entered the Presidential race, making it a three-way contest. Perot inspired citizens and attracted my interest and attention since we were both in the computer business. He actually captured the lead in the polls before resigning while citing Republican dirty tricks planned to ruin his daughter's reputation. In another strange twist, he then decided to re-enter the race after his poll numbers had shrunk. I realized much later that Ross Perot never wanted to be President.

During the campaign, I noticed that Ross Perot constantly attacked George Bush while barely mentioning Bill Clinton. At first, I assumed that it was because Bush was the incumbent, but he strangely continued the trend even when it appeared that Bill Clinton had forged ahead in the polls. It would take years

for me to learn the underlying reasons, involving drug trafficking and POW recovery, as to why Ross Perot despised
George Bush.

Perot's entry into the 1992 race may well have cost Bush
the election. The final numbers were Clinton 43 percent, Bush
38 percent and Perot 19 percent. Bill Clinton was elected
President with the lowest percentage of popular votes since the
Civil War. As a perfect example of media distortion, the *USA
Today* newspaper headlined his victory as a "landslide". Six
years later, when Bill Clinton became the first elected President
to be impeached, the *USA Today* headline instead touted his
"poll ratings surge". These are only a few of the minor media
distortions that those in the impeachment movement would
face for over four years.

MEDIA DISTORTIONS OF THE
JOHN KENNEDY ASSASSINATION

During 1993, my curiosity and interest in government activity began to grow because of the movie JFK. I was one of
the majority of Americans who believed that there had been
more than one gunman in the assassination, but I had no real
details of it. I decided to attend the 30th anniversary of the assassination of John F. Kennedy in Dallas, and I began to learn
how major media organizations could completely and consistently distort facts. The major media organizations had always
told Americans that Lee Harvey Oswald, a lone crazed assassin, fired three shots from the sixth floor of the Texas
School Book Depository in Dallas and killed JFK.

A simple review of the film from Abraham Zapruder clearly
shows that the shot which killed JFK struck him in the right
front temple and had to come from the grassy knoll. No one
ever claimed that Lee Harvey Oswald was on the grassy knoll;
therefore, he could not have possibly killed JFK. In addition,
the famous Altgens photo shows Lee Harvey Oswald standing
in the door of the school book depository as the motorcade is
passing. The identification is unmistakable, despite FBI attempts to convince the public that the individual in the photo
was another person named Billy Lovelady.

The Zapruder film showed that after JFK was hit in the throat, Gov. Connolly turned to see what was wrong and was also hit, then JFK was struck in the right front temple by the third bullet. Gov. Connolly confirmed this sequence of events in testimony before the Warren Commission and House Select Committee. Since the time span of five seconds was too short for one person to have fired all three shots from a manual reload rifle, the Warren Commission concluded that two bullets created all of the wounds to both Connolly and Kennedy. This conclusion required that a single "magic bullet" entered Kennedy's back, turned upward and exited his throat, turned right to enter Gov. Connolly, paused in mid-air for two seconds to account for the time difference between when Kennedy and Connolly were hit, made five more entrance and exit wounds in Gov. Connolly and then appeared in pristine condition on a cot in Parkland Memorial Hospital. The counsel who proposed this magic bullet theory was Arlen Specter, who would eventually become a controversial Senator in the impeachment trial of President Bill Clinton.

MEDIA DISTORTIONS OF THE KING ASSASSINATION

Some light research into the Kennedy assassination at the Georgia Tech and Atlanta libraries led me to the House Select Committee investigation into the assassination of Dr. Martin Luther King. Since he was also from Atlanta, I decided to spend some time researching the general circumstances of his death. Immediately I found a similar distortion of facts by the media. The media claimed that James Earl Ray shot Dr. King in the neck with a single bullet fired from a boarding house a block away and overlooking the Lorraine Motel where Dr. King was staying.

My analysis of investigation evidence matched conclusions that were eventually reached in 1998 expert testimony during the request by James Earl Ray for a new trial. The ballistics expert testimony revealed that the bullet which killed Dr. King "was not of the same lot as the bullets in the five unfired cartridges found associated with the alleged murder weapon". In addition, a spent cartridge found near the crime scene was determined to have been fired from the weapon. The testimony went along way to show that the gun James Earl Ray brought to the scene was not the murder weapon and it confirmed his 30-year contention that he was not the assassin.

Ray was an escaped convict with no known marksmanship expertise. Before the assassination, Ray was funded for over a year to do various types of gun running and other projects for a man he knew only as Raoul. The funds included money to buy a two-year old Mustang and expenses for travel all over the country and to Canada. After the assassination, he traveled back to Canada and received money and passports to London and Portugal. He was caught in London going from Portugal to Belgium. He used as an alias, Eric S. Galt, a Canadian based-intelligence operative who had a top secret security clearance.

In 1977, the House Select Committee on King's assassination resisted nearly all significant efforts to determine who had helped Ray. Ray tried to withdraw his guilty plea three days after being sentenced to life in prison. Eventually Loyd Jowers, who ran Big Ed's Grill beneath the boarding house which was the alleged site used by the assassin, offered to come forward with testimony admitting that he hired a hit man. His involvement was based on orders from reputed mobster Frank Liberto, who, he believed, got his orders out of New Orleans from Carlos Marcello.

Judge Joe Brown was on the verge of granting James Earl Ray a new trial when he was removed from the case after extensive maneuvering by federal officials in Tennessee. Brown, no longer involved in the criminal action request, was eventually rewarded with his own television show. Ray spent 30 years in prison and died in prison without ever receiving a full trial.

Janet Reno, in a phony quest for "accountability", denied the King family the right to waive all criminal prosecution of Jowers in exchange for his testimony. The King family was forced to file a wrongful death civil suit against Jowers to get his testimony on record. In late 1999, more than 30 years after King's death, the King family obtained a small measure of justice when the civil trial jury ruled that Dr. King was killed as a result of a conspiracy, which according to jurors, involved numerous government officials.

MEDIA DISTORTIONS OF THE
ROBERT KENNEDY ASSASSINATION

Since I had researched two of the three major political assassinations of the 60s and was perplexed with what I had found, I decided to review the third, which involved Robert F. Kennedy. Even though his assassination was never investigated by the federal government, I was able to locate books and other information which I expected simply to confirm the original media reports. The media reports had claimed that a lone crazed assassin, Sirhan Sirhan, shot and killed RFK at the Ambassador Hotel in Los Angeles.

The autopsy report and physical evidence showed that RFK was killed by a bullet fired an inch or two away from the back of his head. All witnesses, including the maitre d' who wrestled the gun away from Sirhan, stated that Sirhan was never behind RFK or that close to him. Sirhan fired all eight of his bullets, yet there were at least 10 and possibly as many as 13 bullets fired, based on several independent crime scene analysis conclusions confirmed by one of the investigating FBI agents. Witnesses stated that a man in a security guard uniform, later identified as Thane Eugene Cesar, was behind Robert Kennedy and had drawn his gun drawn.

Cesar was never investigated for involvement in the assassination and his gun was never analyzed. L.A. Police Commission hearings and additional research revealed that 20 key pieces of evidence had been lost missing or destroyed including 2,400 case photographs. The two heads of the special task force that investigated the assassination were CIA operatives on loan to conduct the investigation for the LAPD.

In all three assassinations there appeared to be a federal government cover-up facilitated by the major news media organizations. Therefore, I came to an undeniable conclusion that I could not trust major media organizations to tell me the truth about anything political in nature. However, I was about to get some firsthand, close-up, current experience to validate my conclusion.

MEDIA DISTORTIONS OF THE
REPUBLICAN REVOLUTION

In 1994, Newt Gingrich, the House Minority Whip, adopted many United We Stand platform planks, promised a vote on each issue, put them into a Contract with America and got fellow House Republicans to sign them. For perhaps the first time, voters knew what they were getting ahead of time and could cast their ballots accordingly. The contract was a huge success, sweeping the country with over 70 House seat changes and creating Republican majorities in both the House and Senate.

Since Bob Michael, the previous Republican Minority Leader, was retiring, my Congressman became Speaker of the House while Bob Dole moved from Senate Minority Leader to Senate Majority Leader. In the first 100 days of the new session, the House not only voted on all 10 of the Contract with America planks, but actually passed nine of them. Although some were eventually derailed in the Senate or by a Presidential veto, Newt Gingrich became a hero to many, both locally and nationally.

Since my Congressman was now the Speaker of the House, my interest in government began to peak. One of the first things that I learned was how politicians can lie without conscience.

Since America was awash in a trillion doller debt and billion doller budget deficits, my pet issue, as with so many other Americans, was the balanced budget amendment, which passed the House with a two-thirds majority. I had seen on the Rush Limbaugh show, advertisements from Senate Minority Leader Tom Daschle, stating how he was fighting for a balanced budget amendment. Yet Daschle voted against the amendment, along with other Democrats who had supported a similar amendment when they were still in power. Newly elected Democrat Senator Robert Torricelli, who campaigned for a balanced budget amendment while he was in the House, essentially cast the deciding vote against it.

After the 1996 elections two years later, when Republicans gained the Senate seats needed to pass the amendment, Trent Lott replaced Bob Dole as Majority Leader and never reintroduced the bill even though he had been an advocate of the amendment. I had expected Trent Lott to be a better Senate leader than Bob Dole, but this was only a clue of what was to come. In an additional two years, I would learn how far my expectations were from the truth.

After the first 100 days of the new Congress, Newt Gingrich was on a television special to report that the newly managed, Republican-led House had kept its promise. Dick Gephardt, who went from Majority to Minority Leader after the change in power, followed Newt Gingrich and claimed that the school from where he was speaking was losing its lunch program because of the new leadership commitment to balance the budget. Calls to the school and federal program administrators indecated these charges were false; however, no one in the media ever corrected the facts for the public. I was beginning to learn that it wasn't just Congressmen who were deceptive, but that media organizations could professionally distort political news without anyone's knowing unless they had firsthand knowledge of the circumstances.

One such media distortion occurred when Newt Gingrich appointed Christina Jeffrey as House Historian. I got to meet Christina years later when she ran for Newt's Congressional seat. Christina had suggested that those who are teaching about World War II should also include the Nazi perspective. This was obvious to me because in order to prevent wars you must understand how they start. However, Representative Chuck Schumer, with significant help from the media, falsely portrayed her comments as being anti-Semitic. Gingrich was eventually forced to withdraw her nomination, much to her dismay. Schumer, a Judiciary Committee member who I believe falsely portrayed several other key issues during the impeachment and Waco investigations, eventually became a Senator from New York.

I had expected my Congressman to become a hero for implementing common sense issues like balancing the budget but was frustrated to watch the media consistently portray him as a villain. News articles and reports would appear that implied poor people were going to die if we balanced the budget, even though the budget would still be growing at a rate of one percent per year (instead of five percent). Then, news reports indicated that Medicare and Medicaid would be cut by $270 billion between 1995 and the projected balance year of 2002. In reality, per capita spending was actually increasing from $4,800 to $6,700 per person per year, and this was later negotiated up to $7,200 per year. The "cut" was actually not a cut at all, but an increase of over five percent, yet major news organizations led the American people to believe that the budget was being cut.

Not only did the media attempt to deceive the American people about the balanced budget issue, they began to attack my Congressman simply for mentioning this and other issues. The media used magazine cover stories such as "The Grinch who Stole Christmas" to portray him falsely as some sort of cold, heartless, uncaring individual. In reality, he was almost always promoting local and national charity efforts like Habitat for Humanity, Make a Wish Foundation and an Earning by Learning school reading program.

I was amazed at how the major news media organizations consistently provided false information to the American people. I could understand how a few might be off base because of a liberal bias, but I was witnessing a concerted effort to deceive the American people into supporting a more socialistic agenda. I realized that this was not bias, it was a deliberate, coordinated agenda of deceit that included personal attacks on individuals not conforming to the agenda. I considered the national media organizations as a threat to American freedom and decided that I had to get involved.

I stopped by my Congressman's nearby campaign office and picked up some literature. I also occasionally volunteered to help pass out information, put up yard signs and perform other support functions. I eventually started going to town halls and other meetings that I found helpful in determining what was actually going on in Washington. Things I used to think were boring became essential to protect my freedom.

In 1996, not long after getting involved, I unknowingly received my first clue that my efforts for more honest government may have been misdirected. At a stop on a local campaign bus trip, I saw two guys in a truck that had a sign saying "Ask Newt, who is Callista Bisek?" It would still be two years before a friend I met, who had also become disillusioned with Newt Gingrich, told me that Newt had gotten involved with the Wisconsin Congressional aide. Another year later, after Newt Gingrich resigned as speaker, the American public would know about "Newtie's Cutie" and his subsequent divorce.

It would still be two years before I found out about the socialist history, origins and ownership of major media organizations and how tightly controlled the news information is that flows to and within them. As it turned out, the national news media suppressed the Newt Gingrich affair for about four years while he was the House Speaker, even though it was widely known inside Washington.

I realized just before the affair was publicly exposed that the media uses those situations to control all sides of the political spectrum and implement its agenda. When the impeachment movement caught fire, Newt Gingrich personally delayed the process for over a year and helped withhold devastating evidence from the Articles of Impeachment, all for his supposed adversary, Bill Clinton.

REFERENCES

Michael Brun, *Incident at Sakalin,* Four Walls and Eight Windows.

Kirby Ferris, *A Mountain of Lies,* Rapid Lightning.

Jim Garrison, *On the Trail of Assassins,* Warner Books.

Col. James "Bo" Gritz, *Called to Serve,* Lazarus Publishing.

Dr. Len Horowitz, *Emerging Viruses,* Tetrahedron.

William Pepper, *Orders to Kill,* Carroll & Graf.

Ross Perot, *United We Stand,* Hyperion.

Michael Collins Piper, *Final Judgment,* The Center for Historical Review.

Capt. Joyce Riley, *Gulf War Illness Fact or Fiction?* (video), Alpha-Bet Pictures.

Capt. Joyce Riley, *Gulf War Syndrome* (video), Alpha-Bet Pictures.

Bill Turner & John Christian, *The Assassination of Robert F. Kennedy,* Random House.

JFK Assassination: The Jim Garrison Tapes (video), Westron.

Who Killed Martin Luther King? (video), White Star.

Linda D. Thompson, *Waco II: The Big Lie Continues* (video), American Justice Foundation

Gaylon Ross, *The Elite Serial Killers of Lincoln, JFK, RFK and MLK. RIE*

CHAPTER TWO
THE '90s: DECADE OF GOVERNMENT CORRUPTION

THE CLINTON PRESIDENCY

One of Bill Clinton's first and most important tasks when he began his Presidency in 1993 was to appoint an Attorney General. On the third attempt, after nominations of Zoe Baird and Kimba Wood failed, he was able to confirm Janet Reno. I remember watching Janet Reno on Larry King Live shortly after she was appointed and hearing her state that her major objective was to make the Justice Department more accountable. I was pleased to hear that after the recent fiascoes at Ruby Ridge and Waco. I would eventually realize that her statement on the *Larry King Show* rivaled the biggest lie ever told by Bill Clinton.

During 1993, I had not learned yet where to go for accurate political news and was totally misinformed by major media organizations, which seemed willing to cover up superbly for the Clinton administration. Like most Americans I was totally unaware that Reno quickly fired all 94 U.S. attorneys without a peep as the media focused on events such as a $200 haircut Bill Clinton received while holding up air traffic at L. A. International Airport. In another unprecedented move, Reno fired FBI Director William Sessions on trumped up misappropriation chargers the day before Vince Foster's body was found and quickly pronounced a "suicide" by the media. When questioned, she replied that the firings were a joint decision with Bill Clinton, herself and Webster Hubbell, the Associate Attorney General, who would eventually be indicted for multiple scandals.

Hubbell was perhaps most knowledgeable about the Whitewater scandals, which were plaguing the President. The media had completely concealed the fact that Clinton had helped his Whitewater business partner, James McDougal, bilk what eventually cost taxpayers $60,000,000 from the Madison

Guaranty Savings and Loan that McDougal owned. In addition, there was growing concern about the Travel Office scandal where the Clinton administration fired the entire staff, filed what proved to be false charges against Billy Dale and audited his UltrAir air service. While most of this was concealed from the general public, it was not going unnoticed by the knowledgeable leaders of many different civic organizations.

IMPEACHMENT BEGINNINGS

It was the fall of 1993, when Pat Matrisciana, a Christian film producer, received a phone call from John Hillyer, an NBC cameraman who lived near me in Marietta, Georgia. Hillyer was frustrated over the unwillingness of NBC to report on the evidence of drug trafficking and money laundering in the Clinton administration while Bill Clinton had been Governor of Arkansas. He believed that as President, Bill Clinton posed a serious threat to the security of the American citizens and asked Pat to use his talents to document facts that were being withheld from the American people.

Pat had never done that type of a film before and thought it would be too much of a stretch, so he declined. But John was persistent and contacted Pat several more times before the year was out. Although Pat was living in California, he had once lived in Arkansas and had family there. He was aware of some of the Arkansas corruption and the implications concerning President Bill Clinton. Finally, in January of 1994, he relented and hired John as a cameraman who could also do investigative research for a new film to be entitled *Circle of Power*. It was a monumental decision. For the first time, American citizens would have a television and motion picture film producer who could circumvent the government-related reporting distortions of the television news industry with accurate and reasonably current information.

The video was completed in February of 1994. It was the forerunner to the famous *Clinton Chronicles*, which was completed in June of 1994. That video spurred many other incredible videos such as *Obstruction of Justice, Mena Cover-up,* and *The Death of Vince Foster*. These videos started a whole new cottage industry of factual documentaries containing governmental information that is suppressed by major media organizations. However, John Hillyer never got to see the results of his efforts. Hillyer, a very healthy individual, suddenly died of a heart attack while investigating the Arkansas Development Finance Authority. He became one of many victims on the mysterious Clinton death trail.

COALITION FOR A CONGRESSIONAL IMPEACHMENT INQUIRY

During this time, Floyd Brown of Citizens United and David Bossie had reported numerous articles of information involving Clinton corruption in Arkansas. Most of the evidence so far had focused on Whitewater, along with the money laundering and drug trafficking activity while Bill Clinton was Governor of Arkansas. However, new scandals were beginning to break during the Clinton Presidency, including the FBI file and travel office scandals and the mysterious death of Vince Foster.

The Whitewater, travel office and FBI file scandals were more than enough to warrant a serious Congressional response. So on February 8, 1994, the impeachment movement officially began when Howard Phillips, the Conservative Caucus chairman assembled an organization of over 80 civic leaders, called the Coalition for a Congressional Impeachment Inquiry. Phillips eventually became a Presidential candidate in 1996 for the U.S. Taxpayers and again in 2000 after they were renamed as the Constitution Party.

Both Brown and Bossie joined the coalition. Brown eventually went on to host a talk show, and Bossie became an investigator for the House Government Reform and Oversight Committee under Dan Burton. As his committee got close to uncovering serious wrongdoing, Bossie was fired by Burton who was under political pressure from Democrats and the media.

The coalition recommended that the House Judiciary Committee open an impeachment inquiry and produced a list of 20 questions that required answers. The announcement was made at the National Press Club but received a near total blackout from the major news organizations. It would be three years before I found out that the event had occurred.

Likewise, Congress also elected to ignore the quest for an inquiry. Pat Matrisciana and Lt. Col. Tom McKenney delivered a copy of *The Clinton Chronicles* to every single member of Congress during the 1994 session, the last one with a Democrat Party House majority. The video outlined a clear case of remarkable corruption in Arkansas, but perhaps to nobody's surprise, no one in Congress had the guts to do anything about it.

The change in power to Republican leadership in 1995 resulted in a one-year transitional power struggle with Democrats attempting to sabotage proceedings while they adjusted to their newly found minority status after a 40-year reign as the majority party. However, thanks in part to Howard Phillips and the coalition as well as *The Clinton Chronicles* video, Republicans were obligated to conduct several House and Senate investigations into the serious charges.

CONGRESSIONAL INVESTIGATIONS

Some examples of the investigations and the amazing evidence collected are:

- The Senate Whitewater Investigation collected evidence of embezzlement from Madison Guaranty, extortion of the Small Business Administration and witness tampering at the Resolution Trust Company.
- House Banking Committee investigations corroborated the witness tampering and collected evidence of Mena, Arkansas drug trafficking and money laundering through the Arkansas Development Finance Authority.
- A Senate Judiciary Committee hearing collected evidence that White House Counsel, Bernard Nussbaum and Security head, Craig Livingstone, illegally obtained over 1,000 FBI files on political adversaries.
- A Senate Governmental Affairs Committee determined that the Secret Service agents who contradicted Craig Livingstone's testimony were then investigated by the Treasury Department, which concealed the investigation and lied to Congress twice, stating that the agents were not under investigation.

- A House Appropriations Committee collected evidence that Bill Clinton and Al Gore were aware of and encouraged an INS voter fraud scheme that tripled the normal number of yearly immigrants registered and resulted in 70,000 criminals and 180,000 illegal immigrants' being registered in time for the 1996 election.
- The House Travel Office investigation collected evidence that the Clinton administration filed false charges against Billy Dale, illegally obtained his FBI file and had the IRS audit his air charter service.
- The House Waco investigation collected evidence that Janet Reno approved the CS military gas attack on the Davidians, allowed the FBI to destroy a Davidian building with tanks while people were still inside, and circumvented the Posse Comitatus Act, that prohibits using military equipment and personnel against American citizens.
- The Senate Ruby Ridge investigation collected evidence regarding Janet Reno's refusal to support the conclusion of a Justice Department investigation that found an FBI sniper shot which killed Vicki Weaver was unconstitutional.
- A House Resource Committee and Judiciary Oversight Committee collected evidence that Bill Clinton prevented the State of Utah from mining the same type of clean burning coal as Indonesia, a source of illegal campaign contributions. He did this by declaring 1.7 million acres in southern Utah as a national monument against the will of the people in Utah and the opinions of directors in the Council on Environmental Quality.
- A Senate Campaign Finance Investigation and House Government Reform and Oversight Committee investigation collected evidence that the Clinton / Gore campaigns, the DNC and other Democrat Party candidates had at least seven separate sources of illegal revenue through 11 revenue streams, all traceable to individuals and organizations connected to Communist Chinese military. They also identified numerous instances where the Clinton administration had given the Communist Chinese government sophisticated American military technology over the objections of the our own government agencies, such as the National Security Administration and the Departments of Defense, State and Justice.

Former astronaut John Glenn, the ranking minority member of the Senate Campaign Finance Investigation, chaired by Senator Fred Thompson, appeared to do as much as he could during committee hearings to sabotage the investigation and prevent the Communist Chinese infiltration into the Clinton / Gore campaigns and the DNC from becoming public. Afterwards, Glenn, a man I once admired, was rewarded by the Clinton administration with another trip into space and then portrayed by the media as a hero to the public. I can think of no greater example of how the media has duped the American people than its acclaim for John Glenn, a man I believe is clearly guilty of high treason against America.

Through most of 1995 and parts of 1996, I watched many of the hearings in these investigations, some of which were not completed until 1998. Perhaps the most stunning occurrence of all in the impeachment movement for me, would happen in 1998 when the Republicans were unwilling to use a single iota of this Congressional investigation evidence when they drafted the Articles of Impeachment.

THE DEATH OF VINCE FOSTER

In 1994, Robert Fiske produced a report stating that the death of Vince Foster was a suicide. Fiske, who was appointed by Janet Reno as Whitewater counsel, turned out to be a lawyer for International Paper, Inc., the company that sold Whitewater land to the Clinton / McDougal partnership. Unbeknownst to me because of media distortions, he had reached a conclusion that could not be supported by any of the evidence. In fact, the evidence clearly indicated that Vince Foster was murdered. For example:

- Foster's prints were not on the gun;
- The gun was not Foster's and he had no ammunition for that type of gun;
- The autopsy report showed a rear skull exit wound, but no skull fragments were ever found;
- No bullet was ever found in the park although others dating to the Civil War were found;

- No powder burns were on Foster's mouth, where he allegedly shot himself;
- Powder burns on both forefingers indicate that he tried to push a gun away as he was shot;
- No dirt or grass was on Foster's shoes although his body was found 200 yards into the park;
- Foster's suit, shirt, tie and underwear were covered with carpet fibers (Fort Marcy is definitely not carpeted).

There were so many discrepancies between the conclusion and the FBI lab analysis evidence that the impartiality of Robert Fiske was called publicly into question. Subsequently, a three judge panel decided to appoint Ken Starr as the Whitewater counsel, despite the fact that he had been on Janet Reno's short list when she appointed Fiske. Much investigative work on the death of Vince Foster was contributed by Christopher Ruddy, who had described the discrepancies in many of his news articles for the *New York Post* and *Pittsburgh Tribune Review*. Ruddy left the *Post* for the *Tribune Review* because the *Post* stopped printing his stories. *The New Times* would not cover the story accurately and completely either, even after Reed Irvine, chairman of Accuracy in Media, met with the publisher and took out ads in the magazine. It was an Accuracy in Media ad about the death of Vince Foster in the *Washington Times* that initially triggered my interest in seeking the truth about the Clinton administration.

OKLAHOMA CITY BOMBING

On April 19, 1995, exactly two years after the fatal attack on the Branch Davidians at Waco, I was struck, like the rest of America, by the Oklahoma City bombing, America's most severe terrorist act. It was very disturbing that such an act where hundreds of people were killed could take place in America. I felt particularly sorry for the victims and the people of Oklahoma, who rose to the occasion and epitomized my idea of Americans. It would be almost two years until I realized that the bombing could not possibly have happened the way it was reported.

Eventually I would find disturbing details from Brigadier General Partin, a 25-year weapons expert with two engineering degrees, and other highly qualified sources. Partin showed that a truckload of fertilizer and ammonium nitrate delivered to the Murrah Building in Oklahoma City by Timothy McVeigh could not possibly have blown out concrete posts in the building. Two concrete posts were still standing directly between the truck bomb pit and one of the posts in the back that had been blown out. The truck bomb, which was already too weak to blow out an adjoining concrete post would have had to circumvent the two posts and travel 25 feet through thin air without dissipating in force. Although I knew nothing about weapons, I had enough common sense to know that this was impossible. An aerial view of the damage shown on the cover of an issue of *The New American* magazine, as well as supporting diagrams and articles, illustrated the implausibility of what we had been told. When this became obvious, I noticed that the *USA Today* newspaper curiously cropped the picture of the building so that it did not show its readers the post in question.

Seismic evidence from Oklahoma City and the University of Oklahoma confirmed two unmatched sound waves indicating two explosions. In addition, local television stations in constant contact with federal agencies such as the ATF, reported that there were multiple bombs in the building and not all of them were detonated. In fact, the rescue operation was delayed while the bombs were diffused and removed. Witnesses such as Jane Graham also stated that there were several seconds between the two bomb blasts.

Dozens of witnesses saw another man, who was not Terry Nichols, deliver the bomb with Timothy McVeigh, but the FBI seemed to have no interest in finding him. ATF informant, Carol Howe, other witnesses and a credit card phone bill with a charge made by Timothy McVeigh, implicated three additional individuals of a Neo-Nazi group from Elohim City in the bombing. One of those present in the group at that time, Andreas Streissmeir, is the nephew of a former head of the German Christian Democrat Party who reported to Helmut Kohl.

Even more astounding was the evidence of pre-bomb knowledge the ATF had, as printed later in both *The New*

American magazine and *The Secret Life of Bill Clinton* by Ambrose Evans Pritchard. Carol Howe had penetrated the Neo-Nazi group, found out that it was plotting a bombing, gathered bomb assembly evidence and took ATF agent Angela Finley to targeted bomb sites in Oklahoma City. Her reward for risking her life to give the ATF the information was that the FBI exposed her undercover identification and decided to prosecute her for possessing the evidence that she was under contract to the ATF to collect! Naturally, the charges were dismissed, but the questions of why the FBI refused to investigate the other bombing suspects and why they prosecuted the ATF's own informant have never been answered.

RON BROWN PLANE CRASH

In April of 1996, almost a year later, another tragedy befell America when Ron Brown, Secretary of the Commerce Department, and about 60 other government officials and corporate executives were killed on a trade mission when their plane crashed in Bosnia. The funeral of Ron Brown showed the artificial nature of Bill Clinton perhaps more than any other event. As Bill Clinton left the funeral of his close friend, he was laughing and chatting with Rev. Compolo, who would later become one of his spiritual advisers. When he saw a camera filming them, he stopped laughing, pretended to cry and wiped a fake tear from his eye, all in less than three seconds. The NBC clip was picked up by Rush Limbaugh and played over and over again. Although it showed how phony Bill Clinton was, I would not understand the real relationship between Ron Brown and Bill Clinton for another year.

That understanding occurred after meeting Pat Matrisciana and receiving a phone call from Pat. He said Christopher Ruddy found that Ron Brown had what seemed to be a bullet hole in the top of his head, based on statements of military forensic experts who examined him after the plane crash. Brown was under investigation by seven different government agencies as well as a potential target in a lawsuit by Judicial Watch, which exposed John Huang and the Communist Chinese infiltration of the Clinton / Gore campaigns and the DNC. I did not want to believe this finding because it sounded too incredible. The implications were stunning. Someone would have had to bring down a plane full of people to kill one or two key officials. But the evidence was mounting on this event, too.

The three pathologists who examined Ron Brown confirmed the existence of a perfectly round .45 caliber hole in the top of his head and *The New American* magazine even printed the picture of it. I had read a *Wall Street Underground* intelligence report and knew that the air traffic controller had died of a gunshot wound to the chest, and it was ruled a suicide. That sounded familiar. The report also pointed out that a stewardess, Shelly Kelly, survived the crash but was then found dead on arrival at the hospital.

The intelligence report indicated that a ground crew used a separate beacon to divert the plane into the mountain where the plane crashed after being unable to gain enough height to clear the mountain. This sounded implausible to me because it would require a team of a several people and besides, where would they get a beacon and learn how to use it? Another year would go by before I learned that beacons were used in Operation Watchtower by an American special action team to route drug trafficking planes from Colombia into Panama.

Under normal procedures, many questions could have been cleared up by an investigation, but once again we would find a total cover-up. There was only a partial Air Force safety investigation, no FAA investigation, no NTSB investigation, no airplane manufacturer investigation, and no black box transcripts were ever made public. As in the case of Vince Foster, Ron Brown's X-rays were either lost or destroyed. Comedian Dick Gregory summed it up best when he went to Washington and placed crime scene tape around the U.S. Justice Department.

THE TWA 800 PLANE CRASH

On July 17, 1996, just days before the Atlanta Olympics, another plane crash and cover-up occurred. TWA 800 crashed into the ocean off Long Island, killing everyone aboard, after taking off from JFK airport. At this time I was so focused on the Olympics that I was not even aware of the cover-up that was taking place. Officials eventually stated that the crash was caused by a center fuel tank explosion. It would be three years after the tragedy before I learned that the fuel tank explosion was not the originating event that caused the plane to crash.

Over 130 witnesses stated that they had seen a reddish orange missile streak coming up from the ocean, moving towards the plane or crashing into it. The FBI interviewed 34 of these people, including pilots and military personnel, and found the witnesses to be certifiably credible. Several pictures of the missile streak and the streak of its target missile were taken. One is shown in the background of a photo taken by Linda Kabot, as illustrated in the book by James Sanders, entitled, *The Downing of TWA 800*.

The FAA radar tapes showed another blip converging on TWA 800. The FAA radar technician who analyzed the radar concluded that there were "conflicting radar tracks that indicated a missile". The NTSB reconstruction of the plane, as seen in Sanders' book, clearly showed a large hole on the right side where the missile entered the plane near a galley just in front the right wing. Reconstruction also showed a corresponding hole on the left side where the missile apparently exited the plane. Reddish orange residue containing traces of elements determined to be consistent with rocket fuel were found as early as August 3, 1996, only on seats in rows 17 through 19, which just happen to align with the entry and exit holes in the plane. The cockpit voice recorder and flight data recorder also respectively contained sounds and data consistent with a missile explosion.

So if a missile downed TWA 800, the question remains as to whose missile was it? Some individuals have recognized that TWA 800 was downed by a missile and even provided additional evidence, but they contend that it was a terrorist missile fired by individuals from a rogue nation. However, facts of the crash dispute these assertions.

The altitude of TWA 800, at over 13,700 feet, made it outside the range of any shoulder-based missile system that could have been available to terrorists. The photos and witnesses indicate that the missile was launched from sea, not from land. No other foreign ships with missile launching capability were known to be in the area where the missile was launched. The debris pattern indicated that missile was inert since its entry and exit did not cause an initial explosion. It is not likely that terrorists would use a dummy missile to down a plane.

Several U.S. naval vessels, including the USS Normandy, and P-3 Orion planes were in zone W105 near Long Island on a classified mission to test the Aegis missile system by firing drones to intercept hostile missiles. James Sanders illustrates in his book, priority message R015060, dated 11:07 pm 7/16/96, advising the FAA of phone conversation from a Ms. Cosby of Naval Air Base, Oceana, Virginia, to Mr. Dombrowski of FAA Ron Konkoma, Long Island, (15 miles north of the crash site) that reserved a zone south of Long Island for military use as of 8:00 pm on July 17, 1996. Missile testing activity at the time of the crash has been confirmed by many independent sources, and witnesses saw both the source and target missiles that were fired. The evidence points to a target adjustment failure that resulted in a Navy missile's hitting TWA 800. If a terrorist organization or rogue country had brought down TWA 800, there would be no need for a massive cover-up to hide the missile evidence from the American public.

THE 1996 ATLANTA OLYMPIC GAMES

While I took note of the tragedies and watched some of the investigations during 1995 and 1996, I was still focused on the Olympics coming to Atlanta, the events I would attend and my duties as a badminton line judge, which required some weekend training sessions. The rest of the Olympic experience was also a once in a lifetime opportunity that I wanted to live to its fullest advantage. Therefore, I had tuned out many other activities.

When the Olympic Games arrived, they proved to be an incredible experience exceeding my expectations. I attended the ceremonies, judged on certain days and went to other events each day. At the opening ceremony when Bill Clinton was introduced, I came within an eyelash of screaming at the top of my lungs "Who killed Vince Foster?" Somehow I refrained out of respect for Billy Payne, who had put his heart and soul into getting Atlanta the Olympics. Had I seen the video that I was about to purchase a few months later, I could not have held back.

During the Olympics, I got another taste of media reporting and government cover-up. On Friday night, July 26, my wife and I were returning from a downtown event and walked through the crowded Centennial Olympic Park to enjoy some of the festivities. We left before midnight because I had tickets for a beach volleyball semi-finals the next morning. A little over an hour after we left, a bomb exploded in the park and killed a Georgia woman. A security guard named Richard Jewell was proclaimed a hero for his work both before and after the bomb detonation.

Later the hero became a suspect. The FBI invited him to film a training video where they asked him questions, supposedly for future training of FBI agents. In the middle of the friendly session, Jewell was surprised to find that he was a suspect when the FBI suddenly read him his Miranda rights. Local Atlanta agents testified before Congress that the order to read Jewell his rights came straight from FBI Director, Louis Freeh. Consequently, the local and national media attempted to convict Jewell without a trial, producing numerous false and misleading reports for which Jewell is still collecting damages through court suits and settlements.

I realized immediately that Jewell was innocent, based on the evidence of a phone call from an individual who had alerted authorities about the bomb. The caller had an accent that was in no way similar to Richard's southern drawl. Also, the call was placed from a location that was so heavily crowded that it would be impossible for Jewell to return to his post in the five-minute window of time allotted by the FBI. The FBI and the media both knew this but continued to use Jewell as a scapegoat for the bombing.

The bombing was the only bitter pill in an otherwise up-lifting Olympic experience. The Atlanta Committee for the Olympic Games eventually closed its doors as a financial success and with a tremendous local, national and international respect. Ironically, three years later, after the Atlanta Committee for the Olympic Games had shut down, it became the target of a Congressional investigation because of suspected corruption in the Salt Lake 2002 Winter Olympic bid. After Dennis Hastert replaced Newt Gingrich as Speaker, the House of Representatives decided to spend taxpayer money to investigate the International Olympic Committee bid process, an activity for which it had no jurisdiction. A Commerce sub-committee performed the investigation at the same time it was ignoring the role of the Commerce Department in setting up the 11 illegal revenue streams from the Clinton / Gore campaigns and the DNC to the Communist Chinese government.

Speaker Hastert who controlled this Republican led diversion also appointed Nancy Dorn, a Li Kashing lobbyist, as his top national security aide. Li Kashing is a Hong Kong billionaire who has partnerships in COSCO, the Communist controlled shipping company caught smuggling AK47s into Oakland and China Resources, "AN AGENT OF MILITARY, POLITICAL AND ECONOMIC ESPIONAGE" according to Defense Intelligence Agency and Senate Governmental Affairs reports.

MY AWAKENING

One day in 1996, I heard two co-workers talking about the death of Vince Foster. They mentioned remarkable evidence I described earlier that would lead any rational person to conclude that Vince Foster was murdered, and yet we had been told by the media that he committed suicide. I could not correlate these facts with what the media told me. I immediately reflected back to the Kennedy assassination and the discrepancies there and knew that something was wrong. I went on about my work and kept this information in the back of my mind. Later I found an ad in the *Washington Times* and ordered a report about Vince Foster's death from Accuracy in Media. The report confirmed what I had been told, and I decided to join Accuracy in Media and subscribe to the *Washington Times*. The subscription opened my eyes to a whole new world of factual political information.

A few months later, I was visiting a co-worker in his office, and he had a computer screen saver that showed a picture of Bill Clinton. His screen saver would make Bill Clinton's lips move and his nose grow at the same time. I started laughing, and we talked a little about the President. He told me that Bill Clinton was involved in a drug trafficking operation in Arkansas. I assumed that he was a little biased because if that were true, surely we would have heard about it from the media by now, and Bill Clinton would have never been elected President of the United States.

Shortly after the Olympics, I saw an ad in the *Washington Times* for videos. It was placed by a citizen from Charleston, South Carolina, named Jerry, who was acting as a volunteer distributor, paying for ads out of his own pocket and barely recovering the expense of the ads in video sales. He had previously placed ads at his own expense to encourage Congress to balance the budget. I admired his sacrifice and dedication. However, despite all that I was learning, I was still skeptical of the credibility of the videos and ordered only one about the death of Vince Foster.

When I saw the video I was impressed with lab analysis and other facts that it documented, as well as the dramatic fashion in which it was produced. It confirmed what I had read earlier, and the facts presented could not be disputed. I was upset that I had been taken for an incredible ignorant ride by major news media organizations. I called Jerry back and ordered the remaining set of videos, including *The Clinton Chronicles*, *Obstruction of Justice* and the *Mena Cover-up*.

I was surprised to find that they factually confirmed what my co-worker told me about Bill Clinton's involvement in drug trafficking operations in Arkansas. What bothered me the most was a dramatic documentary of the murders of Kevin Ives and Don Henry entitled *Obstruction of Justice*. They were killed after they stumbled across a drug drop point, and their murders were apparently covered up by the Arkansas medical examiner, who had approximately 20 phony suicide and accidental death rulings documented by the *L.A. Times*. When the people of Arkansas wanted him removed, he was given a raise by Jocelyn Elders and moved to a different department by then Governor Clinton. Seven others with knowledge of the deaths were murdered, and all were still unsolved.

The videos, particularly *Obstruction of Justice*, moved me more than anything ever had before. I HAD to get involved. I could not stand back and let the American government be destroyed by corruption. I called Jerry back and ordered more videos for my friends. I also contacted Citizens for Honest Government (CHG), the organization founded by video producer Pat Matrisciana, and volunteered my services as a coordinator for Georgia along with a meager financial donation.

I thought that I could help make an impact since both Speaker of the House Newt Gingrich and Congressman Bob Barr were in my state. I had met Bob Barr once before at a town hall meeting shortly after he went to Washington, and I knew he had a background as a prosecutor. I had watched him in the Waco investigation and thought he was doing a good job trying to get at the truth. I realized from the investigation that ATF agents never even attempted to serve the warrant on the Davidians peacefully and just started shooting. Evidence that would prove those allegations, like the Mt. Carmel complex front door and ATF videos of the raid, were "lost" by the FBI and ATF. The investigation appeared to be uncovering the truth, so I went to the town hall meeting to express my support and raise the concern that this investigation would not turn into cover-ups like those of the assassinations of John Kennedy and Dr. King. I would later find that although the investigation exposed much of the truth, it did nothing to admit actual wrongdoing on the part of the ATF and FBI or to prevent such a grotesque violation of the Fourth Amendment from occurring again.

THE 1996 ELECTION

As the 1996 election approached, there was a chance that Bill Clinton may not be re-elected. In fact, had the media told the American people the truth about the evidence of criminal activity, bribery and abuse of power that had been collected to date, Bill Clinton could not have even received a double digit voting percentage. However, some interesting factors helped him.

During Bill Clinton's first term, Rush Limbaugh started a half-hour daily TV show. He became popular because he provided a unique, conservative commentary, exposing some of the softer Clinton wrongdoings with information that still could not be found anywhere else on TV. Although he achieved good ratings, his show was always placed in extreme late night or early morning time slots where viewers would be scarce. In spite of this, the show was successful, and he developed a loyal following. He had even received some of the credit for the Republican revolution. However, months before the 1996 election, he surprisingly refused to renew his television show and went off the air.

Ross Perot also entered the Presidential campaign again after United We Stand was converted into the Reform Party. But this time he had lost too much credibility, mostly because of his 1992 election withdrawal. Perot even bought his own election eve television time to expose newly discovered information about illegal donations made to Clinton / Gore campaigns and the DNC from the Chinese Communist government through fundraising schemes established by John Huang. He welcomed the President to defend himself against the allegations on television at Perot's expense, but Clinton naturally declined. It was still one of the finest political speeches that I ever heard, but it went to no avail. Later I would find out that Perot's information had come from Judicial Watch.

Bill Clinton eventually won re-election over Republican Bob Dole, who may have lost even if he were unopposed. Dole, known as the "hatchet man" when he ran for Vice President under Gerald Ford, never attacked Bill Clinton on a single scandal and even stated in one debate how much he liked the President. He never mentioned the Contract with America or never apparently understood what it meant to the citizens. The final results were Clinton 49 percent, Dole 41 percent and Perot eight percent. I am convinced that Bob Dole never actually tried to win the 1996 Presidential election.

The remaining two percent of the 1996 election vote was split between four other candidates who also had a mathematical chance of winning the electoral college. The Federal Elections Commission, which is controlled by Democrats and Republicans, would not allow any third parties in the Presidential debates, even though most were on the ballot in all 50 states.

Three other candidates, Howard Phillips of the U.S. Taxpayers Party (now the Constitution Party), Harry Browne of the Libertarian Party and John Hagelin of the Natural Law Party participated in an independent debate televised by C-Span, the only source of unfiltered political information on television. Former consumer advocate, Ralph Nader of the Green Party did not participate even though he, too, was on the ballot in enough states to win the election mathematically.

There were no media representatives who controlled the questions, so the debate focused on real issues. There were one-minute time limits for responses to questions, so the scope of the issues covered was tremendous. The candidates also offered creative, pro-American solutions not even mentioned by Democrats and Republicans for many issues. It was the finest debate that I had ever seen.

By the time of the election, I was familiar with the mounting evidence of corruption that was building against the President. I concluded that someone could have placed the picture of each of the six Clinton opponents on one side of a die, cast the die, moved the winning individual into the White House and America would have likely had a better President. Once Bill Clinton was re-elected, I knew that I would have to devote personal time and money to help seek his impeachment.

REFERENCES

What Really Happened in Oklahoma City? (video), American Opinion Book Services.

Mena Cover-up (video), Citizens for Honest Government.

TheClinton Chronicles (video), Citizens for Honest Government.

The Death of Vince Foster (video), Citizens for Honest Government.

Investigation into the Activities of Federal Law Enforcement Agencies toward the Branch Davidians, House Government Reform & Oversight Committee & House Judiciary Committee.

Obstruction of Justice (video), Integrity Films.

Martin Gross, *The Great Whitewater Fiasco*, Ballantine Books.

Jerry Longspaugh, *Cover-up in Oklahoma* (video), American Opinion Book Services.

Waco: The Big Lie (video), American Justice Federation.

Ambrose Evans-Pritchard, *The Secret Life of Bill Clinton*, Regnery Publishing.

Christopher Ruddy, *The Strange Death of Vince Foster*, Free Press of Simon & Schuster.

James Sanders, *The Downing of TWA Flight 800*, Zebra.

The Federal Raid on Ruby Ridge, Idaho, U.S. Senate Judiciary Committee.

The New American magazine, Vol. 11 - No. 16, Vol. 11 - No. 95, Vol. 12 - No. 10.

CHAPTER THREE
THE VIEW FROM INSIDE

PERSONAL MEDIA BLACKOUT EXPERIENCES

During the 1996 campaign, I got my first real life taste of media blackout. I was invited by Reform Party members who I met when I gave them videos, to a special *Larry King Live* pre-election show on the Talk Back Live show set at CNN in Atlanta. It featured Presidential candidates, Ross Perot, Howard Phillips, Harry Browne and John Hagelin. Ross Perot was on first by himself because of his friendship with Larry King. I sat directly behind him, in camera view for much of the show.

I decided to ask his opinion of the charges raised by Citizens for Honest Government regarding Bill Clinton's involvement in the Mena drug trafficking operation. I had made friends with one of the hostesses who had decided to start the questioning with me. However, after she relayed the question through her mike and headphones to her producer, she was not allowed to come to me for my question at any time during the entire show.

I then found out that all *Talk Back Live* questions are pre-screened through a producer prior to the show or during commercials without the knowledge of the audience. I returned to the show several other times but was never allowed to ask a question and now realize that the spontaneous appearance of audience participation is totally contrived by the producers.

Afterwards, I decided to bite the bullet and place newspaper ads for the videos like my friend Jerry. I thought I would use the *Atlanta Journal/Constitution* since I had contributed numerous editorials over the years and was viewed favorably by *Journal* editors. I had some experience with ad creation and created my own tactful, local ads for the videos to help spur national sales. I took them to the advertising department, and after a few days the advertising director, Joe Winter, who seemed to be a nice guy in a bad position, called me to tell me the ads were rejected.

I asked who rejected them, and he told me that there was some review board that looks at political ads, but he did not know much about it. I asked why they were rejected, and he said that the board does not explain why, but that I could change them and resubmit them. I asked how would I know what to change if I did not know what was wrong with them. Needless to say, he could not answer that question either.

I realized that Mrs. Cox of the parent Cox Newspapers was a close friend of Bill Clinton, so I tried once again with a different combination of videos that mentioned only the death of Vince Foster and the drug trafficking-related Ives / Henry murders. The ads were rejected again, and I concluded that it was a useless waste of time.

I knew about media blackout of news stories, but I did not know media organizations would even black out paid ads. I was finally beginning to realize that we would have to circumvent the entire national news media to impeach the President of the United States.

PERSONAL EXPERIENCE WITH "SCORCHED EARTH" POLICY

Soon after becoming involved with Citizens For Honest Government, I got to meet Pat Matrisciana, Lt. Col. Tom McKenney and future CHG director John Wheeler on one of their visits to Atlanta. It was then I began to realize the costs Pat was paying to achieve his desire of honest government. I was interested in discussing many things with him, but I spent much of the time getting a taste of what was to be called the Clinton "scorched earth" policy. It seems that two of the people that I knew Pat had hired to help manage the organization appeared to be trying to disable it. Pat said that when they visited his office, one or both apparently broke into Pat's files during the night to get background information. Pat and Tom decided to release them since funding was short anyway. Afterwards, these individuals ordered computers for themselves and tried to bill it to CHG. They also attempted to claim ownership of the web site. CHG eventually was forced to file a civil suit and as a result of the suit, found out that they were under the protection of the FBI. Later, a somewhat distorted version of financial information from the CHG files was leaked to the *Salon* magazine web site, an apparent leader in Clinton "scorched earth" policy. That information was picked up again on CNBC by Geraldo, who became a Clinton "scorched earth" facilitator. The news stories just happened to break right after we had sent out the press releases for our "National Town Hall on Impeachment." We would find out later from a Judicial Watch lawsuit that CHG was on the Clinton enemy hit list.

During this time, two Arkansas police officers sued Pat Matrisciana and CHG for $14,000,000 in damages over the *Obstruction of Justice* video. The suit was based on the word "eyewitnesses" used once in the video in regards to implicating the officers and other named federal officials for further questioning in the investigation of the deaths of Kevin Ives and Don Henry. No other facts presented in the video were challenged. Linda Ives, the mother of Kevin Ives, and Jean Duffey, a former drug task force investigator, eventually explained to me about two police reports that implicated the officers and told me about their discussions with one of the witnesses. However, the judge did not allow the police reports to be entered into evidence. He ruled the reports "prejudicial".

Pat was convinced that the officers filed suit against their will and were funded by someone else. He knew that the officers did not want anymore publicity because Linda Ives, the mother of Kevin Ives, and Jean Duffey, a former drug task force investigator, both strongly believed that they killed her son. In fact, they later stated on local television news that they were "convinced that the officers were the hands on killers of the boys". Despite their pleas the officers were never investigated for the murders. As a result of suit depositions, Pat said that he discovered the officers were deputized by the FBI and trial testimony eventually revealed that a FBI agent suggested to the officers that they sue Pat. The Janet Reno "Department of Injustice" had apparently struck again.

THE "DEPARTMENT OF INJUSTICE"

By now it had become obvious that CHG was not the only victim of the Janet Reno Justice Department. She had already fired all of the U.S. attorneys and the FBI director. The replacement director, Louis Freeh, "mishandled" cases involving the FBI files, FBI lab work, Waco, Ruby Ridge, Richard Jewell, Gary Aldrich, illegal immigration checks and the Oklahoma City bombing. Reno even oversaw the INS while it registered 70,000 criminals and 180,000 illegal immigrants in time for the 1996 election by tripling the number of immigrants normally registered each year .

Reno had also blatantly protected Bill Clinton. She appointed Robert Fiske as Whitewater prosecutor even though he was a lawyer for International Paper, the company that sold Whitewater land to the Clinton / McDougal partnership. She prevented the expansion of the Espy probe to protect Don Tyson, a major Clinton campaign contributor from Arkansas. She stalled investigations into the Clinton administration by making privilege claims for the Clintons that were unanimously rejected by the Supreme Court. She refused immunity for Buddhist nuns to testify about the illegal campaign contributions received at the Hsi Lai temple where Vice President Al Gore held his "community outreach" meeting. She refused repeated requests by the House to appoint a special prosecutor to investigate illegal contributions from the Communist Chinese government despite evidence that the Clinton / Gore campaigns, the DNC and the Democrat Party had seven sources of illegal revenue traceable to the Communists.

Even more disturbing were obstruction of justice allegations involving cases of drug trafficking and organized crime. A drug task force investigation found evidence linking Arkansas drug trafficking to local and state officials. One prosecutor, Dan Harmon, was convicted in 1997 on drug trafficking charges, thanks in part to the persistence of Jean Duffey and CHG. The investigation implicated other officials in drug trafficking and even could have helped solve the murders of Kevin Ives and Don Henry, but Arkansas U.S. attorney, Chuck Banks, shut the investigation down. The FBI then decided that he should be charged with obstruction of justice, but the Justice Department under Janet Reno never charged him.

Another astounding case involved Arthur Coia, a union boss who was a top ten DNC fundraiser, collecting almost $17,000,000 from 1995 through 1996 for the DNC. The Justice Department determined in a complaint that he was "associated with influence from and controlled by" organized crime.

Reports from the National Legal and Policy Center and *Reader's Digest* indicated that Coia was under investigation for extortion, embezzlement, racketeering and death by fire-bombing. The Justice Department planned to take over the union, but after Coia raised the first $4,500,000 with Hillary Clinton at the Fountainbleau Hotel in Miami, the Justice Department signed a consent decree, allowed him to clean up the union and never brought charges against him.

THE FIRST STARR COVER-UP

After the first finding from Ken Starr, concerning the death of Vince Foster, we quickly realized that Janet Reno was apparently not the only one protecting Bill Clinton. In July of 1997, Starr simply confirmed the Fiske ruling that Vince Foster committed suicide in Fort Marcy Park. It was almost beyond belief the two supposedly independent counsels would rule that Foster committed suicide, despite the overwhelming evidence of murder, such as the lack of his fingerprints on the gun that was used to kill him.

Citizens for Honest Government immediately countered with two page ads in the *Washington Times*, explaining the evidence and exposing the fact that Ken Starr may have been compromised since he was retained by a Communist Chinese company named Citisteel. In addition, his employer, Kirkland & Ellis, gave 86 percent of its PAC money to Democrat candidates during the time of the Foster murder investigation. Christopher Ruddy followed with his book, *The Strange Death of Vince Foster*, which outlined hundreds of pieces of corroborating evidence that, I believe, prove beyond reasonable doubt that Vince Foster did not commit suicide in Fort Marcy Park.

The Clinton administration had to be directly involved in the murder of Vince Foster because individuals in the administration produced the briefcase, which was seen in the park by three witnesses, and the suicide note that hand writing experts determined to be a forgery. The suicide note, which turned up all of a sudden in the briefcase on the third search, was such an obvious forgery that any individual could see the pen dots where the letters had been drawn instead of written. This would not be the last time that Ken Starr appeared to cover up crimes that involved the Clinton administration.

DISCOVERING WHY THE MEDIA LIES

By now the media had begun portraying Ken Starr as a biased, overzealous counsel, who was out to get the President. In reality, I knew that he had probably covered up the murder of Vince Foster, and I feared that his team would likely do the same in the future for other serious Clinton offenses. I reflected on all the false reporting of the balanced budget, the new Republican revolution House members who were falsely portrayed as "extremists" and the vicious distorted attacks on Newt Gingrich for ethics charges resulting from two incorrect statements made by his lawyers in regards to his knowledge of the GOPAC political action committee. In contrast, there was a complete media blackout of the activities of a man who would likely become the most corrupt President in American history, assuming that history book authors were more honest than news editors. Finally I thought back to the political assassinations of the '60s and realized that this had been going on for years.

I could not understand it. Obviously one or two TV networks or several newspapers could be biased. But this was not bias. The news was deliberately being distorted and falsely portrayed to Americans consistently by major networks and newspapers. It was a complete distortion of political news dating back to the beginning of my lifetime. How could this possibly be? It began to bother me. My desire to help the impeachment effort and clean up government corruption had been diverted to determining why the media lies so consistently. I had no explanation, was not even close to determining the reason and knew of no way to find out why this was happening.

One day I mentioned this to the co-worker who had told me about the Mena, Arkansas drug trafficking operation. He began explaining how media organizations were generally controlled by the same people. He mentioned that he was a member of the John Birch Society and that they had done a lot of research on this topic. He seemed a little shy to talk about the society because it had been falsely portrayed in the media as some type of "right wing extremist" group. That did not bother me in the least because the media said the same about the new Republican Congress. America needed more of these "extremists" who were willing to balance the budget and restore fiscal integrity to our nation. By this time, I had decades of evidence that the media lied consistently about anything political, and I was more apt to believe the opposite of whatever the media organizations said. After reviewing the society literature, meeting some members and reading a book authored by one of them, I realized that the media had performed a character assassination on this group that was second to none. Nowhere had I seen more caring, astute individuals who were truly concerned for America.

The society had already produced a special issue of *The New American* magazine that documented amazing links between many media moguls and the Council on Foreign Relations. The issue traced the positions of leadership that the members of the CFR had attained. It included wire service chairmen, network news presidents, managing editors, editorial page editors, TV news anchors, magazine editors, political columnists and many other key positions of power in the media world. The issue also traced the socialist and even fascist roots of the CFR and quoted the Congressional record from 1917 where Congressman Oscar Callaway explained how J.P. Morgan interests had bought two dozen of the largest national newspapers in March of 1915 and installed their own editors. It outlined a one world government strategy of the council and its sister organization, the Tri-Lateral Commission, and explained how the plan would be implemented at the expense of American sovereignty. Finally, I had the answer I had been seeking. It was the only logical explanation for why the media organizations could lie so consistently.

But *The New American* magazine issue went further. It also showed how CFR members dominated many government agencies, monetary institutions such as the Federal Reserve and public policy foundations such as the Rockefeller Foundation. All Presidents since Richard Nixon, with the exception of Ronald Reagan, were CFR members, and many of their cabinet members were as well. It also explained how the Federal Reserve was neither federal nor did it have adequate reserves. Essentially, the members of a single organization dedicated to global socialism helped set American political agendas, controlled American monetary policy and manipulated public opinion to implement their agenda. For the first time, I now knew what George Bush meant when he talked about the "new world order."

The issue also listed many Democrat Party Congressional members that belonged to the CFR as well as key Republicans like Newt Gingrich, Jim Leach and Henry Hyde. My society friends tried to enlighten me that Newt and Bill Clinton were actually on the same team. I had just been fed an overload of information and could not even begin to digest such a strange concept. Newt and Bill Clinton were diametrically opposed in almost every way. It would be another year before I could finally conclude that the person most responsible for protecting Bill Clinton was Newt Gingrich.

PROMISE KEEPERS

The scope of what I learned was depressing because it forced me to realize the obstacle that we faced in impeaching Bill Clinton. We would have to circumvent the entire national news media and there may even be politicians and others who pretend to be on our side but end up deceiving us. The battle was only just getting started, and I was losing hope that anything could be done to rectify the corruption in Washington.

Then along came an event that restored my faith. On October 4, 1997, one million men, organized by a former Colorado coach, Bill McCartney, convened on the mall in Washington to pray for America. It was an incredible spectacle. I stayed with my mother in Richmond, Virginia, took the train to Washington and met lots of great people. I looked forward to going because I believe that America is a blessing from God, the Constitution was divinely inspired and that we have a duty to maintain the American form of government so as to preserve the freedom and power that we have been given.

I went to support a rally by the Coalition of Politically Active Christians, organized by the founder, Charles Phillips. It took place in a park between Union Station and the Capitol. It had many great speakers anchored by Alan Keyes and included a fabulous Ohio-based gospel choir. Since it was a separate event from the Promise Keepers rally, I felt somewhat guilty afterwards that I did not get to participate in the full Promise Keeper event and pray with them. Shortly thereafter, I returned

to D.C. with Pat Matrisciana and stopped by Congressman
Barr's office for a few minutes to discuss plans for filming an
event with him. Inspired by Promise Keepers, we then prayed
in the House chambers, Senate chambers and on the Capitol
steps. I believe the Promise Keepers concept of a million
citizens praying for our government may be the only hope
Americans have left.

GETTING INVOLVED

My experiences with media blackouts and the Clinton
"scorched earth" policy had left me frustrated but only made
me more determined to help expose the truth. I did not really
know how to proceed, and then suddenly an interesting coincidence occurred. I was at a party with many of my Vietnamese
friends, where I was introduced to Jimmy, who knew
Congressman Bob Barr. Jimmy also became one of my friends,
and he told me that he would invite me to a future meeting with
the Congressman. It wasn't long before I got to see Bob Barr
again at breakfast and once more at a meeting in Chinatown.
This time I brought him *The Clinton Chronicles* and *Death of
Vince Foster* videos. I was generally uncomfortable with
politicians and did not expect anything ever to come of it. Little
did I know, that his response would exceed my wildest expectations.

A few months later, Congressman Barr wrote a letter to the
House Judiciary Chairman, Henry Hyde, requesting a formal
impeachment inquiry. Then he followed that up with a letter to
Hillary Clinton which was published in the *Wall Street Journal*.
That letter complimented the work she had done on the Nixon
impeachment inquiry and stated that it was excellent
groundwork for the Clinton impeachment inquiry. Based on the
Nixon impeachment inquiry investigation, which was co-authored by Hillary Rodham, Bernard Nussbaum and other
lawyers, the grounds for impeachment of Bill Clinton had
already been exceeded.

Henry Hyde responded that a Presidential impeachment
inquiry was "premature". By now it was 1997, and I was familiar with evidence in many of the 11 Congressional
investigations into the President. I knew full well what a
ridiculous position Henry Hyde had taken, but I did not know

why. I decided that if the House Judiciary Committee would not began an inquiry and establish the Articles of Impeachment, that we the citizens would have to produce our own indictment of the President to get the facts out. Unbeknownst to me, former Congressman Bill Dannemeyer had already drafted four Articles of Impeachment based primarily on the FBI file case and the Travel Office firing scandal. He had apparently already circulated them to some friends in Congress, including Henry Hyde. Bill Dannemeyer told me later that his concern had peaked after receiving videos about the Waco massacre produced by the American Justice Federation in Indiana. Like myself and many other Americans, he was deeply disturbed by the abuse he saw and decided to get involved.

I concluded that I had a golden opportunity to go over Henry Hyde's head since my Congressman was Speaker of the House. I produced signs, bumper stickers and a 25 count Citizens' Presidential Impeachment Indictment of major allegations. I described evidence to support each allegation and referenced it to the appropriate source. The indictment covered criminal activity in Arkansas, abuses of power in Washington, treason and bribery with the Communist Chinese government and a whole host of obstructions of justice that the President apparently committed with Attorney General Janet Reno to cover up the other crimes. I then began to pepper the constituents of the Speaker of the House, Newt Gingrich, with these indictments at every town hall or other meeting, in hopes that they would pressure him to move on impeachment.

The response was great. Over half of the people that received a copy of the indictment burst out in a joyous smile and seemed so relieved that someone was actually doing something about Clinton administration corruption. Some people ignored me, but no one ever seriously even challenged me or the evidence I had compiled.

I received wonderful encouragement, and even people who disagreed me were frequently fun to have met. One little old lady saw my "Impeach Clinton" sign at a tax reform town hall and said, "You must be a very sick man." Another lady saw my "Honk for Impeachment" bumper sticker at a traffic light and waved her finger in a circular motion around her ear to give me the "crazy" sign. I wanted to pass an indictment to her through the window, but I could not stop laughing.

Many others honked and waved their approval as they passed by. The district obviously supported impeachment. A friend named Bill, whom I had met recently told me prophetically that "it doesn't take a whole lot of effort to accomplish something significant." I hope that all American citizens now know that he is right and realize what they can help accomplish.

PAULA JONES SUES BILL CLINTON

During this time Paula Jones filed what would prove to be a historically significant sexual harassment civil suit against Bill Clinton because it forced him to testify. We were familiar with her suit because Pat had already videotaped her telling her story for *The Clinton Chronicles*. In fact, Pat was placed under a gag order by a judge, at the request of Clinton attorney Bill Bennett, in response to the suit. Anyone who saw *The Clinton Chronicles* knew she was credible, but the media organizations which could not black out this story, chose to portray her as a floozy.

One apparent example was the actions of the *Washington Post*, which obtained an exclusive on her story and sent Michael Isikoff to cover it. After Isikoff interviewed her, he realized that she was credible and returned to Washington with the facts. When the *Post* editors found out that Isikoff articles were not going to destroy her, they refused to print them. Isikoff and the editors got into an argument which resulted in Isikoff's leaving the *Post* for *Newsweek* magazine, another Clinton apologist. It was clear to us from this event that the *Washington Post* was also on the Clinton "scorched earth" team.

After Jones filed her suit she was audited by the IRS, despite the fact that her husband made only $30,000 a year. Bill Clinton also had Janet Reno file a privilege claim to seek a ruling that he could not stand trial while he was in office because he was commander in chief of the military. Finally on May 27, 1997, the U.S. Supreme Court issued a unanimous decision that allowed the case to go forward. Over a year later, her case would be thrown out of court by Judge Susan Webber

Wright, a former student of Bill Clinton. Judge Wright ruled that even if everything that Paula Jones claimed were true, she still did not prove any damages. We would later learn that Bill Clinton had perjured himself several times during the testimony, and Judge Webber Wright, by holding him in contempt of court, was forced to make the same conclusion.

THE TAX REFORM DIVERSION

During 1997, I was temporarily set back by a hernia operation as the Republicans diverted attention from Clinton corruption to tax reform legislation. National tax reform debates sponsored by Citizens for a Sound Economy and Citizens for an Alternative Tax System started around the country. The debates typically featured Billy Tauzin, a national sales tax proponent, and Dick Armey, a flat income tax proponent, extolling the virtues of their proposals and taking questions from the audience. By now I had become addicted to C-Span, and I watched the tax reform testimony of witnesses who had been persecuted by the IRS for taxes that they legally did not owe. I was excited about the possibly of a national sales tax to eliminate this and many other tax problems. I found out that the Tauzin / Armey debate was coming to Atlanta. I thought I could let myself have a diversion for a day or two and that I might even be able to work an impeachment-related question into debate if I attended. Then I found out that the debate would occur on the evening of the day that I was to be hospitalized for a hernia operation.

Fortunately for me, hernia operation techniques had improved over the previous two decades to the point where doctors could simply add a supporting mesh screen to cover the tissue tear rather than attempt to sew it back up. Therefore, although it takes a day or two for recovery and two weeks to get back to normal, I decided to attend the event after I got out of the hospital. Needless to say, my wife, who was already not too pleased about the time I was spending on the impeachment effort, was irate about my desire. Somehow, I was able to get her to agree to attend and help get me there.

Their debate was advertised on two radio stations, and thousands of people were there. It was hosted by Neal Boortz, who had replaced Sean Hannity as Atlanta's top talk show host after Sean's move to the *Hannity and Colmes* show on Fox News television in New York. Newt Gingrich and Bob Barr also attended, and the questions that were asked were, for the most part, extremely intelligent. It was the most successful of all of the debates, and yet C-Span did not televise it. It was the first inkling of a revelation I would receive next year when I found that C-Span may not be quite the non-partisan network I thought it was.

My wife let me out at the Galleria. I limped up the escalator, slipped into the main room that held only about 250 attendees, saved her a seat, found her and led her back into the main room where the debate would be held. When it was time for questions, I limped into the line. When my turn came, I held up my wrist with the hospital band still attached, thanked the sponsors, host and Congressmen and told them how much I wanted to attend because of the historic nature of the event. Even Billy Tauzin started to clap. I had already realized that this was not the appropriate time for an impeachment question, so I mentioned that I saw in the hearings how the IRS had persecuted citizens over disagreements about income owed and asked Dick Armey how a flat income tax would solve that problem. Naturally, he could not effectively answer that question or many others. He was outgunned by his opponent, Billy Tauzin, the content of their proposals and the audience that was about 95 percent in favor of a national sales tax to replace the income tax.

Republican Congressman throughout the country began scheduling tax reform town halls, including Newt Gingrich, who had two on consecutive weekends. The time had come to pressure Newt publicly for impeachment, but I was not sure how best to do it since the town halls were supposed to be limited to tax questions. In addition, Newt was somewhat intimidating because he was brilliant, articulate and extremely knowledgeable. I went to the first town hall just to listen and pass out indictments and decided to wait for the second town hall, which ironically would occur at Centennial High, a newly built school named after the Olympics, a previous two-week passion of mine.

Newt mentioned at the previous town hall that he would like to send out a survey to the citizens asking them about their preferences for tax reform. However, he was reluctant to do that because it would cost about $60 million. When it was my turn for a question, I first recognized the fact that he had endured more false press attacks than anyone I had ever known and thanked him and his wife, Marianne, for having the determination to withstand them and continue to represent us. The crowd cheered.

I then mentioned that my concern with the IRS was that Bill Clinton had used it to persecute political adversaries, and I reeled off the names of a few organizations that have been audited. I then suggested that the $60 million he needed for the survey was the exact amount of money that it cost us to shut down Madison Guaranty. I said that we should make James McDougal pay the money back and that if he could not, Bill Clinton should pay it back because he was warned five years in advance of Madison's insolvency by two government agencies.

Before I could even finish my sentence the crowd was cheering again. Finally I mentioned that other evidence indicated Bill Clinton had committed treason and bribery with the Communist Chinese government. I concluded urging Newt to "unite the Republican Party, impeach the most corrupt President in the history of our nation and save this country for our children and our grandchildren."

The crowed cheered again and Newt, who unbeknown to most of us, had held up the impeachment inquiry for months, was in a minor predicament. He could not confront me because his supporters were on my side. Therefore, Newt, who always gave us straight answers, did not respond, became somewhat red-faced and simply went to the next person. Despite all of his antagonistic confrontations with an unfairly hostile press, it was the only time I had ever seen Newt seemingly a little embarrassed.

BOB BARR'S H. RES. 304

I also began attending town halls and functions for Bob Barr and found that his constituents were already pressuring him to move forward on the impeachment issue. This personal firsthand experience flew in the face of another media lie that claimed Bob Barr was driven simply his own partisan motive. His former background as a U.S. attorney made him the perfect person to carry the impeachment banner in Congress, and his constituents wanted him to take the lead.

Several national civic leaders were encouraging him to have a press conference, and he actually went to the point of calling one and then canceling it, apparently after pressure from Newt. We, as citizens, began calling conservative talk show hosts like Rush Limbaugh and got no support whatsoever. Barr was careful and even somewhat reluctant to proceed. He would have to take on the entire Washington power structure with little support from the people allegedly claiming to be on his side, and he would risk becoming a victim of "scorched earth" policy. Yet, if he didn't, he would lose respect from his constituents. It appeared to be a no win situation. Then more developments occurred to help push him over the top.

The John Birch Society decided to join the effort and form the Impeach Clinton ACTION Committee. ACTION stands for Activate Congress to Improve Our Nation. I was ecstatic. The society was loaded with the most knowledgeable, caring people that I had met, and they were organized in every Congressional district in America. They could help apply significant pressure in support of the impeachment effort.

In addition, Howard Phillips rallied the organizations in the Coalition for a Congressional Impeachment Inquiry via some conference calls to obtain a pledge from them to support an impeachment resolution. Finally, on November 5, 1997, three and a half years after the coalition was formed, Bob Barr introduced House Resolution 304, Presidential Impeachment Inquiry, with 17 brave co-sponsors. Despite the historic nature of the event and a press conference with a multitude of civic organizations supporting the resolution, the introduction of the impeachment inquiry received a complete national TV blackout with the exception of Fox News network.

The President shrugged off the entire event with the comment, "Bob Barr carries the water buckets for the NRA." We decided that Bob Barr deserved something better. Pat, Tom and John came to Atlanta for another meeting that happened to be on the same day as one of Bob Barr's town hall meetings.

We decided to attend the town hall, and in recognition of his courage, to present him with an engraved glass flame award that he eventually placed on the credenza in his local office. On the marble base of the award was a gold plaque inscribed with the sentence: "Thank you for carrying the water buckets of the American citizens."

FORCING THE MEDIA TO CHANGE TACTICS

The introduction about H. Res. 304 was a watershed event because now the Republicans were threatening to expose some of the evidence that they had collected about criminal activity in Arkansas, using government agencies to persecute political adversaries and the millions of dollars that had likely been funneled into the Clinton / Gore campaigns and Democrat Party candidates by the Communist Chinese military. If the Republicans included this evidence in the Articles of Impeachment, the media would be forced to report it to the American people, and the public would finally figure out what Bill Clinton had done to them.

The major media organizations had covered up the criminal activity in Arkansas to get Bill Clinton elected, covered up his abuses of power to get him re-elected and were covering up the Communist Chinese infiltration of the Clinton / Gore campaigns and Democrat Party to avoid his impeachment. H. Res. 304 threatened to expose the media organizations, and they were now in a dilemma.

Within a month, the same media organizations that had blacked out every attempt to expose Clinton corruption and even participated in the "scorched earth" policy, began attacking Bill Clinton on issues related to sexual morality, which they had covered up all along. At the same time, Attorney General Janet Reno suddenly authorized Ken Starr to look into sexually related allegations with White House intern, Monica Lewinsky, whose affair with Clinton had almost nothing to do with the scope of his investigation. In addition, Judge Susan Webber Wright ruled that witnesses like Lewinsky could be called in the Paula Jones suit.

The media could have broken the story five months earlier in July, when Monica had an incident at the White House gate where she was refused entry while Elanor Mondale was visiting Bill Clinton. In fact, Michael Isikoff was apparently prepared to break a sex-related Clinton scandal at that time for *Newsweek* when all of a sudden former White House intern and Clinton campaign worker, Mary Caity Mahoney, was murdered at the Georgetown Starbucks, where she was a manager.

Reports indicated that Mary Caity Mahoney was shot five times in the head by two men who apparently used silencers on their guns, left $4000 in the store and locked the doors when they left. Two co-workers were shot once in the head and also killed. Only the *Washington Weekly* followed up on the murders after the initial reports. The *Newsweek* story was canceled, and the murders received a national media blackout. Several reports quoted Monica Lewinsky as saying that she "did not want to end up like Mary Mahoney."

The media accomplished three things with the focus on the Lewinsky sexual matter. First, it diverted attention from the real crimes and redefined the impeachment movement as a matter about sex. Second, it made the media appear more un-biased since it was finally attacking Bill Clinton on one of his shortcomings after covering up all of the criminal, treasonous and tyrannical activity that gone on during his Presidency. Third, it fooled most Americans into thinking that Bill Clinton simply had a personal problem and was no threat to their freedom or the American form of government. It was a brilliant strategy that would surely deceive the majority of American citizens into opposing impeachment. We had to find ways to strike back, circumvent the media with the truth and counter the "immaculate deception."

REFERENCES

House Appropriations Subcommittee Meeting, 4/4/97.
What Really Happened in Oklahoma City? (video), American
    Opinion Book Services.
The Clinton Chronicles (video), Citizens for Honest
Government.
Investigation into the Activities of Federal Law Enforcement
Agencies toward the Branch Davidians, House Government
    Reform & Oversight Committee, House Judiciary
    Committee.

Obstruction of Justice (video), Integrity Films.
Jerry Longspaugh, *Cover-up in Oklahoma* (video), American
  Opinion Book Services.
 Ethics Watch (various issues), National Legal and Policy Center
Reader's Digest, 4/96.
Chris Ruddy,*The Strange Death of Vince Foster*, The Free
  Press of Simon & Schuster.
Year of the Rat, Ed Timperlake & Bill Triplett, Regnery
  Publishing.
The Federal Raid on Ruby Ridge, Idaho, U.S. Senate Judiciary
  Committee.

CHAPTER FOUR
THE IMMACULATE
DECEPTION

NATIONAL TOWN HALL ON IMPEACHMENT

To combat the sexual diversion and maintain focus on the real corruption that generated the impeachment movement we needed a national event. Now that the H.R. 304 had been introduced, national support had been confirmed and the media had begun to turn, Bob Barr seemed more open to do an impeachment-related event with us. We knew that the major media organizations would attempt to distort the event, so we settled on the concept of a town hall to keep everything as refined as possible.

We rented the Cobb Civic Center theater, which was in Bob Barr's district but was also near Newt's adjoining district, We wanted to put pressure on Newt since Barr had mentioned that Newt was holding up at least a hundred more co-sponsors for the resolution. We had a very limited budget for advertising, but the event still drew about 400 people in all. The town hall was free, and we scheduled a reception afterwards for a small fee at a nearby hotel. We divided the event into three phases, a background on impeachment, the allegations and an audience question and answer period.

I did the logistical support and local marketing while John Wheeler did the agenda and press releases. John's contacts and experience were the key to success. He even knew local contacts that became invaluable in their assistance. Our three primary coordinators were Sherry for on-site support, Monica for press contacts and Gene for the stage. My wife and our friends, Jerry and Judie, handled the entrance and product table, along with John Wheeler's son, John Christopher. All were godsends that I would like to acknowledge more fully, but given the now proven Clinton "scorched earth" policy, I feel I must withhold their last names for their protection.

Our only significant problem, aside from countering the Clinton "scorched earth" policy, was that we could not find a host. Most local and national talk show hosts were petrified at the thought of hosting such an event. Because of the complete media blackout of Clinton corruption there was little public understanding or support for impeachment. The hosts were obviously aware of the corruption, but appeared afraid that we would be crazed lunatics ranting and raving at the President.

Therefore, John and I decided to host it ourselves, with his introducing of the speakers and my conducting the town hall. This was a superb idea because it meant we had no major media organization representatives on the stage. We had put our hearts and souls into the event and knew how we wanted to conduct it. We minimized our roles to keep things moving and to the point. Cathy McDonald, the widow of Larry McDonald, knew many of the speakers and was very articulate in helping co-host with John. The audience was well aware that the media would attempt to distort its reaction and was very refined, despite numerous outbreaks of applause.

The event started with Pastor Robert Rutherford giving a stirring opening prayer that moved the audience to applause. Steve Fitchen of the National Legal Foundation then outlined some remarkable historical facts and precedents of impeachment. Herb Titus followed by contrasting the Nixon and Clinton administrations brilliantly. Howard Phillips then added his fascinating perspective while challenging Congress and Newt Gingrich to do their jobs. Bob Barr, our keynote speaker, then closed out the segment to several standing ovations.

Congresswoman Helen Chenoweth called in to explain why she co-sponsored H. Res. 304 and Larry Klayman, who was in the middle of preparing depositions in the FBI file case, also called in to report his progress. Pat Matrisciana covered some fascinating experiences in Arkansas and also received a standing ovation. Former Congressman Bill Dannemeyer used his vast experience to detail the abuses of power in Washington, and John McManus closed the second segment with a stunning presentation on the Clinton global agenda.

We decided to circumvent the expected poor TV media coverage by hiring our own filming crew, renting a satellite truck to beam the program up and buying satellite time to send the program to all networks and affiliates. Despite all this, we received only brief, but relatively positive media coverage on each local Atlanta station and national TV network, including *ABC World News Tonight.* We got good coverage from the local *Marietta Daily Journal,* but the *Atlanta Constitution* distorted the event, using a reporter who works directly for Cox Newspapers. He employed a frequently used technique that gave us broad coverage but focused on irrelevant peripheral issues and completely avoided all substantive content in the town hall.

In terms of total coverage, the media blackout continued. NET decided not to cover the event after being bought out just before the town hall by new owners who eventually changed the channel to America's Voice and canceled all Free Congress programming. However, C-Span, the only vehicle for unfiltered political news on TV, was even more disappointing. Despite the historic nature of the first event of its kind in history and the fact that we paid for all filming expense, bought the satellite time to send it to them, hired the same contract video firm that they used in Atlanta and offered them full operational control, C-Span refused to carry the town hall live or taped even though they had no other significant programming scheduled. C-Span would later carry two town halls organized by anti-impeachment Congressmen, Chris Shays (CT) and Bobby Scott (VA).

INCREASING INVOLVEMENT
AND KNOWLEDGE

The National Town Hall on Impeachment led me to a number of new friends who helped stimulate involvement within several metropolitan communities. We began having regular monthly meetings to show videos and disseminate information. I compiled visuals all of the Clinton scandals, computerized them and began giving presentations throughout the metro area. I also began doing presentations for the Impeach Clinton ACTION committee in other states.

I became good friends with Chuck, who agreed to host many of the video showings at his antique mall. He also sent me several informative books and numerous articles to help keep me abreast of the many events that were happening at once. Another person named Victoria, that I met at the town hall, organized an impeachment meeting all by herself. She did the flyers, got some local press coverage and turned out 30 people single-handedly without spending any money on advertising. It was a perfect example of what can be done by a committed citizen.

Eventually I cut a video for a public access channel, was a guest several times on a public access TV show, was a guest on several radio talk shows and even guest hosted a couple of talk shows for John Bennett, the Citizens for Honest Government radio show host, on the American Freedom Network. Don Weideman, founder of American Freedom Network, was one of the first individuals to arrange for radio shows to be broadcast through the Internet. It was a fabulous technology that meant anyone with a computer could get the truth.

I quickly became paranoid when I first started my activities. During my first guest appearance on John Bennett's show, I gave a no holds barred account of the evidence that I had assembled against Bill Clinton and placed into our 25 count Citizens' Presidential Impeachment Indictment. The very next evening the studio burned down. A day after that I returned to an airport to get in my car, only to find the door ajar and the battery run down because the interior light had been on for a couple of days. It took me about a month before I convinced myself that the fire was an accident and that I did not shut the door tightly when I got out of the car.

CLINTON RULE BY EXECUTIVE ORDER

When I was a guest on the John Bennett show, we received a call from Randy Yarborough, another talk show host who was nice enough to send me some research work on executive orders by Dr. Gene Schroder. I had a growing concern that Bill Clinton was systematically dismantling the American form of government with unconstitutional executive orders.

In 1994, Bill Clinton had already implemented Executive Order 12919, which allows the federal government to take over private property under any emergency that he defined, no matter how bogus. Specifically listed are food, water, energy, transportation, health resources, materials and supplies. In 1996, he implemented Executive Order 12986, which appeared to grant immunity to international agencies which take the property of American citizens for conservation purposes. In 1998, he implemented Executive Order 13083, which allowed the federal government to take over specific state government functions for uniformity, cost effectiveness or other regulatory purposes defined by the federal government.

He had also previously issued Presidential Decision Directive 25, which required American troops to serve under foreign United Nations commanders. This resulted in the suit by Michael New, a decorated soldier who refused the unconstitutional order. In the first week of 1999, Bill Clinton would follow this up with Executive Order 13107, which basically subordinated the Bill of Rights to the United Nations.

Paul Begala of the Clinton administration summed up the presidential perspective best when he said; "Stroke of the pen, law of the land, kinda cool". His unconsitutional, anti-American attitude was no problem for MSNBC, which hired Begala as a talk show co-host.

This Executive Order threat was so serious that it forced me to deviate from the impeachment shortly to see if I could get the Republican Congress to deal with them. I thought that this may not be hard since the first sentence of the Constitution states that "All legislative power granted herein is vested in the Congress of the United States...."

I had the opportunity to discuss the severity of this problem with John Ashcroft, the Missouri Senator who was chairman of the Senate Constitutional Subcommittee. During his brief Presidential campaign, Ashcroft was in Georgia for a Saturday afternoon Christian Coalition function and a Sunday morning sermon at Peachtree Corners Baptist Church. A friend of mine named Lew and I expressed our concern about the Executive Orders and he told us that they applied only to the Executive Branch. We explained that although that was the original intent, the Clinton Executive Orders illegally affected private citizens but Ashcroft did not seem to believe us. I went home, copied three of the orders, highlighted the parts that were illegal, presented them to him at the Sunday service and sat on the front row while he preached the sermon a sang two songs. Although he promised to have someone get back in touch with me, that was the last I ever heard from him or anyone on his staff. During one of my impeachment presentations I mentioned the ignorance that Ashcroft demonstrated about the Clinton Executive Orders and an attendee asked me if I believed him. I thought for about three seconds and replied "No, he had to know. He is the Chairman of the Senate Constitutional Subcommittee".

Congressman Barr introduced legislation on the steps of the Georgia Capitol to stop Executive Order 13083, and many local activists went there to support him. Still, I was bothered by the frustrating prospect of introducing legislation to stop orders that were unconstitutional in the first place, particularly since the legislation could be vetoed.

I then asked Newt Gingrich about it, and he told me Tom Delay's office was checking into it. I called Delay's office only to find that it was such a low priority that no one was working on it. Finally I found a concurrent resolution that was introduced by Congressman Metcalf to void all orders that exceeded the authority of the Executive branch but discovered that it specified no procedure by which to accomplish voiding the orders. In addition, since the bill was only a resolution, it had no basis in law. Thus, the Republicans had proposed three separate solutions to address one threatening issue, and none of the solutions actually solved the problem. I was finally beginning to wonder if Republicans were a true opposition party to Democrats. Before long I would have my answer.

PREPAREDNESS COMES TO ATLANTA

During one of my presentations in a different state, one of the attendees showed me a brochure indicating that Preparedness '98 was coming to Atlanta. It was an excellent exposition and seminar about getting ready for the year 2000. It covered psychological, physical and political aspects. Preparedness gave me the opportunity to meet some interesting people including Steve Vaus, Terry Reed and Bo Gritz. Steve would later put together the Dear Mr. President campaign, using the voices of young children to ask the President to get them out of trouble when they commit the same acts that he did, such as lying. Steve would also experience media blackout of his paid advertising campaign. But Terry Reed and Bo Gritz provided new revelations for me.

Chuck had given me a copy of the book *Compromised* by Terry Reed. Reed claimed to be a pilot in the Contra operation when Barry Seal, a DEA drug informant and CIA pilot, was assassinated. Reed had implicated both Ollie North and former President, George Bush, in the Mena, Arkansas drug trafficking operation, which he claimed for some period of time was tied to the Contra re-supply effort. I was aware of George Bush's strange background, including his sealed financial records, his membership in the secretive Skull and Bones group at Yale and his mysterious involvement in anti-Castro Cuban activities around the time of the Kennedy assassination. Some researchers already believed that he had knowledge of the Kennedy assassination, and now he was implicated in drug trafficking.

I knew about the involvement of Bill Clinton because CHG videos explained that he was the only authorized payer for the Arkansas Development Finance Authority, which was established by Webster Hubbell and used as a money laundering agency for the Mena drug operation according to ADFA director, Larry Nichols. I was also aware that the money appeared to be laundered through Lasater and Co., owned by Dan Lasater, the President's friend, campaign contributor and apparent cocaine supplier. Lasater, a former employer and apparent supplier of Roger Clinton, was convicted of drug distribution in a case that involved giving cocaine to teenage girls. He was later pardoned by Bill Clinton after serving five months in jail.

I had met Ollie North briefly once and found the charges that Terry Reed raised were hard to believe. I had heard the allegations before when they were raised by talk show host Joe Maddison at a live radio debate with Ollie North at a Washington, D.C. restaurant. Maddison was supported during the debate by a professor who I found to be quite credible with his research in the Kennedy assassination. Terry and his wife, Janis, were quite convincing. Terry graciously answered any question that I had, and Janis talked with me several times over the course of the event. Their sincerity and the debate began to raise serious doubts in my mind about Ollie North.

I also got to meet Bo Gritz, one of America's most decorated Vietnam veteran, whose book, *Called to Serve*, implicated the CIA and DOD in Southeast Asian drug trafficking. This was just a little too much of a stretch for me to think that both our current and former Presidents, who are members of opposing political parties, could be involved in illegal drug trafficking operations. One could possibly be involved, but two from opposite parties? I was reminded by John Birch Society friends that both were members of the Council on Foreign Relations and the Tri-Lateral Commission; however, the concept was still just too difficult from me to perceive at the time.

BILL CLINTON COMES TO ATLANTA

As publicity of Clinton wrongdoing grew, protesters were appearing most everywhere he traveled. My stomach turned when I found that he decided to come to Atlanta to attend a fundraiser for Democrat Michael Coles, a cookie company founder who ran against Republican Senator Paul Coverdell. I had met Michael Coles two years earlier in a park when he was challenging Speaker Newt Gingrich for his 6th District Congressional seat. I explained to him at that time about Clinton corruption in Arkansas and sent him the *Obstruction of Justice* and *Mena Cover-up* videos. He promised me that he would view them and get back to me. I called his office a half a dozen times, extending to months after the elections. Neither he nor anyone in his office ever responded.

I determined from this experience that Michael Coles would simply be part of the corruption if he ever were elected to public office. I concluded that we could not let Bill Clinton come to town without showing him we cared about what he had done to America. I decided to try to help organize my first protest ever on that day, August 9. My friends, Jerry, Bill and Victoria and many others, including the "Chicken Men", turned out with impeachment signs.

The heavily pro-Clinton Atlanta police tried to move us to areas where the cameras could not record us and literally ordered us off a public sidewalk at one time, falsely claiming that it was the property of the hotel that Clinton was visiting. In one case they ordered another man who was not with us to cross the street and then arrested him for jaywalking while he crossed.

Despite their efforts and the interesting way in which most local news stations avoided covering us, one local station decided to balance its coverage by including one of the "Chicken Men" and me. They asked me what I thought about Michael Coles' having Bill Clinton do a fundraiser for him. My response was "I am amazed that Michael Coles would tie his campaign to what I believe is the most corrupt President in U.S. history." To my astonishment, I made the first five minutes of the six o'clock news.

As Bill Clinton left downtown, I was the last person with an impeachment sign just as he entered the interstate. He looked at me, saw the sign, smiled and waved as though he appreciated the publicity, even if it was negative. I marveled at his confidence, but it would only be just over another week before his attitude began to change.

Perhaps the most interesting part of Bill Clinton's visit for me was making contact with General Barry McCaffrey, his appointed drug czar, who was appearing with him at a drug prevention rally. He was also scheduled to appear at *Talk Back Live* in the afternoon, so I went there again, this time to raise the issue of government involvement in drug trafficking. I had raised that issue with one of his staff members months earlier at a meeting. Just seconds after the staff member told me that he had plenty of time to discuss any issue, the staffer said that he had to leave.

At *Talk Back Live*, I tried to get a watered down question past the host and producer while we were live, but I could not. I eventually was forced to ask the general a question while they were cleverly prescreening during the commercial breaks. I asked him to address it live, but naturally he would not. However, after the show I caught him off line. Three times I raised the issue of drug trafficking in Mena, Arkansas and asked for help in resolving the murders of Kevin Ives and Don Henry. All three times the general turned and walked away from me without saying a word. I decided that the war on drugs and its drug czar were frauds.

BILL CLINTON IS TRAPPED

By now the media attacks on Bill Clinton's sexual morality were reaching a frenzy while the evidence of his other crimes were completely blacked out. Clinton had testified in the Paula Jones suit that he did not have sex with Monica Lewinsky and repeatedly denied having an affair with her to the press. In one pressure situation, he pointed his finger and sternly uttered his famous quote, "I want you to listen to me. I am going to say this again. I did not have sexual relations with that woman,... Miss Lewinsky."

Linda Tripp, who was an assistant in Bernard Nussbaum's office and one of the last people to see Vince Foster alive, approached Starr's office, telling him she had taped some of her conversations with Lewinsky and proved that Bill Clinton was lying about their affair. Lewinsky, then in a bind, decided to switch lawyers and eventually cooperated with Starr's team by giving them truthful testimony in exchange for immunity which was agreed to on July 28, 1998.

Her testimony created another major problem for the President. It seems that during one of his trysts with Lewinsky he left a deposit on her dress. Lewinsky did not have the dress cleaned, based on advice from Tripp, and the Starr team sent it out for DNA testing. The mess on the dress caused Clinton to confess. On August 17, 1998, after Tripp and Lewinsky testified before the Starr grand jury, Bill Clinton testified in a special deal with Ken Starr via closed circuit television from the White House.

It was a now famous disaster, which had him redefining the word "is" regarding the state of his relationship with Lewinsky. He also redefined the word "alone" regarding his time together with her when they met in the Oval office. That night Bill Clinton went on national television to admit his "inappropriate relationship". Clinton had committed perjury in the Paula Jones civil suit trial and likely in the Starr grand jury trial as well. Three days later, on August 20, Clinton bombed an aspirin factory in Sudan that was allegedly making chemical weapons and bombed targets in Afghanistan to retaliate for bombed African embassies. The Afghanistan government had nothing to do with the bombings and the allegations against the asprin factory were proven to be unfounded. We would soon learn that he planned the bombing without consulting a single one of his Joint Chiefs of Staff.

Paula Jones appealed Judge Wright's ruling and eventually settled her suit out of court for $850,000. She was the victim of an IRS tax audit immediately after filing her suit, despite the fact that her husband made only $30,000 a year. Tripp, along with another White House aide, Kathleen Willey, were victims of many harassing incidents.

Willey went public with information that Clinton had made sexual advances to her in the White House when she asked to move from volunteer status to paid staff. The Willey incident occurred on the day her husband was found shot to death in a northern Virginia park. His death was also ruled a suicide, much like the death of Vince Foster. Ed Willey was one of eight people involved in Clinton-related campaign financing who mysteriously died. These people were part of a bigger list containing around 70 names of people related to Bill Clinton who mysteriously died of suicide, unsolved murder, plane and car crashes or heart attacks.

THE STARR REPORT

During the time, anticipation was growing because the Starr team had announced that they would produce a report to Congress, which may identify impeachable offenses. Starr had jurisdiction over the FBI file scandal, the Travel Office scandal and Whitewater-related activity. Yet the major media organizations suggested that his report would likely include only the sexual scandal. It was almost inconceivable that Starr would leave out impeachable offenses from all of the investigations he had conducted into the Clinton administration during the last four years. The Starr team had only begun the sex scandal investigation during the previous year, so it would be very unusual if that were completed before the other investigations had finished.

Sure enough though, the Starr report was released on September 9, 1998, and the media organizations were found to be correct. The report built a credible case for impeachment based on six counts of perjury and essentially five counts involving obstruction of justice, but all exclusively involved the sexual activity of Bill Clinton, primarily in regards to Monica Lewinsky. It was apparent that someone on the Starr team was leaking information to the media.

The Starr report still created a frenzy when it was placed on the Internet. It was also produced in book form, which generated significant public interest, despite the fact that none of the more serious evidence and crimes were included in it.

Despite its limitation, the report did attract attention to the topic of impeachment. All of a sudden, conservative and even non-conservative talk show hosts, all who thought impeachment was crazy a year earlier, were beginning to use the dreaded "I" word.

Starr had spent four years and $40 million investigating the other scandals. His team had reportedly recovered about $30 million in various fines and obtained nearly 20 convictions, making it the second most successful investigation in history. However, every time the trail led to Bill Clinton or his close associates the investigation would go nowhere in spite of the evidence.

We were somewhat suspicious of Starr because we believed he had already covered up the murder of Vince Foster; however, for him to ignore four years of investigative research and evidence was still a surprise. We had known for over a year that the media organizations would deliberately focus on sexual-related problems to protect Bill Clinton, but we did not know that Ken Starr would become an accomplice to the scheme.

REFERENCES

Col. James "Bo" Gritz, *Called to Serve*, Lazarus Publishing.

The National Town Hall on Impeachment (video)- March 14, 1998, Citizens for Honest Government.

New American magazine special report, Conspiracy for Global Control.

Terry Reed & John Cummings, *Compromised*, Shapolsky Publishers.

Obstruction of Justice (video), Integrity Films.

Dr. Gene Schroder, *War and Emergency Powers*, American Agriculture Movement.

CHAPTER FIVE
THE MILLENIUM BETRAYAL

THE IMPEACHMENT INQUIRY BEGINS

The lack of evidence and limited scope of the Starr report were cause for serious concern, but there was still the primary avenue that would rectify even a compromised independent counsel. The opposition party, called Republicans, controlled both sides of Congress and had the authority to include whatever it felt was appropriate in Articles of Impeachment.

Since the success or failure of the impeachment conviction hinged on the evidence included in the articles, I decided to ask Newt about what might be included. He had always given his constituents straight answers even if it meant disagreeing with them. I caught Newt after a special event at his campaign headquarters one Saturday just before the House inquiry vote and simply asked him if Articles of Impeachment are created would they include evidence of other impeachable offenses collected in some of the 10 or so Congressional investigations. I was somewhat relieved when he replied, "That's exactly what would happen."

On October 8, 1998, the House of Representatives voted 258-176 to open an impeachment inquiry. Unbeknown to me, an hour or so later, a report from the CIA Inspector General regarding CIA drug trafficking allegations was also publicly released and would eventually demonstrate that I had acquired a false sense of relief.

THE MARCH FOR JUSTICE

In October, just before one of my impeachment presentations, my friend, Victoria, told me about something called March for Justice in Washington, D.C. It was a rally organized by members of Free Republic, a non-profit web site founded by Jim Robinson, a software developer, who had created the web site in his spare time. He was attempting to gather concerned citizens together by announcing the March for Justice exclusively through the web site. I was skeptical and told her I did not really want to go, especially since it was on Halloween. In a couple more weeks, I had a dramatic change of mind.

A few days before Halloween, I received a call from someone named Roger, who would also eventually become a good friend. Roger, who was an attendee of our National Town Hall on Impeachment, called to say he had a discount air ticket that was not being used and that I could have it for a paltry sum of about 50 bucks. He also convinced me, without hardly trying, of the importance of the event. I decided to go. Victoria also went, and Roger met us there.

It was an incredible event at the Washington Monument attended by about 5,000 people. The speakers included Alan Keyes, Bob Barr, Larry Klayman, Gary Aldrich and many others. There was every kind of custom sign and costume imaginable. One guy posed in a full PLA uniform carrying a model of a nuclear missile, while his friend had a Bill Clinton mask and a suit with dollar bills sticking out of it. Another was dressed as a cigar, in reference to what Monica did with a cigar during one of her trysts with Bill Clinton. C-Span reluctantly decided to cover the event after some significant pressure. The event was particularly historic since it was probably the first major Washington rally held to impeach an American President, and it had been arranged and promoted almost exclusively over the Internet by volunteers.

THE 1998 ELECTION

The March for Justice took place the weekend before the election. The Clinton corruption was expected to be a boon for Republicans in the 1998 elections. However, the Republicans never made Clinton corruption an issue in the election, except for a few last ditch commercials that briefly mentioned soft points such as "What do we tell the children?" In fact, Republicans had no real agenda at all. As a result, the Republicans broke even with Democrats in the Senate and lost five seats of their majority in the House since most of the American public believed that the impeachment movement was merely about sex.

One of the Republican leaders behind the campaign strategy was House Speaker Newt Gingrich. That was particularly interesting since Newt had promised earlier that he would mention real Clinton corruption in every one of his speeches. Many House Republicans were already upset with him because they felt he had compromised the conservative agenda. After the election, a handful of them reportedly went to Newt saying that they would vote for Minority Leader Dick Gephardt as Speaker. That would be enough to offset a new razor-thin Republican majority and cause the Speaker position to change hands back to Democrats.

Newt decided to resign the position to heal the division in the party. Since he would no longer be Speaker, he also decided to resign his House seat after winning his district by a 70 percent to 30 percent margin. Bob Livingston, the Appropriations Committee chairman who had already solicited House Republicans to be the next Speaker after Newt left, was selected to succeed Newt. It was a stunning turn of events. The Clinton administration was riddled with corruption, but the Speaker of the House resigned.

JUDICIAL WATCH INTERIM IMPEACHMENT REPORT

A significant portion of the Clinton administration corruption had been expertly assembled via documents and testimony compiled into a newly released Interim Impeachment Report to Congress from the lawyers at Judicial Watch. The report outlined impeachable offenses in the Travel Office and FBI file cases and the China scandal, which had been originally uncovered when Judicial Watch founder, Larry Klayman, deposed John Huang.

In the Travel Office case, the Clintons had fired Billy Dale and the Travel Office staff to bring in their own friends. This was actually an acceptable practice for the President, but the Clintons went much further. They filed frivolous charges against Billy Dale, which were dismissed in two hours by a grand jury. After he was fired, the IRS suddenly showed up to audit Billy Dale's Altair air charter service, and his FBI file was believed to be illegally obtained when Craig Livingstone told the FBI that Dale was being "considered for access".

In the FBI file case, White House Counsel Bernard Nussbaum signed for, and Security Chief, Craig Livingstone, appeared to illegally obtain, over 1,000 FBI files, mostly on Clinton adversaries. Nussbaum had access to both Clintons, and two FBI agents were told by White House Counsel William Kennedy that Hillary Clinton hired Livingstone. The FBI agent statments were later corroborated in a documnet uncovered by Judicial Watch. Two Secret Service agents contradicted Livingstone's testimony that his list of individuals was left over from the Bush administration. The agents were later illegally investigated by the Treasury Department. There was also a six-month gap of file access records that were either lost or destroyed.

In addition, the Judicial Watch Interim Impeachment Report laid out against the President a serious case of jeopardizing national security. The report showed how the President had forced the hiring of John Huang at the DNC and Commerce Department and how Huang had received a top secret clearance and made many phone calls back to Lippo Group subsidiaries. He also helped arranged seats on trade missions in exchange for donations. The report was impressive and similar to what we had expected from Ken Starr. Larry Klayman gave it to House Judiciary Chairman Henry Hyde, who said the House Judiciary Committee would consider it in the Articles for Impeachment. It turned out to be another broken Republican promise.

STARR TESTIFIES

The majority Republican Judiciary Committee conformed to the Republican election strategy by delaying any movement on the Starr report until after the 1998 elections. When they did, they decided to call special counsel, Ken Starr, for testimony instead of the fact-based witnesses. For over a year, Starr had been badgered by major media organizations, which portrayed him as a conservative Republican out to get the President. We knew that this was one of the biggest lies of all.

Christopher Ruddy had done some interesting reporting in regards to the Starr appointment and ongoing investigation. He found that Starr, who had been on Janet Reno's short list when she appointed Robert Fiske, had staffed the team with many liberal Democrats, including Mark Tuohey, who had thrown a party for Janet Reno in his house. Starr hired Sam Dash, who later tried to claim that Starr had ethically overstepped his bounds. Starr also hired Miguel Rodriguez, a liberal Democrat who was sincerely trying to solve the Vince Foster murder. Rodriguez complained to Starr that Tuohey was interfering with the investigation, and when Starr did nothing, Rodriguez resigned, citing ethics problems. Starr even failed to conclude that the White House had produced talking points that someone had apparently given to Monica Lewinsky.

During the hearing, Starr handled himself almost flawlessly. He showed that his case had merit and that he was far from having any bias. He even received a standing ovation from many of the people in the hearing room when he concluded. But during the testimony, he casually dropped a couple of bombshells. He told Clinton defense lawyer, David Kendall, that he did not find impeachable offenses in the Travel Office investigation or the FBI file investigation, and he stated that he had not made a determination in Whitewater. Perhaps the most incredulous statement in his testimony was when he testified, "The controversy surrounding the death of Vince Foster has dissipated because of our thorough and accurate reporting."

During the testimony, Congressman Barr asked Starr point-blank if he had interviewed Mack McLarty, the chief of staff, in regards to the FBI file case. Starr answered that he believed that his staff had done so. In reality, the Starr team had not interviewed McLarty, and I believe Starr had to know it.

Larry Klayman of Judicial Watch had been making a point on talk shows for several weeks that the depositions he had taken in the Judicial Watch lawsuits indicated that Starr had not interviewed chief of staff McLarty or records manager, Terry Good. This was significant because evidence uncovered by Judicial Watch indicated that McLarty was the individual who changed the FBI file acquisition procedure to bypass the FBI resident White House liaison, Dennis Sculimbrene. Even if that were not true, it was virtually impossible to determine that no impeachable offenses existed without interviewing both of them.

I found it fascinating that Starr had been portrayed as a strong Christian with high moral values when in reality, it seemed that he had repeatedly done everything within his power to protect Bill Clinton. I concluded that Starr had, in all likelihood, lied multiple times under oath, protected Bill Clinton's illegal use of FBI files and persecution of Travel Office staff members, and worst of all, covered up the murder of Vince Foster.

It was already clear that the Starr report would not be adequate for an impeachment conviction. Former Congressman Dannemeyer and I, along with many other concerned citizens, exerted as much pressure as possible on the House Republican leadership and House Judiciary Committee members to include in the Articles of Impeachment, more serious Congressional evidence before sending the articles to the House floor for a vote. It would prove to be a fruitless effort for all of us.

THE DEPARTMENT OF INJUSTICE

The China scandal had just been fully detailed in the new book, *Year of the Rat*, co-authored by Ed Timperlake and Bill Triplett, investigators in the Burton and Thompson committees. The information from the investigations had been accessible for almost two years, but now the American public had a simple, readily available document that they could read to find out the severity of the problem. The book showed that the Clinton / Gore campaigns and the DNC had seven sources of illegal revenue traceable through 11 revenue streams to the Communist Chinese government. Several of the sources were known Communist Chinese agents and/or members of Asian organized crime. The book also illustrated some of the very sophisticated military technology that the Clinton administration gave the Communist Chinese government over the objections of the Department of Defense, Department of State, Department of Justice and the National Security Administration.

However, no amount of information seemed to make a difference. Janet Reno had already refused three separate 1997 House requests for an independent counsel to investigate DNC fundraising. In addition, FBI Director Louis Freeh recommended an independent counsel, but Reno ignored him. Justice Department investigator, Charles Labella, was hired and after a preliminary study also recommended an independent counsel, but Reno refused again, and Labella returned to San Diego as acting U.S. attorney, a position that he was later denied.

The House Government Reform and Oversight Committee, chaired by Dan Burton, requested the memos, and Janet Reno refused to comply, so they voted to hold her in contempt. Finally she allowed the House Judiciary Committee counsels to review the memos at the Justice Department but not to take any notes about the content. Both the minority counsel and majority counsel, David Schippers, who had been recently hired by Henry Hyde, were Democrats. The House Judiciary Committee members were not allowed to see the unredacted memos.

Schippers wanted to pursue the more serious charges and eventually proved to be another Democrat who seemed sincere in wanting to do the right thing. However, House Republican leaders eventually shut down his efforts and refused even to vote on the contempt recommendation by the House Judiciary Committee.

RESIGNATION AND IMPEACHMENT ENDORSEMENTS

By now endorsements for resignation and impeachment were growing. We had already gotten long-term informal support from the U.S. Taxpayers Party, which was eventually and appropriately renamed to the Constitution Party. The California Republican Party became the first political organization to pass an impeachment resolution, which was co-authored by Ray Morton, whom I met at Promise Keepers. It called for the impeachment of both Bill Clinton and Al Gore. Soon after, a few other state Republican Parties followed suit.

In June of 1998, the Libertarians became the first national party to pass an impeachment resolution. Then Paul McHale from Pennsylvania became the first Democrat to call for resignation. He was immediately attacked by Geraldo Rivera, a Clinton "scorched earth" facilitator, who appeared to distort McHale's military record before eventually backing off. It took tremendous courage for McHale to speak out against Clinton. My own representative, Newt Gingrich, who was supposed to be the leader of the opposition party, had gone remarkably silent and would remain so, despite the fact that months earlier he said he would mention Clinton corruption in every speech.

ROSS PEROT JOINS THE FRAY

In the midst of all of the hoopla, the Reform Party came to Atlanta for its annual convention. I knew the state director, Anne Merkl, who had given Congressman Barr an award for opposing fast track at one of the town halls I attended. I had also met some of the other members during my election eve experience at *Talk Back Live* in 1996. I had never been to a political convention before, so I decided to attend.

I found the platform debate interesting but noticed a large controversy over the issue of qualifying delegates from the State of New Jersey. I ended up spending a lot of time talking to the New Jersey delegates. I concluded that Vice President Pat Benjamin, who was from New Jersey, had heisted control of the delegation in a power play that was supported by President Russell Verney. I noticed that Russell Verney had lost the respect of many of the members and that was part of the reason why membership was dropping. While I was there, I tracked down Dale Barlow and asked her to run for President. I had remembered her from watching the last Reform Party convention.

I sized up the situation quickly because I had my own experience with Verney when I tried to get Ross Perot to speak at our National Town Hall on Impeachment. I sent Citizens for Honest Government videos to Ross Perot by way of Verney, but they were never acknowledged. Verney, a former Democrat Party state chairman, had told me at the time that "Whitewater was a two-bit land deal", and I challenged him on it. I was sure that was a lie because of the clear evidence that Bill Clinton assisted James McDougal in bilking what eventually cost us $60,000,000 of taxpayer money from Madison Guaranty after being told by his State Department and the Federal Home Loan Bank Board about Madison's insolvency in advance of its closure. A couple of members at the convention confirmed to me that they were not surprised since they had similar experiences with Verney's credibility.

The highlight of the convention was the Saturday evening speech by Ross Perot, which was carried live on C-Span. I got to sit on the third row. He spoke mostly about the need for Bill Clinton to resign and got about 15 standing ovations in roughly

20 minutes. I was bobbing up and down like a jack-in-the-box. He questioned Clinton's ability to lead, his sexual immorality, his drug usage and his potential threat to this nation.

I shook his hand afterwards and told him what a great speech it was, but inside something still seemed strange. Missing from the speech were virtually all of Clinton's serious crimes, including criminal activity in Arkansas, treason and bribery with the Communist Chinese government, abusive use of government agencies to persecute political adversaries and the obstructions of justice involving drug trafficking and organized crime.

Shortly thereafter, Perot went on the *Larry King Live Show* again to announce a campaign to force Bill Clinton to resign. I was suspicious because Perot never mentioned the serious crimes and never sought the impeachment of Bill Clinton, only his resignation. Many organizations had already collected millions of impeachment petitions, but Perot wanted to start collecting resignation petitions and take them to Washington on Pearl Harbor Day. I would show up there on Pearl Harbor Day, but Ross would be nowhere to be found. He later turned the petitions over to Senator Joseph Lieberman, a Connecticut Democrat who voted to dismiss the case against Bill Clinton without even hearing the evidence. This convinced me that the Ross Perot and the Reform Party leadership were not really on our side.

NATIONWIDE RALLIES

By now the impeachment inquiry had triggered a series of rallies across the country. Citizens for Honest Government had done one in Los Angeles that drew thousands of people and had to be run twice back to back to accommodate everybody. There were three rallies in the San Fransisco Bay area that also drew thousands to each one.

I got involved with these when a future friend named Dan called Citizens for Honest Government and told them he was putting on a rally in San Diego. They asked me to call and see if he needed any assistance because I had helped organize the National Town Hall on Impeachment. I called Dan, related some of my experiences to him, and we became good friends.

He already had most everything under control and was planning a fabulous event in the heart of Balboa Park, complete with props, guest host and a superb Ben Franklin impersonator. Since I had been closely supporting the Presidential impeachment effort of Bob Barr, he invited me to bring a message from him and speak. I simply could not turn that invitation down. I loved San Diego, could not wait to see the event and had years of thoughts balled up inside of me that were dying to get out.

I had done many presentations around town, but these were technical in nature and let the audience make up their own minds based on the facts that I assembled. A public speech at a rally was something different because it had to stir the crowd into a frenzy of emotion. I was not satisfied with many of the speeches that I had heard and wanted mine to be stronger and more factually based. I struggled to come up with a workable structure that would not be a boring recital of facts. I had also heard many great lines and seen many catchy signs by now and wanted to share them with the audience. Finally I came upon a concept of presenting the case against Bill Clinton in single bullet fact points with some props to support my case and related applause lines dispersed throughout after every two or three points.

Dan had assembled a great array of speakers and drew several hundred people. I was scheduled to go later in the program, but a couple of speakers were a little behind schedule in showing up, so Dan wanted to move me up to second speaker. I was sandwiched between Mason Weaver, the dynamic talk show host who authored *It's OK to Leave the Plantation* and former Congressman Bill Dannemeyer, another superb speaker who was to draw a standing ovation. It was a pressure situation, but I never knew it. I was so fired up to get out on the stage that I could barely wait. The speech concept worked great; I was able to have one of the most factual presentations with many rounds of applause. Dan had a fabulous rally. I spent the night at his ranch and was hooked on public rally speaking after that.

After I got back, I left a message for another organizer that I tracked down on the Free Republic web site to see how her rallies had gone. Her name was Jennifer, and when I got her return voice mail message, I was captivated. She was so articulate, sincere and passionate about her cause that I played her message over and over. She had organized two rallies that had drawn several hundred people each. It would be just a short time before I got to meet her and see her in action.

In the meantime, Jim Robinson received another call from Gary Aldrich, who after talking with Bob Barr, asked him to do another rally in Washington for the Judiciary Committee hearings. It was on short notice, less than a month after the first one, but Jim agreed and another 500 people returned for a rally at the Capitol steps. Most of the same speakers returned to make it another great event. Jennifer also attended and requested that her name be added to the agenda. Since it was a smaller event, they agreed, and when her turn came, she stole the show, proving that passionate citizens make the best speakers.

A MARCH FOR TRUTH

When had I talked to Jennifer on the phone, she mentioned to me that someone from the Atlanta metro area was organizing a rally in Washington for Pearl Harbor Day, December 7, the Monday after the second Free Republic rally. I was surprised because I didn't know about the rally, and I did not know the organizer, whose name was Michelle. I was still on a high from San Diego, so I called her to find out if she needed another speaker or any other help.

She told me that she had attended the National Town Hall on Impeachment, was frustrated with Clinton administration and felt that she had to do something about it. She already had a permit for Lafayette Square Park across from the White House. I was amazed to find out she had organized the rally with some other folks from different parts of the country, and they had marketed it exclusively through the Internet at a cost of next to nothing.

But Michelle had run into some problems and told me there was a lot of work left to be done. I found out that her funding was undependable and the agenda was still not together even though there were only a couple of weeks left until the event. Eventually the organization in Washington, D.C. that was to help sponsor it backed out, and we were left on our own. It was crunch time.

Michelle had done an incredible job in proving that a couple of people could organize a rally for a great American cause remotely through the Internet. We could not let it fail. I helped her with the agenda and the funding, and we took up a collection at the rally to help offset some of the costs. Debbie from Virginia stepped in to handle the logistics and also contributed some funds. It was a true citizen-sponsored, citizen-organized and citizen-funded event.

The agenda turned out to be great. We got Howard Phillips to attend, along with Carmen Pate of Concerned Women of America and Paul Weyrich, who had established the Heritage Foundation, Free Congress Foundation, America's Voice TV channel and the *American Investigator* TV program. Pat Matrisciana just happened to be planning a visit to town that weekend. So he and John Wheeler spoke, and Pat filmed the event for his next video, *The Real Crimes of Bill Clinton*. He got great shots of the crowd chants at the event and filmed the long line parading in front of the White House, led by Piper George, our bagpipe player and by now, regular rally attendee. In the front of the line was a little girl carrying a sign saying "Lying is bad, Mr. President." She had figured out what 44 Democrat senators and over 200 Democrat representatives could not understand.

ARTICLES OF IMPEACHMENT

On the following Friday, December 11, the Judiciary Committee voted along party lines to move four Articles of Impeachment onto the House floor. The Articles were: perjury in Grand Jury testimony, perjury in the Paula Jones civil suit, obstruction of justice and abuse of power. Three articles passed 21-16 and one article passed 20-15, with Lindsey Graham casting the only dissenting Republican vote. All articles related solely to the charges in the Starr report.

While most people would expect that moving articles of impeachment out of the Judiciary Committee at long last, would be a great relief to those in the impeachment movement, many of us knew better. All of the evidence of the serious Clinton crimes collected in 10 other investigations authorized by the Republican Congress had been ignored by the Republican majority on the House Judiciary Committee. The evidence included criminal activity in Arkansas, abusive use of government agencies to persecute political adversaries, treason and bribery with the Communist Chinese government and a whole host of obstructions of justice with Janet Reno, even involving drug trafficking and organized crime.

The relatively pitiful Articles of Impeachment meant that the Republicans were helping the major media organizations to continue deceiving the American people into thinking that Bill Clinton simply had a personal problem and that the impeachment movement was just a matter about sex. Most Americans had been completely shielded from the real evidence, and many thought that the people who started the impeachment movement were some kind of sex police.

The Republican leadership helped the media mislead the American people into thinking there was no smoking gun in all of the rest of the evidence. I felt seriously betrayed because I knew better. It appeared that Republicans deliberately wanted the impeachment to fail in the Senate. The only question was: "Who made this decision and why?" Former Congressman Dannemeyer had asked Chairman Hyde several times but never got a straight answer, even though they were friends. Hyde had publicly claimed that those decisions were "above my pay grade." I was determined to find out what happened.

The next day, Saturday, December 12, Newt Gingrich was having his final town hall before his resignation became effective. I decided that I could get my answer from him. I had already asked Congressman Barr why the evidence was excluded, and he dodged my question by saying that, "We are concentrating on these charges for now." While I thought that Barr represented our interests much better than Newt, Barr was a little more reluctant to field pointed questions openly, perhaps because of his CIA background prior to becoming a U.S. attorney. One of the things I liked best about Newt was that he would always give his constituents a straight answer even if he did not agree with them.

I went to the town hall, wearing my impeachment button and peach ribbon that Roger had given me at the first large

Free Republic rally. I had made many friends there because I had passed out indictments at many previous town halls. The town hall attendees paid Newt Gingrich many compliments and touted his accomplishments. I noticed that one participant had already asked him why the China evidence was not included in the Articles of Impeachment. Newt's reply was that the Cox Committee was looking into that and the investigation was not yet finished.

When it was my turn, I wanted to start with a compliment, so I told Newt that I hated to see him go, but there was some poetic justice in the fact that he would still be Speaker the next week when "I believe that the House or Representatives will stand with the citizens of this country and against the media and vote to impeach President Bill Clinton." The crowd applauded.

I then followed up on the China question by mentioning that there was already enough evidence collected by the Burton and Thompson committees to prove both treason and bribery. In addition, evidence from a total of 11 other Congressional investigations showed criminal activity in Arkansas, abuses of power in Washington and a whole host of obstructions of justice. "I'd like to know why all of this evidence was left out of the Articles of Impeachment." I concluded by saying, "And, Newt, I ask this question because many people within the impeachment movement are concerned that the Republican Party leadership has done this in a deliberate attempt to fail the impeachment process in the Senate."

I had begun to walk away from the mike when Newt brushed the question off by replying "Go ask Bob Barr". Despite all of the confrontations that he had with the major media organizations, it was the first time that I had ever seen Newt not answer a question candidly. I was particularly surprised since I was his constituent, but I knew that I had struck a real nerve.

Since it was Newt's special day, I didn't want to come back and tell him that I already asked Bob Barr and we had asked Henry Hyde, too. Their response and Newt's evasive answer made me realize that the House Republican leadership and not the House Judiciary Committee majority had ultimately made the decision. Impeachment manger Lindsey Graham confirmed this to me later. David Schippers eventually fingered Newt for preventing a full investigation and having two-faced positions on what evidence should be considered for impeachment.

I realized that the John Birch Society had been right all along and it was Newt who had held up the evidence all of this time. The man who I once admired more than any other Congressman turned out to be the protector of perhaps, the most corrupt President in U.S. history as the leader of the "opposition" party.

CAN C-SPAN BE TRUSTED?

I was still contemplating the Republican designed impeachment failure the next evening, Sunday, the 13th, when I turned on C-Span and found out that it was broadcasting Newt's town hall. I was glad that my question would be made public and other Americans could reach the same conclusion that I had. I thought that it was strange that even though the audience cameras were in place during the shooting, the video focused on Newt the whole time and did not zoom in on any people asking the questions, as C-Span normally does. I watched the entire event carefully and saw myself first, sitting in the audience and then standing in line. When the time came for my question, all of a sudden the next person in line was asking his question. I had been cut straight out of the town hall in one of the most professional editing jobs I had ever seen. I was flabbergasted because I thought that C-Span did not edit events.

On Monday, I called C-Span and had a great deal of difficulty reaching the production department. I left my request for an explanation with viewer services and followed up on it after a few days. When I found out they had done nothing, I decided to get some help. I described what had happened in an Email to a national list that we had established and on the Free Republic web site.

The friends I had developed nationwide peppered C-Span with calls, faxes and Emails until we finally got a believable answer. At first, C-Span gave us several blatantly false replies. One C-Span representative said that they did not edit events until I explained that we had the tape and witnesses to prove otherwise. Another C-Span representative said it was a glitch in

production until I explained how it was one of the most professional editing jobs I had ever seen.

Finally, when we persisted, a third C-Span representative
checked the tape logs and found that there was a change of tape
at the 74-minute mark of the town hall which was about when I
asked my question. I was still suspicious, but I accepted that
answer and E-mailed it back to all of the people who had
helped me. I found out later in an Email reply that a friend in
South Carolina had a similar experience when his live question
for Brian Lamb was edited out of the posted transcripts. These
occurrences, added to my experience with C-Span during our
National Town Hall on Impeachment, made three strikes for
the only network that I depended on to tell me the truth.

CLINTON IMPEACHED

The following Thursday, December 18, was supposed to be impeachment eve. By now many American citizens were communicating
via Email and web sites like www.FreeRepublic.com. The citizens
had visited local offices of their representatives and bombarded
them with faxes, Emails, calls and letters. The Capitol
switchboard numbers were frequently jammed with their calls.
Millions of petitions had been signed, collected and sent to
Congress by dozens of civic organizations. Many concerned
citizens participated in town halls and talk shows, explained
facts to their friends and even attempted to pressure media organizations to tell the truth. Although all of this effort was
almost totally unreported by the major media organizations, it
was the final key to impeachment passage. More and more un-
committed representatives were forced to announce their
support for impeachment.

Reports indicated that in the morning Bill Clinton was told
he did not have the votes to stop his impeachment. Less than
four hours later he issued a bombing strike against Iraq, which
had been cooperating with weapons inspectors for several
months and had even let inspectors enter Baath Party headquarters just days earlier. Iraq had been out of compliance with
weapons inspections months before, and Bill Clinton had done
nothing. Former U.N. weapons inspector, Scott Ritter, confirmed that Iraq had shuffled its weapons during that period
and had begun cooperating again.

Bill Clinton had needlessly jeopardized the lives of American troops just to save his position of power. The Democrats screamed that our troops were now in harm's way; therefore, we should support them by postponing the impeachment vote. In a heated internal meeting, the Republicans decided to delay beginning the impeachment debate for one day until Friday.

On Saturday, December 20, the full House of Representatives continued the impeachment debate from the previous evening and held the impeachment vote. Bob Livingston, the prospective Speaker Elect who was expected to be the victim of a Clinton "scorched earth" attack for secret sexual escapades, challenged the President to resign. Some of the House Democrats, acting almost like a band of demons, began yelling "you resign" as he was speaking. Livingston then stunned America by saying that he would set an example for the President and resign. He read the rest of his prepared speech, which outlined the terms of his resignation.

After a few more hours of debate, votes were taken. The first article, perjury before a Grand Jury, passed 228-206; the second article, perjury in the Paula Jones civil suit, failed 205-229; the third article, obstruction of justice, passed 221-212; and the fourth article failed 148-285. The brave Democrats who voted for the passed impeachment articles included Reps. McHale (PA), Goode (VA) Steinholm (TX), Hall (TX) and Taylor (MS). Republicans who voted against the first impeachment article included Reps. Shays (CT), King (NY), Houghton (NY), Morella (MD) and Souder (IN). Souder voted for the third article of impeachment which passed despite the fact that Republican dissenters were joined by Reps. Johnson (CT), Boehlert (NY), Regula (OH), Castle (DE), Kim (CA), Leach (IA) and McHugh (NY)

Many of the Democrat members of the House walked out briefly during the first vote for a pre-staged press conference just outside the Capitol. They wanted an unconstitutional censure motion that would criticize the President with no consequences. After the votes, the morally bankrupt Democrat House members assembled on the White House lawn for a pep rally where Vice President Gore proclaimed Clinton to be "one of the greatest Presidents" ever.

Nevertheless, there was some relief. The House had finally impeached Bill Clinton, and we had achieved a major objective even if it was for the wrong reasons. We overcame a massive media distortion campaign that was protecting the most powerful person in the world.

The House then voted for the Republicans on the Judiciary Committee to become the managers of the prosecution's case. These included: Barr (GA), Buyer (IN), Bryant (TN), Canady (FL), Cannon (UT), Chabot (OH), Gekas (PA), Graham (SC), Hutchinson (AK), Hyde (IL), McCollum (FL), Rogan (CA) and Sensenbrenner (WI).

Roger, Victoria, my wife and I celebrated with Victoria and her family at her house. It was supposed to be a Christmas party, but it turned into more of an impeachment party. The rest of the guests seemed happy with House vote as well. None of us were out to put an indelible stain on Bill Clinton's record; we were out to save America from what we believed may be the most corrupt President in U.S. history. We also knew that the Republican Party had left us a procedure designed to fail the required two-thrids majority Senate vote, but we still did not know why.

SENATE TRIAL

While the new year brought on anticipation of the Senate trial, the media wasted no time in formulating its attack. One strategy was to imply that Republicans had to cater to Democrats for the sake of bipartisanship while the other was to force a premature conclusion and prevent the evidence from being exposed. The major media organizations only had one question before the trial: "When will it end?" They never asked questions like "How will you determine the truth?" or "How will you ensure that all of the evidence is presented?" They simply wanted it to end before it began. NBC even withstood tremendous pressure in delaying its interview of Juanita Broaddrick until after the impeachment trial was over, claiming that it needed more time to check facts. Broaddrick explained in the interview how Bill Clinton had raped her while he was running for Governor in Arkansas.

The Senate trial had not even begun before it was corrupted when the Republican-led Senate unanimously adopted procedures to redefine the Constitutional concept of a trial that is used in courtrooms throught America today. They set artificial time limits and decided to vote on what evidence they would hear and what witnesses they would call. They implemented numerous delaying tactics such as making their own motions, debating on the motions, debating on what witnesses to call and redeposing all witnesses before they testified. They kept testimony closed to the public and ignored all of the precedents set in previous impeachment trials, including those of judges and of former President Andrew Johnson.

The senators, led by a 55-45 Republican majority, then used those procedures to sabotage the House managers' case by eliminating all of the potentially hostile witnesses. The Senate demanded that Hyde reduce the witness list, and he seemed to comply eagerly. Only Monica Lewinsky, Vernon Jordan and aide Sydney Blumenthal, all relatively supportive of the President, testified. The managers had requested only two weeks to present their entire case, including the brief questioning and cross examination of about 10-12 witnesses that they felt were essential to their case. The impeachment trial of Andrew Johnson similarly called 25 witness in just over five days. All of this was done under the phony argument of bipartisanship, a thinly veiled excuse that allowed compromised Republicans to pander to corrupt Democrats who were trying to destroy the Republic.

Although 27 of the Democrats had already voted to convict Judge Walter Nixon on the same charge, perjury before a grand jury, the Senate actually attempted to dismiss the case without hearing any witnesses. The motion to dismiss was made by Robert Byrd, who was frequently known to walk around with a Constitution in his pocket. The motion failed 56-44, with Democrat Russ Feingold crossing party lines to hear witnesses and the rest of the evidence. The vote for an unprecedented, unconstitutional motion that contradicted the sole power of impeachment provided to the House under the Constitution, exposed Byrd and most of the remaining Senate Democrats as Constitutional frauds.

Even more stunning was the refusal by Senate Republicans to uphold their Constitutional duty and hear the case. After eliminating all hostile witnesses and potentially damaging evidence, they decided to take the vote. Naturally, both articles failed. The first article of perjury failed, 46-54 with surprise "no" votes from Senators Fred Thompson, John Warner, Slade Gorton and Richard Shelby.

Arlen Specter, whose wife had received an appointment from Bill Clinton, actually referenced a provision of Scottish law to vote "not proven" instead of not guilty. It was somewhat fitting since he and the rest of the Senators had voted not to allow the House managers to prove their case fully. However, he did not explain when he was sworn to uphold Scottish law instead of the U.S. Constitution.

The second article of obstruction failed at a 50-50 vote with Republican Senators Collins, Jeffords, Chafee, Snowe and Specter voting with the Democrats, as was somewhat expected. It was particularly interesting that Specter, who was one of the last few Senators to vote, did not invoke his Scottish law claim but instead cast a straight "no" vote that prevented the second article from at least having a majority in favor of it.

Most of us knew that the handwriting was on the wall for the Senate trial before it started because of the trial procedure vote. Some of us had held out some hope since we knew that if Bill Clinton was to be removed, it would have to be by surprise because of the danger he posed in bombing countries to avoid his impeachment.

After witnessing the behavior of the House Democrats, the Senate Democrat votes were no surprise. The Democrat Party had become morally bankrupt and a threat to the freedom of every American citizen. It officially condoned anti-American activities of Bill Clinton involving tyranny, fascism and communism. Democrats were perfectly willing to subvert the Constitution, Declaration of Independence and Pledge of Allegiance by implementing an unprecedented double standard of justice in America for:

- A President vs. a judge who would be impeached;
- The commander in chief vs. a military officer or soldier who would be court-martialed;

- A government executive vs. a corporate executive who would be fired;
- An elected official vs. a private citizen who would be jailed.

THE REPUBLICAN BETRAYAL

The Republicans were even more disgusting. They could have gotten the necessary 12 Democrat Senate votes for the two-thirds majority needed to convict Bill Clinton at any time simply by conducting a REAL trial and using the Congressional investigation evidence of criminal activity, abuse of power, treason and bribery in the Articles of Impeachment. Even a threat to use the evidence would force Democrat Senators to convict Bill Clinton on perjury and obstruction or be forced to dismiss real crimes such as treason, which would expose them as frauds.

I began to reflect on the incredible Republican betrayal. Despite overwhelming detailed evidence that Bill Clinton, Janet Reno and many Democrats implemented a treasonous, fascist regime, Republican leaders, after conducting reasonable investigations, established a systematic, multi-year cover-up of Democrat crimes. Ironically, two Republicans portrayed as heroes of the conservative and impeachment movements were responsible for much of the protection for Bill Clinton.

In early 1997, after many of the investigations were complete, Congressman Barr wrote a letter to House Judiciary Chairman, Henry Hyde (IL), suggesting an impeachment inquiry. Hyde, who is proclaimed as a hero of the impeachment movement for his elegant speeches in the Senate, stated that an impeachment inquiry was "premature" and delayed action on the inquiry for almost a year.

On November 5, 1997, Congressman Barr filed the H. Res. 304 impeachment inquiry with 17 co-sponsors. Speaker Newt Gingrich, a key adversary of Bill Clinton and acknowledged hero of the conservative movement, worked behind the scenes to prevent additional co-sponsors from signing onto the inquiry. Congressman Barr estimated that he would have probably had 150 co-sponsors had it not been for his friend, Newt Gingrich. Based on the eventual House impeachment vote, it is fairly easy to tell that Barr was correct.

After the Republican-led House voted to begin an impeachment inquiry in October, 1998, the House Judiciary Committee, chaired by Henry Hyde, elected to use only evidence from the Starr report for the impeachment. Hyde, who said that the original inquiry was "premature", now claimed that there was not enough time to investigate the more serious charges against Bill Clinton.

Newt Gingrich resigned after suppressing Clinton corruption through the 1998 election and then recommended Denny Hastert (IL) for his replacement as Speaker of the House. Hastert concurred with Hyde and avoided any confrontations by continuing protection for Bill Clinton from any charges based on the more serious crimes. Therefore, when the Republican House Judiciary Committee finally acted on the impeachment inquiry, it left out all of the evidence of serious, freedom threatening, impeachable offenses including the criminal activity in Arkansas, treason and bribery with the Communist Chinese government, abusive use of government agencies to persecute adversaries and a whole host of obstructions of justice involving drug trafficking, money laundering and organized crime.

Much of the drug trafficking and money laundering evidence was suppressed by House Banking Committee Chairman, Jim Leach (IA), who conducted an investigation into Mena, Arkansas, activities but never produced a report. Likewise, incriminating evidence regarding the FBI file case was collected by the Senate Judiciary Committee, but Chairman Orrin Hatch (UT) never produced a report. Evidence regarding Whitewater criminal activity and the death of Vince Foster was produced in a set of volumes by the Senate Banking Committee and its Chairman, Alfonse D'Amato, but no action was taken.

Republicans on the House Judiciary Committee were reluctant to deal with the more serious crimes since they had no support from the Republican leadership. In December of 1998, the House Judiciary Committee voted to send the Articles of Impeachment, based exclusively on the Starr report, to the House floor for a vote. The House of Representatives passed two of the four articles, and the charges were sent to the Senate where the Republican Judiciary Committee members served as case managers.

When the Articles of Impeachment reached the Senate, all 100 Senators, led by a 55-45 controlling Republican majority, voted to establish procedures that allowed them to refuse to hear the hostile witnesses and damaging evidence that would be presented in a normal impeachment trial. Henry Hyde, under pressure from Republican Senate leader, Trent Lott, then dealt the case a fatal blow by personally reducing the witnesses list from at least 12 to three, all supportive of the President.

Four Republican Senators from New England, Jeffords (VT), Chafee (RI), Snowe (VT) and Collins (ME), spoke out against conviction during the trial proceedings, and the Democrats, knowing that the Republican led Senate was preventing the evidence from being presented, held firm for acquittal. Thus, the failure to convict Bill Clinton rested almost exclusively on the shoulders of the "opposition" Republican party.

The Republican betrayal continued after the impeachment trial was over. As more evidence from the Cox Committee confirmed many likely acts of treason, the majority of Republicans did nothing about it. The Republicans refused to make Janet Reno accountable for justice obstructions, and they even let the independent counsel law expire, eliminating the last line of protection that American citizens have against collusion between Democrats and Republicans.

We knew when the impeachment movement started that the Democrats would likely protect Bill Clinton at all costs and we would have to overcome them We also knew that the major media organizations would continue to distort nearly all political news about Bill Clinton to keep him in office, as they had done for almost two decades. We were prepared to fight a protracted battle to circumvent them. We suspected that Ken Starr would fail to find impeachable offenses in the FBI file case, the Travel Office firing scandal and Whitewater because he had likely covered up the murder of Vince Foster. We knew that the impeachment process could compensate for a corrupted independent counsel. What we did not fully realize was that there are no REAL opposing political parties.

If the Republican Party were a true opposition party, nearly every member of the party would have explained on national television how Bill Clinton had jeopardized the freedom of our friends and family. If the Republican Party were a true opposition party, Bill Clinton would have been forced to resign in 1995 when Republicans gained control of Congress. If the Republican Party were a true opposition party, it could have destroyed the Democrat National Committee solely with evidence of bribery by the Communist Chinese government.

Republican leaders withheld nearly all of the serious evidence of wrongdoing by the Clinton administration in the House and refused to hear true damaging witnesses and evidence against the President in the Senate. Republican leaders illustrated how our two-party system is a fraud that has completely compromised the United States government.

MY ENCOUNTER WITH RUSH

A few months later, I got an opportunity to ask Rush Limbaugh about the Republican impeachment betrayal during a radio show focusing on third parties just after Pat Buchanan declared his switch to the Reform Party. The breadth of Rush's audience is so widespread that three of my friends, Dick in Pennsylvania, Ed in Mississippi and Harry from Georgia, who was working out of state, all heard me on the air. I called in on "open line Friday" which is not really open since the callers are still screened about their subject. I got passed the substitute screener by stating that I did not see any difference between Republicans and Democrats and wanted Rush to explain why I should vote Republican instead of third party. This is the classic position that Rush loves to defend so the screener allowed me to have the first question.

When I got on the air I thanked him and quickly explained that the Republican led House had evidence of criminal activity in Arkansas, abuse of power in the FBI file case and IRS audits, 50 potential acts of treason that I had documented, and a bribery scheme involving 11 illegal revenue streams traceable to individuals and organizations directly connected to the Communist Chinese military. I then mentioned how the Republican led Senate established trial procedures to sabotage the impeachment effort. Rush was polite enough to let me finish but responded with: "That's old news". It sounded like he thought it was OK for Republicans to sellout America as long as they did it a few months ago. I said: "Well let me bring it up to date for you. The Cox Committee report has now been released and hardly any Republican will mention the treasonous activity that it documents about the Clinton Administration".

Rush replied: "What does any of this have to do with Pat Buchanan?" I quickly answered: "If the Republican party cannot protect the American citizens against the treason, bribery, tyranny and fascism committed by the Clinton Administration, then what good are Republicans as alternatives to Democrats?" For the first time, I noticed about five seconds of dead silence on Rush's show. He then feebly replied "Well, a lot of people have said that the Republicans have been too soft about that" and went on to the next call. About an hour later, perhaps after he received an irate private call from the RNC, Rush referred back to me stating: "You heard the anger in his voice", "He said you should never vote for any Republicans." He then began attacking me on the air and stating how wrong I was. His tirade started one hour after being speechless when I asked him what I think is the political question of the decade.

WHY THE BETRAYAL?

I had to know why the Republicans protected Bill Clinton so consistently. Conservative talk show hosts like to say that they are spineless and scared of the media. Some even say that they are stupid and inexperienced at majority leadership. These arguments are provably false, and I believe they are deliberate distortions.

Anyone who has watched Congressional business conducted on C-Span knows that Republican Congressional members are at least as intelligent and articulate as their Democrat counterparts and in many cases, more so. Most importantly, Republican (and even Democrat) Congressional offices were swamped with calls, faxes, Emails and letters supporting both impeachment and conviction by a wide margin. I personally verified non partisan letters collected on the internet and found them to be running as high as 10-1 or better for conviction. Therefore, the Republicans knew that they had the support of their constituents if they voted to convict.

Another excuse frequently mentioned for Republicans is the fact that the Clinton administration held and used numerous

FBI files against their adversaries, and this may have played some part in the reluctance of many Congressmen to confront the President. For Newt Gingrich, his unreported affair with Calista Bisek that dated to 1993 could be one factor since his FBI file was likely updated with information about the affair when he became Speaker of the House, and it is a near certainty that the Clinton administration illegally obtained his file. But Henry Hyde continued to protect Bill Clinton even after a decades old affair had been exposed.

Henry Hyde originally stated that impeachment inquiry was "premature" then claimed that there was not enough time to investigate the more serious charges against Bill Clinton, and he was eventually responsible for reducing the witness list from at least 12 mostly hostile witnesses to three supportive ones. His latter two actions came after his affair was exposed, thereby eliminating the FBI files as the likely excuse. Ironically, Hyde received a standing ovation at a dinner for the House impeachment trial managers a few months after the trial.

It is also important to understand that Newt Gingrich, Henry Hyde, Jim Leach, John Chafee and Olympia Snowe are all members of the Council on Foreign Relations (CFR). My involvement led me to realize that CFR members control the national news media, Democrat Party agenda and key Republican leadership posts. The handful of Republican CFR members in Washington were instrumental in protecting Bill Clinton. Given that there are only a few other Republican CFR members in Congress, this is more than just coincidence.

Since the number of Republican CFR members is relatively low, CFR membership cannot explain the consistent protection offered to Bill Clinton by all of the opposing Senators and even some members in the House of Representatives. I concluded that there had to be even more to it. I suspected what the real motive was after meeting Terry Reed and Col. Bo Gritz and receiving the book, *White Out,* from my friend Chuck.

I then discovered an article by Michael Ruppert and a link to his web site while scanning Free Republic one day. Michael is a former LAPD narcotics officer, who once confronted CIA Director Deutch concerning three CIA drug trafficking operations during a now famous L.A. town hall. Michael had put together a variety of newsletters, videos, of government investigation reports about America's best kept secret. I spoke with him by phone when ordering his material and found that he had reached the same conclusion about the Republican betrayal that I had from a completely different angle, only he had facts to support his conclusion.

Michael discovered that Volume II of the CIA Inspector General's report on drug trafficking allegations was released to the web on October 8, 1998, an hour after the Judiciary Committee voted to begin an impeachment inquiry. He also had found that Ken Starr, while in the Justice Department, helped draft a memo to the CIA that alleviated CIA reporting requirement responsibility for any knowledge they may gain about drug trafficking operations. I studied the material he had assembled on several different drug operations and reviewed the highly credible sources he had on video tape. I combined all of this with what I had already read and learned from Bo Gritz and Terry Reed. As explained in Chapter 10, the trail of overall control and responsibility for the drug operations invariably traced back to one individual: former Vice President, George H. W. Bush.

If Bill Clinton continued releasing this type of information about George H. W. Bush, it would destroy the year 2000 presidential candidacy of his son, George W. already the favorite for the Republican presidential nomination. Therefore, it is obvious that Republicans were forced to leave serious evidence out of the Articles of Impeachment and sabotage the Senate impeachment trial to preserve the candidacy of George W. Bush. However, this was not my most significant discovery. The national news media generally portrayed those who believed in CIA drug trafficking as crazed lunatics, much the same way it portrayed those who wanted to hold Bill Clinton accountable to the same laws as the rest of the citizens. The controlled national news media was not just discrediting one political side but was deliberately discrediting honest people on BOTH sides of the political spectrum so that the media controllers could compromise the majority of politicians in Washington and implement their own agenda.

REFERENCES

Investigation of Illegal or Improper Activities in Connection with 1996 Federal Election Campaign 1-6, Hearing 1-10, Senate Governmental Affairs.

Investigation of Political Fund Raising Improprieties and Possible Violations of Law #1-4, House Government Reform and Oversight Committee.

Hearing on the Impeachment Inquiry of William Jefferson Clinton, House Judiciary Committee.

Alexander Hamilton, James Madison & John Jay, *The Federalist Papers*, (reprinted by) Mentor.

Byron Preiss & David Osterlund, *The Constitution of the United States*, (reprinted by) Bantam Books.

Ed Timperlake & Bill Triplett, *Year of the Rat*, Regnery Publishing.

Judicial Watch, Interim Impeachment Report to Congress.

II
The Real
Corruption

CHAPTER SIX
THE REAL CASE FOR IMPEACHMENT

The impeachment movement was initiated in 1994 by dozens of civic leaders based upon evidence of serious wrong-doings that occurred while Bill Clinton was Governor of Arkansas. Between 1995 and 1998, the Republican-led Congress conducted more than a dozen investigations into the Clinton administrations in Arkansas and Washington. They confirmed many facts upon which the original allegations were based and in some cases, found even more. The following summarizes allegations that have been made against Bill Clinton along with supporting evidence, which the Republican led Congress either collected or had access to, but refused to use in the Articles of Impeachment:

EMBEZZLEMENT AT MADISON GUARANTY

Those who have been tricked into believing that Whitewater was a two-bit land deal need only to look at the case of Madison Guaranty to find the truth. James McDougal, Bill Clinton's close business associate, Whitewater partner and fundraiser, was convicted on 18 counts of fraud for bilking millions of dollars from Madison Guaranty Savings & Loan. The total cost to American taxpayers was more than $60,000,000 when it was shut down by the Resolution Trust Company in 1989.

Evidence indicates that Governor Clinton was warned about Madison's potential insolvency in 1983 by aide Marlin D. Jackson. He was warned again on June 21, 1984, by Arkansas Securities Department chief, Lee Thalheimer, and the Federal Home Loan Bank Board whose limited investigation concluded that the "viability of the institution is jeopardized" because of "unsafe and unsound lending practices". So what did he do to resolve the potential problem before it got out of hand?

Bill Clinton replaced Thalheimer with Beverly Bassett, who came from a law firm that had worked for Madison Guaranty. She was also the sister of his Washington County campaign chief. Clinton got McDougal to retain Hillary Clinton and the Rose Law Firm to produce an accounting study that concluded Madison was solvent. The study was quickly accepted by the revamped Securities Department, and Madison was allowed to continue its existence until 1989. Without the assistance of Bill Clinton, James McDougal would likely not have been able to embezzle the Madison funds.

The federal government agency that exposed the problems with Madison Guaranty was called the Resolution Trust Company (RTC). RTC investigator, Jean Lewis, submitted the first criminal referral, which helped convict Arkansas Governor Jim Guy Tucker in September of 1992. She submitted nine more criminal referrals later. Afterwards, procedures were changed to shift responsibility to the Legal division, and the case was transferred to the Rose Law Firm with its lead billing attorneys, Webster Hubbell and Vince Foster. Lewis was eventually removed from the Madison case. She and her supervisors, Richard Lorio and Lee Ausen, both lifelong Democrats who supported her investigation, were given a two-week administrative leave and escorted from the office. White House Associate Counsel, William Kennedy, another former Rose partner, was finally forced to release notes revealing that the White House had acquired inside knowledge of the criminal referrals.

In 1994, one week after prosecutor Fiske was appointed to investigate Whitewater, the Rose Law Firm began shredding documents, despite protest demonstrations outside the building. Two employees resigned, and one stated that he saw many files being shredded with Vince Foster's initials. During the same week, a fire destroyed records on the 14th floor at the Worthen Bank, which was co-owned by the Lippo Group, a major Clinton donor. These events continued a suspicious trend from March of 1992 when all files on the Mena drug trafficking investigation were removed by Clinton staff members from the Arkansas Attorney General's office, just before Freedom of Information Act requests could be filed by local news organizations.

EXTORTION OF THE SMALL
BUSINESS ADMINISTRATION

David Hale, who made Small Business Administration backed loans through his company, testified that Bill Clinton pressured him to make a $300,000 "disadvantaged persons" loan to Susan McDougal because the Clinton Whitewater partnership would receive some of the proceeds. Susan McDougal was the wife of James McDougal, owner of Madison Guaranty. She was certainly not a "disadvantaged person" unless admiring Bill Clinton would qualify her for that status. Her loan was never repaid, and McDougal was also charged but acquitted of stealing $150,000 from Zubin and Nancy Mehta, a California couple for whom she worked. Susan McDougal was eventually convicted in regards to the Small Business Administration loan, but a judge freed her from prison a few months after the conviction using the grounds that back problems warranted her release on medical conditions.

Bill Clinton testified that he had no knowledge of the loan to Susan McDougal. His testimony was contradicted by James McDougal, David Hale and Trooper L.D. Brown, the former president of the Arkansas State Police Association. Susan McDougal was jailed for refusing to answer whether or not Bill Clinton had knowledge of the loan and she actually demanded immunity from perjury for her testimony.

Clinton's testimony that he has no knowledge or connections to Madison Guaranty other than the Whitewater loan with McDougal also appears to have been contradicted by McDougal, Madison chairman John Latham and Rose attorney Richard Massey. McDougal stated that Bill Clinton stopped by his office one morning while jogging and asked him to give Madison business to Hillary Clinton at the Rose Law Firm, which he did as requested. But Hillary Clinton claimed that a junior partner, Richard Massey, brought in the Madison account. Massey testified, "That is NOT my recollection." Latham confirmed that McDougal made the decision, and McDougal also provided documents to support his claim and contradict both Clintons.

James McDougal stated that Clinton asked Hale about the loan after a meeting between Hale and McDougal concerning

Madison Guaranty. Arkansas Trooper L.D. Brown, a former Clinton bodyguard who was also a past president of the Arkansas State Police Association, told the FBI and Whitewater prosecutors that Clinton said to Hale in a tunnel under the state Capitol steps, "You're going to have to help us out. We're going to need to raise some money." Brown told the Associated Press, "There's no question that Clinton was pressuring Hale." Brown reported a bribe offer to change his testimony in June of 1997 while in London. McDougal joined the Clinton death count when he had a heart attack under mysterious circumstances while in prison.

GRAND LARCENY AND MONEY LAUNDERING AT ADFA

As Governor, Bill Clinton established the Arkansas Development Finance Authority, ADFA, to issue state bonds for projects such as school and college construction. Webster Hubbell, the Rose Law firm partner, drafted and introduced Act 1072, the legislation that created ADFA. Larry Nichols, ADFA marketing director, stated that the first loan provided by ADFA was $2.85 million to a company named Park-O-Meter, which among other things, allegelly retrofitted airplane nose cones to carry drugs. Webster Hubbell was the secretary/treasurer of Park-O-Meter, which was owned by his father-in-law, Seth Ward.

Larry Nichols explained how ADFA was used by Bill Clinton to reward friends and campaign contributors with many times more than their contributions in the form of loans that were never to be repaid. For example, Nichols stated on *The Clinton Chronicles* video that Don Tyson, the Tyson Foods owner who was investigated as a major drug traffic suspect, contributed over $600,000 to Clinton and received $10,000,000 from ADFA. Bill Clinton totally controlled ADFA by appointing all board members.

Larry Nichols also explained how ADFA was used as a money laundering agency for Barry Seal's drug trafficking operation that ran between 1982 and 1986 from the airport in Mena, Arkansas, where family members of deceased Colombian drug lord, Pablo Escobar, lived. Then Governor Clinton issued $664,000,000 in bonds to Lasater & Co., which was owned by Bill Clinton's campaign contributor, fundraiser and convicted cocaine distributor, Dan Lasater. Former Clinton bodyguard, L.D. Brown, went on a flight where drugs were flown back to Arkansas. He stated during an interview that when he told Clinton about it, Clinton was aware of Seal's operation and knew that it was "Lasater's deal."

As much as $100,000,000 a month was reportedly transferred between ADFA and other banks, including Bank of Commerce & Credit, BCCI, which created one of the worst scandals in savings and loan history when it collapsed in 1985 and was shut down in July, 1991. As President, Clinton dismissed charges against the head of BCCI, Clark Clifford, who was the former LBJ Defense Secretary. Bank records show that the laundering abruptly ended when Barry Seal was assassinated in February of 1986 after he was ordered to be confined at a Baton Rouge Salvation Army halfway house just before he was scheduled to testify before a grand jury. Seal's attorney was Richard Ben Veniste, the Lead Democratic Counsel for the Senate Whitewater hearings.

THE KEVIN IVES AND DON HENRY MURDERS

On August 23, 1987, a train ran over the bodies of Kevin Ives and Don Henry as they lay across railroad tracks in Saline County, Arkansas, during the middle of the night. Fahmy Malak, the Arkansas State medical examiner, ruled that the deaths were accidental because the boys were under the influence of drugs and had fallen asleep on the tracks. The parents did not believe the examiner and spent over a year trying to get a second opinion while Malak did not comply with court orders for information. Finally during a second autopsy, Atlantan Joe Burton and six other forensic experts determined that Don had been stabbed in the back, and Kevin's skull was crushed before it was mutilated by Malak during the initial autopsy.

The *L.A. Times* found nearly 20 suspicious or obviously inaccurate death rulings by Malak, even ones that favored Clinton's mother, a nurse anesthetist who apparently had two patients die while under sedation for minor surgery. Other questionable death ruling examples include a suicide ruling for

Raymond Albright, who was shot in the chest five times, and a natural cause death ruling for James Milam, who was decapitated. Malak reported directly to Jocelyn Elders, who instead of firing him, gave him approximately a 40 percent raise. When the citizens held protest demonstrations and forced his resignation in 1992, Clinton created a new position in the state health department for Malak. Clinton told reporters that Malak was "stressed out", and Elders stated on video that "Arkansas owes Dr. Malak a great debt and a real apology."

Further investigation revealed that Ives and Henry had stumbled across a drug trafficking drop point known by the drug pilots of Barry Seal as A12. The drugs were dropped regularly out of planes flying from Colombia to Mena, Arkansas, and then picked up by ground crews that frequently included local government officials and policemen. Police deny the existence of the rifle that was the possible murder weapon used to kill Kevin Ives, even though it was videotaped as it was collected from the scene. They also deny the existence of the tarp that engineers saw covering the bodies of Ives and Henry as they lay on the tracks. From 1988 to 1995, seven people with knowledge of the death of Ives and Henry, including some of those who were on the tracks that night, have also been murdered. No one has ever been charged in any of the murders.

ABUSE OF POWER IN THE FBI AND TREASURY

Clinton White House Counsel, Bernard Nussbaum, appears to have authorized Craig Livingstone, White House Personnel Security Office Director, to acquire confidential FBI files of over 900 officials using a list of names he gave the FBI. By contrast, in the Nixon administration Charles Colson was indicted and convicted on one count of possession of an FBI file. Livingstone was identified in reports as a former bouncer with a history of drug use and no qualifying experience for his position.

Livingstone and his supervisor, William Kennedy III, a former Rose Law Firm partner, testified that they did not know who hired Livingstone. I found this particularly amazing since I know of no one who has ever gotten a job without knowing who hired him. FBI agents Dennis Sculimbrene and Gary

Aldrich stated that Kennedy told them Hillary Clinton had hired him. A document leter uncovered by Judicial Watch also confirmed that Hillary Clinton hired Livingstone.

Livingstone claimed in June 1996 testimony that the list of names he gave the FBI was left over from the Bush Secret Service agents, since it contained many key Republican adversaries. However, Secret Service agents testified that no such list was left over. Livingstone's executive assistant, Mari Anderson, who apparently hid in fear for three months in Georgia, testified that Livingstone and Anthony Marceca had unrestricted file access. She also stated that six months of entries in the file check out logbook were missing. Marceca, a White House Personnel Office employee, invoked the 5th Amendment and refused to testify. Bill Clinton has maintained that this was "a completely honest bureaucratic snafu".

During the FBI file investigation by the Senate Judiciary Committee, Secret Service agents Libonati and Undercoffer provided testimony refuting Craig Livingstone's claim that the list of 900 names he gave the FBI was left over from the Bush administration. On October 2, 1996, after their testimony, Treasury Department Inspector General Valerie Lau opened an investigation into the agents' notes, as indicated by the testimony, and Email message of Assistant Inspector General James Cottos. The investigation was based on a memo from Donald Goldberg, a Congressional staffer, who was hired in 1997 by the White House Office of Legislative Affairs. The *Washington Times* reported that Emily Coleman, head of Eastern region investigations, admitted that on October 9, 1996, she destroyed the original case-tracking document, created a new one without the names of the agents and backdated it to October 2, 1996. Afterwards, Lau told Congress on two separate occasions that the agents were not under investigation. Senator Grassley called for and received her resignation.

Former Clinton aide, George Stephanopoulos helped to conceal damaging information in a related Judicial Watch law suit. A federal judge found that his testimony was "not truthful" and his memory loss was "not believable". His untruthfulness apparently qualified him to join Sam Donaldson, Barbara Walters and others at ABC where he was hired as a commentator.

BLACKMAIL AT THE IRS

Since the election of Bill Clinton, the IRS has made politically biased rulings and audited over a dozen organizations and individuals that have opposed Clinton policies or exposed corruption in his administration. Some organizations that have been audited include:

- Heritage Foundation,
- National Rifle Association,
- Christian Coalition,
- Citizens Against Government Waste,
- Freedom Alliance,
- Western Journalism Center.

Paula Jones also was audited immediately after her lawsuit was filed even though she was not working and her husband made only $30,000 a year. IRS agent Thomas Cederquist told the Western Journalism Center that their audit was not random, but political, and the outcome would be determined in Washington. The IRS also requested extensive detail on the publishing of articles about the death of Vince Foster, even though it had nothing to do with income. The Heritage Foundation was forced to produce a 75-foot stack of paper in response to IRS questions that wanted detailed data on each seminar, lecture and publication from 1994 through 1996. After a four-year wait, the National Policy Forum was denied tax exempt 503(c)4 status by the IRS even though it operated almost identically to the Democratic Leadership Council which had the status.

No known pro-Clinton organizations were audited during this period. The discrepancy in audit targets perhaps can best be explained by the fact that the person appointed by Bill Clinton to head the IRS during many of these audits was Margaret Richardson, a close family friend and 1992 Presidential campaign worker.

IRS audit abuses also continued in the Travel Office scandal. David Watkins, Clinton's director of the Office of Administration, fired Billy Dale and the Travel Office staff on May 19, 1993. Multiple communications by Watkins, Mack McLarty and William Kennedy from May 12-17 revealed that

Hillary Clinton ordered the firings to provide business for TRM, Inc., a travel agency partially owned by Harry Thomasson, a campaign fundraiser.

On May 20, 1993, Dale's air charter service, UltrAir was visited by three IRS employees who showed up to perform an audit. Mari Anderson, Livingstone's executive assistant, testified that around the same time, Livingstone asked her to check out Billy Dale's FBI file for White House personnel. In December 1993, after banning Dale from the White House, Livingstone's office requested and received his raw background file from the FBI, under the grounds that he was "being considered for access." The Clintons later brought against Dale, embezzlement and mismanagement charges, which were dismissed by a federal jury in two hours of deliberation. The taxpayers reimbursed Dale's attorney $400,000.

In 2000, a bi-partisan congressional committe finally determined that the White House had made illegal requests for information from the IRS on at least two occasions. One request came directly from the office of Vice President Al Gore.

VOTER FRAUD AT THE INS

The Immigration & Naturalization Service (INS) typically registers about 300,000 immigrants per year for citizenship. In 1996, it registered 1.1 million before the election, including 180,000 illegal immigrants and 70,000 criminals. In an April 4, 1997 House Appropriations Committee meeting, INS head Doris Meissner, confirmed that the INS was working closely with the Vice President and his office to register the immigrants. Meissner and other INS employees also acknowledged the existence of Email messages from the Vice President's office to the INS stating Bill Clinton's frustration and concern that the registration process may be going too slowly. His concern seemed to be that it would be completed in time for the election.

MORE WASHINGTON SCANDALS

The Clintons spent about $1,700,000 of taxpayer money to build and maintain a database of contributors at the White

House under the direction of Hillary Clinton. Many of the data sources were illegally collected from White House public property. In addition, Bill Clinton used 103 White House coffee klatches to raise nearly $27,000,000 from over 1,500 individuals who attended. The Pendleton Act, as well as Sections 600, 607 and 641 in Title 18 of the federal criminal code, prohibit the use government property or taxpayer funds to solicit personal or political contributions. Bill Clinton claimed that visits took place in his residence; however, videos released in October 1997 showed that many occurred in the Oval Office.

Dozens of other contributors received overnight stays at the White House for no apparent reason other than that they were a donor. This was confirmed in a 1995 memo from Clinton to then DNC finance chairman, Terry McAuliffe that said, "Ready to start overnights right away." for those who contributed "50,000 or more".

In March 1994, Webster Hubbell, a former Rose Law Firm partner, quit his appointment as Associate Attorney General, the third highest U.S. Justice Department position, to stand trial for embezzling $482,410 from Rose clients and evading $143,747 in taxes. Hubbell is the individual most knowledgeable about the Clintons' Arkansas activities and even kept the Whitewater partnership files. Between March and December when he was convicted, Hubbell received over $700,000 from 10 contributors, such as the Lippo Group, and has no plausible explanation of what work he did for the money. During this time he also had over 70 meetings with 20 different Clinton administration officials, including three with the President. Officials, including Mickey Cantor, Mack McLarty and Erskine Bowles, solicited money and favors for Hubbell from many sources.

DRUGS AND DRUG TRAFFICKING

Bill Clinton's brother, Roger, told undercover agents, when he was videotaped snorting cocaine and busted for distribution by the DEA, "I have to get some for my brother. He has a nose like a vacuum cleaner." Witness Sharline Wilson stated that she had seen then Governor Clinton snorting cocaine at a party with his brother Roger. Larry Nichols stated that Clinton was hooked on cocaine. Dr. Samuel Houston, former physician of Bill Clinton's father-in-law, stated on *The Clinton Chronicles* video that Clinton was admitted to the Little Rock Medical Center and treated for a drug overdose. He also noted that Clinton was regularly treated for a sinus condition that could be caused by the destruction of membrane from snorting cocaine. Bill Clinton consistently refused to release all of his medical records.

As Governor and President, Bill Clinton maintained close relationships with drug traffickers. Dan Lasater, his friend, campaign contributor, fundraiser and suspected supplier, was convicted on cocaine distribution charges in a case that involved giving cocaine to teenage girls in exchange for sex. He was sentenced to 30 months in jail but was quickly pardoned by Clinton after five months. Another Clinton associate who owned a lumber company, was reportedly caught transporting cocaine in a truck with a lumber facade. Jorge Cabrera, a convicted felon who donated $20,000 to the DNC, had his picture taken with Al Gore at the 1995 White House Christmas party. Twice In the 1980s, Cabrera plea bargained after being indicted on charges of drug trafficking, racketeering and managing a continuing narcotics operation. In January of 1996, undercover agents arrested Cabrerra, a Cali cartel operative, with over 5,800 pounds of cocaine, most likely from the Cali cartel.

As President, Bill Clinton took amazing steps to facilitate drug trafficking within the U.S. In 1997, he decertified Colombia in the "war on drugs". In 1995, his DOD appointee removed radar tracking on planes coming from Colombia and Peru. From 1993 to 1994, Clinton eliminated the money laundering division of the U.S. Justice Department, cut over 80 percent of the White House Office of National Drug Control Policy, cut 355 Drug Enforcement Administration members, cut customs drug interdiction budget by one-third and cut $500,000,000 from Defense Department, anti-drug and other drug treatment and prevention budgets.

COMMUNISTS BRIBE THE DEMOCRATS

Senate campaign finance investigation testimony confirmed that many illegal large foreign contributions were accepted by the Clinton inaugural fund, Clinton defense fund and Democrat National Committee (DNC), in conjunction with Presidential fundraisers. Many of the illegal revenue streams were traced to individuals and organizations connected to the Communist Chinese military. The pattern of repetition and deception for illegal foreign contributions showed that they were not accidental. Here are some reported examples:

- Indonesians Sonya and Arief Wiriadinata, who were sent to a White House meeting by Mr. Riady, donated $450,000 even though they filed no U.S. tax return.
- Charles Yah Lin Trie donated $350,000 to the DNC and $640,000 to the legal defense fund in sequentially numbered money orders received from various cities by people who strangely have the same handwriting.
- Ted Seong, head of the Communist controlled Pagoda Red Mountain Cigarette Co., donated $400,000 to the DNC before Democrats attempted to implement anti-tobacco legislation, against American companies.
- Yogesh Gandhi donated $325,000 to the DNC despite having liens filed against him for non-payment of taxes.
- The Cheong Am American Co. donated $250,000 to the DNC, despite having raised no funds ever in the United States.

Nearly $1,000,000 in funds raised by Bill Clinton's long time friend, Charlie Trie, was traced through the Communist controlled Bank of China to a Chinese resident of Macao named Ng Lap Seng, also known as Mr. Wu. Senate testimony from the FBI showed that Ng was involved with the People's Consultative Congress, a panel that advised the Chinese government and Communist party on business and economic matters.

The investigations have resulted in more than 100 non-cooperative witnesses including:

- over 35 witnesses pleading the Fifth Amendment,
- over 20 witnesses requiring immunity for their testimony,
- over 10 witnesses leaving the country and
- over 10 foreign nationals refusing to be interviewed.

John Huang, the former U.S. President of the Lippo Group, was the DNC's Asian fundraiser for most of the illegal campaign contributions. The Indonesian based Lippo Group had a partnership with the Chinese Communist government controlled China Resource Holding Co. to own the Hong Kong Chinese Bank jointly, also known as Hua Ren Jituan in China. Under Hong Kong law, the partnership provided China Resources with access to all Lippo corporate information. China Resources was found by the Cox Committee to be an agent of "political, economic and military espionage" according to investigators from the Defense Intelligence Agency and Senate Governmental Affairs.

Huang left Lippo with a $780,000 bonus and took a large pay cut to join the Commerce Department. While at Commerce, he was given a top secret clearance, received over 100 intelligence briefings and reviewed dozens of top secret documents. To join the DNC, Huang took another large pay cut and was reissued a new security clearance. He also maintained a separate office at Stephens, Inc., owned by Jackson Stephens, the Lippo Group's Worthen Bank partner who made a $3,000,000 loan to the Clinton campaign in 1992.

Huang's security clearance was issued by the Commerce Department Chief of Personnel Security and reissued by the Defense Industrial Security Clearance office without the standard full-field FBI background checks. Commerce Department phone logs showed that he made nearly 400 calls to Lippo or its subsidiaries. DNC Finance Director Richard Sullivan testified that Bill Clinton urged him to hire John Huang, former U.S. President of the Lippo Group. Nolanda Hill, a business associate of Ron Brown, testified in a Judicial Watch law suit that Bill Clinton pressured Brown to hire Huang at the Commerce Department.

The Senate Campaign Finance investigation and the House Government Reform and Oversight investigation found that the Clinton / Gore campaigns and the DNC had seven sources of revenue traceable through 11 revenue streams to Communist Chinese controlled companies or individuals connected to the People's Liberation Army. These money streams provided millions of dollars in illegal campaign contributions dating back to when Bill Clinton was still Governor of Arkansas. An

April 17, 1996, DNC memo indicated that Bill Clinton was overseeing the fundraising efforts.

TREASONOUS TECHNOLOGY TRANSFERS

What did the Communist Chinese government get for its money? Bill Clinton transferred export technology decisions from the State Department to the Commerce Department in 1996. This weakened export controls and increased security risks. During his administration, *American Investigator* reported that over 1,000 dual use and military technologies were transferred to the Communist Chinese government. U.S. exports to China included:

- top-secret encryption
- missile guidance
- MIRV technology
- 46 supercomputers
- fighter bomber "hot section" range technology
- nearly complete missile and strategic bomber factories
- global satellite positioning
- patent database information

Bill Clinton became the first President in history to transfer military technology to a Communist nation over the objections of his own government agencies. Some of the transfers raised objections from the:

- Defense Department
- National Security Administration
- State Department
- Justice Department
- Judiciary Committee
- Congressional members

Bill Clinton apparently even allowed encryption technology to be transferred to China after he had prevented it from being transferred to Australia, one of our allies.

Clinton also met Long Beach, California, officials at the White House in September 1995 and visited them in August 1996 to support the Communist controlled, China Ocean

Shipping Co. (COSCO) takeover of the Long Beach naval station. American military intelligence believes COSCO, which has a business relationship that controls both sides of the Panama Canal, is a front for Chinese military operations. No national security review of the takeover was conducted even though COSCO had been caught shipping 2,000 illegal AK-47s into the Oakland port.

The weapons came from Poly Technologies, just days before Wang Jun, the chairman of their parent company, China International Trust Investment Company, met with Bill Clinton at the White House. Wang Jun, who gained White House access without a backround check, is a renowned arms dealer and son of Wang Zhen, a general involved in the Tiananmen Square massacre.

After the House voted on impeachment, the Cox Committee determined that the technology transfers and policy changes of the Clinton administration were massive. A separate chapter of this book is allocated to describe them in detail.

REPAYING THE CONDUIT

The conduit for much of the Communist Chinese money flow was the Lippo Group, an Indonesian company owned by the Riady family, who are ethnic Chinese. They have many business investment interests such as the financing of coal mining in Indonesia and China through their Hong Kong Chinese Bank.

A leading export of Indonesia is a unique form of clean burning, low sulfur coal, that is mined in the coal fields of Kalimantan Island, formerly known as Borneo. This super compliance coal is the only coal that meets the U.S. Clean Air Standards Act, and the largest deposit of it in the world is at the Kaiparowits plateau in southern Utah. The plateau area included 62 billion tons of coal valued at over a trillion dollars, about four billion barrels of oil and approximately three trillion cubic feet of natural gas.

Three million tons of coal that would produce 1,000 Utah jobs were about to be mined by the Kentucky-based company, Andalex Resources. However, Bill Clinton made the coal-mining project unfeasible by declaring 1.7 million acres in southern Utah as the Grand Escalante National Monument. The area is larger than the states of Delaware and Rhode Island combined.

The declaration was kept secret from Utah officials until midnight of the night before Clinton made the announcement, which actually occurred in northern Arizona instead of Utah. In protest of the declaration, the people of the Utah district immediately voted Democrat Rep. Richard Orion out of office and replaced him with Republican Chris Cannon, who went on to serve as a House manager in the impeachment trial. Twenty-nine counties also filed suit against Bill Clinton's decision which was based on the 1908 Antiquities Act. Kathleen McGinty and Linda Lance, the head and associate director of the Council of Environmental Quality, stated in Emails that the lands were "not really endangered" and "not threatened", respectively. It seems obvious that Bill Clinton did not make the declaration because he was concerned about the enviroment.

This New Attorney General

After the nominations of Zoe Baird and Kimba Wood had failed, Bill Clinton was able to have the U.S. Senate confirm Janet Reno as Attorney General of the United States. One of her first actions was to file a brief in the U.S. vs. Knox case. Reno sought to reverse the conviction of a child pornographer on the grounds that child pornography is a form of free speech rights protected by the First Amendment of the Constitution. She received a rebuke from the U.S. Senate by a 99-0 vote.

Around that time, Janet Reno appeared on CNN's *Larry King Live* and stated that her major objective was to make the Justice Department more accountable. This was pleasant news after the recent fiascoes at Ruby Ridge and Waco. However, she established an immediate track record that was diametrically opposed to any accountability.

WACO

When Janet Reno took office she was faced with a stand-off between federal agents and the Branch Davidians at Mount Carmel, near Waco, Texas. The ATF had brought in dozens of agents in an attempt to serve a search warrant on David Koresh, allegedly for having an automatic weapon. House

Waco Investigation testimony in 1995 revealed that the ATF could have picked up Koresh while he was out several times in the days before the February 28, 1993, raid. The ATF falsely told the military that Davidians were manufacturing drugs so that the ATF could receive military training that would normally violate the Posse Comitatus Act. Federal agents later accused Koresh of abusing children, although Texas Human Services had found no such abuse in two investigations.

More disturbingly, no substantial evidence was ever presented that indicated the ATF attempted to serve the warrant peacefully. In fact, the ATF had even contacted press reporters and indicated that there may be a major shoot-out when it served the warrant. The Davidians claimed that the ATF shot first. Most videotapes of the raid and the front door, which contained bullet holes that could validate or disprove the Davidian claims, were either lost or destroyed by the ATF and FBI. The videos that were provided showed that the ATF was not under fire as they climbed onto the roof using ladders and stood behind cars firing at the Davidians.

On April 19, 1993, after a stand-off with the Davidians, the FBI attacked the church and living complex with tanks, helicopters, automatic weapons and deadly CS military tear gas, which is internationally banned in warfare. The CS gas powder was dissolved in methylene chloride and propelled by carbon dioxide, both potentially suffocating agents. This dissolution method releases a deadly hydrogen cyanide. Reno approved the CS military gas attack that led to the deaths of over 80 men, women and children who had never committed any crime.

Videos, debris, Forward Looking Infrared (FLIR) tape and testimony from the survivors corroborate that the FBI started the fire that killed most of the Davidians on April 19. The FLIR tape shows pyrotechnic explosions immediately after the last gas insertions at the gym and second floor right front corner, the areas where fires first started. Pyrotechnic M-651 gas canisters, which disperse gas by burning and are fired from an M-79 grenade launcher, were found at the gym and right front corner of the Davidian property. Survivors Derek Lovelock and David Thibodeau saw fireballs igniting their paths while racing through the property from the gym and second floor of the right front corner, respectively.

The FLIR tape clearly showed heat images from automatic weapons fired at the Davidians as they tried to escape from the burning kitchen / dining area in back of the complex. FLIR creator and former Defense Department Night Vision Lab Manager, Edward Allerd, stated that "nothing in nature could duplicate the thermal signature" of the automatic weapons' fire shown. Infraspection Institute confirmed Allerd's findings after being contracted to analyze the tape for *60 Minutes*, whose producers then withheld the Institute's analysis from the American public

At least three Delta Special Forces members, two tanks, helicopters, communications equipment and 40-50millimeter military ammunition were part of the assault. Over 360 military ferret rounds of gas were fired into all windows of the Davidian buildings, despite manufacturer warnings that the ferrets could kill anyone that they struck. An aerial videotape also showed one tank destroying a Davidian building while people were still inside. Autopsy reports indicated that six bodies found in the rubble of that building were crushed to death.

Despite all of the evidence, Reno stated that she "could not find anything wrong" with FBI actions in Waco. She confirmed the FBI claim that the Davidians set themselves on fire based on a barely audible recording of the Davidians that had no supporting evidence. Janet Reno also could find no violation of the Posse Comitatus Act which expressly prohibits the use of military equipment and personnel to enforce laws against American citizens unless authorized by the U.S. Constitution or an act of Congress.

RUBY RIDGE

Janet Reno refused to support the conclusion of a Justice Department investigation that found an FBI sniper shot which killed Vicki Weaver at Ruby Ridge, Idaho, in 1992 was unconstitutional. Senate testimony showed that an FBI sniper killed Vicki Weaver by shooting her in the head as she held her baby while standing with the door open on her front porch. The FBI snipers were shooting at the Weavers from over 200 yards away using rifles with 10 power scopes.

In bone chilling Congressional testimony, the snipers and Assistant FBI Director Larry Potts, stated that they had the right to shoot and kill anyone if that person was holding a gun. Chairman Arlen Specter pointed out that such a situation did not warrant the use of deadly force according to FBI policy. On the House floor, Idaho Representative Helen Chenoweth called for the resignation of Potts, who was also responsible for the Waco disaster. Potts is a personal friend of FBI Director Freeh, who was appointed by Reno. Randy Weaver's attorney called for Lon Horiuchi, the sniper who killed Vicki Weaver, to be tried for murder based on the Justice Department investigation. Instead, Horiuchi and Potts received paid leave for over two years. The State of Idaho decided to pick up the ball and charge Horiuchi with manslaughter in the shooting, but he was eventually found not guilty, as expected, after his case was moved to a judge in federal district court. Some accountability was achieved through the judicial system when Randy Weaver was able to obtain a $10,000,000 settlement in a wrongful death suit. However, Horiuchi was later put in charge of a Waco sniper post that the FLIR tape indicates fired on the Davidians.

CREATING THE DEPARTMENT OF INJUSTICE

Another one of Janet Reno's first acts as Attorney General was to fire all 93 United States attorneys, a move unprecedented in American history. She stated that the replacement of all U.S. attorneys was a "joint decision" with the White House. Her liaison with the White House was the third highest ranking Justice Department official, Associate Attorney General, Webster Hubbell, who is now a convicted felon.

In another historically unprecedented move, Janet Reno fired FBI Director William Sessions on a trumped up charge of transportation misappropriation. Sessions was forced to leave immediately on July 19, 1993 and the next day the body of Chief White House Counsel, Vince Foster, was found in Fort Marcy Park. Sessions was eventually replaced with Louis Freeh, based on a recommendation from Robert Fiske, one of Clinton's former lawyer partners.

THE FEDERAL BUREAU OF INVESTIGATION

Under Freeh, the FBI entered the most incompetent, unaccountable period in its history as illustrated by the following evidence, most of which was collected in Congressional investigations:

- Louis Freeh promoted his close friend, Larry Potts, despite the Assistant FBI Director's responsibility for both the disastrous Waco and Ruby Ridge sieges;
- Freeh's FBI illegally gave Clinton administration personnel over 900 files, including those on political adversaries. Freeh's FBI General Counsel, Howard Shapiro apparently even briefed White House Counsel, Jack Quinn, on the information;
- Freeh's FBI failed to process criminal background checks on citizenship applications resulting in over 70,000 criminals' being granted U.S. citizenship in time for the 1996 elections;
- Freeh ordered agents to read Richard Jewell his Miranda rights while Jewell was cooperating to supposedly film a training video. The order was issued by phone over the unanimous protest of all involved Atlanta FBI agents;
- Freeh's FBI was cited along with the ATF by 13,500 Oklahomans who were granted a new grand jury investigation into the alleged government cover-up involving the Oklahoma City bombing;
- Freeh's FBI crime labs were accused by agent Fredric Whitehurst of tainting evidence in high profile cases including the Oklahoma City bombing case;
- Freeh's FBI agents interrogated agent Gary Aldrich about his book, *Unlimited Access*, as well as agent Dennis Sculimbrene about his Craig Livingstone background inquiry that linked the Livingstone hiring to Hillary Clinton;
- Freeh refused to get the FBI involved in the Vince Foster death investigation, which was handled by the park police, despite the fact that Foster was the highest ranking government official to die of unnatural causes since the assassination of John F. Kennedy.

THE VINCE FOSTER MURDER

Vince Foster, the chief White House Deputy Counsel and the Clintons' personal lawyer, allegedly committed suicide in

Fort Marcy Park by placing a gun into his mouth and literally blowing his brains out. The conclusion was reached by independent prosecutor Robert Fiske, who happened to be the lawyer for International Paper, Inc., which sold land to the Clinton / McDougal Whitewater partnership. However, FBI lab analysis, witness testimony and other physical evidence illustrate that Foster could not have committed suicide in the park or anywhere else. Some examples of the evidence are:

- Although the coroner's report showed a skull exit wound, no exit wound fragments or bullet were found in the park.
- Foster's fingerprints were not on the gun, but another print was on it.
- Foster's family stated that he did not own the gun which had been untraceable since 1913.
- A search of Foster's ammunition showed he had no bullets for that type of gun.
- No powder burns were on his mouth, but there were powder burns on both of his forefingers.
- There was abnormally little blood at the scene.
- His glasses had no powder burns, and they were found almost 20 feet from his body.
- No grass or dirt was found on Foster's shoes even though he would have walked over 100 yards through the park to the point of the suicide.
- Foster's suit, shirt, tie and underwear were covered with carpet fibers.

Evidence indicated that Bernard Nussbaum, White House Counsel, turned over Foster's briefcase to the authorities. However, three different witnesses said that they saw the briefcase in Foster's car at Fort Marcy Park. So how did it get back to the White House? Did it fly or walk? On the third search of the briefcase, a suicide note, supposedly written by Foster, suddenly appeared in it. The suicide note was declared a forgery by several different handwriting analysts. The forgery was so obvious that anyone could see many letters that had several pen dots indicating the letters were drawn. No fingerprints were found on the note even though it was torn into 28 pieces.

OBSTRUCTIONS OF JUSTICE FROM
THE DEPARTMENT OF JUSTICE

Janet Reno failed to implement a 1993 FBI investigation recommendation to prosecute Chuck Banks, the former Arkansas U.S. attorney who was to be tried for obstruction of justice for shutting down a federal drug investigation that implicated many people within the state and local governments. The investigation found compromised local judges and prosecutors, drug trafficking at Mena, money laundering through ADFA, suppression and distortion by the media and information about the murder of Kevin Ives and Don Henry, as well as five other subsequent deaths.

Assistant U.S. Attorney Bob Govar, who resigned in protest of the shutdown, received much information from Jean Duffey, the head of a drug task force investigation that was also shut down by Judge John Cole. Duffey was attacked with 200 false press articles, threatened with imprisonment on an illegal warrant issued by the same judge, pressured to turn over her investigation to the people she was investigating and forced to flee the state temporarily when her mother received a tip from a police dispatcher that she would be killed if imprisoned.

Despite confiscation of task force evidence, Dan Harmon, a prosecutor that she implicated, was tried and convicted in Arkansas during June of 1997 on five drug-related felony counts, each carrying a maximum of 20 years in jail and a $150,000 fine. Harmon was convicted in 1990 on tax evasion but had his suspended law license reinstated after Winston Bryant, the Arkansas Attorney General under Governor Clinton, testified on his behalf. To date, no one has been charged in any of the murders, despite contentions of the task force undercover agents that the murders were easily solvable.

THE JUSTICE DEPARTMENT AND
ORGANIZED CRIME

The Reno Justice Department shut down the prosecution of Arthur Coia, the head of Laborers International Union of North America, who was investigated by the Justice Department over several years for corrupt labor union practices such as extortion, conspiring to prevent free elections and even death by fire bombing. The National Legal and Policy Center reports explained how Justice concluded in its 1994 complaint that Coia was "asso-ciated with, influenced from and controlled by" organized crime.

His union political action committee, Laborers' Political League, contributed over $4.5 million to the Democrat National Committee and its candidates. In February of 1995, Coia helped Hillary Clinton raise millions of dollars in a Miami Beach fundraiser at the Fountainbleau Hotel for the top of-ficials of his union. In February of 1995, the Justice Department suddenly dropped the complaint against Coia, signed a consent decree, withheld his prosecution and told him to clean up his own union. Officials of the Janet Reno-led Justice Department declared that the consent decree was "the finest, most practical resolution that's ever been reached in a case of alleged mob influence." Coia thanked them by being vice chairman of a May 1996 gala that raised over $12,000,000 for Democrats. Coia was eventually convicted on an unrelated felony.

ATTORNEY GENERAL OR CLINTON DEFENSE LAWYER?

Soon after her Senate confirmation, Janet Reno became the defense lawyer for President Clinton. She began her clever defense by appointing Robert Fiske as a special independent prosecutor to investigate the Clintons' Whitewater dealings even though Fiske was a lawyer for International Paper Inc., the company that had sold land to the Whitewater partnership of Clinton and McDougal. Fiske was also a lawyer for the Bank of Commerce and Credit, which received laundered drug money transfers from the Arkansas Development Finance Authority (ADFA), according to ADFA marketing director Larry Nichols. Questions concerning the impartiality of Fiske mounted after he ruled that Vince Foster committed suicide. In 1994, he was replaced by Ken Starr, who was selected by a three-judge panel, despite the fact that Starr had been on Janet Reno's short list when she appointed Fiske.

During 1994, Janet Reno barred expansion of the probe into the affairs of Agriculture Secretary Mike Espy so that it would not include Don Tyson, the Clinton campaign contributor who was accused of bribing Espy. The investigation of Mike Espy, conducted by independent prosecutor Donald Smaltz, is believed to have revealed evidence that Don Tyson may have been involved in drug abuse, drug distribution, money laundering and even murder for hire. Much of the evidence already existed in Arkansas State Police intelligence files as shown on *The Clinton Chronicals* viedo. Tyson, owner of Tyson foods, had contributed over $600,000 to various Clinton campaigns. Tyson Foods counselor, James Blair, was the individual who turned a $1,000 cattle futures investment into $100,000 for Hillary Clinton.

During 1997, Reno filed amicus briefs with the Supreme Court in an attempt to support the claim by Bill Clinton that he should be shielded from the Paula Jones sexual harassment civil suit until he left office on the grounds that he was the commander in chief of the U.S. armed forces. The Supreme Count ruled unanimously, by a 9-0 count, against Reno.

Also in 1997, Reno attempted to compromise the Kenneth Starr investigation by challenging an 8th U.S. Court of Appeals ruling that found the Hillary Clinton personal attorney client privilege claim did not apply to White House lawyers who were paid by American taxpayers. The ruling, which was challenged in the U.S. Supreme Court, involved Vince Foster and Rose Law Firm billing record matters that Hillary Clinton discussed on July 11, 1995, with White House Counsels Miriam Nemetz and Jane Sherbourne. The Supreme Court refused to hear the case.

COVERING UP FOR COMMUNISTS

For almost the entire Clinton term, the Reno-led Justice Department repeatedly attempted to stymie Judicial Watch in its freedom of information suit against the Commerce Department, even though the Justice Department's role was to make sure that the Commerce Department responded properly. The Judicial Watch suit was responsible for the John Huang deposition, which led to the exposure of millions of dollars in illegal contributions to the Democratic National Committee and Clinton campaigns. In February 1996, Judicial Watch also subpoenaed Ron Brown, who was killed in the plane crash in Croatia during April 1996, while he was preparing for the deposition. An assistant U.S. attorney in the Justice Department filed numerous motions to delay the case, made repeated objections that were overruled during testimony and terminated a deposition against orders of the judge, who ruled that his conduct was "totally improper" and "totally scandalous."

The cover-up continued into 1997 as Reno also refused to grant immunity to four Buddhist nuns who had contributed $5,000 apiece to the Democratic National Committee at a fundraiser in the Hsi Lai Buddist temple in Hacienda Heights, Califorina, during April 1996. The event was attended by Vice President Al Gore who claimed he did not know it was a fundraiser even though evidence showed that virtually everyone on his staff knew it was a fundraiser, and dozens of early 1996 documents confirmed that it was.

The nuns, who like Buddist monks, are sworn to poverty, were unwilling to testify as to where they got the money unless granted immunity. Reno admitted that the Justice Department would not prosecute the nuns but refused to grant immunity which helped conceal the illegal foreign source of the contributions. The Senate committee granted immunity to the nuns by votes of 15-1 and 13-3. The nuns testified that the related temple financial documents had been shredded.

Pictures showed two Communist Chinese agents sitting beside Al Gore and a Buddist monk at the fundraiser. The agents were, Maria Hsia, who helped John Huang with several fundraisers and Ted Sioeng, the head of the Communist controlled Pagoda Red Mountain Cigarette Co. Hsia was convicted an all five counts of campaign finance violations against her. Sioeng, who was also connected to Asian organized crime, gave $400,000 to the DNC just before the Democrat Party launched its anti-tobacco legislation against American companies under the guise of preventing teen smoking. Were they really trying to prevent teen smoking or were they repaying the Communists by giving them a foothold into the American cigarette market?

Janet Reno refused three separate House committee requests in 1997 to appoint a special counsel to investigate the Democratic National Committee and Presidential fundraising scandal, despite clear evidence of treasonous policies made by Bill Clinton in exchange for contributions. The requests were made by the Judiciary Committee in March and September, as well as the Government Reform and Oversight Committee in August.

In addition, FBI director Louis Freeh recommended an independent counsel, but Reno ignored him. Justice Department investigator, Charles Labella, who was hired and after a preliminary study, also recommended an independent counsel. Reno refused again, and Labella eventually resigned from the Justice Department. The House Government Reform and Oversight Committee, chaired by Dan Burton, requested the Freeh and Labella memos, and Janet Reno refused to comply. The committee voted to hold her in contempt, but the House never brought the contempt finding to the floor. Finally, Janet Reno allowed the House Judiciary Committee counsels, both Democrats, to review the memos at the Justice Department but not to take any notes about the content. Reno refused to let House Judiciary Committee members see the memos without redaction.

Despite the evidence presented in this chapter about Chinese infiltration into the American government, Reno said she could see no evidence that a special prosecutor was needed and even failed to notify the White House when the FBI informed her of Chinese attempts to influence the 1996 presidential elections. Assistant Attorney General, Joel Klein, added the final insult to American intelligence after the Justice Dept. received an initial favorable ruling in the Microsoft anti-trust case. He stated that "no person or corporation is above the law".

THE REAL STATE OF THE UNION

On January 20, 1999, President Bill Clinton gave his State of the Union address after he was impeached for perjury and obstruction of justice. Two years earlier, Bill Clinton had given a State of the Union speech where he declared that "The era of big government is over" and then minutes later in the same speech, announced roughly 17 new government programs requiring unfunded mandates. He already had established a track record of lying without conscience and now the additional awkwardness of a perjurer giving a State of the Union speech left him little credibility. It was difficult for a listener to believe what, if anything, he said was actually true. Therefore, I began to consider the events of the past two years and reflect on the real "state of the union". I considered that:

- President Bill Clinton, an impeached perjurer, who almost assuredly committed multiple felonies, was in control of America;

- The President had set up a state of tyranny in America by using the FBI, IRS, INS and Treasury Department to persecute his political adversaries;
- The President and his political party, the Democrats, committed bribery by selling their souls to the Communist Chinese military through at least seven separate sources of illegal revenue;
- The President committed multiple acts of treason by being the first to export sophisticated military technologies to a Communist government over the objections of his own goverment agencies, including the DOD, NSA, Justice Department and State Department;
- The President planned the bombing of Sudan and Afghanistan without consulting his Joint Chiefs of Staff and bombed Iraq two weeks after it began complying with U.N. inspections, but just hours after finding that he could not stop his impeachment;
- The President established executive orders to rule America by a dictatorship that can legally take away property of any American citizen and subordinate his/her rights to the international agencies;
- The President had kidnapped the American justice system by dismissing the FBI director, firing every single U.S. attorney and installing Janet Reno as an Attorney General, to serve as his defense lawyer;
- The Attorney General turned the Justice Department into the "Injustice Department" by filing phony privilege claims for the Clintons and preventing the investigation of the Communist Chinese money flow into the President's campaigns and political party;
- America's alternate hope, the independent counsel law, was proven useless after two special counsels ruled that Chief White House Counsel, Vince Foster, committed suicide without getting his fingerprints on the gun that was used to kill him;
- Major media organizations had systematically protected the President by keeping the American public almost totally uninformed;
- Most amazing of all, the opposing Republican Party, which controlled Congress, did not think that any of this was an election issue in 1996 or 1998.

The real state of the union and the evidence presented here is not just an indictment of President Bill Clinton and his administration. It is also an indictment of the Republican-led Congress which collected much of this evidence in Congressional investigations and then opted to protect Bill Clinton by not using it.

REFERENCES

Investigation of Whitewater Development Corporation and Related Matters #2-4, Senate Banking Committee.

Inquiry into U.S. Park Police Investigation of the Death of White House Deputy Counsel Vincent Foster, Senate Banking Committee.

Investigation into the Activities of Federal Law Enforcement Agencies toward the Branch Davidians - 1995, House Government Reform & Oversight Committee & House Judiciary Committee.

Investigation of Illegal or Improper Activities in Connection with 1996 Federal Election Campaign 1-6, Hearings 1-10, Senate Governmental Affairs.

Investigation of White House Travel Office Firings and Related Matters, House Government Reform and Oversight Committee.

Investigation of Political Fund Raising Improprieties and Possible Violations of Law #1-4, House Government Reform and Oversight Committee.

Behind Closed Doors: The Abuse of Trust & Discretion in Establishment of the Grand Escalante National Monument, House Resource Committee.

Senate Judiciary Committee Investigation into FBI Background Files (videos), C-Span.

Senate Governmental Affairs Committee Meeting 11/3/97.

House Appropriations Sub-committee Meeting 4/4/97.

Judicial Watch, Interim Impeachment Report to Congress.

Human Events - Case For Impeachment.

Ethics Watch Vol. 3 No. 1 - Vol. 5 No. 1, Ken Boehm & Peter Flaherty, National Legal & Policy Center.

Eugene Methvin, "The Clintons and the Union Boss," *Reader's Digest* 4/96.

London Sunday Times, 2/2/97.

Washington Times 2/9/97, 4/5/97, 12/26/96-12/30/96, 4/11/97-

4/18/97, National Weekly Edition 3/23/97, Vol. 4, No.25.

American Spectator, 7/97, 10/97.

China Trilogy (videos), American Investigator, Free Congress Research & Education Foundation.

Quid Pro Coal (video), American Investigator, Free Congress Research & Education Foundation.

The Clinton Legacy (video), Accuracy in Media.

The Clinton Chronicles (video), Citizens Video Press.

The Mena Cover-up (video), Citizens for Honest Government.

The Death of Vince Foster (video), Citizens for Honest Government.

Obstruction of Justice (video), Integrity Films.

William Gazecki, Michael McNulty, Dan & Amy Gifford, *Waco, Rules of Engagement* (video), Somford.

Martin Gross, *The Great Whitewater Fiasco,* Ballantine Books.

Jack Thompson, *The Truth About Janet Reno* (video), American Forum.

Christopher Ruddy, *The Strange Death of Vince Foster*, Free Press of Simon & Schuster.

Linda D. Thompson, *Waco: The Big Lie* (video), American Justice Federation.

Linda D. Thompson, *Waco II: The Big Lie Continues* (video), American Justice Federation.

CHAPTER SEVEN
THE UNHOLY NATO ALLIANCE

THE BOMBING OF YUGOSLAVIA

To expose the Republican Senate betrayal, two more citizens, Pat and Andrew, had joined forces to begin another web based rally, named March on Washington '99. Pat represented True Blue Patriots of Ohio and Andrew, from Massachusetts, was active in picketing NBC and eventually forcing them to air the Juanita Broaderrick interview where she stated that Bill Clinton raped her. I had grown somewhat weary but agreed to put together another agenda that included Bill Triplett, Larry Klayman, Michael Ruppert, Pat Matrisciana, Clliff Kincaid representing Accuracy in Media, former Vice Presidential candidate, Herb Titus, Bob Djurdjevic, a Serbian computer consultant who founded the Truth in Media web site and each of the organizers. We quickly adjusted the focus of this rally after March 24, when Bill Clinton began another atrocious bombing campaign, this time against the country of Yugoslavia.

In December, four hours after he was told he did not have enough votes to stop his impeachment, Bill Clinton had issued a bombing strike against Iraq. In August, when the sex scandal broke, Bill Clinton bombed Sudan and Afghanistan without consulting a single one of his Joint Chiefs of Staff during the planning. Iraq was bombed despite the fact that two weeks earlier, Iraq had begun complying again with U.N. weapons inspections. The bombs in Sudan were dropped on what was proven to be nothing more than a pharmaceutical plant. The ones in Afghanistan were in retaliation for the bombing of African embassies, which the national news media told us was the responsibility of an alleged Arab terrorist named Osama Bin Laden. However, this time Bill Clinton had actually joined Osama Bin Laden in support of the Kosovo Liberation Army (KLA), which was trying to force the province of Kosovo to secede from Yugoslavia.

The bombing of Yugoslavia was much worse since it was not an isolated strike, but a sustained bombing campaign. In addition, Bill Clinton had solicited and received the support of the North Atlantic Treaty Organization, (NATO). Nine of the 19 countries in the NATO alliance agreed to support the physical attack but America was doing about 90 percent of the bombing. Not a single country would have agreed to the attack without American initiation and leadership. The bombing was initiated exactly one month before the 50th anniversary celebration of NATO, held in Washington, D.C. That anniversary triggered nearly 2000 demonstrators to come to the capital for an April 24 anti-war protest that was blacked out by all of the national news media organizations except C-Span.

The new bombing campaign completely overshadowed the evidence of treason that had surfaced in the recently released Cox Committee report. Therefore, Yugoslavia would be the fourth country to fall victim to American bombs impeccably timed near the peak of a Clinton scandal.

THE PHONY WAR TRIGGER

In his March 24 speech, Bill Clinton justified the bombing of Yugoslavians by referring to a "massacre" where Serbian police allegedly lined up Albanians in a ditch and shot them. I was familiar with the lies about this incident, thanks to my friend Will Grigg, who wrote a tremendous cover story about it for *The New American* magazine in the previous month.

The alleged incident occurred at Racak on January 15th when the Serbian police forces were accompanied for the entire day by an Associated Press TV crew and two journalists, who saw no such massacre. The television footage reportedly showed Serbian police entering an empty town that was controlled by the KLA, engaging in a fierce battle with the KLA, who were dug into hillside trenches and then withdrawing from the town in the afternoon. Remaining KLA members then immediately returned to the town, but no bodies were seen. The bodies appeared the next day in trenches with little blood and few cartridges around them. The battle timing and fierceness of the battle indicated that THE TRENCHES WERE NEVER CONTROLLED BY SERBS WHEN THE BODIES WERE PLACED THERE.

The "massacre" was announced by Clinton administration official William Walker, whose account was denounced by French news sources, Le Figaro and Le Monde, based on the evidence they reported. Belarus and Finnish forensic experts who came to Yugoslavia could not verify the claims of massacre. Thus, America began bombing Yugoslavians based on false reports about an event that was likely staged. America entered the Vietnam War in much the same way after what are now considered false reports about a North Vietnamese attack on American ships in the Gulf of Tonkin. The false attack led Lyndon Johnson to create the Gulf of Tonkin resolution, which he used to place 550,000 troops in Vietnam, 58,000 of which never returned alive.

THE FALSE NATO CLAIMS OF GENOCIDE

NATO, and particularly Britain Prime Minister Tony Blair, backed up Clinton claims to the hilt with additional charges of genocide. Genocide against Albanians by Yugoslavian leader Slobodan Milosevic was the excuse that NATO used for bombing Yugoslavians. But when pressed for "ethnic cleansing" numbers in a March 25 Senate briefing, the Clinton administration stated that about 2,000 people, including 700 Serbs, were killed in the year before the bombing. Only a few dozen people had been killed during 1999 before the bombing.

In reality, there was a civil war between the Yugoslavian government and the KLA, who wanted Kosovo to secede from Yugoslavia against the will of Serbs and even most Albanians. Serbian hostilities were directed at the KLA, not Albanians, 100,000 of whom live peacefully in Belgrade as one of 26 Yugoslavian cultures.

Even after extensive residential area bombing drove hundreds of thousands of Kosovars from their homes and unleashed para-military forces that the government could no longer control, Kosovo Democratic Initiative spokesman, Fatmir Seholi, stated "As an Albanian, I am convinced that the Serbian government and security forces are not committing any kind of genocide."

I soon found out that false claims of genocide or oppression were used several times in the 20th century to justify invasions. In 1931, Japan invaded and occupied Manchuria allegedly to protect it from Chinese terrorists. In 1935, Mussolini invaded Ethiopia to free Ethiopians who were allegedly enslaved by their emperor. In 1938, Hitler invaded the Czech Republic to end alleged ethnic violence against native Germans there, just before he committed genocide against the Jews. NATO took chapter, page and verse directly from the Hitler and Mussolini war tactics.

THE ILLEGALITY OF THE WAR

NATO was established as an alliance of mostly European nations and chartered only to defend them against invasion, not to attack other sovereign countries. NATO violated three of its own articles as well as United Nations and Geneva convention principles when it bombed Yugoslavians, who have never attacked another country. Despite the illegalities, the U.N. Security Council failed to pass a resolution condemning the bombing, and the U.N. war crimes tribunal gathered "ethnic cleansing" evidence on Slobodan Milosevic during the bombing, while doing nothing to hold NATO leaders accountable for their breeches of all fundamental international law. Thus, the U.N. proved itself far too prejudiced to mediate any international crisis.

NATO conducted a sustained bombing campaign, which any rational person would agree is clearly an act of war. Bill Clinton violated Article 1, Section 8 of the U.S. Constitution by participating in the war without approval by Congress, which holds exclusive power to declare war. Thirty-one Congressmen filed an unsuccessful suit when, without their approval, Clinton also violated the 60-day limit for introduction of any hostilities in the War Powers Act. In fact, not one parliament of any nation in the entire world passed a resolution endorsing the war, thus NATO acted outside the will of all governing bodies, even those of its own participating countries.

THE FALSE MEDIA PORTRAYAL OF THE KLA

What kind of organization would stage a massacre? The media repeatedly portrayed the Kosovo Liberation Army as a group of freedom fighters attempting to liberate the ethnic Albanians from Kosovo. Will Grigg of The *New American* magazine and several other sources reported that they were actually drug funded Arab terrorists who received arms, equipment, money and training from forces of Osama Bin Laden, the terrorist who was accused of bombing two embassies in Africa. This KLA profile is based on our own State

Department, FBI and military intelligence reports, as recently as 1998, a year before the bombing started. The reports of drug allegations were also confirmed by the German, Swedish and Czech Republic police forces as well as the Strategic Research Institute of the U.S., which stated that it believed more Albanians may have died at the hands of the KLA than at the hands of the Serbs. Despite all of these reports, our Senators wanted to arm the KLA, and our President essentially gave them our air force.

In addition, America and other NATO countries supported the KLA covertly before and during the war. *PBS News Hour* reported on July 15, 1998, that selected Vietnam War veterans were training the KLA in Albania. After the bombing started, the *London Sunday Telegraph* reported on April 18 that the British special forces SAS unit had two training camps near the Albanian capital of Tirana. Jane's *Defense Weekly* publication confirmed on April 20 that France, Britain and U.S. special forces were working undercover in Kosovo. Canadian Parliament member, David Price, confirmed on April 19 that 50 Canadian soldiers were also working with the KLA in Kosovo to assist in bomb guidance. Apparently, they did not understand that water supplies, television stations and com- mercial power plants are not military targets.

Perhaps the most interesting report was released on April 8 from Jurgen Reents, spokesperson for the German PDS Party. It claims that the CIA founded the KLA by funneling funds through drug smuggling operations in Europe. It also says that the CIA formed a joint operation with the German Secret Service, to sow ethnic divisions in Yugoslavia and encourage its break-up. This effort to destabilize Yugoslavia, called Operation Roots, has been going on since the beginning of the Clinton Presidency, according to the report. The report also states that when Milosevic and Rugova were close to an agreement in 1998, the CIA stepped up KLA attacks on Yugoslavian police units. This is reminiscent of the fate of South Vietnamese President Diem when he wanted to reach an agreement with the North Vietnamese.

The German report was somewhat corroborated by addi- tional reports indicating that Osama Bin Laden was a CIA operative during the conflict in Afghanistan and that Richard Armitage was in the Balkans negotiating oil leases a few months before the bombing started. Armitage was implicated by Col. Bo Gritz and other authors regarding Southeast Asian drug operations originating in Burma during the late 1970s. Armitage, the former Assistant Secretary of Defense in the Carter and Reagan administrations, was supposed to be in charge of POW recovery at the time.

THE ARTIFICIAL RAMBOUILLET PEACE PLAN

Although our own government intelligence reports indicated the KLA was a drug funded terrorist organization, that was attempting to get Kosovo to secede from Yugoslavia, the KLA was seated as representative of Kosovo Albanians at the Rambouillet conference. In reality, it appears that the majority of Albanians did not want Kosovo to secede from Albania. Two weeks before the bombing started, Doug Bandow, Senior Fellow at the Cato Institute, testified for the House International Relations Committee that on his recent visit to Kosovo, he could not find any Albanians who wanted to secede from Yugoslavia.

Nevertheless, NATO organizations made no serious attempt to negotiate peace at the Rambouillet conference and, in fact, attempted to goad Yugoslavia into a war, as shown in the Rambouillet accords. The accords specify that NATO and the European Union have final authority on all civilian matters, including how the Kosovo economy will run and that NATO personnel have total immunity, unrestricted access and use of nearly all services in Kosovo free of cost. These opressing accords clearly outline a colonization and occupation of Kosovo as shown in the following Chapter, Section and Article samples:

- **Chapter 4a, Article I**—"The economy of Kosovo shall function in accordance with free market principles." (Kosovo has vast mineral resources, including the richest mines for lead, molybdenum, mercury and other metals in all of Europe. The capital to exploit these mainly state owned resources would undoubtedly come from the U.S. and western Europe.)

- **Chapter 5, Article V**—"The CIM shall be the final authority in the theater regarding interpretation of the civilian aspects of this Agreement, and the Parties agree to abide by his determinations as binding on all Parties and persons." (The CIM is the Chief of the Implementation Mission, to be appointed by the European Union countries.)

- **Chapter 7, Article XV**—"The KFOR [NATO] commander is the final authority in theater regarding interpretation of this Chapter and his determinations are binding on all Parties and persons."

The following appendix sections further illustrate the unreasonable demands of NATO:

- **Section 6a**: "NATO shall be immune from all legal process, whether civil, administrative, or criminal."

- **Section 6b**: "NATO personnel, under all circumstances and at all times, shall be immune from the Parties' jurisdiction in respect of any civil, administrative, criminal or disciplinary offenses which may be committed by them in the FRY." (Federal Republic of Yugoslavia)

- **Section 7**: "NATO personnel shall be immune from .... arrest, investigation, or detention by authorities in the FRY."

- **Section 8**: "NATO personnel shall enjoy, together with their vehicles, vessels, aircraft, and equipment, free and unrestricted passage and unimpeded access throughout the FRY including associated airspace and territorial waters."

- **Section 11**: "NATO is granted the use of airports, roads, rails, and ports without payment of fees, duties, dues, tolls, or charges occasioned by mere use."

- **Section 15**: "The Parties (Yugoslav & Kosovo governments) shall, upon simple request, grant all telecommunications services, including broadcast services, needed for the Operation, as determined by NATO... free of cost."

One likely commercial motive for NATO member demands was control of the multi-billion dollar Trepca mining complex,

22 state owned mines and processing plants of Stari Trg, the third leading producer of zinc and lead in the world. Under the plans, the silver, gold, lead, zinc and $17 billion in coal reserves would be exploited by conquering NATO invaders. Mining director, Novak Bjelic, summed it up when he said: "The war in Kosovo is about the mines, nothing else."

(Note: His prediction was proven correct at 4:30 am on August 14, 2001, when 3,000 NATO soldiers shut it down after storming a recently reopened Zvecan lead smelting plant, the only portion of the Trepca mining complex that was functioning at the time. Bernard Kouchner, head of the United Nations Mission in Kosovo, declared the Trepca mines as environmentally unsound based on a recommendation from the International Crisis Group that was set up by George Soros, the multi-billionaire Bilderberg conference participant. Two hours after the raid, the NATO soldiers confiscated the equipment of the Zvecan radio station and closed it, too. Kouchner has yet to explain the environmental threat posed by the radio station or justify the environmental damage done by the original NATO bombing. To implement the International Crisis Group recommendation of foreign management and administration, NATO turned full control of the complex over to a newly formed consortium called ITT Kosovo Limited, a partnership of Swedish based Boliden Contech, French based TEC-Ingenierie, and the American company, Morrison Knudsen, which has several connections with major American defense contractors.)

AMERICAN TAXPAYER FUNDED MURDER OF CIVILIANS

Day after day, Americans were befuddled to find that much of the NATO bombing was directed not at the Yugoslavian military, but at the Yugoslavian citizens. The civilian targets hit by NATO included dozens of city bridges, water purification facilities, power generation stations, television stations, marketplaces, buses, a heating plant, a hotel, a refugee convoy, a passenger train, an engine factory, the Chinese Embassy and dozens of residential areas.

Many facilities were struck deliberately based on NATO claims that they were military targets. Even we Americans who are victims of a dumbed-down education system should be able to tell that the previously mentioned facilities are not military targets. For example, power plants do not provide energy for tanks, bomber fighters or warships, and only a fraction of one percent of plant output might actually be used by a military base. In addition, nearly all military bases have back-up generation capability for their critical functions, so bombing a power station serves nothing more than turning the lights out for civilians. Thus, I believe NATO blatantly lied by claiming that these and other bombings were for military purposes.

Over 2,000 civilians were killed in two months, three times the number of apparent Serbian military deaths and far more than the number that Milosevic was accused of killing in the year before the bombing. The web site, *www.truthinmedia.org*, posted pictures of the atrocities to allow visitors to draw their own conclusions. Over 90 percent of this death and destruction was conducted with American equipment, troops and munitions.

A series of incidents that clearly illustrated the evil of NATO, began on April 14 when a refugee convoy was bombed. NATO and our news media outlets reported that Yugoslavia bombed the convoy, despite obvious total air supremacy of NATO forces. Serbian television, which replayed parts of American newscasts nightly to explain how Americans were being deceived, proved that NATO had bombed the refugees. On April 23, after admitting that it had bombed the convoy, NATO then bombed the Serbian television building, killing innocent civilians whose only crime was that they had told the truth.

NATO spokesmen claimed that the "propaganda" of the Serbian television justified the bombing, and then later appeared to lie under pressure by stating that the TV station was a military target. A Yugoslavian television station is no threat to American citizens. When NATO decided to kill people who said things that it did not like, it proved to those of us who still have a brain and access to the truth, that NATO had become an evil, fascist alliance.

MARCH ON THE PENTAGON

Fortunately, there were still some people left in America who knew what was actually happening and cared enough to try and stop it. Thousands of them descended upon Washington again on June 5, 1999, for a March on the Pentagon. The march appropriately began at the Vietnam Veterans memorial, where Bob Djurdjevic was joined by a host of Orthodox Christian ministers and other Serbian speakers such as Sladjana Dankovic, who had recently returned from Yugoslavia. After a couple of hours there, we marched across the Memorial Bridge carrying signs such as "Clinton, Blair and NATO are war criminals".

As we marched across the bridge and down a Virginia highway that led to the Pentagon, the effect was dramatic. For as far as the eye could see, there was nothing but a mass of humanity occupying the bridge and roadway that had been closed to traffic. Some marchers played instruments, and most shouted many different slogans during the brief journey which took a little less than an hour. While crossing the bridge, I thought about the many Yugoslavians who went to stand on their own bridges in hopes that NATO would avoid bombing the bridge and killing more civilians.

When we got to the Pentagon, Sara Flounders and Brian Becker of the International Action Center led another large rally with many speakers. Particularly effective speakers included former Attorney General Ramsey Clark, who summarized how the conflict really started; Pacifica Radio talk show host, Amy Goodman who exposed many media lies; and professor Brian Lituchy, who provided interesting details on Western involvement in the creation and destruction of Yugoslavia over several decades.

Despite having about 5,000 people present, the rally was blacked out by most media outlets. However, C-Span, which had also broadcast Serbian television newscasts, decided to carry the Pentagon portion of the rally live and on tape delay. Despite its coverage, many Americans never knew that the largest anti-war protest since the Vietnam era had just taken place.

It was interesting to note that the entire political spectrum was in attendance, from military veterans and proponents all the way to anti-Pentagon Communist Party members. Regardless of political philosophy, everyone knew that what we were doing was wrong. The widespread backlash against the war may have had an impact. Within a week, the 72-day bombing campaign stopped, and I felt a sense of gratification for having attended. However, throughout the afternoon there, I noticed the distinct smell of pesticide and could not help but wonder if the Pentagon area had been sprayed with some sort of potentially hazardous chemicals. Another year would pass before I began to learn about the long history of chemical experiments such as "Chemtrails" that have been conducted on American citizens without their knowledge.

THE NATO "PEACE" PLAN

The peace plan that was accepted by the Yugoslavian parliament was not much different than the Rambouillet accords and basically called for NATO occupation and colonization of Kosovo. As Serb troops withdrew from Kosovo, the military damage assessment became obvious. As expected, NATO had lost almost no casualties and a few airplanes and NATO bombs had killed over 2,000 civilians, 3-1/2 times the 600 Yugoslavian soldiers who lost their lives, mostly as a result of ground fighting with the KLA. In addition, the Serbians had lost only three tanks that they left in Kosovo, and they had perhaps another 10 out of their total of 300 that had sustained some damage.

The military casualties were so light that it raised the question of why Milosevic decided to surrender, since he and the Yugoslavian government accepted what was close to the original NATO terms. The casualty count also raised the question as to whether NATO was actually targeting the Yugoslavian military at all. There were no reports of military bases being struck by bombs, yet NATO bombs did billions of dollars in damage to civilian facilities. It appeared that the portrayal of Slobodan Milosevic as a villain by NATO and the national news media was a scam.

As the bombing stopped, the news media continued to portray Milosevic as a villain by entering Kosovo and repeatedly documenting claims of genocide against him and the Yugoslavian army. However, there were a couple of problems with these claims. All of them occurred AFTER the bombing started and were conducted by PARA-MILITARY forces that the Yugoslavian government could not control during the bombing. Other than Racak, I could not find a single one of the daily claims of genocide, that occurred before the bombing started and was traceable to Slobodan Milosevic.

WHY THE MEDIA LIED

Yugoslavian leaders repeatedly claimed that they were victims of two wars, one of bombs and the other of false words used by the media to justify the bombing. The national news media reported virtually anything that NATO said, unchallenged. They reported that Milosevic had ordered the killing of Albanian leaders who were later found to be alive. They reported that Serbians had slaughtered Albanians and buried them in mass graves, which were later found to be individual graves with flowers on them. They reported that Yugoslavians had bombed a refugee convoy that was actually bombed by NATO. They reported that city bridges, water supplies, television stations and power plants were military targets.

American news media likely deceived Americans about the war to maintain domestic support for it and satisfy their vested interests. CBS and NBC are owned by Westinghouse and General Electric, respectively, which are two of the largest American defense contractors. News network parents can frequently profit from war by gaining new munitions and technology contracts. Likewise, CNN benefits tremendously from global conflicts that increase ratings and profits handsomely whenever America is involved in war. In addition, the immediate parent company of ABC is Capital Cities, which had on its board, a former director of the CIA, an organization specializing in masters of deception.

Consistent nightly misinformation cannot simply be excused as incompetence. Chinese General Sun stated thousands of years ago that "All war is based on deception." The military, CIA and CFR connections of the media obviously played a significant role in the daily media deception.

AMERICA DEMILITARIZED

The result of the war was devastating to America as well as Yugoslavia. The Yugoslavian war increased America's reputation as a terrorist country while draining our cruise missile supply. Nuclear warheads on the remaining cruise missiles were replaced under emergency contract with traditional warheads so that they could be used to bomb Yugoslavians. America was now forced to supply thousands of troops to Kosovo, even though our troops were already spread out all over the world.

Many of our existing troops were placed under the command of NATO or the United Nations, neither of which had any regard for the U.S. Constitution or American law. *The New American* and other sources reported that NATO Secretary General Javier Solana, who directed the fascist attack on Yugoslavians by our military, was actually a Spanish Marxist.

Without nuclear cruise missiles and domestic troops we are vulnerable to attack. I am convinced that the degradation and subordination of our military is no accident. It is a deliberate, long term effort by Bill Clinton, his predecessors and many globalists in his administration and Congress to demilitarize America so that it can be subordinated to a one world government body controlled by a global fascist regime, that is staffed by non-elected rulers.

AMERICA MOVED TOWARD FASCISM

As a result of the war on Yugoslavia and many other Presidential scandals, America moved far past Lyndon Johnson socialism and deep into Bill Clinton fascism against the will of most American citizens. It started when Bill Clinton was not held accountable for using the FBI, IRS, INS and Treasury to persecute his adversaries. It continued as Bill Clinton ruled America by unconstitutional Executive Orders and was not challenged by the Republican opposition. It was completed in a shammed impeachment effort when:

- House Republicans ignored Congressional evidence of his more serious crimes;
- Senate Republicans set up procedures to avoid hostile witnesses and damaging evidence against him; and
- Senate Democrats admitted that he was guilty but established a new double standard of American justice by refusing to hold him accountable for charges that were presented.

Worst of all though, were the bombings that covered his political scandals. The bombings, particularly in Yugoslavia, occurred against the will of the American people, who lost total control of their government.

THE THREATENING GLOBAL
FASCIST PRECEDENT

When Bill Clinton and NATO joined forces to bomb Yugoslavians, it established a new precedent for a threatening global fascist dictatorship. NATO, a global organization, manufactured a "Hitleresque" excuse to invade a country, bombed hundreds of its civilian facilities, killed thousands of its citizens and created hundreds of thousands of refugees from the people it claimed to be helping. NATO did so by breaking the basic principles of international law without the consent of a single legislature in the entire world. NATO participants aligned themselves with KLA terrorists attempting to overthrow the government for the apparent purpose of eventually exploiting the mineral resources of the victims and establishing themselves as the sole world power.

The U.N., another global organization, did nothing to stop the aggression and is even attempting to prosecute the victims for war crimes, while imposing a double standard of justice for NATO to absolve it of guilt. These atrocities were committed under NATO and U.N. world leaders, none of whom are elected by citizens.

Those responsible for the atrocities include globalist leaders, who desire to form a worldwide, unaccountable, ruling class of elite, and the media organizations who deliberately misinform audiences to achieve that objective and their own vested interests. Our national news media missinformed Americans about NATO and key world events in the same manner that the German media misinformed Germans about Adolf Hitler.

REFERENCES

Independent Commission of Inquiry to Investigate U.S./NATO War Crimes against the people of Yugosalvia, Ramsey Clark, Independent Commission of Inquiry.

The U.S. / NATO War in Yugoslavia: Eight Myths, International Action Center.

The New American magazine, Vol. 15 No. 6.

The New American magazine, "Special Report: Are you Ready for the New World Army?"

NATO in the Balkans, various contributing authors, International Action Center.

The Recak Killings a Massacre?, archive of authors, Strategic

Issues Research Institute of the U.S.

Richard Becker, The Rambouillet Accord, International Action Center.

Christophe Chatelot,Were the Racak dead really coldly Massacred?, Le Monde.

Bob Djurdevich, Daily accounts of the war on Yugoslavia, Truth in Media.

Sara Flounders, "Kosovo: 'The war is about the mines'," International Action Center.

Diana Johnstone,"The 'Racak Massacre' questioned by French Media," International Action Center.

Gloria La Riva, *NATO Targets* (video), International Action Center.

Jerry Seper, Some KLA rebels trained & financed by bin Ladin, *Washington Times*.

Tony Snow, Is Kosovo Really that Bloody?, NewsMax.com from Creators Syndicate, Inc.

Gary Wilson,Who is the KLA?, International Action Center.

Gary Wilson, The Balkans: Lies vs. Facts, International Action Center.

Benjamin Works, *Kosovo - Getting Worse?*, Strategic Issues Research Institute of the U.S.

CHAPTER EIGHT
AMERICA: THE BEST GOVERNMENT COMMUNISTS CAN BUY

THE COX REPORT

The bombing of Yugoslavia obscured much of the information in the Cox Report from the public. While the Burton and Thompson Committee investigations identified some key technology that the Communist Chinese government had received for its illegal contributions, they had only scratched the surface of what the Communist Chinese military had actually gotten.

The House Select Committee investigating technology transfers to China, provided more devastating details. The committee, referred to as the Cox Committee, after Committee chairman, Chris Cox produced the bi-partisan, unanimously approved Cox Report as an end product. The declassified version contained roughly 700 pages, while the classified version contained another 300 pages. Some of the factual highlights from the report by chapter are as follows:

THE COX REPORT - PRC Accquisition of U.S. Technology

The Chinese Communist Party controls all state, military, commercial and political activities in the PRC. The Communist Party's eight-member Central Military Commission heads the People's Liberation Army. General Liu Huaqing, the former vice chair of the Central Military Commission and father of Col. Liu Chao Ying, was involved with dozens of Hong Kong and western countries engaged in illegally acquiring advanced U.S. technology.

The PRC has more than 3,000 front companies in the U.S. with technology targeting and acquisition roles. The U.S. has no procedure in place to track PRC front companies and their technology acquisition activity.

In June 1993, Bin Wu and two other PRC nationals were convicted of smuggling third generation night vision equipment to the PRC. In 1997, Peter Lee passed classified techniques to the PRC regarding detection techniques for nuclear submarines. In 1985, he passed classified information to the PRC about laser created nuclear explosions.

THE COX REPORT - PRC Theft of U.S. Nuclear Warhead Design Information

The PRC has stolen classified information for over two decades on all the most advanced U.S. thermonuclear warheads, including all those currently deployed and several associated reentry vehicles. The thefts are continuing to the present. The thefts include the W-88 Trident D-5, W-56 Minuteman II, W-62 Minuteman III, W-70 Lance, W-76 Trident C-4, W-78 Minuteman III, Mark 12A and W-87 Peacekeeper. All are recent except for the W-70 design information the PRC stole in the late 70s from the Lawrence Livermore national labs.

The CIA learned about the thefts in 1995 from a Chinese informant who provided an official PRC document classified as secret. The CIA determined that the informant was directed by the PRC intelligence services. The thefts occurred primarily at Los Alamos, Lawrence Livermore, Sandia and Oak Ridge labs.

Peter Lee, a scientist at Los Alamos and Lawrence Livermore, admitted to passing submarine detection information to the PRC and was convicted in 1997 of passing classified data on miniature nuclear fusion explosions to the PRC.

A suspect in the W-88 theft, Wen Ho Lee, was identified in 1995 and investigated by the FBI beginning in 1996. However, he maintained his security clearance and continued to work in one of the most sensitive divisions at Los Alamos until 1998.

(In 1999, Le was jailed and charged with downloading 400,000 pages of classified secret nuclear design, construction and testing codes onto portable tapes and refusing to tell authorities the whereabouts of the tapes. Nine months later he received a plea bargain when the Clinton Administration refused the to release documents ordered by Judge Parker for Lee's trial. Subsequent testimony at a 9/26/00 Joint Senate Committee hearing revealed that Lee denied he downloaded the data until proven that he had done so and Lee deleted classified files from a disk so that they would not be found.)

The PRC also may have acquired classified U.S. nuclear weapons computer codes from the labs.

Foreigners can visit labs even though a definitive assessment of risks vs. benefits has never been performed.

No procedures are in place to prevent or detect the movement of classified information to unclassified sections of the computer systems at the labs.

The Department of Energy briefed the Secretary of Energy about thefts in late 1995 and early 1996. The Department of Energy briefed the Deputy National Security Advisor in April 1996. It also briefed the CIA director, FBI director and Attorney General during this period. The deputy, Sandy Berger, who was promoted to National Security Advisor, stated in writing that the President did not learn about the successful PRC espionage until early 1998.

PDD 61, issued in February 1998, required the Energy Department to implement counterintelligence measures that would not even be minimally effective until 2000 according to the Cox Committee.

THE COX REPORT - High Performance Computers

High performance computers appear to have been diverted by the PRC for these unauthorized military uses:

- Upgrading and maintaining nuclear weapons
- Equipping mobile forces with high technology weapons
- Building a modern fleet of combat support aircraft and submarines
- Conducting anti-submarine warfare
- Developing a reliable accurate ballistic and cruise missile force
- Equalizing a battlefield with electronic information warfare
- Improving command, control communications and intelligence capabilities

The PRC may have received over 600 high performance computers since 1996, all over 2,000 million theoretical operations per second (MTOPS) and two over 10,000 MTOPS.

High performance computers recently sold to the PRC could be used for:

- Nuclear weapons development
- Information warfare
- Cryptography
- Military command and control
- Intelligence collection
- Intelligence instrument research and development
- Development of high technology
- Ballistic and cruise missiles
- Ballistic missile defense
- Mobile force development
- Designing submarine nuclear reactors
- Combat simulation

The PRC is seeking high performance computer software for:

- Satellite launch and missile guidance simulation
- Computer assisted design and manufacturing systems
- System simulators
- Applications of artificial intelligence

Three dimensional nuclear explosion simulation requires a computer capacity of one million MTOPS without test data for advanced nuclear weapons. These numbers decrease for more rudimentary nuclear weapons or depending upon how much test data exist.

Prior to 1994, licenses were required for computers over 195 MTOPS. In February of 1994, Japan and the U.S. agreed to raise the limit to 1,500 MTOPS.

Between 1993 and 1995 the NSA withdrew from high performance computer licensing reviews.

Export Administration Regulation revisions in 1996 made exporters responsible for determining whether a license is required.

The 1998 National Defense Act required exporters to notify Commerce of any computer over 2,000 MTOPS shipped to tier three countries such as the PRC.

In June 1998, the U.S. and PRC agreed on relatively useless conditions to verify post shipment computer use in the PRC. Some flaws in the agreement are:

- The PRC considers the request to be non-binding;
- The PRC insists that the verification be conducted by its own ministries;
- The PRC does not allow U.S. Embassy and Consulate personnel to attend verification unless invited;
- The PRC controls all scheduling of the verification;
- The PRC permits verification only for the first six months after the computer arrival.

A few examples of cases involving export violations are:

- On December 20, 1996, New World Transtechnology pled guilty to illegal export of a computer to a PRC nuclear equipment factory in August of 1992 and again in October, 1992. It paid a $10,000 fine and $600 assessment fee.
- On April 18, 1997, Compaq was fined $55,000 for alleged violations of computer export laws between September 17, 1992, and June 11, 1993.
- On June 12, 1997, Digital Creations Corp. of New Jersey was fined $800,000 for violating the Export Administration Act with regards to the PRC. It pled guilty in 1994 for exporting a DEC computer to the PRC illegally.
- On June 17, 1997, Lansing Technologies pled guilty to export violations for illegally exporting a DEC computer vector processor and data acquisition system in 1992.
- In July of 1998, IBM of East Europe and Asia was fined $8.5 million on 17 counts of violating U.S. export laws by shipping computers to a Russian nuclear weapons lab.

A Commerce Department license review between January 1, 1992, and September 23, 1997, showed:

- One export license to Hong Kong was rejected
- 100 licenses to the PRC were rejected
- 37 licenses to Hong Kong were approved, two of those in the 11,000 to 12,800 MTOP range.

THE COX REPORT - PRC Missile
and Space Forces

Qian Xuesen, a Chinese citizen trained in the U.S., worked on classified missile systems including the Titan intercontinental ballistic missile (ICBM) program. He was born in Shanghai in 1911 and left China in 1935 during Japanese occupation. He received a Masters from MIT and a Ph.D. from CalTech where he worked in the jet propulsion laboratory and became an expert. He was recruited by the U.S. Army Air Force for its long range missile program and eventually began working on the Titan. Qian was accused of spying for the PRC but was not charged and was allowed to return to China, along with four other Chinese members of the Titan design team. He became the chief project manager of the CSS-4 ICBM (Long March 2) which is targeted on the U.S. now. The CCP awarded him an honorary rank of Lieutenant General in the PLA, and President Jiang Zemin awarded him the highest honor a PRC scientist can achieve in 1991.

The PRC has gotten much technology from Russia. The Russian designer of the SSX27 claims that its advanced penetration capability will allow it to penetrate any ballistic missile defense.

The PRC proliferated complete ballistic missile systems or components to Iran, Pakistan, North Korea and Saudi Arabia.

THE COX REPORT - Hughes Satellite
Launches in the PRC

China Great Wall Industries Corperation launched Hughes Space and Communications International, Inc. satellites from the PRC in 1992 and 1995, but explosions occurred before they reached orbit. Launch failure investigations that determined how to improve the rocket, resulted in the transfer of technical information to the PRC when the transfer was approved by government officials. Hughes' claim of government approval in 1992 is not fully substantiated. In 1995, a Commerce Department official improperly issued a clearance for Hughes, which sought Commerce approval even though it knew that the jurisdiction belonged to the State Department.

In the 12/21/92 Optus B2 failure the Hughes launch investigators, Peter Herron and Stephen Cunningham, submitted to the Defense Technology Security Administration (DTSA) view slides of a failure analysis paper prepared by Hughes' chief technologist, Al Wittmann, in June of 1993. The paper detailed how Wittmann believed that a fairing was the cause of the launch failure and how the fairing could be improved for a forthcoming launch. DTSA approval of the view slide transfer to the PRC appears in a 6/25/93 facsimile signed by Lt. Col. Coates, who said that he did not recall approving the transfer and did not have the authority to do so.

In the 1/26/95 Apstar 2 failure, the Hughes launch investigative team was composed of many of the same individuals. By July 1995, Wittman and Spencer Ku determined that the PRC had added some additional fairing rivets but did not restructure the fairing based on the previous failure recommendation, and therefore, the changes were inadequate. Hughes Export Control Coordinator Leedle and others acknowledged that a State Department license was required to transfer failure analysis information to the PRC. However, Commerce licensing officer, Gene Chritansen, sent a letter to Leedle on 8/24/95 authorizing Hughes to release the detailed failure design analysis to the PRC. A 12/7/98 Defense Department report indicated that failure investigation transfer had damaged our national security.

Charlie Yah Lin Trie whose families and business contributed $220,000 to the DNC between 1994 and 1996, received $100,000 in May 1996 from CP Group, shareholders in Asia Pacific Telecommunications and the Apstar satellite program. During the same period that Trie made his contributions he received $1.5 million by wire transfer from foreign sources.

THE COX REPORT - Loral Satellite Launch in the PRC

On 2/15/96 a Long March 3B carrying Intelstat 708 crashed after liftoff from the PRC, the third PRC launch failure in 38 months involving rockets carrying U.S. payloads. In April 1996, the Great Wall China Industry Corperation invited Dr. Wah Lim, Loral's Senior V.P. of Engineering and Manufacturing, to chair an independent review committee that would conduct a failure investigation. The first meeting of the committee took place on 4/22/96 where William Schweickert, Loral Technology Control Manager, claimed he told the committee that Loral did not have a license for the meeting. The preliminary report of the investigation containing a conclusion that an inertial measurement unit within the rocket control system had failed, was faxed to the China Great Wall Industry Corperation on 5/7/96 by the committee secretary, Loral's Nick Yen, without any U.S. Government approval.

Around May 14, Robert Kovac, a DTSA Export Analyst read about the transfer in *Space News* and called Loral's Export Control Officer, who met with State and Defense Departments' licensing personnel the next day. In June of 1996, the U.S. Government issued a cease and desist letter regarding investigation activities to Loral and Hughes which had members on the review committee. In 1997, the Defense Department concluded that "Loral and Hughes committed a serious export control violation" and recommended referral to the Justice Department for possible criminal prosecution. Lim refused to be interviewed by the Cox Committee, despite Loral's agreeing to a voluntary disclosure.

In August 1996 the Defense Department prepared a classified assessment citing 18 violations of the Independent Review Committee. The State Department prepared a corroborating report, and the DTSA recommended referral to Justice for possible criminal investigation.

The crash into a mountainside occurred at 3:00 a.m. local time, but Loral and Intelsat employees were not allowed onto the debris field for 12 hours. The media reported that PRC officials were seeking out satellite encryption devices that protect the satellite from unauthorized messages once it is in orbit. Loral engineers determined that the satellite encryption devices were never shipped back to Loral at Palo Alto.

THE COX REPORT - Launch Site Security in the PRC

U.S. satellite manufacturers hire a security force to provide physical security for the satellite prior to launch. Only one company has bid for the contracts, and the conduct, professionalism and abilities of the personnel of that company have been sharply criticized by Defense Department monitors.

If the PRC has unrestricted access to a satellite for two hours, it could gain valuable information that is not publicly available. The PRC could learn virtually everything about a satellite with unrestricted access for 24 hours. PRC could gain this information via sophisticated X-ray and other equipment while remaining completely undetected.

A Defense Department monitor stated that we, as a nation, cannot afford to allow an industry to police itself when it comes to national security, and that if restrictive measures are not levied against the industries, our technology will be compromised to such a staggering level that our highest level of technology advancements will be available to our international competitors before it comes off the research and development floor.

During 1993 to 1996, Commerce issued three export licenses for satellites to be launched in the PRC without Defense monitors present and without reimbursing the Defense Department for monitors.

After the Intelstat 708 crash, a Defense Department monitor advised Loral management to delay piece recovery until a meeting between Loral, the PRC and the monitor could be held to avoid technology transfers in the recovery effort. Loral upper management ignored the advice, and the satellite encryption technology was never recovered.

A former Loral security manager argued against having the Chinese program manager placed in charge of security during the Intelstat 708 launch because the manager's objective of launching the satellite took precedence over security. He was overruled by Loral management. The manager also had Chinese nationals photographed in front of the satellite, which is a violation of security rules.

Only Pinkerton Aerospace offers foreign launch security since Launch Security Services International went out of business in 1996. One Defense Department monitor reported that problems with security guard forces included:

- Sleeping on job;
- Reporting to work under the influence of alcohol;
- Poor reporting on daily logs and at shift changes;
- Routine bus trips into the town to meet prostitutes ;
- Overall lack of respect for management;
- Reporting to work with a sleeping bag.

Satellite companies also have a cost incentive not to hire an adequate number of security guards.

THE COX REPORT - Commercial
Space Insurance

China Great Wall Industry Corperation set up the review committee for the Intelstat 708 failure to provide adequate reporting so that it could stay in the launch business and prevent cancellations.

It invited Dr. Wah Lim of Loral (and formally of Hughes), to chair the committee. On May 13, 1996, Lim sent a copy of the preliminary report to Paul O'Connor, Vice President of Marsh and McLennan, one of the prospective insurers for the next launch of the Apstar-1A.

Lim hired Nick Yen as secretary for the committee. Yen advised O'Connor that "The IRC may require a technical export license for the subject matter which may result in a revised version in wording. However, the technical contents and assessment in the report as faxed in this package remain valid."

On May 31, 1996, O'Connor advised China Great Wall Industry Corperation of the formal State Department decision that the release of the IRC interim report was not allowed.

THE COX REPORT - U.S. Export Policy
Toward PRC

The 1979 Export Administration Act established control of American export regulations. The 1996 Economic Espionage Act provided additional regulations to the Export Administration Act.

In 1995, new CIV licensing exceptions were issued by the Commerce Department for items under export controls that were destined for civil use; a new CTP license exception raised the super computer export limit from 2,000 MTOPS to 7,000 MTOPS.

Key Executive Orders that loosened U.S. export controls included:

E.O. 12981 - 1995:
Eliminated need for Commerce referrals to State, Defense Energy and U.S. Intelligence;

E.O. 13020 - 1996:

Transferred commercial communication satellite and "hot section" range technology export authority from the State Department to Commerce;

E.O. 13026 - 1996:

Required Justice Department review of encryption applications from Commerce Department.

The Commerce Department failed to provide the Cox Committee with classification requests that vendors had submitted to determine licensing requirements for commodities they were preparing to export.

In the spring of 1996, Bill Clinton approved new NSC commodity classification procedures that transferred commodity jurisdiction to Defense and Commerce Departments and included an appeal process to the President.

The countries participating in the Coordinating Committee on Multi-Lateral Export Controls (COCOM) agreed on consistent export controls for items to China and the Soviet Union since 1972.

In October 1988, U.S. President Reagan approved a plan to permit the export of U.S. satellites to the PRC for launch on PRC rockets, provided the PRC followed conditions defined in an agreement signed in December 1998. The agreement specified security safeguards to prevent unauthorized technology transfers to the PRC, required the PRC to apply fair trade market principles, limited the number of launches and assumed responsibility and liability for any damage done by space objects.

In 1990, Congress passed the Foreign Relations Action with additional sanctions prohibiting exports of satellites, U.S. munitions list items and crime control and detection equipment as a result of the Tiananmen Square massacre.

George Bush authorized three waivers to the act, and Bill Clinton authorized nine waivers, including one on 2/18/98 to Loral that bypassed Justice, which was investigating Loral for an earlier illegal transfer.

On 10/23/92, regulations were issued to transfer certain satellites from the State Department munitions list to the Commerce control list.

On 9/29/93, Commerce issued a report "Toward a National Export Strategy - Report to U.S. Congress" which quoted Bill

Clinton in Chapter Five as saying, "One reason I ran for President was to tailor export controls to the realities of a post Cold War world."

The State Department's Warren Christopher objected to the March 1996 Clinton decision to transfer all commercial communication satellite export control from the State Department munitions list to the Commerce control list.

Commercial communication satellites having nine identifying characteristics were transferred from the State Department munitions list to the Commerce Department control list in October 1996. Commercial satellite authority was returned to State by Congress in 1999 under the Strom Thurmond Defense Act. Jet engine hot section range technology was transferred to Commerce in October 1996, and encryption item authority was transferred to Commerce during December 1996.

In May of 1992, the U.S. imposed foreign policy controls on super computers, defined as those above 195 million theoretical operations per second (MTOPS) in a bilateral agreement with Japan, the other exporter.

Prior to 1994, COCOM countries agreed that licenses would be required to export computers of more that 12.5 MTOPS to the PRC. In January 1994, COCOM raised the limit to 260 MTOPS, and that was published in the *Federal Register* on 2/24/94. On 3/30/94, the Clinton administration removed licensing requirements on computers up to 1,000 MTOPS exported to COCOM controlled countries.

In October 1995, the Clinton administration announced further export regulation changes that allowed the PRC to receive computers up to 7,000 MTOPS without a license. Commerce published these licensing requirements in the *Federal Register* on 1/25/96 as revised Export Administration regulations using a four-tier structure of countries based on their security risk. The Clinton administration also removed all supercomputer licensing requirements to most industrialized nations.

More favorable export controls, such as a 10,000 MTOPS supercomputer non-licensing limit, have remained for Hong Kong even after it was taken over by the PRC. The Cox Committee stated that "a sizable number of Hong Kong enterprises serve as cover for PRC intelligence services, such as the MSS."

Defense Intelligence Agency Analyst, Nicholas Eftimiades, and Senate Governmental Affairs Committee investigator, Thomas Hampson, stated that China Resources Co., a PRC owned corporation that is based in Hong Kong, is "an agent of economic, military and political espionage". It is also a partner of the Lippo Group, whose principal executive in the U.S. was John Huang.

Huang left Lippo to join Commerce in late 1993 as Principal Deputy Assistant Secretary of Commerce International Economic Policy. He had a top secret clearance, and his superiors even requested him to increase it to the sensitive compartmented information clearance held by his predecessor.

Between October 1994 and November 1995, he received 37 briefings from the Office of Intelligence Liaison at Commerce and had access to dozens of classified cables each day. During his 18 months at Commerce, Huang made 394 calls to Lippo Group headquarters, subsidiaries, consultants or partners.

For additional communications, Huang used a visitor's office across the street at the D.C. branch of Stephens, Inc., another Lippo Group partner. He also met with PRC Embassy officials in D.C. on at least nine occasions. His other office and visits with PRC officials were unknown to anyone at Commerce.

THE COX REPORT - Manufacturing Processes

COCOM, Coordinating Committee for Multi-lateral Export Controls, restricted exports to the PRC of machine tools having a linear positioning accuracy no better than 10 microns because they could be used for nuclear weapons development.

In 1996, the Wassenaar Agreement and Nuclear Suppliers Group generally required export licenses for lathes and milling machines better than 6 microns and grinding machines better than 4 microns.

On 6/24/94 and 7/28/94, the export of McDonnell Douglas machine tools from a closing Columbus, Ohio, plant to the PRC was discussed by State, Defense, Energy, Commerce and an Arms Control Disarmament Agency (ACDA) at an Advisory Committee on Export Policy (ACEP) meeting. No agreement to export was given because of the concerns expressed by Defense and ACDA that the tools or other existing PRC tools would be diverted to the PLA. ACEP later voted to export the tools with 14 conditions.

China Aero Technology Import and Export Corp (CATIC) violated the conditions by distributing the tools to various unauthorized military locations. McDonnell Douglas reported this to Commerce on 4/4/95. No action was taken by Commerce until the Defense Technology Security Administration requested a formal investigation on 10/4/95.

Once an investigation began, the Commerce Department refused the November 1995 request from its L.A. field office to issue a temporary denial order against CATIC.

THE COX REPORT - Appendices

Loral employees were instructed by their lawyers not to answer questions and three Loral lawyers claimed attorney certain client privileges after Loral waived the privileges for voluntary disclosure.

The CIA impeded the Cox investigation by tipping off Hughes with a "courtesy" notice that the Cox Committee might interview Hughes employees. The CIA even detailed to Hughes the potential lines of questioning. The Cox Committee did not agree to the "courtesy" notification and was concerned that the CIA had given Hughes the opportunity to destroy evidence and pressure employees to be less candid.

Chairman Cox testified that the Justice Department attempted to insert itself as an intermediary for information requests between the committee and all government agencies because an investigation was in progress. However, Justice did not provide other agencies with necessary progress information about its investigation. The Cox Committee spent a major part of its resources retracing Justice Department steps despite protests of harm to the investigation. (Note: The sincerity of its investigation was demonstrated one day after the Cox Report was released, when Justice gave John Huang immunity for the entire campaign finance scandal in a plea bargain on an unrelated 1992 charge. Previous evidence indicated that Huang arranged most of the seven sources of revenue traceable through 11 streams from Clinton / Gore campaigns and the DNC to individuals and organizations directly connected to the Communist Chinese military.)

Defense Technology Security Administration (DTSA) employees testified that senior managers frequently overruled valid national security concerns regarding DOD positions on dual-use license applications. But the DOD refused to allow the Cox Committee to interview the six most senior DTSA managers, refused to let them interview DTSA employees unless a DOD observer was present and refused to allow DTSA employees to answer a survey by mail.

HIGH TREASON

As the media continued to focus only on the fact that the Chinese had stolen most of our classified nuclear design information, the real story that the media deliberately avoided was how government agencies and individuals, particularly in the Clinton administration, helped the Chinese Communists obtain the information and technology they sought. Slowly the facts became a little more obvious as to why Bill Clinton would strongly support an illegal, immoral, unconstitutional and fascist war against Yugoslavia and why he would even go to the extent of lying about genocide to initiate it. After considering the Burton, Thompson and Cox Committee investigations and statements from their members and other supporting sources, I compiled the following breakdown by department and individual of 50 reported unexplained potential acts of treason that I believe may have been committed by the Clinton administration.

TREASON AT COMMERCE

- The Clinton administration, primarily through Commerce, loosened export controls to transfer over 1,000 military and dual use technologies to Communist controlled companies and organizations in China.
- Commerce gradually raised the PRC supercomputer export limit from **12.5 to 7,000 MTOPS** (million theoretical operations per second), a near **600-fold increase** over the previous limit in force during Janurary 1994. As a result,

the PRC received over 600 supercomputers, which can be used for nuclear weapons design.

- Commerce approved the illegal release of a 1995 PRC launch crash analysis and approved export of sophisticated jet fighter "hot section" range technology that helps planes fly farther.
- Commerce refused the November 1995 request from its L.A. field office to issue a temporary denial order against CATIC after it violated the agreement conditions for distributing sophisticated McDonnell Douglas machine tools to various unauthorized PLA military locations.
- Commerce revised the Export Administration Regulations in 1996 to make exporters responsible for determining whether a license is required instead of the federal government.

TREASON AT ENERGY

- Former Energy Secretary, Hazel O'Leary, removed the color coded security badges for visitors at weapons labs.
- Hazel O'Leary, suspended background checks during 1993 and 1994 for visitors to at least of two nuclear labs.
- In 1995, Hazel O'Leary, overturned the decision of the Energy office in Oakland and allowed a former employee to retain his classified status after his status has been removed by the Oakland office for releasing sensitive classified information to unauthorized people.
- Hazel O'Leary gave a classified diagram of the W87 nucular warhead to a reporter for *U.S. News and Report* which published it in the July 31, 1995 issue.
- In 1995, an assistant to Energy Secretary O'Leary prevented Notra Trulock from briefing Congress about nuclear lab security breeches because she thought it might hurt the President's China policy.
- The Intelligence and Arms Control director newly appointed by Hazel O'Leary removed Jay Stewart from his position as Foreign Intelligence Director and destroyed all documents from his "Russian Fission" program after it detected a loss of nuclear weapons control by the Soviets in 1993.

- Former Energy Secretary, Fredrico Pena, issued a "gag order" at a weapons lab to prevent any Energy employee from interacting with Congress or providing documents without formal approval.
- In October 1998, Energy, under Secretary Richardson **gave a Chinese national all of the key computer parts needed to create one of the most powerful computers in the world (150,000+ MTOPS). The parts, valued at $9,000,000, were sold for $30,000,** and the transaction was not exposed until the manufacturer was alerted when the Chinese national contacted them with questions regarding re-assembly.
- In 1999, Secretary Richardson claimed that security problems at Energy had been corrected despite Cox Report statements that it would require several years for the Energy Department to minimally address security concerns.
- In 1999, Energy Security Chief, Col. Ed McCallum, who pointed out many security lapses, was placed on adminis- trative leave by Secretary Richardson, who claimed McCallum passed classified information while interviewing a whistle-blower.

TREASON AT THE CIA

- The CIA alerted Hughes about the questions that the Cox Committee would ask them against the will of the com- mittee.
- A CIA intelligence officer was pulled from a panel drafting Presidential Decision Directive 25 after he objected to intel- ligence sharing in international peacekeeping efforts and opposed U.S. troop involvement in civil wars.

TREASON AT DEFENSE

- The U.S. Navy reversed Lt. Jack Daly's highest rating ever for a promotion, making it the worst evaluation of his career after he was struck in the eye by a laser while monitoring a Russian ship and notified a House Intelligence Committee member about the incident.
- The Defense Technology Security Administration (DTSA) refused to grant the Cox Committee private interviews of its

employees and refused to allow its employees to fill out Cox Committee surveys.

TREASON AT STATE

- The State Department gave a 24-hour advance notice of American intent to search the Russian ship suspected of having the laser that injured Lt. Col. Jack Daly and his Canadian co-pilot.
- A government agency believed to be the State Department leaked advance notice of American intent to arrest Chinese officials for the smuggling of 2,000 illegal AK47 into Oakland by COSCO. This helped protect Wang Jun, who had recently met with Bill Clinton at the White House. Wang is the son of PLA General, Wang Zhen, and the head of the COSCO parent company, CITIC.

TREASON AT THE NSA

- The National Security Administration, NSA, withdrew from high performance computer licensing reviews between 1993 and 1995.
- After being briefed about major security breeches and theft in the nuclear labs in 1995, Sandy Berger failed to brief the President for two years.
- In 1995, the NSA assisted in producing NIE 95-19, a document that ruled out a rogue missile threat to the U.S. The GAO found the document to be overstated with numerous analytical shortcomings, while former CIA director, Robert Gates, who headed an independent review, found the document to be "politically naïve" and "foolish from every perspective" in regards to the threats posed to Alaska and Hawaii.

TREASON BY THE PRESIDENT

- Bill Clinton became the only President in U.S. history to give military technology to a foreign country over the objections of his own government agencies. He did this not once, but four times on three separate transfers over objections of four different agencies. The technology was not sent to an ally, but to a **Communist** government whose Communist Chinese Party and People's Liberation Army literature refers to America as its main enemy.

- In March 1996, Bill Clinton transferred all commercial communication satellite export control from the State Department munitions list to the Commerce control list over objections by State Department Secretary Warren Christopher.

- Bill Clinton issued Loral a waiver for a satellite launch over objections from the Justice Department while Loral was under investigation for illegally transferring launch crash analysis information to China.

- Bill Clinton approved the transfer of fiber optic communications equipment over objections from both Defense and the NSA.

- Bill Clinton issued Executive Orders 12981 and 13020, which moved much of the export authority to Commerce and eliminated intelligence referrals to other departments.

- Despite security briefings by Energy in 1995 and the NSA in 1997, Bill Clinton initially claimed that he was not briefed until 1998.

- Bill Clinton terminated American involvement in the Coordinating Committee on Multi-Lateral Export Controls (COCOM), whose members had agreed on consistent export controls for items to China and the Soviet Union since 1972.

- Bill Clinton lobbied for COSCO to take over the Long Beach naval base after it was caught smuggling 2,000 illegal AK 47's into Oakland and after its parent company chairman, Wang Jun, son of PLA General Wang Zhen, met with Clinton in the White House.

- Bill Clinton orchestrated the illegal campaign fundraising scheme that produced **seven sources of revenue** traceable through **11 illegal** revenue streams to organizations and individuals directly connected to the **People's Liberation Army**, including three **Communist agents** and three members of **Asian organized crime**.

- Bill Clinton pressured Ron Brown to hire John Huang, the illegal campaign fundraiser, at Commerce despite his lack of qualifications.

- Bill Clinton pressured DNC Finance Chairman Sullivan to hire John Huang at the DNC despite his lack of qualifications.
- Bill Clinton repeatedly lied about national security, stating over 100 times that no missiles were pointed at the U.S..
- Bill Clinton said in March of 1999 that he had not been told about espionage at the labs after he had been briefed by several cabinet members.
- Bill Clinton refused to release documents requested by Judge Parker for the espionage trial of Wen Ho Lee.

TREASON AT JUSTICE

- Attorney General Janet Reno granted immunity for the entire campaign finance scandal to John Huang, key organizer of the 11 illegal revenue streams traceable from the DNC and Clinton / Gore campaigns to the Communist Chinese military.
- The Reno Justice Department refused several times to tap the phone line of nuclear design theft suspect Wen Ho Lee, the only individual whose phone tap was denied out of more than 2,000 FBI requests, even though the Justice Department had been briefed about the lab thefts in 1995.
- The Reno Justice Department delayed a search warrant for the computer and documents of Charlie Trie, thus giving him the time needed to remove key information.
- Janet Reno refused seven requests to appoint an independent counsel to investigate all of the numerous detailed allegations of illegal campaign contributions from the Communist Chinese military to the Clinton / Gore campaigns and the DNC.
- In 1996-7, Lee Radek of the Reno Justice Department's Office of Public Integrity sent cease and desist orders to the L.A. U. S. Attorney regarding the investigation of the Hsi Lai temple fundraiser attended by Al Gore.
- The Reno Justice Department attempted to impede information requests from the Cox Committee by demanding that all requests be routed through them.
- Justice Dept. lawyer Laura Ingersoll, and her boss Lee Radek refused to allow FBI agents Ivian Smith, Daniel

Wehr, Kevin Sheridan and Roberta Parker to get a search warrant while Charles Trie destroyed business and travel records for four months;

- Laura Ingersoll allegedly told FBI agents "Not to persue any matter related to solicitation of funds to the president. That's the way the American political process works";

TREASON IN THE JUDICIAL BRANCH

- Judge Norma Holloway, a Carter appointee, bypassed the normal random selection of judges and assigned cases involving Webster Hubbell and Charles Trie to Clinton appointed judges;
- Clinton appointed Judge Paul Friedman ruled on Friday October 9, 1998 that it was not illegal for foreign nationals to contribute unlimited amounts of "soft money" political contributions used for general campaign purposes;
- Judge Paul Friedman threw out a total of 19 Justice Dept. campaign finance related charges against Charles Trie, Maria Hsia and Pauline Kanchanalak in addition to 6 other charges that were dropped as a result of his ruling;
- Judge Paul Friedman "erred" in his dismissal of charges against Maria Hsia according to a D.C. Circuit Court of Appeals ruling on May 18, 1999. Hsia was eventually convicted of all five counts against her.
- Judge Paul Friedman refused to jail Charles Trie to keep him from fleeing overseas after being informed by a federal prosecutor that Trie applied for a Taiwanese passport after being forced to surrender his U.S. passport when charged with campaign finance violations;

THE PAYOFF

Many of the technology transfers began occurring before the Clinton / Gore campaign and the DNC received illegal contributions from China. The contributions were documented long before the impeachment votes by the House Government Reform and Oversight Committee and the Senate Campaign Finance Committee.

Eleven illegal streams of revenue were traced from the Clinton / Gore campaigns and the DNC to individuals and organizations directly involved with the Communist Chinese military. As a whole they form an incredible bribery scheme that was obviously used by the Communist Chinese government to gain prohibited American technology. Some reported examples of this intricate arrangement are:

- Charles Yah Lin Trie, a member of Asian organized crime, donated $350,000 to DNC and $640,000 to Clinton defense fund in sequentially numbered money orders from various cities sent in by different people who happened to have identical handwriting. The Trie funds were traced to the Communist controlled Bank of China and to Ng Lapseng, an advisor to both the Communist Chinese Party and Communist Chinese government;
- PLA Col. Liu Chao Ying, daughter of PLA General Liu Huaqing, gave Johnny Chung $300,000 from Chinese General Ji Shengde, who told Chung that he wanted to give it to Bill Clinton because "We like your President." Chung, who passed about $100,000 of that money along, also donated $366,000 to the DNC, a figure well beyond his personal means;
- Ted Sioeng, head of the Chinese Communist controlled Pagoda Red Mountain Cigarette Co. donated $400,000 to DNC. Immediately afterwards, the Democrats tried to help Sioeng get a foothold in the American market by introducing a significant amount of anti-tobacco legislation against American companies under the guise of concern about teen smoking;
- Sonya and Arief Wiriadinata donated $450,000 to the DNC but filed no U.S. tax return. Arief is the Indonesian gardener who can be seen on White House videos shaking the hand of the President and saying "Mr. Riady sent me." The Riadys own the Lippo Group, which jointly owns the Hong Kong Chinese Bank with China Resources, an "agent of political, economic and military espionage" according to investigators from the Defense Intelligence Agency and Senate Governmental Affairs Committee;
- The Worthen Bank, jointly owned by the Lippo Group and (Jackson) Stephens, Inc., made a key $3,000,000 loan to Bill Clinton in 1992, which catapulted his Presidential campaign from near collapse to success;

- The Communist Chinese controlled arms company, Norinco, partnered with Thailand's CP group, which retained Pauline Kanchanalak, who raised nearly $600,000 for various Democratic Party candidates;
- Maria Hsia, a known Communist Chinese agent, supported four fundraisers for Vice President Al Gore and formed the Pacific Leadership Council with John Huang to raise money for the DNC. Hsia can be seen in a picture sitting with Al Gore at the Hsi Lai temple fundraiser;
- John Huang, the former Lippo U.S. President at the epicenter of Chinese espionage against America, raised about $2,000,000 for the DNC after Bill Clinton pressured DNC Finance Chairman Sullivan to hire him;
- Nina Wang, who gave $50,000 to help restore Bill Clinton's boyhood home, also funded $7,000,000 for American training of PLA officers, including two involved in the Tiananmen Square massacre;
- The Communist Chinese controlled company, Costind, partnered with Chun Hua Yea, who gave $37,000 to the DNC;
- Other mysterious illegal campaign contributions were also received. For example, the Korean company, Cheong Am American, donated $250,000 to DNC but never raised U.S. funds, and Yogesh Gandhi donated $325,000 to DNC but had liens filed against him for non-payment of taxes;

During the Congressional investigations, over 100 witnesses either pleaded the 5th Amendment, required immunity for testimony, left the country or refused to be interviewed because they were foreign nationals. In addition, China refused to provide bank records or allow Congressional investigators to enter the country. On the American side of the scheme, an April 17, 1996, DNC memo uncovered by the House Government Reform Committee investigation confirmed that Bill Clinton oversaw all fundraising. As expected, Bill Clinton was not only aware of the freedom threatening fundraising scheme, he orchestrated it.

CONCLUSION

The sheer number of potentially treasonous acts involving the Clinton administration and the Communist Chinese government indicate Bill Clinton orchestrated a clear pattern of events that will jeopardize the security of American citizens for decades to come. His obvious motive was the 11 illegal revenue streams received from individuals and organizations directly involved with the People's Liberation Army. However, whether or not a quid pro quo existed is irrelevant since treason and bribery are independently impeachable offenses.

The known evidence may present the clearest case of treason and bribery that has ever existed in America. Therefore, perhaps even more stunning than these acts committed by a Democrat administration, is the unwillingness of the "opposition" leadership in the Republican controlled Congress, to protect the American citizens as China acquires the best government money can buy.

Equally disturbing is the fact that Chinese generals who had operational, tactical and general responsibility for the Tiananmen Square massacres such as Xu Huizi, Wang Zhen and Chi Haotian, have been welcomed to Washington by the Clinton administration.

The national news media outlets have attempted to convince the American people that only a couple of hundred pro-democracy students were killed at Tiananmen Square by repeatedly showing a picture of a tank stopping for a Chinese student. However, on June 3 and 4, 1989 the tanks did not stop as thousands of non-violent pro-democracy students were crushed to death and machine gunned by the PLA.

On the morning of June 4, the Chinese Red Cross announced that 2,600 people had already been killed. On the same day, the Swiss Ambassador who had diplomatic responsibility for the International Red Cross confirmed 2,700 civilian deaths. But the killing continued that day as NATO intelligence estimates eventually reached 6,000 deaths. One of the most knowledgeable organizations of all was the Hong Kong Communist Party newspaper, Wen Wei Po, which reported that 5,000 people were killed and 30,000 injured.

However, it was not just the students that were murdered by the PLA, according to Toronto Globe and Mail reporter Jan Wong and London Observer correspondent Dr. Jonathan Mirsky. When parents of some students gathered in front of the Beijing Hotel on East Changan Ave. PLA troops opened fire killing dozens of them and even the white gowned nurses and doctors from Beijing's Capital Hospital who had rushed to the scene in an ambulance.

By nearly all accounts the PLA unit responsible for most of the killing was 27th Group Army, formerly commanded by General Chi Haotian, who met with Bill Clinton in the White House.

REFERENCES

The Select Committee on U.S National Security and Military/ Commercial Concerns with People's Republic Of China, House Select Committee (Cox Committee).

Investigation of Illegal or Improper Activities in Connection with 1996 Federal Election Campaign 1-6, Hearing 1-10, Senate Governmental Affairs.

Investigation of Political Fund Raising Improprieties and Possible Violations of Law #1-4, House Government Reform and Oversight Committee.

Bill Gertz, *Betrayal*, Regnery Publishing.

Ed Timperlake and Bill Triplett, *Red Dragon Rising,* Regnery Publishing.

Ed Timperlake and Bill Triplett, *The Year of the Rat*, Regnery Publishing.

China by any other Name (video), American Investigator, Free Congress Research & Education Foundation.

Low Road to China (video), American Investigator, Free Congress Research & Education Foundation.

Red Gold Rising (video), American Investigator, Free Congress Research & Education Foundation.

The New American magazine, "Special report: Treason in the White House," Vol. 18. No. 4.

HOW THE CHINESE COMMUNIST GOVERNMENT INFLUENCED THE AMERICAN POLITICAL SYSTEM

TREASONOUS TECHNOLOGY TRANSFERS

COCOM- Coordinating Committee on Multi-Lateral Export Controls

ACEP- Advisory Committee on Export Policy
ACDA- Arms Control Disarmament Agency

Strategic Defense Initiative
Aegis Missile Tracking
Peter Lee
Energy Dept
Sub Detection
Heat Shield
Reentry Vehicle
Electromagnetics
Missile Guidance
Nuclear Weapons Labs
Energy Intelligence
W56 Minuteman2
W62 Minuteman3
W76 Trident C4
W78 Minuteman3
W87 Peacekeeper
W88 Trident D5
Wen Ho Lee
FBI
COCOM
Justice Dept
CIA
Cox Committee
President Bill Clinton
Loral
Executive Order 12981
Executive Order 13020
National Security Admin
State Dept
Defense Tech Sec Admin
Hughes
Review Committee
Defense Dept
ACEP
ACDA
Commerce Dept
1996 Launch Crash Analysis
1992 Launch Crash Analysis
1995 Launch Crash Slides
1995 Launch Crash Analysis
Communication Encryption
Satellite Encryption
Launch Insurers
Fiber Optic Equipment
Machine Tools
Super Computers
Fighter hot sections
Saudi Arabia
North Korea
Iran
Pakistan
Peoples Republic of China

reinstated security clearance for
stolen by
removed color coded security badges at
stopped briefing to Congress by
suspended background checks at
data stolen for
theft suspected is
refused phone tap for
briefed in April 1996
briefed in 1996
briefed in 1998 by
vetoed in 1994 by
restricted by
withdrawal made by
granted waiver during investigation to
claimed not briefed until 1998 by
briefed in 1995
claimed privilege to
CEO gave $10K to party
briefed in 1997
eliminated export intelligence referrals by
moved export authority to
raised PRC export limit from 12 to 2000 mflops
stopped reviewing
objected to
investigated illegal transfer by
impeded requests by
did not provide vendor product class requests to
gave briefing about Cox questions to
impeded interviews by
conducted
approved
prepared
contained
chaired
cited 16 violations by
objected to transfer of
approved transfer of
approved export of
revealed loss of
released to
illegally to
illegally given to
given to
illegally given by IRC to
not retained by
gave CSSX7 and M11 to
gave weapons assistance to
gave CSS6 missiles to
gave CSS8 and C802 missiles to
600 given to
stopped release of
approved

CHAPTER NINE
THE DEATH TRAIL

The Clinton administrations have been directly involved in the cover-ups of the murders of Kevin Ives, Don Henry and Vince Foster. Although two independent counsels ruled that Vince Foster committed suicide, it is obvious to any halfway intelligent human being that a man cannot shoot himself without getting some portion of his fingerprints or palm prints on the gun. All the other evidence I previously described in this book also debunks the suicide rulings. I believe the evidence clearly shows that Vince Foster was murdered and both independent counsels lied.

In regards to Clinton administration involvement in the cover-up of Vince Foster's murder, evidence indicated that Bernard Nussbaum, the White House Counsel, turned over Foster's briefcase to authorities. However, three different witnesses said that they saw the briefcase in Foster's car at Fort Marcy Park. On the third search of the briefcase, a suicide note, supposedly written by Foster, suddenly appeared in it. No fingerprints were found on the note even though it was torn into 28 pieces. The suicide note was declared a forgery by several different handwriting analysts. The forgery is so obvious that anyone can see many letters that have several pen dots indicating the letters were drawn.

In the case of Kevin Ives and Don Henry, after the parents proved that Fahmy Malak, the Arkansas State medical examiner, had made false rulings in their deaths, the *L.A. Times* documented nearly 20 suspicious or obviously inaccurate death rulings that he had made. Afterwards, Bill Clinton introduced lagislation to give an approximate 40 percent raise to Malak, who reported to Jocelyn Elders. When the citizens held protest demonstrations and forced his resignation in 1992, Bill Clinton created a new position in the state health department for Malak. Clinton told reporters that Malak was "stressed out", and Elders stated on the *Obstruction of Justice* video that "Arkansas owes Dr. Malak a great debt and a real apology."

Therefore, based on the protection that Bill Clinton gave Malak directly, I believe it is clear that he personally participated in the cover-up of the murders of Kevin Ives and Don Henry.

There are also many other mysterious deaths of individuals who in some direct or indirect way are related to the Clinton administration even though there is no direct evidence implicating anyone in the administration. The number of mysterious deaths has grown to the point where it even surpasses the approximate 55 mysterious deaths involving the assassination of John F. Kennedy. These strange reported deaths generally fall into four categories:

- Suicides;
- Unsolved Murders;
- Plane or car crashes;
- Heart attacks.

I have compiled the following partial list of about 70 individuals many of whom became adversaries of the Clinton administration. The list is in reverse chronological order beginning with the most recent incidents. It includes the date of death, official cause of death, their connection and the unusual circumstances surrounding their death:

Carlos Ghigliotti 4/2000 Unknown
Thermal image expert who told House Committee that FLIR video indicates federal agents fired shots at Branch Davidians and was to be retained for Davidian civil suit after first expert suffered a stoke. Decomposed body found at his home with no signs of a break-in or struggle.

Lt. Col. Mark Cwick 9/99 Car crash
HMX-1 helicopter pilot who transported Bill Clinton and other officials around Washington area. Died when a car he attempted to pass moved in front of him, causing him to swerve off the road.

Daniel Dutko 7/23/99 Bicycle accident
Co chair of DNC's Leadership 2000 fund raising, vice chair for DNC finance in 1996, vice chair of finance for Clinton/ Gore in 1995. Died of multiple head injuries in bicycle accident.

David Drye 6/99 Plane crash
Friend of *The Clinton Chronicles* producer, Pat Matrisciana, who was scheduled to fly with him to Washington. Plane lost one engine on take-off and a second engine while immediately attempting to land.

Ann Drye 6/99 Plane crash
Friend of *The Clinton Chronicles* producer, Pat Matrisciana, who was scheduled to fly with her to Washington. Plane lost one engine on take-off and a second engine while immediately attempting to land.

Major Marc Hohle 4/99 Helicopter crash
Pilot for Bill Clinton during first year of Presidential term in 1993. Died In same HMX-1 Unit as Mark Cwick.

Cpl. Eric S. Fox 3/99 Suicide after car crash
Helicopter crewman in same Marine Corps HMX-1 Unit as Mark Cwick and Marc Hohle. Found in school yard with gunshot wound to head after car ran off the road and hit a guard rail earlier in the evening.

Johnny Franklin Lawhon 3/29/98 Car crash
Transmission shop owner who found $27,000 check from Madison Guaranty Savings and Loan to Bill Clinton in car trunk. Died in single car crash with no witnesses when run off the road by a semi for a second time in the weeks after turning over the check to Ken Starr's team.

James McDougal 3/8/98 Heart failure
Clinton Whitewater business partner and campaign fundraiser convicted of fraud. Prison staff apparently denied his nitroglycerin heart medicine, gave him a diuretic and prescribed a "near fatal" 60 milligram daily Prozac dose, according to examiner.

Ron Miller 10/12/97 Unknown
Gave Congressional investigators recorded tapes of Gene and Nora Lum's illegal campaign contributions. The Lums, who were sentenced to prison, hired Ron Brown's son, Michael, to funnel $60,000 to Ron Brown, according to Nolanda Hill's testimony.

Mary Caity Mahoney 7/7/97 Unsolved murder
Former White House intern who worked with Asian groups and in Clinton 1992 campaign. Shot five times in head while two co-workers shot once at Georgetown Starbucks in triple murder by men who left $4,000, in the store apparently used silencers and locked doors when they left.

Pamela Harriman 2/5/97 Heart failure
Top 1991 DNC fundraiser appointed by Bill Clinton as ambassador to France. Bill Clinton was chairman of her PAM PAC (political action committee).

Neil Moody 8/25/96 Car crash
Stepson of Vince Foster's ex-wife, Lisa Foster, who was remarried to Judge James Moody, on 1/1/96. Believed ready to expose evidence from Lisa Foster's private papers and was last seen in an argument just before he drove off and crashed.

Aldo Frascoia 8/18/96 Plane crash
Secret Service agent who maintained White House security equipment. White House claimed pilot of plane turned around and called for help before crashing in Tetons, but no such record exists at Jackson Aviation or FAA Salt Lake center.

Jeremy Boorda 5/16/96 Suicide
Admiral who knew of the naval technology China received for donations. Died days after giving officers' mess presentation that included the naval technology given to China under Clinton policy.

Niko Jerkic 4/5/96 Suicide
Head of Maintenance and Operations who was air traffic controller for Brown's plane at Cillipi airport in Dubrovnik. Died of shotgun blast to chest three days after Brown's plane crashed and before being interviewed by investigators.

Ron Brown 4/2/96 Plane crash
Commerce Department Director and former DNC chairman. Had perfect cylindrical .45 millimeter round hole in top of head; X-rays now disappeared; NBC video shows Clinton immediately faked tears for camera after laughing while he was leaving Brown's funeral.

James Lewak 4/2/96 Plane crash
High level CIA officer who prepared the Daily Intelligence Brief for the President. No investigation by FAA, NTSB, Air Force safety report or airplane manufacturer into crash near Cillipi airport at Dubrovnik, Bosnia, Croatia.

Adam Darling 4/2/96 Plane crash
Confidential assistant to Ron Brown. Familiar with investigations of Ron Brown by Justice, FDIC, FBI, Commerce IG, Energy, Senate Judiciary and Reform and Oversight Committee.

Charles Meissner 4/2/96 Plane crash
Assistant Secretary of Commerce for International Trade. Placed John Huang on a Commerce Department contract that allowed him to retain his security clearance.

Shelly Kelly 4/2/96 Accidental death
Stewardess who initially survived the Ron Brown plane crash. Dead on arrival at hospital after reportedly helping at crash scene for nearly 12 hours.

William Colby 2/28/96 Accidental death
Ex-CIA director, Strategic Investment contributing editor, head of Operation Phoenix in Vietnam. Helped expose fake Foster suicide note, drug cartel control of U.S. Goverment, CIA mind control project and Castro assassination attempt. Drowned in canoe while wearing no life jacket and leaving a partically eaten dinner on the table.

Barbara Alice Wise 11/30/95 Natural causes
The 14 year Commerce Department employee who shared suite with John Huang. Nude, bruised body found locked in her Commerce Department office; autopsy results remained unpublished.

Ken Michael Trentadue 8/1/95 Suicide
Held in the Oklahoma prison about the same time as Timothy McVeigh. Garrotted with a bed sheet and violently beaten so badly that body wounds prove suicide ruling is virtually impossible. Reno Justice Department has resisted pressure from Senate Judiciary to get truth.

John Hillyer 7/10/95 Heart failure
Cameraman filming Arkansas drug activities and investigator with Citizens for Honest Government. Collapsed in dentist's office before his investigative information on ADFA could be produced.

Mike Samples 6/95 Unsolved murder
Witness in Ives and Henry grand jury investigation. Shot to death; 7th witness (or potential witness) in Ives/Henry murders to be killed.

Florence Martin 10/94 Unsolved murder
Accountant who reportedly had documents and PIN# to Barry Seal's laundered bank account. Shot three times in head; (Barry Seal's Cayman Island account at the Fuji Bank was reportedly worth $1.46 million.)

Calvin Walraven 7/28/94 Suicide
Informant in cocaine distribution trial of Jocelyn Elders' son. Died of shotgun blast to head 10 days after testifying against Jocelyn Elders' son.

Stanley Huggins 7/1/94 Viral pneumonia
Attorney investigating Madison Guaranty Savings and Loan. Principal of Memphis law firm heading investigation into Madison Guaranty Savings and Loan for Resolution Trust Company agency.

Bill Shelton 6/12/94 Suicide
Fiance of Kathy Ferguson an Arkansas police officer critical of the Ferguson suicide ruling. Died of gunshot wound to back of head at her grave site.

Kathy Ferguson 5/11/94 Suicide
Nurse and ex-wife of Trooper Ferguson, who brought Paula Jones to Clinton; potential witness in Jones' civil suit. Found shot after packing bags to leave town; autopsy contradicted by six nurses, and Dr. Houston who stated she had a gunshot wound to BACK of head.

Dr. Donald Rogers 3/3/94 Plane crash
Arkansas dentist on his way to interview with foreign journalist about Bill Clinton. Rogers radioed that plane fuel read
empty, apparently due to electrical problems since tank was determined to be nearly full.

Hershel Friday 3/1/94 Plane crash
Clinton Presidential Campaign Finance Committee
member. Plane apparently exploded for unknown reasons.

Gandy Baugh 1/8/94 Suicide
Attorney for Dan Lasater, Clinton friend and fundraiser
with access to Governor's mansion. Lasater was pardoned by
Clinton after his drug distribution conviction. His company was
allegedly used to launder money through ADFA.

Ed Willey 11/30/93 Suicide
Presidential Campaign Finance Committee manager.
Husband of Kathleen Willey who was found dead in northern
Virgina woods on the very same day that his wife was groped
by Clinton, according to her testimony.

Jerry Parks 9/26/93 Unsolved murder
Presidential Campaign Security Chief. Ambushed and shot
a dozen times while driving home from restaurant after files he
compiled on Clinton's sex scandals were stolen from his home.

Stanley Heard 9/10/93 Plane crash
Appointed by Clinton as Chairman of National Healthcare
Advisory Committee. Also personally treated Clinton's mother,
stepfather and brother.

Steven Dickson 9/10/93 Plane crash
Counsel to Chairman of National Healthcare Advisory
Committee. Was flying with Heard when they called to report
fire on board aircraft they rented after Heard's personal aircraft
developed trouble.

Jon Parnell Walker 8/15/93 Suicide
Senior RTC specialist investigating Whitewater. Fell from
an apartment balcony.

Vince Foster 7/20/93 Suicide
Chief White House Counsel and personal attorney for Clintons. No fingerprints on gun; gun and ammo not his; no dirt / grass on shoes after walking in park; no blood at scene in park; clothes covered with carpet fibers; suicide note shown to be a forgery.

Paul Wilcher 6/22/93 Suicide
D.C. attorney who delivered an approximate 100-page affidavit to Janet Reno detailing Mena, Arkansas, drug running. Cause of death still unknown.

William Barkley 5/19/93 Helicopter crash
Secret Service agent who was a former Clinton bodyguard. Escorted Clinton to carrier *U.S.S. Roosevelt* for Bosnia peace mission talks.

Brian Hassey 5/19/93 Helicopter crash
Secret Service agent who was a former Clinton bodyguard. Escorted Clinton to carrier *U.S.S. Roosevelt* for Bosnia peace mission talks.

Scott Reynolds 5/19/93 Helicopter crash
Secret Service agent who was a former Clinton bodyguard. Escorted Clinton to carrier *U.S.S. Roosevelt* for Bosnia peace mission talks.

Tim Sabel 5/19/93 Helicopter crash
Secret Service agent who was a former Clinton bodyguard. Escorted Clinton to carrier *U.S.S. Roosevelt* for Bosnia peace mission talks.

John Wilson 5/19/93 Suicide
D.C. Councilman attempting to expose Clinton corruption. Hanging.

Conway Lebleu 2/28/93 Murder
ATF agent who was a former Clinton bodyguard. One of four agents killed while attacking Branch Davidians. Killer is unknown.

Todd McKeahan 2/28/93 Murder
ATF agent who was a former Clinton bodyguard. One of four agents killed while attacking Branch Davidians. Killer is unknown.

Robert Williams 2/28/93 Murder
ATF agent who was a former Clinton bodyguard. One of four agents killed while attacking Branch Davidians. Killer is unknown.

William Robertson 2/23/93 Helicopter crash
V Corps Deputy commanding general Europe who   figured prominently in Bosnia-Serbia peacekeeping operations. With carrier *U.S.S. Roosevelt* before crash in Germany.

William Densberger 2/23/93 Helicopter crash
V Corps Chief of Operations and Plans who figured prominently in Bosnia-Serbia peacekeeping operations. With carrier *U.S.S. Roosevelt* before crash in Germany.

Robert Kelly 2/23/93 Helicopter crash
V Corps Chief of Intelligence who figured prominently in Bosnia-Serbia peacekeeping operation. With carrier *U.S.S. Roosevelt* before crash in Germany.

Gary Rhodes 2/23/93 Helicopter crash
V Corps Spec. crew chief who figured prominently in Bosnia-Serbia peacekeeping operations. With carrier *U.S.S. Roosevelt* before crash in Germany.

Ed Cauley 1/93 Unknown
Campaign Finance Chairman in Arkansas. Found dead in hotel room.

Jim Wilhite 12/21/92 Skiing accident
Vice Chairman of Arkla, whose Chairman and CEO was Mack McLarty, White House Chief of Staff. Similar sking accident circumstances as deaths of Sonny Bono and Michael Kennedy.

Paula Gober 12/9/92 Car crash
Clinton speech interpreter for the deaf. No witnesses to single car crash.

Paul Tully 9/24/92 Unknown
DNC Political Director who authored Clinton and Democratic Party strategies. Was found dead in hotel room, and cause of death still unknown.

Victor Raiser 7/30/92 Plane crash
National Finance Co-Chairman of Clinton for President Campaign. Cause of crash undetermined.

Montgomery Raiser 7/30/92 Plane crash
Son of National Finance Co-Chairman of Clinton for President Campaign. Cause of crash undetermined.

Dan Casalaro 8/10/91 Suicide
Reporter investigating ADFA, Mena, PROMIS. Found in Martinsburg, West Virgina, hotel with wrists slashed over 10 times. Many other mysterious deaths have been related to the PROMIS scandal.

Jordan Ketelson 7/90 Unsolved murder
Potential witness in Ives and Henry grand jury investigation. Convicted drug dealer who knew Keith McKaskle.

Richard Winters 7/89 Unsolved murder
Witness in Ives and Henry grand jury investigation. Shot during apparent staged robbery attempt.

Keith Coney 5/17/89 Motorcycle crash
Potential witness in Ives and Henry grand jury investigation. Told friends he was at tracks when Ives and Henry were killed; Officers at scene believed his throat was cut before his motorcycle crashed.

Jeff Rhodes 9/89 Unsolved murder
Potential witness in Ives and Henry grand jury investigation. Told parents he knew too much about Ives and Henry murders before being shot in head and set on fire.

Boonie Beardon 3/89 Disappeared
Potential witness in Ives and Henry grand jury investigation. Friend of both Keith Coney and Greg Collins who is believed to be dead; only the T-shirt he wore was found.

Greg Collins 1/89 Unsolved murder
Scheduled to testify at Ives and Henry grand jury investigation. Shotgun blast to face.

Keith McKaskle 11/7/88 Unsolved murder
Cooperated with prosecutor on Ives and Henry investigation. Stabbed 113 times.

Don Henry 8/29/88 Accidental death
Died at Mena, Arkansas, drug drop point A12. Second forensic exam found stabbing in back; *L.A. Times* documented 20 false death rulings by Arkansas medical examiner.

Kevin Ives 8/29/88 Accidental death
Died at Mena, Arkansas, drug drop point A12. Second forensic exam found skull crushed with rifle butt; examiner got 40 percent raise from Jocelyn Elders and new job from Clinton.

Barry Seal 1/86 Murder
Mena, Arkansas, drug ring head turned DEA informant. Shot to death after being forced by judge to stay at a Salvation Army halfway house before he testified about drug trafficking for Arkansas grand jury.

Judy Gibbs 1985 Accidental death
Penthouse cover girl who lured politicians into compromising sexual encounters. Burned to death in fire at her home after calling 911; was cooperating with investigators; Bill Clinton flew with state police over her house after it burned.

Susan Coleman 2/15/77 Suicide
Former Clinton law student who was pregnant. Shot to death while seven months pregnant, reportedly with Clinton's child.

It is mathematically unfeasible that these deaths could all have happened as they are described by the official causes. Eventually one must reach the inevitable logical deduction that there are individuals or an organization willing to systematically eliminate those people who pose some threat to Bill

Clinton, particularly those who have inside knowledge of more severely damaging evidence and threaten to use it.

This raises many questions as to who is ultimately behind the deaths and why it has been so important to keep Bill Clinton in office. Was he chosen and groomed to be President since his days in college and in Europe where he conducted anti-American demonstrations? Was he designated to disintegrate America in the same way that the Soviet Union was disintegrated? Why are the major media organizations keeping so much information secret? Why is the opposing political party protecting him? The answers to some of these questions can be found in the subsequent chapters.

REFERENCES

Christopher Ruddy, *The Strange Death of Vince Foster*, Free Press of Simon & Schuster.

Christopher Ruddy & Lt. Col. Steve Cogswell, *The Death of Ron Brown* (video), Vortex.

Kenn Thomas & Jim Keith, *The Octopus*, Feral House.

Vincent Foster: The Ruddy Investigation, United Publishing.

Bill Clinton's Rise to Power (video), Bozeman American Trust.

The Death of Vince Foster (video), Citizens for Honest Government.

Obstruction of Justice (video), Integrity Films.

Vortex Issues, Volume 1 Nos. 10-11, newsmax.com.

CHAPTER TEN
AMERICA'S DARKEST
SECRET

DRUG TRAFFICKING HISTORY

Government-sponsored drug trafficking has actually been going on for hundreds of years. In fact, the recent turnover of Hong Kong to China has direct connections to drug trafficking, which has been almost totally unreported by our media.

When Britain colonized India in the late 1590s and early 1600s, Britain began to manufacture opium there in the mountainous northeastern regions. It used ships to distribute it to China where they traded it for items such as tea, silk and textiles, part of which generated funds to continue colonization. In the 1830s and 1860s Britain fought two wars with China as China attempted to stop the influx of opium into its destabilized country. Britain eventually won the right to lease Hong Kong from China for 99 years. Therefore, the historical roots of the fabulous economy in Hong Kong can be traced, at least in part, to opium profits.

The worldwide drug market has grown into an estimated $500 billion a year market, a number roughly one third the size of the U.S. government's total annual income. Americans are believed to spend $50 billion a year on drugs. American government involvement actually predates the CIAs beginning with its predecessor, the Office of Strategic Services (OSS).

Subsequent CIA and American military-related worldwide drug trafficking operations have code names such as Operation Amadeus, Pegasus, Watchtower, Triangle, Morning Gold and Burma Road. There have been several government investigations that have reached significant conclusions about government-sponsored drug trafficking operations, but these were primarily limited to Central American drug connections with the Contras.

THE CONTRAS AND COCAINE

The first major story linking the Contras, CIA and drug trafficking was written by Associated Press journalists Robert Parry and Brian Barger, who had begun a series of articles in 1985. It was suppressed by AP editors in the United States who had growing concern about its increasingly damaging content which included links to Panamanian head, Manuel Noriega. However, a Spanish language editor unknowingly translated the story and put it out on the AP Latin American wire, where it was picked up and run on the front pages of Spanish language newspapers throughout the world in December of 1985. Parry then convinced the AP to produce a watered down version on the English language wire. Thus, one of the most important stories of the decade was suppressed by the Associated Press and broken to the American public almost completely by accident.

The story led with the claim that "Nicaraguan rebels operating in northern Costa Rica have engaged in cocaine trafficking in part to help their war against Nicaragua's leftist government, according to U.S. investigators and volunteers who work with the rebels". It linked the Costa Rican drug trafficking to the Contra group of Edwin Pastora, a CIA-created group run by Adolfo Calero and Enrique Bermudez, and a Contra splinter group led by Sebastian Gonzales Mendiola, who was indicted in Costa Rica and a CIA-sponsored Cuban émigré group which oversaw the operations.

KERRY COMMITTEE

Parry and Barger were prohibited from writing any more stories about the Contras and drugs by the AP Washington Bureau chief, according to Parry. Both left the Associated Press; however, their articles triggered a 1986 investigation by the Senate Foreign Relations Subcommittee on Terrorism, Narcotics and International Communications. The subcommittee received testimony over more than two years about CIA-sponsored drug trafficking in Central America in conjunction with the Iran Contra affair that was supervised by Oliver North.

The investigation concluded that: "It is clear that the individuals who provided support for the Contras were involved in drug trafficking. The supply network of the Contras was used by drug trafficking organizations, and elements of the Contras themselves received financial and material assistance from drug traffickers". The drug traffickers had exploited "...the clandestine infrastructures established to support the war and that the Contras were receiving assistance derived from drug trafficking". However, the investigation, led by Senator John Kerry, reached few substantive conclusions regarding direct CIA or American military involvement other than conclusions such as "The military and intelligence agencies turned a blind eye to the trafficking."

DARK ALLIANCE

More recently, CIA drug trafficking attention was generated after the *San Jose Mercury News* published a three-part series called "Dark Alliance", written by Gary Webb, who had written previous articles on the danger of California asset forfeiture laws that allowed police to confiscate property without trial. The series, which began in a Sunday edition during August of 1996, linked the Nicaraguans to America's crack plague. It described how a group of Nicaraguan exiles set up a cocaine ring in California and established ties with the black street gangs of South Central Los Angeles who manufactured crack out of shipments of powder cocaine.

The series was summed up in the lead paragraph that stated: "For the better part of a decade a San Francisco Bay Area drug ring sold tons of cocaine to the Crips and Bloods street gangs of Los Angeles and funneled millions of dollars in drug profits to a Latin American guerrilla army run by the CIA." The drug ring was headed by Norwin Meneses (Cantero), who was in charge of security and intelligence for the Contra FDN group, headed Adolfo Calero and Enrique Bermudez who were apparently installed in their positions by the CIA.

Meneses' contact in Los Angeles was Danilo Blandon, who left Managua just before Meneses did in 1979. Blandon had earned a master's degree in marketing from the University of Bogota in Colombia before heading an export program for the Somoza dictatorship that fell shortly after he left. Blandon had developed close ties to the U.S. Commerce and State Departments while in the position. Blandon hooked up with "Freeway" Ricky Ross through exiled Nicaraguan dealer Henry Corrales and by 1983 was passing as much as 100 kilos of cocaine a week at attractive undercutting prices to Ross, who distributed most of it in South Central Los Angeles.

In 1991, the DEA arrested Blandon for cocaine trafficking. Although the U.S. Probation Office recommended a life sentence, after cooperating in other cases he served only a little over two years. In the spring of 1995, the DEA approached Blandon to set up a sting operation against Ross, who had already been arrested, served time in an Ohio prison and had just returned to L.A. The sting was successful although it is not clear if Ross actually agreed to buy drugs from Blandon again, since he still had retained much of his property after serving his time. Blandon returned to Nicaragua, and Ross was back to prison when Webb went to see him and decided to do the story.

Webb, who eventually resigned from the newspaper after being transferred against his will, went on to author the book entitled, *Dark Alliance*. The book provided more details to the "Dark Alliance" series of articles, confirmed Parry and Barger's original AP stories and provided some evidence of CIA involvement in that:

- Contra FDN leaders Enrique Bermudez and Adolfo Calero were handpicked by the CIA and on its payroll;
- Blandon's federal grand jury testimony stated that he was instructed by Bermudez to raise money for the Contras and that "the ends justify the means";
- Meneses' admitted to Webb that he was involved with the Contras after being shown a picture of himself with Adolfo Calero;
- A 1986 FBI report indicated that Blandon and Lister were involved in drug trafficking and arms supply for the Contras;
- A police report stated that Blandon's arms supplier Ronnie Lister mentioned he "worked with Scott Weekly of the CIA" when his house was raided;
- Blandon's attorney acknowledged that the CIA "winked at this sort of thing".

CIA INSPECTOR GENERAL REPORTS

Despite the evidence, several conservative news media organizations attacked Webb and his book. However, most fundamental facts were confirmed and never substantially refuted in Volumes I and II of the declassified CIA Inspector General reports that were released by Frederick Hitz in January and October of 1998, respectively.

Although the reports denied any CIA involvement, the first part of Volume I admitted that:

- Blandon and Meneses donated thousands of dollars to the Contras;
- Blandon had a personal relationship with Contra leader, Eden Pastora,
- Blandon supplied Pastora with rent-free housing and two vehicles in Costa Rica;
- Blandon met four times with Enrique Bermudez who solicited support for the Contras from him.

The second part of Volume I addressed the "Frogman Case" in San Francisco where swimmers were arrested with 430 pounds of cocaine as they attempted to swim ashore from a Colombian freighter in 1983. Also arrested were Nicaraguans Julio Zavala and Carlos Cebezas, who had some of their assets confiscated. Two Contra leaders sent letters requesting that $36,000 in seized funds be returned because the money actually belonged to the Contras. A CIA cable written shortly after a CIA attorney met with the responsible prosecutor, indicated that the money was returned at the CIA's request.

Hitz testified about the reports before the U.S. House Permanent Select Committee on March 16, 1998, and denied CIA involvement in drug trafficking. In his opening statement regarding the second part of Volume I, he told Congress: "CIA officials mistakenly identified one of the Contra members as a former CIA asset, and there was a concern that the depositions might expose a Contra support group in which the CIA had an operational interest." In regards to the meeting, he also told Congress that, "The CIA attorney cannot recall the facts of the case or the meeting in question." His testimony seems laughable if it were not for the underlying depth of corruption that exists.

In Volume II, the CIA acknowledged six cases where it was not deterred from using organizations or individuals involved in drug trafficking. Several pages are devoted to the activities of John Hull, who reportedly received cocaine at his airstrips, but the pages never identify whether or not he was a CIA asset. Hull and Oliver North were indicted in Costa Rica for drug trafficking.

The report also explained that Moises Nunez could not answers questions relating to his involvement in Costa Rican drug trafficking because he revealed that since 1985 he had engaged in a clandestine relationship with the National Security Council (NSC). Oliver North headed the Central American Contra operations at the NSC.

POWDER BURNS OF A DEA AGENT

Perhaps the most important aspect of Volume II was its tacit confirmation of some basic charges regarding El Salvador operations as raised by DEA Agent Celerino Castillo and later documented in his book, *Powderburns*. Castillo recruited an informant at the Ilopango air base in El Salvador, who recorded dates, times, pilots and plane numbers of drug trafficking and arms supply flights being flown by the Contra support network.

One hangar was operated by the CIA under control of Felix Rodriguez, and the other by the NSC under control of Oliver North. Both reported to Donald Gregg, the National Security Advisor to then Vice President George Bush. Rodriguez set up operations at the air base immediately after meeting personally with George Bush on January 22, 1985. When Castillo raided the house of a cocaine pilot in San Salvador, he found weapons, vehicles and communications equipment belonging to the U.S. Embassy. He confronted Ambassador Edwin Corr and was told, "It's a White House operation, Cele, stay away from it."

But DEA agent Castillo went further than just accusing the CIA of involvement in drug trafficking. He produced a written statement claiming that the CIA was complicit in the murders of several individuals in Guatemala by Guatemalan Military Intelligence (G-2). He even cited names, dates and case file numbers of the people who were murdered.

In DEA file # TG-86-0005, Castillo stated that the trafficker, Jose Ramon Parra Iniguez (Mexican passport
A-GUC-043), was tortured and murdered while his two
daughters were raped and murdered "by CIA and DEA assets
with the approval of the CIA." In addition, Colombian pilots,
Adolfo Leon Marales-Arcilia (a.k.a. Adolfo Morales-Orestes),
Carlos Alberto Ramirez, and Jiro Gilardo Ocampo were
brutally tortured and murdered in the presence of both a DEA
and CIA agent. In all cases the bodies were gruesomely dis-
membered. It seems that the CIA, DEA and Guatemalan
military lost sight of the fact the murder and torture are far
worse crimes than drug trafficking.

THE LEGNDARY BARRY SEAL

Terry Reed, a CIA operative and Contra co-pilot, exten-
sively documented in his book, *Compromised*, how Contra
shipments and drugs were being transported by pilots under the
control of Barry Seal. Seal is considered to be the most notorious American drug smuggler of all time, but his CIA and
military connections can no longer be credibly denied.

Seal served as a pilot for the U.S. Army Special Forces
Division in the early 1960s where he was active in the CIA
backed Bay of Pigs operation. The video, *In Search of the Drug
Lords*, by Daniel Hopsicker, recently published an astounding
January 1963 photograph of Seal in Mexico with CIA agents
Felix Rodriguez and Frank Sturgis. Sturgis is also pictured in
the House Select Committee investigation of the Kennedy assassination as he celebrated with Fidel Castro after they
overthrew Batista in Cuba several years earlier.

In 1965, at the age of 26, Seal became a pilot for TWA. He
lost that job when he was busted for smuggling 14,000 pounds
of C-4 explosives into Mexico in 1972. He and six other defendants gained a mistrial when the U.S. Attorney introduced
an automatic weapon that had nothing to do with the charges.
The Baton Rouge advocate published an editorial that asked
"Why False Evidence in Government Trial?". Two years later
an Appeals Court answered that question when they denied
motion for a retrial because the prosecution had committed "intentional misconduct".

In the mid-1970s, Seal set up the bulk of a major drug and
gun running operation between Colombia and America while

becoming the chief link between the Medellin cartel and the Southeastern United States. In 1982, while facing the threat of prosecution in Louisiana, he moved his operation to the Mena, Arkansas, airport. Mena had been used for CIA drug operations as far back as 1972, according to Michael Ruppert, who interviewed two of the pilots.

In 1983, Seal was first nailed by the DEA for smuggling 200,000 Quaaludes into a Fort Lauderdale airport. He was convicted in 1984 and faced 10 years in prison but had his sentence postponed after the DEA refused, but then later agreed, to use him as an informant.

After he had relocated to Mena, the CIA approached Seal about carrying loads of supplies and guns to Central America. Seal's drug runs were a perfect cover for the covert operation, and Seal naturally agreed since it meant federal protection for his planes and pilots. The CIA also equipped his planes with the latest electronic gear, including remote control hidden cameras for the C123 that Seal soon purchased from CIA contractor, Harold Dean.

Seal provided some bonus cooperation when he arranged a sting of Nicaraguan Sandinistas by videotaping Fredrico Vaughn and some other Sandinista soldiers loading 1,200 pounds of cocaine into Seal's C123 at the Los Brasiles air strip in Nicaragua on June 25, 1984. The CIA claimed that Vaughn was an associate of Interior Minister, Tomas Borge, although it appears that Vaughn had CIA contacts as well. The Managua home phone number that Seal claimed belonged to Vaughn was actually used for U.S. military intelligence between 1981 and 1986. The photographs that Seal took were eventually used by Ronald Reagan in a dramatic nationally televised address that supposedly exposed drug trafficking in the Sandinista regime that the Contras opposed.

Seal's cooperation eventually netted him a sentence of six months' probation on the Florida smuggling charges after he received supporting testimony from DEA agents. However, in December of 1984, Seal was caught again, this time flying a load of marijuana into Louisiana.

On February 20, 1985, Emile Camp, Seal's best friend and co-pilot for many of his runs, was killed when his state-of the-art equipped Seneca plane crashed into a mountain near Mena. Terry Reed may have summed up the crash best when he said:

"I still think his crash was sabotage. His plane left Baton Rouge with three hours of fuel. He crashes two hours later. There is no post crash fuel and no fuel in the engine lines. Couple that with the fact that he crashed in a heavily wooded area, miles off course, while executing an instrument approach to Mena in VFR conditions."

By the summer of 1985, Seal was exposed and the Medellin cartel knew that it had been taken. Seal sold the C123 back to Harold Doan, and it eventually ended up in the service of the Contra re-supply effort headed by Oliver North. The plane, nicknamed "Fat Lady" by Seal, was the same one that carried Eugene Hasenfus when it was supposedly shot down by the Sandinistas in October of 1986, just before expiration of the two-year old Boland Amendment, which prevented inter-ference in the Nicaraguan government.

According to Reed, Seal believed that he had an ace in the hole, which may have turned out to be a liability. Seal confided to Reed that he received documentation and videotapes from a DEA informant indicating Jeb and George W. Bush were also into drug use. Details subsequently revealed that they were caught on videotape in a DEA sting operation picking up two kilos of cocaine for personal use from a plane owned by Seal at the Tiamiami airport in Miami.

The tape has still yet to surface publicly; however, Daniel Hopsicker and Mike Ruppert found that the plane model type is a Beechcraft King Air 200, with FAA registration number N6308F and serial number BB-1014. They traced the own-ership of the plane through several individuals and organizations connected to various government officials and agencies. Its current owner is none other than the State of Texas, where it frequently was used by George W. Bush per-sonally, as Governor.

In a plea bargain arrangement on the Louisiana charges, Seal testified in three major drug cases during 1985, helping to obtain convictions on all three in exchange for an agreement that his sentence would not exceed that which was given in Florida. However, DEA agents did not testify on Seal's behalf at his trial in Louisiana.

On December 20, 1885, Baton Rouge U.S. District Court judge, Frank Palozola, effectively set Barry Seal up to be ex-ecuted by sentencing him to probation having a nighttime confinement, in the Baton Rouge Salvation Army halfway house on Airline Highway. The sentence which prohibited personal body guards, was featured in a movie about Seal's life, entitled *Double-crossed.*

Seal was placed in a federal witness protection program that offered no protective agents. He was assassinated on February 19, 1986 by a Colombian hit team headed by Jose Coutin, a Miami-based CIA asset whose gun shop supplied weapons to the Contras, according to Daniel Hopsicker, who also made some other startling discoveries.

Seal's attorney, Larry Unglesby, told Hopsicker that he once challenged Seal by telling him that, "I cannot represent you effectively unless I know what is going on." Seal gave him a phone number and told him to identify himself as Seal to the answering party. Unglesby said, "I dialed the number and a pleasant female voice answered 'Office of the Vice President'." When Unglesby identified himself as Seal, he was transferred to an admiral who hung up on him when he identified himself as Seal's attorney.

Sam Dalton, a criminal trial attorney for the hit men who killed Seal, also had a corroborating story for Hopsicker. Dalton gained access to the trunk of Barry Seal's Cadillac through discovery. But the FBI entered the Baton Rouge Police Department and illegally seized the contents of the trunk.

Dalton was forced to start a legal battle to gain access to the trunk, but neither the FBI nor CIA would honor his subpoena for the evidence. Eventually a courageous state judge threatened to hold them in contempt, and the FBI returned the trunk after ransacking it. Dalton explained that, "Some of the things that had been in it, we didn't get back. But they missed a few things that indicated just how valuable the trunk was. That's where we found George Bush's personal phone number."

THE HASENFUS PLANE CRASH

Information about the Contra supply network that was established in violation of the Boland Amendment was exposed when Barry Seal's former C123 plane was shot down by the Sandinistas over Nicaragua in October of 1986. Pilots Bill Cooper, William "Buzz" Sawyer and a Nicaraguan were killed.

Eugene Hasenfus, a "kicker" who pushed shipments out of the plane, parachuted to safety. However, the details of the crash are very suspicious, as explained to Terry Reed by Israeli agent, Amiram Nir, a former consultant to the Israeli Prime Minister on terrorism. For example:

- The plane flew miles off course directly over a Sandinista military camp;
- The plane contained documents from prior flights including flight dates, crew member names, descriptions of the munitions carried and the coordinates of the drop zones;
- Cooper was carrying his Southern Air Transport ID card, a direct link to the CIA against CIA covert operation procedures;
- Hasenfus was carrying a parachute over hostile territory against CIA covert operation procedures;
- Hasenfus, who stated that the plane was hit by a surface-to-air missile, would have no way of knowing that;
- There was no evidence of profuse bleeding normally associated with crash victims killed by impact, thus indicating the bodies were already dead prior to the crash;
- Nicaraguan autopsies indicated the bodies had been dead for up to 12 hours before the crash;
- The remains of the plane that was put on display in Managua indicated that the plane exploded from inside out;
- The Nicaraguan co-pilot had his throat cut.

Israel participated in Central American drug trafficking and arms supply operations as a partner of the United States. Nir claimed that CIA employee, Felix Rodriguez, was likely a double agent involved in killing the pilots before the plane took off. Reed confirmed that Hasenfus was capable of flying and bailing out of the C123 by himself, but Nir was unsure whether Hasenfus was a willing or unwilling accomplice. Rodriguez certainly would have no qualms about killing people since he reportedly was an assassinations manager in the notorious Phoenix program that may have killed as many as 40,000 Vietnamese who allegedly had Communist ties.

Nir's claim that the crash had been staged as a shoot down was further substantiated when the bodies of Cooper and Sawyer were never returned to America for autopsies and burial because of national security reasons. Therefore, it appears obvious that, at a minimum, the CIA protected the killer of its own operatives even if Rodriguez were not involved in the killings. Israel must also be a suspect in the downing of the C123, particularly considering its motives at the time and the Mossad track record of killing American agents in Operation Watchtower, as documented in this book and several other sources.

Nir mentioned that Israel wanted to end its involvement in the operation since key documents were stolen in a break-in at its embassy in Mexico City. Nir also said that Israel was concerned about the balance of power shift if Russia were ruined economically and Communism were destroyed. In the spring of 1988, Nir resigned and moved to London. He was killed in another mysterious plane crash in November of 1988 over Mexico.

The C123 is not the only plane crash in which Israel would have a motive for foul play. Just recently, EgyptAir Flight 990 crashed after leaving New York on Halloween morning 1999, carrying 30 Egyptian officers who had been trained in the U.S. on modern Apache helicopters. In July, the plane of John F. Kennedy, Jr. crashed on the third anniversary of the TWA 800 crash and the 30th anniversary of the car crash at Chappaquidick, where Senator Ted Kennedy left Mary Jo Kopechne in the car to drown. John Kennedy was in the process of interviewing Isreali Mossad agents for a follow-up article in *George* magazine on the assassination of former Prime Minister Yitzhak Rabin, as reported by Catherine Crier of Fox News.

Although *George* magazine normally treats politics somewhat superficially, the March 1997 issued contained a devastating investigative interview with the mother of assassin, Yigal Amir. She and journalist Linda Gradstein provided detailed evidence that he was encouraged to shoot Rabin by Avishai Raviv, an operative of the Shin Bet, an Israeli equivalent of the FBI and Secret Service.

The article apparently caused some serious contention between Kennedy and Michael Berman, a key *George* magazine investor. Kennedy certainly had a special place in his heart for the story since most serious researchers into the assassination of his father have concluded that CIA elements involved with the anti-Castro Cuban movement played a direct role in his father's murder.

CHIP TATUM AND OPERATION PEGASUS

Much of the information authored by Terry Reed was further confirmed by Gene "Chip" Tatum, an Army helicopter pilot from 1982 to 1986 and a CIA agent from 1986 to 1992. Tatum was ordered to fly drugs from Fort Campbell, Kentucky to Mena, Arkansas. Tatum stated that he was a commander in the Contra supply operation called Pegasus and that Rep. Henry Hyde (IL) was responsible for finances of the unit.

On CIA orders, he had infiltrated the 3/498th Medical company without its knowledge. Tatum documented many flight plans where he flew Contras and civilians in "Medevac" helicopters to or from Pamerola air base in Honduras or Ilopango air base in El Salvador. The flights frequently contained cocaine disguised as medical supplies, which Tatum accidentally discovered one day when a cooler was dropped and had to be resealed. Tatum reported the find to Donald Gregg and Oliver North, both who independently told him that the cocaine was evidence of Sandinistas manufacturing drugs, and it was going to the world courts.

Tatum stated that the operation involved Oliver North, Felix Rodriguez, Gen. Manuel Noriega, Israeli Col. Michal Harari, Willam Barr, Donald Gregg, Bill Clinton and George Bush. Recipients frequently included Dan Lasater and Clinton security chief, Raymond "Buddy" Young, who were sometimes assisted by Jerry Parks, the security company owner who was later murdered.

Both Reed and Tatum describe separate meetings that they attended where the subject of missing drug money on the Panama to Arkansas route was discussed at the highest government levels. Reed stated a meeting occurred in Arkansas shortly after Barry's Seal's assassination in 1986. It included Oliver North, Felix Rodriguez, Bill Clinton, his aide, Bob Nash, and William Barr, an attorney for CIA proprietary Southern Air Transport, whom he did not know at the time.

Tatum stated that a meeting occurred during 1985 in Central America and included William Barr, CIA agent Joe Fernandez, Gen. Manuel Noriega of Panama, Gen. Gustavo Alverez of

Honduras and Michael Harari. Tatum also stated that the amount in question was $100,000,000 and that Oliver North, George Bush and Bill Clinton all participated by phone.

At the 1986 meeting Reed stated that Barr accused Clinton of siphoning off extra money through the Arkansas Development Finance Authority and told him that they were moving the operations out of state. Barr, whose code name was Robert Johnson, was eventually appointed Attorney General of the United States by George Bush.

DRUG TRAFFICKING DISGUISED AS POW RECOVERY

Government sponsored drug trafficking began long before the Contra movement. In 1978, Defense Intelligence Agency Director, Gen. Eugene Tighe, called Ross Perot and asked him to front a private sector effort to determine whether or not U.S. prisoners of war (POWs), those missing in action (MIA), were alive and being held against their will in Southeast Asia. Perot had gained fame for his rescue of EDS personnel in Iran just prior to the hostage crisis. The rescue was so dramatic and surpassed the government handling of the hostage crisis so thoroughly that it was made into a famous TV movie entitled, *On Wings of Eagles*.

Perot contacted Col. Arthur "Bull" Simmons, who had rescued the EDS employees in Iran and Col. Bo Gritz, one of the most decorated soldiers of the Vietnam era. In April of 1979, Bo Gritz went to Southeast Asia and determined in one month that there were POWs left there. He sent Perot a TWX message on May 17 telling him "the problem is real".

His conclusion was since confirmed by refugee reports, intelligence documents, numerous individuals in the intelligence community, DIA satellite photography and a famous picture taken on May 25, 1990 of three live prisoners of war still held in captivity. The Pentagon continually denied the authenticity of the evidence and disputed any testimony confirming live POWs, despite estimates that over 2,000 POW/MIAs were left in Southeast Asia after the Vietnam War. When confronted by the families of POW/MIAs at a National League of Families convention in July of 1992, George Bush replied, "Shut up and sit down."

Gritz spent the next few years attempting to track down POWs and bring them back to the United States. He had frequently arranged to do so, but each time his efforts were sabotaged by individuals within the American government. Gritz and Perot eventually suspected that Richard Armitage, who was in charge of the POW recovery effort, was not doing his job.

In 1986, Gritz made a journey to Burma to meet with General Khun Sa, who reports indicated, may have some MIAs or help in locating them. Khun Sa could not locate any for Gritz but provided some stunning information to him almost by accident.

Khun Sa had set up the world's largest heroin production capability in the mountainous Shan territories of the Golden Triangle within Burma. He had an army of people who protected the drug production and constantly fought Burmese Communists and occasional Thai incursions. However, Khun Sa offered to stop virtually all heroin and opium production and distribution at the Golden Triangle. In exchange, he asked for some American assistance in converting heroin and opium production to legitimate crops and for recognition of the Shan provinces as independent, so that they would no longer have to sell heroin to fight the Red Burmese.

Gritz knew that America was already prepared to recognize the Shan provinces. Although disappointed that no POWs could be located, he returned to Washington optimistically with a videotaped offer to eliminate 900 tons of opium and heroin annually from the world market and expose those U.S. government officials who had been dealing with Khun Sa for the last 20 years. Gritz was not only surprised to find out that there was no interest in Washington for the offer, but he and his partner, Scott Weekly, began to incur the wrath of the federal government, which seem to increase its support for Khun Sa's adversaries in Burma and Thailand.

Gritz went to see Khun Sa again in May of 1987, and even though he did not have concurrence from the U.S. Government, Khun Sa was willing to provide the names of previous U.S. government officials with which his organization had done business. Khun Sa assembled his generals who had just withstood a remarkably well-timed attack by the Red Burmese, and they provided some amazing names, probably without realizing the magnitude of the information. Several key top level CIA personnel stationed in Southeast Asia were named as well as:

- Santos Trafficante, head of the Miami Mafia;
- Ted Shackley, CIA Deputy Director of Covert Operations, who reported to George Bush;
- Richard Armitage, then Assistant Secretary of Defense for International Security Affairs in charge of POW recovery.

According to the generals of Khun Sa, Trafficante handled "civilian" U.S. distribution, Shackley handled international operational aspects, and Armitage handled financial transactions and money laundering.

VIETNAM WAR: FIGHTING COMMUNISM OR MOVING DRUGS?

If that were true, Armitage would be the last person to want POWs returned home, since some of them would likely have knowledge of the operations. Many of the POWs were in Laos covertly during the Vietnam War. Although America was not supposed to have any presence in Laos, it became the home of the largest covert operation in American history. American military personnel allowed drug shipments to pass from Burma through Laos. Laos became a gateway for drug distribution from Burma while some of the profits appear to be used to fund the Vietnam War.

America became involved in Vietnam to prevent the spread of Communism by Ho Chi Minh, a Communist connected North Vietnamese nationalist, who originally sought help from American President Dwight Eisenhower but was rejected. The Vietnam situation escalated into a war for America when North Vietnamese allegedly fired on American ships in the Gulf of Tonkin. Afterwards, Lyndon Johnson signed the Gulf of Tonkin Resolution in the mid-60s and escalated American involvement to 550,000 troops, 58,000 of whom did not return alive.

It is now reasonably well-established that the North Vietnamese did not really fire on American ships. The Gulf of Tonkin situation was a false war trigger, nearly identical to the alleged massacre in Rajak that was used to justify NATO bombing of Yugoslavia. In reality, Yugoslavia was fighting a civil war with the KLA over the secession of Kosovo. The KLA was found to be a drug-funded terrorist group supported by America in much the same way as America supported the Contras.

Gritz's discovery raises a very disturbing question. We know that the Vietnam War was falsely triggered, and American officers have explained how the war dragged on because politicians never allowed Americans to fight to win. Laos, home to the largest covert operation in American history, is perfectly positioned between Vietnam and Burma drug production. Were we in Vietnam to defeat communism, or were we there to establish and control Southeast Asian drug trafficking?

BUSH: "GET BO GRITZ"

A disillusioned Gritz returned to America and shared the information of CIA and military drug connections with Ross Perot and officials in Washington. However, Washington was far from thrilled with his findings. Gritz, who naturally used special identification while traveling for his clandestine POW recovery efforts, found himself as a target of a Justice Department criminal prosecution. The charge was using a false passport WHILE HE WAS ON THE COVERT MISSION. The Justice Department spent two years attempting to prosecute Gritz for the operation that he was requested to perform by Defense Intelligence Agency Director, Gen. Eugene Tighe, through Ross Perot.

Gritz was eventually acquitted on April 21, 1989, before he could give a word of incriminating testimony about CIA and military personnel engaged in Southeast Asian drug trafficking. As he left the courtroom, U.S. Attorney William Maddox was pressured by TV news personnel to explain why the government had spent two years prosecuting a bogus charge. Maddox admitted and even repeated to TV news reporters that he had gotten a call from George Bush who told him to "Get Bo Gritz".

WHY ROSS PEROT DISLIKES
GEORGE BUSH

Unbeknown to Gritz, the information he discovered also corroborated previously collected evidence by the Christic Institute. In addition, Ross Perot had apparently already verified Armitage's drug financing involvement through federal, state and local law enforcement authorities by October of 1986. Related articles subsequently were written by Ben Bradlee, Jr. for Globe News Co. on January 11, 1987, and by George Church, Jonathan Beaty and Bruce van Voorst of *Time* magazine on May 4, 1997.

The astounded Perot made a trip to the Pentagon, backed the 6 foot, 275 pound Armitage into a corner, confronted him with the allegations and demanded his resignation. Naturally, Armitage denied everything, and Perot, not satisfied with his answers, went to see his fellow Texan, George Bush, the Vice President of the United States. After Perot explained the details, Bush told Perot to see the "proper authorities". In reality, George Bush was the proper authority since Executive Order 12333 and Presidential Decision Directives 2 and 3 put Bush in charge of all covert operations not long after the assassination attempt on President Ronald Reagan.

When Bush ran for President and won the following year, Perot established United We Stand, the forerunner of the Reform Party, to oppose him in 1992. Perot constantly attacked Bush during the campaign even after Clinton pulled ahead in the polls, and he eventually cost Bush the 1992 election. He apparently could not reveal his true motive for fear of being destroyed by the CIA dominated national news media, which concealed the information from the American public.

Despite the videotapes from Gritz and the corroborating evidence assembled by Ross Perot from federal, state and local authorities, Armitage was protected at all costs by the very top level of the American government, including the Vice President of the United States, George Bush. His covert activities appear to have continued for decades. In 1998, the *Washington Times* reported that he was negotiating oil leases and development contracts for U.S. firms in Albania and "the former Yugoslavia". His timing is fascinating since the trip occurred the year before Yugoslavian refineries and production facilities were destroyed by NATO.

THE AMERICAN MILITARY AND
ORGANIZED CRIME

The link that Gritz discovered between the CIA, Defense
Department and organized crime was furthered by the discovery of Col. Albert Vincent Carone a few years after his
death in 1990. His existence was not publicly known since virtually all records of his existence were electronically destroyed
after his death. Carone was a New York Police Department detective and Colonel in the Army Reserve. Michael Ruppert
pieced together much of the story of Albert Carone from
Carone's daughter, Dee Ferdinand and other sources during his
own exclusive research as publisher of the *From the Wilderness*
newsletter.

Between 1940 to 1946, Carone was in the U.S. Army,
Pacific Theater, where he received his first intelligence
training. Between 1946 and 1966, he was a NYPD patrolman
and detective who was issued badge number 3283 and assigned
to the 81st precinct, the 42nd precinct in Manhattan and a
Chinatown precinct during the course of his service. Carone
was on periodic active Army reserve while he was with NYPD.
He went on full time active reserve in 1956, was commissioned
as a second lieutenant and eventually crossed over into the
CIA, according to his daughter.

In 1980, Carone was apparently caught in sodomy with two
twelve-year old boys which he said were provided to him.
Carone retired after he was committed to and released from
South Oaks psychiatric hospital which was run by his brother,
Pat.

The book, *Franklin Cover-up*, by former Nebraska State
Senator, John DeCamp, details just such a covert child sex
slave operation beginning around that time. Decamp, who
headed Operation Baby Lift in Vietnam, was part of a committee investigating a satanic, Omaha based, child sex slave
operation that supplied young boys to politicians in
Washington D.C. and elsewhere. Implicated in the heinous
scandal were the Omaha police chief, the regional FBI director
who protected him and the publisher of the Omaha World
Herald, which continually distorted the investigation and subsequent trials. Decamp, a Republican, believed that the head of
the ring was a man named Larry King, who sang the National

anthem at the 1984 Republican National Convention. Although the key investigator died in a small plane crash with his son, King was eventually indicted and convicted on unrelated charges. Decamp uncovered evidence that the boys attended at least one party where then Vice President, George Bush, was also present.

Immediately after retirement Carone went on active reserve as a commissioned officer, moved to Rio Rancho, New Mexico, in 1980 and began traveling worldwide. He had black, maroon, olive drab and navy blue passports, one of which was in the name of Albert V. Rodgers. His service number, 04639528 USAR, contains an 046 prefix believed to indicate he was an officer in military intelligence.

During this time Carone had frequent contact with James Robert Strauss, a CIA operative whose code name was Cherub. The Ferdinands believed that Strauss was the one who closed down many of the accounts and records of Carone after his death and before they could get to them. The offices of Senator Pete Domenici told the Ferdinands that Strauss was nothing more than a con-man and that they were advised by CIA that it had no connection with Strauss. However, a civil suit filed by American Airlines for non-payment of fares indicates that Strauss flew all over the world on what could only be a government travel account, considering the extensive charges accumulated.

Carone's personal phone book had several interesting entries discovered by Michael Ruppert who summed it up this way: "I visited Dee Carone-Ferdinand in New Mexico and while staying with Dee and her family I was allowed to examine Al Carone's personal phone book. It was closed with rubber bands and there were other loose pages inside. In the pages of the book proper, I found the home address and telephone number of CIA Director William Casey on Long Island. On a loose piece of note paper inside the book I also found the home address and telephone number of Pauley Castellano, head of the Gambino Mafia family." Carone also knew Joe Percilia, the Columbo family crime member believed to handle all CIA transactions.

In 1994, Dee Ferdinand confirmed Carone's mob contacts this way: "I knew Santos Trafficante as 'Uncle Sonny', Joe Percilia as 'Joe Pickles'. I grew up with them around all the time. My father knew Joe Black, Vito Genovese, Carlo Gambino, Benny Eggs, Matty 'the Horse' Aienello, Jimmy Bruno, Joey Lugosa and Pauley Castellano. Most of them were at my wedding. My father was an NYPD detective so we had two rooms full of people at my wedding, and no one from one room ever talked to the people in the other."

On the federal government side, Dee Ferdinand confirmed that Carone worked with Richard Stillwell and Paul Helliwell of the Army Intelligence Support Activity (ISA), which was reportedly disbanded for corrupt activities. She confirmed that Carone knew Bill Casey, who lived in Locust Valley, Long Island, when Carone lived in Wantagh, Long Island, until 1980. She also confirmed that Carone knew Oliver North. Carone told her about a mission named Amadeus and that he mentioned North's alias "20 or 30 times" when talking about Nicaragua and Mexico. Coincidentally, there is an Amadeus restaurant directly across the street from a bank in San Juan, Puerto Rico, where Carone and the CIA conducted numerous financial transactions.

Dee Ferdinand was able to locate Strauss after visiting Mid-Valley airport, believed to be the destination for drug shipments. Mid-Valley is heavily populated by retired Air Force officers. It has a fascinating uncontrolled airport with two north/south runways less than a mile long and immediately adjacent to railroad tracks. In addition to standard hangars, there are 15-20 large homes with attached hangar garages, where it would be possible to taxi a multi-engine aircraft into them and close the doors for total privacy.

In 1985, Carone became depressed over a mission in Mexico where he told his daughter that innocent people and two DEA agents were inadvertently killed. The mission he referred to was later confirmed by Strauss to be near Veracruz. Carone suddenly became ill, was treated at Presbyterian and St. Joseph's hospitals in Albuquerque and eventually died of "chemical toxicity of unknown etiology" on January 7, 1990. After his death, nearly every record of his existence was lost or destroyed including:

- Military records;
- NYPD records;
- New York and New Mexico driver's licenses;

- Most medical records;
- Insurance policies given to his attorney, Robert Fuentes, who claims that he gave them back to the family;
- Bank accounts, including a joint account #3330690, held at Albuquerque Federal (now BOFA) with daughter Dee, who has some of the canceled checks.

Carone was buried with military honors including a 21 gun salute in a Santa Fe national cemetery, and his headstone was upgraded from Staff Sergeant to full Colonel after Carone's daughter, Dee Ferdinand, made contact with the offices of Ted Shackley. Later she received a letter from Patricia Moore, the Chief of Inquiries, dated November 26, 1991, stating that "Extensive searches at this Center and at the National Archives and Records Administration Center in St. Louis, Missouri, failed to locate Mr. Carone's military records." The Army's denial came despite the fact that Dee had in her possession:

- A diploma for successful completion of a Counter Intelligence Corps course dated 7/23/54;
- Several letters of commendation from the First Army Intelligence School, Ft. Slocum, N.Y., Post Intelligence Office, Fort Hancock, N.J.;
- Several Army course completion certificates including an Army Intelligence school certificate signed by Major John Murphy (MPC) and Col. Thomas Larner stating that, as a Sergeant, he successfully completed a AR-CIC Investigations Course from 10/16/56 to 10/26/56;
- Orders to Active duty and special orders from the New York military district;
- Oath of Office certificate from the New York Guard.

The need to destroy all of Corone's military and personal recoreds speak volumes about his involvement with the CIA and the mafia.

THE MURDER OF DEA AGENT "KIKI" CAMARENA

The Mexican operation that Carone referred to near Veracruz likely involved DEA agent Enrique "Kiki" Camarena and SETCO, a Honduran air freight company owned by Juan Ramon Matta (Ballesteros). Contra leader Adolfo Calero testified before Congress during the Iran Contra investigation that SETCO received funds from "bank accounts established by Oliver North".

Volume II of the CIA Inspector General's report stated that SETCO was selected to transport goods for the Contras from late 1985 to mid-1986 by the Nicaraguan Humanitarian Assistance Office of the State Department. SETCO apparently got this contract and others despite the known existence of a DEA profile indicating SETCO was smuggling cocaine into the U.S. and a 1983 U.S. Customs Service report stating that its owner was a "Class I DEA violator".

Juan Matta Ballesteros was a Honduran drug dealer who had been arrested and merely deported in 1970, after bringing 26 kilos of cocaine into Dulles International Airport. In 1975, he set up a partnership with Mexican drug lord, Felix Gallardo, and transported huge amounts of cocaine from Colombia to Mexico.

The Gallardo cartel included partners Ernest Fonseca Carillo and Rafael Caro Quintero. One DEA account indicated that it was the largest cocaine operation in history, moving as much as four tons of cocaine a month. All of the partners were being investigated by Camarena, who had already directed raids on two of their largest plantations and was unraveling their ties to Mexican politicians and the Mexican secret police (DFS), which received funds from the CIA.

On February 7, 1985, Camarena was kidnapped in front of his office by five gunmen who witnesses believed to be members of the Mexican secret police (DFS). Camarena and his pilot, Alfredo Zaval Avelares, who had also been kidnapped, were driven to a ranch owned by Felix Gallardo near Veracruz. The were brutally tortured the following day and then murdered the next.

Gallardo, Matta Ballesteros and Caro Quintero were eventually tracked down, arrested and convicted of various charges in the murder of Camarena and his pilot. One intriguing witness was Lawrence Harrison, a DEA informant who was hired by the DFS to install high-tech electronic bugging equipment. In their book, *White Out*, Cockburn and St. Clair describe DEA reports and testimony from the trial of Camarena defendants and two other trials in Los Angeles where Harrison stated that:

- He developed a system to monitor Camarena's office for the DFS;
- He installed and managed a bugging operation at the house of Guadalajara drug lord, Ernesto Fonseca, while on the DFS payroll in 1983;
- He recorded hundreds of conversations between drug traffickers and the Mexico City DFS;
- Fonseca made a drug deal with two Americans who claimed that they were being protected because they worked with Contras;
- Fonseca had a visitor named Theodore Cash, pilot of CIA proprietary, Air America, who had previously testified that he had worked for the CIA for ten years;
- Gallardo told him that they were being protected because they sent weapons and money to the Contras;
- The CIA used Gallardo's ranch to train Guatemalan troops, who slaughtered and tortured 19 Mexican federal judicial police officers during an unexpected raid on the ranch.

Witness Enrique Plascencia Aquila told the DEA that he saw Matta at Fonseca's house at a meeting where they passed around a photograph of Camarena and planned the details of his kidnapping. Therefore, the DEA knew that Matta was involved soon after the murder. The CIA Inspector General's Volume II report may have provided the final insult to the Camarena murders when it indicated that SETCO was selected by the State Department to transfer goods for the contras. AFTER it became clear that its owner, Juan Matta Ballesteros, was involved in plotting the murder of DEA agents.

OPERATION WATCHTOWER

Ted Shackley, the CIA deputy director who reported to George Bush and was implicated by General Khun Sa in Southeast Asian drug trafficking, had his own deputy named Thomas Clines. Shackley and Clines were assisted in Southeast Asia by CIA operatives, Ed Wilson and Frank Terpil. Shackley, Clines, Wilson, Terpil and Felix Rodriguez were eventually transferred to the JM/WAVE group in Miami, the largest CIA office in the country outside of the Washington headquarters. They focused on South American drug operations and were apparently involved in military related drug operations that have been pieced together by former LAPD narcotics officer Michael Ruppert, among others. Wilson and Terpil were implicated by several American military personnel as the controlling agents in Operation Watchtower, a series of three missions that took place between December of 1975 and March of 1976.

The operation established three electronic beacon towers beginning outside of Bogota, Colombia and continuing northeast to the border of Panama. The purpose of the operation was to guide aircraft carrying drugs so that they could fly undetected by normal air traffic control from Bogota, Colombia, into Albrook Air Station in Panama. The planes were met by Panama Defense Force officers led by Col. Manuel Noriega, Ed Wilson of the CIA and an Israeli national called "Mike", who was later identified by Pvt. William Tyree as Israeli Army Col. Michael Harari, a former Mossad intelligence agent who headed an assassination team.

Tyree was a U.S. Army Special Forces team member (SAG-7 & SAG10) who participated in Watchtower, provided details about it and subsequently identified the people meeting the planes. Upon completion of the missions, Tyree returned to Fort Devens, Massachusetts, where he lived in an apartment with his wife, Elaine, whom he married in December of 1977. Elaine was a U.S. Army member who was also an informant for the Army Criminal Investigative Division. She kept a diary of illegal activities happening at Fort Devens, according to affidavits by Bill Tyree and Elaine's friend, Tina Gregory. In October 1978, Bill and Elaine Tyree began to receive threats about the diaries, and on January 30, 1979, Elaine was murdered.

In April and May, 1979, Bill Tyree was investigated for the charge that he murdered his own wife, but no probable cause was found. Earl Michael Peters (SP4), who had befriended Tyree and then later admitted to Tyree that he killed Elaine, was charged with the murder. Apparently Peters was noticed at the scene, and there were even photographs of his entering and leaving Tyree's apartment at the time of the murder. Col.

Edward Cutolo, Tyree's immediate superior, had put the apartment under surveillance after Tyree reported the threats to him. Erik Aarus, a drug dependent buddy of Peters, according to the affidavit of Kenneth Garcy, was also charged and subsequently convicted in February of 1980.

However, District Attorney John Droney attained a ruling from the Massachusetts Supreme Court that struck down the murder charge against Peters and reinstated the charge against Tyree. On the ruling, the Supreme Court actually granted itself exclusive jurisdiction to prosecute the Tyree case, in violation of state statues.

Droney was a target of Operation Orwell, where Devens military personnel conducted covert surveillance on the top Massachusetts politicians, judges and prosecutors to compromise them. Droney had apparently been compromised by a closet homosexual relationship where he admitted to his lover that his office had helped cover up the police murder of a convicted felon who had escaped from the East Cambridge jail. Tyree participated in Operation Orwell and was on the team that monitored Droney.

Droney sent a remarkable letter to Cutolo using Middlesex County, Massachusetts District Attorney letterhead, as illustrated in *The Tyree Papers* assembled by Michael Ruppert. The letter, delivered in person by Lt. Dywer, contained:

- An acknowledgment of an agreement between them;
- A commitment that Peters would not be arrested for the Elaine Tyree homicide;
- A request for the audio-visual material collected concerning the relationship between him and to the escaped convicted felon;
- A request not to mention the material related to his alternative lifestyle;
- A recommendation to destroy the surveillance material collected at the Tyree residence on January 30, 1979.

Tyree was subsequently convicted in February of 1980, based, in part, on the testimony of Aarus and the fact that there was no break-in since Peters had befriended Tyree, asked to store a shotgun at his apartment and later got an apartment key from Tyree so that he could pick up the shotgun. Fifteen years

later in November of 1995, Aarus swore in an affidavit that Bill
Tyree was not involved in the murder of his wife; however,
Tyree remains in prison at Walpole, Massachusetts, today.

Nine additional key individuals with knowledge of
Watchtower have subsequently lost their lives, including five
Special Forces colonels, two National Security Administration
employees and even a member of Congress. They are:

- Sgt. John Newby, who worked with Bill Tyree on Operation
  Watchtower and Operation Orwell, also received
  threatening phone calls in October of 1978 and died that
  same month when his parachute failed to open;
- Col. Robert Bayard, who supplied photographs of Michael
  Harari and Mossad operative, David Kimche, was murdered
  in Atlanta, Georgia, in 1977 as he went to meet David
  Kimche;
- Col. Edward Cutolo, Tyree's immediate superior at Fort
  Devens who also commanded the final Operation
  Watchtower phase, died in 1980 in a one-car accident while
  on a military exercise at Skullthorpe, England, just before
  he was to meet Harari;
- Col. A.J. "Bo" Baker, the original commander of Operation
  Watchtower, died shortly thereafter, while trying to de-
  termine if Harari had killed Cutolo;
- Col. James Rowe, who provided the picture that helped
  Tyree identify Michael Harari and provided drug trafficking
  information to the CBS *60 Minutes* staff, which declined to
  use it, was assassinated on April 21, 1989, in the
  Philippines three days after Harari arrived;
- Paul Neri of the NSA, who tried to help Rowe and Baker
  determine if Harari had killed Cutolo, died on April 29,
  1989;
- Hugh Pearce of the NSA, who met with Col. Rowe and
  Congressman Larkin Smith about going public to call for a
  full investigation, died in June of 1989 in a helicopter accident;
- Congressman Larkin Smith (R-MS,5th), who met with
  Pearce and Rowe about conducting a Congressional investigation into the incidents, died in a plane crash on August
  13, 1989;

- Col. Richard Malvesti, who was assisting Col. Rowe and Bill Tyree, died on July 26, 1990 after his parachute failed to open on a routine jump.

New evidence has since revealed that the Elaine Tyree diaries, taken illegally from her apartment, were kept and delivered to CIA headquarters by Col. Albert Vincent Carone, whom Tyree believed to be the paymaster of several drug operations. The evidence has triggered a civil suit by Bill Tyree who identified Carone, as did the daughter of Edward Cutolo. Named in the suit along with the CIA, are:

- Governor Paul Celucci, who ignored the recent appeals of Tyree, and coincidentally had a former law partner, William Kittridge, who defended Erik Aarus in 1980;
- Attorney General Scott Harshbarger, who defended Peters in 1987 and failed to comply with court orders to return the diaries in 1985 and 1987;
- George Bush, whom the suit claims provided "express direction" for Carone to retrieve the diaries.

Also named in the suit are Oliver North and Bill Clinton for their roles in facilitating various related drug operations that have been previously discussed.

The assistant district attorney who helped John Droney was none other than John Kerry, who went on to become a U.S. Senator from Massachusetts. In 1986, Kerry, in his role as chairman of the Senate Foreign Relations Subcommittee on Terrorism, Narcotics and International Communications, received testimony about CIA-sponsored drug trafficking in Central America. The investigation thoroughly documented Contra involvement in drug trafficking, but it did not reach significant conclusions about CIA and military involvement or ensure that those responsible were held accountable for their activities.

Cutolo attained his position by succeeding his superior, John Shalikasivili, as commander of the 10th Special Forces Group, Airborne. Since Shalikasivili was the commander of the group that carried out Operation Watchtower, he would surely be a the likely originator of it. In 1994, President Bill Clinton appointed him as Chairman of the Joint Chiefs of Staff.

THE HUB IN A CIA DRUG
TRAFFIC WHEEL

There is a single common thread in nearly all of the drug operations described in this chapter. That thread is George Bush, whose life is quite secret since most of his financial information and college records are sealed. We know that after returning from his stint in the Navy, George Bush, like father Prescott Bush, son George W., and successor Bill Clinton, attended Yale University. Like his father, as a senior, George Bush was a member of the mysterious Skull and Bones Society, which seems rooted in opium smuggling and some pro-slavery advocates as explained by author Webster Tarpley. It has become a breeding ground for Bush's fellow CIA operatives and fellow CFR members.

Skull and Bones, the Russell Trust Association, was founded from the Yale graduating class of 1833, by William Huntington Russell of Middletown, Connecticut. His second cousin, Samuel, established Russell and Company, a huge opium syndicate that acquired opium from Turkey and smuggled it under the protection of the British Empire into China, where it was prohibited. The smuggling eventually led to the previously described wars between Britain and China.

Sometime after graduating from Yale in 1948, Bush helped form Zapata Corporation, a now fairly obvious Houston-based, CIA front company, which established oil drilling equipment in the Caribbean. Rodney Stich, in his book, *Drugging America*, states that investigators, CIA operatives and CIA cable analyst, Michael Maholy, revealed that Zapata Petroleum, Zapata Off Shore and Zapata Cattle Co. were heavily involved in drug trafficking.

The oil rigs were apparently used to carry out the drug operations. Drugs would be off-loaded from ships onto the drilling platforms and then taken into the nearby coastal areas in helicopters that were constantly carrying supplies and personnel. Maholy had learned about this both through cable traffic and his observations while on the rigs, which provided the perfect cover.

CIA AGENT BUSH

During that time period, as early as 1961, George Bush was almost assuredly a secret CIA agent. This was revealed by

Joesph McBride, who found an FBI memorandum buried among 98,755 pages of FBI documents released to the public in 1977 and 1978, as a result of Freedom of Information lawsuits. The memo was dated November 29, 1963, and writtten from FBI Director J. Edgar Hoover to the Bureau of Intelligence and Research at the State Department. It summarized the briefings given by the FBI's W.T. Forsyth to Capt. William Edwards of the Defense Intelligence Agency and George Bush on November 23, 1963, the day after the Kennedy assassination and just before Lee Harvey Oswald was killed.

The memo entitled "Assassination of President John F. Kennedy, November 22, 1963" explained the pro and anti-Castro Cuban sentiment in Miami communities regarding the assassination. It stated that "the substance of the foregoing information was orally furnished to Mr. George Bush of the Central Intelligence Agency."

The memo was significant because the CIA had repeatedly denied that George Bush was a CIA agent even though its policy is normally one of no comment on employees. In fact, the CIA tried to claim that the reference made by J. Edgar Hoover was to another George Bush in the CIA. When Joesph McBride contacted the other one, George William Bush, Bush told him that "it wasn't me" since he "knew neither one" of the other people involved in the briefing. George William Bush was a "lowly researcher and analyst", by his own description, who only worked at the CIA for six months during 1963-64. George William Bush eventually joined the Social Security Administration in January of 1968 after being employed as a social worker for the Alexandria Department of Public Works from 1965 until then.

The CIA continued to deny that George Bush was a CIA agent or operative even as President Gerald Ford appointed him to head the agency in 1975. Bush, who allegedly had no intelligence experience, was picked by Ford after he fired William Colby, who was cooperating with the Church Committee and the House Select Committee on Assassinations as they were investigating the JFK assassination for the second time.

Colby had already revealed CIA assassination plots against leaders of other countries, such as Fidel Castro of Cuba. Senator Frank Church, chairman of the Senate Select Committee on Intelligence, complained that the Bush appointment was a further attempt to cover up CIA assassination plots by President Ford, a former member of the flawed Warren Commission.

BUSH AND THE BAY OF PIGS

Bush's Zapata Corporation was also involved in another covert CIA operation that involved transportation of anti-Castro Cubans to the infamous Bay of Pigs during their attempted overthrow of Fidel Castro. Fletcher Prouty stated that in his capacity as liaison between the CIA and Air Force at the Pentagon in 1961 he personally "sanitized" two freighters named "Barbara" and "Houston" for use in the Bay of Pigs operation which was code named "Zapata."

The Zapata operation was believed to be controlled from the CIA Miami office by the JM/WAVE group, which was also involved in the Castro assassination plots. Bush's connection to Operation Zapata is particularly intriguing since most serious Kennedy assassination researchers believe that the evidence clearly shows CIA elements from this Bay of Pigs operation were also involved in the assassination of John F. Kennedy, who refused to provide adequate air cover for the invasion. Specific units that have been implicated in the Kennedy assassination plots include the JM/WAVE group and ZRRIFLE assassination team.

The alleged Kennedy assassin, Lee Harvey Oswald, had several contacts with CIA and FBI personnel from the time he had been a Marine until he was killed by Jack Ruby, the day after the assassination. In his new video Daniel Hopsicker published pictures revealing that in the 1950s, Oswald and Barry Seal were in the same Civil Air Patrol unit commanded by David Ferrie, a CIA pilot. Ferrie also had contacts with the Carlos Marcello crime family in New Orleans and even flew Marcello back to America after he was deported, according to the person who picked up Ferrie at the airport.

While Oswald was in Dallas, his handler was George de Morenschildt, a CIA operative, who was shot to death just as he was about to be questioned by the House Select Committee on Assassination in 1976. Mark Lane and other authors reported that his personal telephone book was located after his death and found to contain the entry, "Bush George H.W. (Poppy) 1412 W. Ohio also Zapata Petroleum Midland".

Kennedy had agreed to one covert air strike against Cuban fighter planes on an airfield in Cuba to incapacitate them to the degree they could not stop the Bay of Pigs invaders. The CIA had made the strike from Guatemala using Cuban pilots in airplanes disguised to look like those of Cuba. They claimed to the United Nations that those pilots were defectors. However, the damage was not complete, and Kennedy refused a CIA request for another bombing run needed to ensure the safety of the landing party. Cuba had asked the U.S. and the U.N. to interview the pilot, and Kennedy was concerned about repercussions of finding direct U.S. involvement in the invasion.

The 1,500 invading anti-Castro Cubans were killed or captured by Castro forces who had been alerted and were waiting for them at the Bay of Pigs. The captured forces realized that they had been betrayed as soon as they were let out, and some even started firing back at the freighters. From that day on Kennedy was considered a traitor among those involved in Operation Zapata.

REAGAN ASSASSINATION ATTEMPT

In 1980, George Bush ran in the Republican primaries against Ronald Reagan where he uttered his famous quote that proposed Reagan financial policies were "voodoo economics". In spite of the quote, Reagan picked Bush as his Vice President after being coerced by his advisors, according to some authors. I was surprised to find out years later that Reagan and Bush were never that close.

George Bush gained unprecedented power as Vice President through control transfers of covert operations and national security matters from Ronald Reagan. The transfers were accomplished via Presidential Decision Directives and the signing of Executive Order 12333 in December of 1981. The power shift began after the March 30, 1981, assassination attempt on Ronald Reagan by John Hinckley. Like the Kennedy assassination, George Bush also had a direct connection to the Reagan assassination attempt as documented by Webster Tarpley in his book, *George Bush: The Unauthorized Biography*.

On Tuesday, March 31, the *Houston Post* published a copy-righted story under the headline: "Bush's son Was to Dine with Suspect's Brother". The lead paragraph read: "Scott Hinckley, the brother of John Hinckley, Jr., who is charged with shooting President Reagan and three others, was to have been a dinner guest Tuesday night at the home of Neil Bush, son of Vice President George Bush, the *Houston Post* has learned."

The article went on to state that Neil Bush admitted on Monday, March 30, that he had met Scott Hinckley once in the recent past and knew him. Neil Bush also stated that he knew the Hinckley family and referred to large monetary contri-butions made by the Hinckleys to the Bush 1980 Presidential campaign. Scott Hinckley, the Vice President of Vanderbilt Energy Corporation, lived in Denver as did Neil Bush. John Hinckley, Jr. lived on and off with his family in nearby Evergreen, Colorado.

Neil's wife, Sharon, stated that she knew the woman who was coming with Scott Hinckley to the dinner. She also con-firmed that the Hinckleys "..have given a lot of money to the Bush campaign." Both Sharon and Neil stated that they did not know or recognize Scott's brother, John.

On April 1, 1981, the *Rocky Mountain News* carried Neil Bush's confirmation about the dinner party. The article also ex-plained that Scott Hinckley had come to a surprise birthday party for Neil at the home of Neil and Sharon Bush on January 23, 1981. Scott had come to the surprise party with the same female friend of Sharon Bush. On the same day, the office of then Vice President Bush confirmed the dinner party, but both Neil Bush and the office stated that they had not received any campaign contributions from the Hinckleys.

The Bushes were never questioned or investigated in regards to the assassination attempt, the contributions or their connections with the Hinckleys, even though George Bush would have the most to gain from an assassination of Ronald Reagan. The national news media made the somewhat lu-dicrous claim that John Hinckley admired actress Jodi Foster and thought that shooting the President would somehow win her love.

There is no known evidence that would suggest anyone in the Hinckley family had knowledge of John Hinckley's in-tentions. Assume for a minute though, a four person family, each having close associations with 100 other families in a 280 million person population. I am not a mathematician, but it seems to me that the odds of the Vice President's family being that closely connected to the family of the man who attempted to assassinate the President are about 700,000 to one. Surely that justifies a serious investigation.

THE REAL GEORGE H.W. BUSH

In regards to Nicaragua, three government investigations have confirmed, at a minimum, that:

- Nicaraguan Contras were supported by traffickers who transported drugs into America;
- The Contra supply line was used by traffickers who transported drugs into America;
- The CIA was aware of the drug trafficking operations but did nothing to stop or even hinder them.

These allegations can no longer be credibly denied. Two of the leaders of the Contra supply effort were Oliver North of the National Security Council and Felix Rodriguez of the CIA.

However, it is obvious that the CIA is far more than just a passive onlooker and that Contra related drug trafficking is only the tip of an iceberg in terms of CIA drug trafficking scope. Despite repeated denials by the CIA, the evidence presented by CIA operatives, Special Forces colonels, DEA agents, police officers and trial witnesses makes a clear case that:

- The CIA ran drug smuggling operations for the Contras from El Salvador through Felix Rodriguez;
- The CIA controlled operational aspects of Southeast Asian drug traffic originating in Burma;
- The CIA was ultimately in control of Operation Watchtower drug trafficking conducted by American military personnel between Panama and Colombia;
- The CIA was involved in Caribbean drug smuggling operations through the Zapata Corporation;
- The CIA was involved in Mena, Arkansas, based smuggling operations from various points in Central America through Barry Seal.

The evidence presented by CIA operatives, Special Forces colonels, DEA agents, police officers and trial witnesses illustrates that the scope of the corruption extends well beyond the CIA. The evidence establishes a clear, coordinated effort among elements in American government agencies and other foreign organizations to facilitate drug trafficking, money laundering, protection for those who are caught and elimination of those who get in the way. For example, this evidence indicates that:

- The Israeli Mossad was a partner with the United States in Central American drug trafficking operations and possibly others as well;
- American Defense Department and military personnel were used in Panama and Colombian drug trafficking operations for worldwide money laundering and as a link to organized crime figures for drug distribution in America;
- Elements of the CIA, DEA, Israeli Mossad and the American military were involved in other heinous crimes including multiple murders;
- Those government officials involved in drug trafficking and other heinous crimes were protected and promoted by the highest level of the American government, specifically United States Presidents, Bill Clinton and George Bush.

Even though all of the allegations of money laundering, drug trafficking, drug use and obstruction of justice made against Bill Clinton may well be true, the following evidence indicates that George Bush is the real cocaine kingpin of America:

- Bush oversaw Contra operations through his security advisor, Donald Gregg, who controlled both Oliver North and Felix Rodriguez;
- Bush oversaw the Burma drug trafficking operations through his CIA deputy, Ted Shackley;
- Bush protected Dick Armitage after he was confronted about his involvement in Southeast Asian money laundering and drug trafficking by Ross Perot;

- Bush attempted to prosecute Bo Gritz for using a fake passport while on a covert mission after Gritz had uncovered the Southeast Asian drug trafficking operation;
- Bush's Zapata oil rigs were found by investigators and a CIA cable analyst to be involved in smuggling drugs;
- Two attorneys verified that CIA operative and drug smuggler, Barry Seal, had Bush's phone number;
- Operation Watchtower began immediately upon the appointment of Bush as CIA Director;
- Bush is accused in the Tyree suit of ordering Albert Carone to obtain the Tyree diaries illegally to prevent Operation Watchtower from being exposed.

There are implications that we need profits from drug trafficking to fight communism. But if the billions of dollars collected from all of the government-sponsored drug trafficking operations were actually used to fight communism, it would have been eradicated worldwide by now. I believe that most of the profits are going to fund George Bush's New World Order and implement the global agenda of the Trilateral Commission and Council on Foreign Relations.

George Bush may have taken the Skull and Bones heritage to a new level. While cocaine has replaced opium and airplanes have replaced Clipper ships, the founding principle seems to be the same. Use government endorsed drug trafficking to gain wealth and power by feeding selected groups of people dope to enslave and control them.

But the Bush legacy does not end with just drug trafficking. His shocking, seldom revealed background is perhaps, best explained in *"George Bush: the Unauthorized Biography"*. Authors Anton Chaitkin and Webster Tarpley may have produced the most important book written in the 1990s. At the time of this writing, the manuscript is still available for viewing on the web at *www.tarpley.net*.

George H.W. Bush has the dubious distinction of being connected to two presidential assassination endeavors as well as the resignation of a third president. Bush is linked to the Reagan assassination attempt through the ties between his son, Neil, and Scott Hinckley, the brother of attempted assassin, John Hinckley. Bush is linked to the Kennedy assassination through the anti-Castro Cuban elements of the CIA, Barry Seal, Lee Oswald and George De Morenschildt, the man believed by many assassination researchers to be the CIA operative handler for Oswald. It is just too difficult to accept the many million-to-one odds that a President or Vice President could have coincidental connections to two separate presidential assassination efforts.

Although political opposites, both Kennedy and Reagan were populist, independent minded individuals who gained power somewhat outside of the traditional political power structure. Reagan succeeded through his fame as an actor and Kennedy succeeded from the fortunes of his father, Joe Kennedy. Their backgrounds instilled them with a unique unwillingness to completely buckle under to the Washington power structure. This common trait may ultimately be what made them assassination targets.

THE ULTIMATE INSIDER

To the contrary, George H. W. Bush has been the ultimate insider since his birth to Dorothy Walker and Prescott Bush. His father, Prescott, was a Yale classmate of Roland "Bunny" Harriman, younger brother of Averell Harriman. Prescott, "Bunny" and several other Skull and Bones members from their Yale class of 1917 would later become core partners in Brown Brothers Harriman, the world's largest private investment bank. Averell's father, stock broker E.H. Harriman, had gained control of the Union Pacific Railroad in 1898 with credit arranged by William Rockefeller and by Kuhn Loeb & Co.'s private bankers, Otto Kahn, Jacob Schiff and Felix Warburg. William Rockefeller, treasurer of Standard Oil and brother of Standard founder John D. Rockefeller, co-owned National City Bank (now Citibank), which then became the primary bank for the railroad. After E.H. Harriman issued tens of millions of dollars in tainted railroad stock, mostly through the Kuhn Loeb Co., President Theodore Roosevelt denounced him as being an "undesirable citizen." because of "cynicism and deep-seated corruption".

In 1914, Bonesman Percy Rockefeller, son of William, took control of Remington Arms, a major supplier of rifles, ammunitions, machine guns and Colt automatic pistols to America, its allies and even Czarist Russia. Remington Arms supplied nearly 70% of the U.S. rifles and over 50% of allied small arms ammunitions used during World War I. In 1918, just after World War I started, Samuel P. Bush, father of Prescott, became chief of the Ordnance, Small Arms and Ammunition Section of the War Industries Board. Just months later, he was the director of the Facilities Division, despite having no arms experience and a background exclusively in railroading. The War Industries Board was run by Bernard Baruch, whose brokerage firm handled many Harriman speculations. His assistant was Clarence Dillon, a Wall Street private banker. Samuel Bush worked closely with Percy Rockefeller and Remington Arms through his positions at the War Industries Board.

Prescott Bush met Dorothy Walker in the fall of 1919. They were engaged in 1920 and married in August 1921. On May 1, 1926, Prescott Bush joined W.A. Harriman & Co. as vice president, reporting to Dorothy's father, the president, George Herbert "Bert" Walker. Walker, was a Missouri power broker and son of a dry goods wholesaler who specialized in English imports. He founded the W.A. Harriman & Co. private bank in November 1919 and became its president. Averell Harriman was chairman and controlling co-owner with his brother "Bunny" and Percy Rockefeller was a director and founding financial sponsor. After the 1931 merger with British-American banking house Brown Brothers, Prescott Bush became managing partner of the resulting company, Brown Brothers Harriman, the world's largest private bank. He also managed the personal investments of the Harriman brothers.

In 1920, Harriman created the world's largest private shipping line by re-starting Germany's Hamburg-Amerika, whose commercial steamships had been confiscated by the United States at the end of the First World War. The deal was made possible through the capital supplied when George Walker arranged the merger W.A. Harriman & Co., with the Morton & Co. private bank. Walker also organized the American Ship and Commerce Corp. as a unit of W.A. Harriman & Co., with contractual power over Hamburg-Amerika's affairs. Through some still secret arrangements with U.S authorities the ships became the property of the Harriman enterprise, which gained "the right to participate in 50 percent of all business originated in Hamburg" and had "complete control of all activities of the Hamburg line in the United States." for 20 years.

In 1925, George Walker and Averell Harriman headed a syndicate that rebuilt Madison Square Garden. George personally managed most aspects of Averell's horse racing interests. By 1930, George Walker was New York State Racing Commissioner and president of the Belmont Park racetrack. In 1924, Prescott and Dorothy had a newborn baby boy who they named George Herbert Walker Bush after his grandfather George Herbert "Bert" Walker who propelled them into the upper echelons of the Eastern Establishment. Thanks to his father and grandfathers, George H.W. Bush was the classic example of an individual born with a silver spoon in his mouth, however, that spoon was also coated through profiteering in world war.

THE BUSHES, HARRIMANS AND NAZIS

In 1942, just after the U.S. entered World War II, America was preparing its first assault against Nazi military forces and George H.W. Bush was an 18-year-old who had just begun training to become a naval pilot. At that time, Prescott Bush was managing partner of Brown Brothers Harriman and director of Union Banking Corporation, which was owned almost exclusively by his friend "Bunny" Harriman. The bank was established by an agreement between Averell Harriman and Fritz Thyssen. The Thyssen family and business partners are acknowledged as the most important German financiers of the Adolf Hitler takeover in Germany.

In August of 1942, the U. S. government ordered the seizure of all Hamburg-Amerika property under the Trading with the Enemy Act. On Oct. 20, 1942, the U.S. government also took over Union Banking Corporation as part of a seizure ordered against all Nazi banking operations in New York City. The U.S. Alien Property Custodian issued Vesting Order 248 to seize its stock shares, all of which were owned by "Bunny" Harriman, Prescott Bush three Nazi executives, and two other Bush associates. On Oct. 28, the government issued orders seizing two Nazi front organizations run by the bank: the Holland-American Trading Corporation and the Seamless Steel Equipment Corporation. On Nov. 17, 1942 Nazi interests in the Silesian-American Corporation, a mining and steel production conglomerate managed by Prescott Bush and his father-in-law George Walker, were also seized under the Trading with the Enemy Act but the Nazis' U.S. partners were left to continue business.

A 1942 U.S. government investigative report stated that Union Banking Corporation was interlocked with the German Steel Trust, led by Fritz Thyssen and his two brothers. After the war, further Congressional investigations revealed that German Steel Trust produced these proportions of total German national output:

- 50.8% of Nazi Germany's pig iron
- 41.4% of Nazi Germany's universal plate
- 36.0% of Nazi Germany's heavy plate
- 38.5% of Nazi Germany's galvanized sheet
- 45.5% of Nazi Germany's pipes and tubes
- 22.1% of Nazi Germany's wire
- 35.0% of Nazi Germany's explosives

The German Steel Trust, Germany's largest industrial corporation, was organized in 1926 by Wall Street banker, Clarence Dillon, former comrade of Samuel P. Bush at the U.S. War Industries Board. Friedrich Flick was a major co-owner with Fritz Thyssen. While preparing for the war crimes tribunal at Nuremberg, the U.S. government found that Flick "contributed large sums" to the Nazi Party and the German SS private armies (black and brown shirts). Flick was sentenced to seven years in prison for his role in the buildup of the Nazi war machine but he served only three years. Prescott Bush and George Walker directly supervised the Flick-Harriman partnership involving German Steel Trust and Union Banking Corporation.

The Silesian-American Corporation, partnership, owned two-thirds by Frick and one-third by Harriman interests, controlled mines and steel production facilities in both Germany and Poland. They included the Polish Upper Silesian Coal and

Steel Company, which employed 25,000 men and accounted for 45 percent of Poland's total steel output, much of which was exported to Germany, and 12 percent of the coal production. A *New York Times* article on March 19, 1934 reported that: "The company has long been accused of mismanagement, excessive borrowing, fictitious bookkeeping and gambling in securities. Warrants were issued in December for several directors accused of tax evasions. They were German citizens who fled and were replaced by Poles. Herr Flick, regarding this as an attempt to make the company's board entirely Polish, retaliated by restricting credits until the new Polish directors were unable to pay the workmen regularly." Prescott Bush alerted Averell Harriman about the problem and the dispute continued for several years with the Polish government demanding taxes on the facilities. It was finally settled in September 1939 when Nazi tanks and bombs invaded Poland. The Nazi army thus initiated World War II after being equipped by Flick and Harriman with materials taken from Poland during a depression.

Hitler had previously received several seals of approval from key Jewish individuals or organizations. One came from the Jewish representative of American Ship and Commerce Corp. Its shares were held by the Harriman Fifteen Corp. which also held Consolidated Silesian Steel. Harriman Fifteen Corp was run by Prescott Bush and Bert Walker. On March 7, 1933, American Ship and Commerce Co. notified Max Warburg of Hamburg, Germany that Warburg was to be the designated representative on the board of Hamburg-Amerika. On March 27, 1933, Max Warburg, assured his American sponsors the Hitler government was good for Germany and there was no cause for any alarm whatsoever.

On March 31, 1933, two days after the letter from Warburg, the American-Jewish Committee and B'nai B'rith issued a formal, official joint statement requesting "that no American boycott against Germany be encouraged" and they advised "that no further mass meetings be held or similar forms of agitation be employed". The American Jewish Committee was controlled by the Warburgs, and B'nai B'rith, forerunner of the Anti-Defamation League, was heavily influenced by the Sulzbergers of the *New York Times*. They continued with the defense of Hitler throughout the 1930s and blunted the fight mounted by many other concerned Jews.

On March 29, 1933, two days after Max Warburg's letter to Harriman, Max's son, Erich Warburg, sent a cable to his cousin Frederick M. Warburg, a director of the Harriman railroad system. He asked Frederick to `"use all your influence" to stop all anti-Nazi activity in America, including "atrocity news and unfriendly propaganda in foreign press, mass meetings, etc."

Hamburg-Amerika officials testified before Congress, in 1934, of astounding corporate support for the Nazis. The line provided free passage to individuals going abroad for Nazi propaganda purposes. A supervisor from the Nazi Labor Front rode with every Hamburg-Amerika ship. New York office employees were directly organized into the Nazi Labor Front organization. The line subsidized pro-Nazi newspapers in the U.S.A., as it had done in Germany against the constitutional German government. The U.S. embassy in Berlin even reported that when the German government attempted to preserve Constitutional freedom by ordering that the Nazi private armies be disbanded, Hamburg-Amerika purchased and distributed propaganda attacks against the German government.

THE BUSH / FARISH FORTUNES

When George H.W. Bush was elected Vice President in 1980, his personal wealth was relegated to a blind trust managed by his closest friend and confidante, William ("Will") Stamps Farish III, one of the richest and most secretive men in Texas. Farish owns and boards the studs that mate with the mares of Queen Elizabeth II. On her visits to America, she often stayed at the Farish house.

Will's grandfather, William Stamps Farish, was the key organizer of Texas based Humble Oil, which later merged with Standard Oil of New Jersey (now Exxon). John D. Rockefeller appointed Farish as chairman of the merged company in 1933 and in 1937 he became President and Chief Executive Officer. On March 25, 1942, William Stamps Farish pled "no contest" to charges of criminal conspiracy with the Nazis. Farish, as CEO, managed a worldwide partnership between Standard and German based I.G. Farben, a key corporate supporter of Adolf

Hitler. The merger opened the Auschwitz slave labor camp on June 14, 1940, to produce artificial rubber and gasoline from coal based on patents supplied by Standard Oil to the Nazis without the knowledge of the U.S. government. The Hitler regime supplied the camp with political opponents and Jews, who were worked to near death and then often murdered.

During a Senate investigating committee hearing led by then Senator Harry Truman of Missouri, the Justice Department submitted a letter written to Standard president Farish by vice president Frank Howard and dated October 12, 1939, shortly after the beginning of World War II in Europe. The letter concerned a renewal of their earlier agreements with the Nazis and explained the objective of a meeting with three I.G. Farben executives in Holland:

"We did our best to work out complete plans for a modus vivendi which could operate through the term of the war, whether or not the U.S. came in..."

At the hearings, communications between Standard and I.G. Farben from the outbreak of World War II were released to the Senate. Other damaging evidence indicated that Farish or his organization:

- Were supplying gasoline and tetraethyl lead to Germany's submarines and air force;
- Deceived the U.S. Navy to prevent them from acquiring certain patents that were supplied to the Nazis; and
- Had arranged to deceive the U.S. government into not seizing certain Nazi-owned assets.

When grandson, Will Farish, was 25 years old he was a personal aide to George Bush during his unsuccessful 1964 campaign for the U.S. Senate. When Bush was elected to Congress in 1966, Farish, who invested some of his Nazi created inheritance in Bush's Zapata Oil Company, joined the board of Zapata. Zapata put oil-drilling rigs in certain locations of great strategic interest to the American intelligence community. As explained earlier, these rigs were also used as drug transshipment points.

BUSH AND THE SUPERIOR RACE

A significant American political event for Hitler, the Third International Congress on Eugenics, was held at New York's American Museum of Natural History August 21-23, 1932 and supervised by the International Federation of Eugenics Societies. The Congress proceedings were dedicated to Averell Harriman's mother; who had paid for the founding of the race-science movement in America back in 1910 and built the Eugenics Record Office as a branch of the Galton National Laboratory in London. Averell Harriman personally arranged with the Hamburg-Amerika Line to transport Nazi participants from Germany to New York for the meeting. Topics included racial purity, "Mental Aberration and Race Hygiene" race-mixing and sterilization of the unfit. The ensuing movement was dedicated to these topics as well as execution of the insane, criminals and the terminally ill.

Immediately after World War II, Henry Kissinger brought Nazi scientists who conducted human experimentations in Nazi death camps to America under Operation Paperclip. In 1950 and 1951, John D. Rockefeller III and John Foster Dulles, then chairman of the Rockefeller Foundation, went on a series of world tours, focusing on the need to stop the expansion of the non-white populations. In November 1952, the Rockefeller family funded the Population Council with tens of millions of dollars. The American Eugenics Society moved into the office of Population Council from its old headquarters at Yale University. The International Planned Parenthood Federation was founded in the London offices of the British Eugenics Society. But most importantly, many of the Nazi human experimentations were essentially reborn under the guise of "population control".

As a Congressman, former President George H.W. Bush, brought two "race-science" professors to the Republican Task Force on Earth Resources and Population on August 5, 1969, about two weeks after the moon landing. As Task Force chairman, he invited Professors William Shockley and Arthur Jensen to explain to the committee how runaway birth rates for black Americans were forcing inferiority onto the American population. Afterwards, Bush personally summed up for

Congress the testimony the advocates had given to the Task Force.

Bush's thinking on this subject was influenced by family friend, Gen. William H. Draper, Jr., the founder and chairman of the Population Crisis Committee, and vice chairman of the Planned Parenthood Federation. Draper had previously formulated plans to depopulate poorer countries whose non-white population was perceived as threat to national security. He established the "Draper Fund", helped to fund a eugenics conference and joined the Rockefeller and Du Pont families to promote eugenics as "population control". After being advised by Gen. Draper, the Lyndon Johnson administration began to finance birth control in tropical countries through the U.S. Agency for International Development (USAID).

Draper was hired by Clarence Dillon at Dillon Read & Co. to handle the Thyssen account. In January 1926, Dillon Read created the German Steel Trust and German Credit and Investment Corporation, Thyssen's short-term banker. Draper was director, vice president and assistant treasurer of the German Credit and Investment Corp. He provided financial management for Thyssen and German Steel Trust clients. They helped sponsored Hitler's rise to power, the buildup of the Nazi war industry and even war activity against the United States.

The German Credit and Investment Corp. (GCI), had the same New Jersey address as U.S. & International Securities Corp. (USIS), whose directors were Clarence Dillon and his son C. Douglas Dillon. In the Senate Banking Committee's 1933 "Pecora" hearings, USIS was exposed as a speculative pyramid scheme that had swindled stockholders of hundreds of millions of dollars and may have led to the Great Depression of the 1930s. The Nazi regime surrendered in May 1945 and in July, General Draper was appointed head of the Economics Division of the U.S. Control Commission. He was called to Europe to take apart the Nazi corporate cartels. Draper, who financed and managed Nazi enterprises in treasonous acts against the U. S., was now authorized to decide who would by exposed, who lost or kept their businesses and who could be prosecuted for war crimes.

Draper and his colleagues demanded that Germany and the world accept the collective guilt of the German people as the explanation for the rise of Hitler and the Nazi war crimes. This was a keenly convenient precept for Draper, Bush, Harriman and all of their colleagues who funded the Nazi war machine.

The population control programs advocated by Draper have essentially been adopted by the American government and funded by American taxpayers to the tune of 1/3 billion dollars per year. The expert advisor in these matters for the George H.W. Bush White House was chief White House legal officer, Clayland Boyden Gray, whose father, Gordon, organized North Carolina experiments that formed basics of the present worldwide sterilization program.

The experiments were conducted during 1947, in Winston-Salem and nearby Orange County, North Carolina. Underwear mogul James Gordon Hanes, a trustee of Bowman Gray Medical School, financed the project. Bowman Gray was the principal owner of R.J. Reynolds Tobacco Co. and father of Gordon Gray. Gordon named the medical school after his father and used inherited cigarette stock shares to found the school, which already a eugenics center. Gordon's aunt, Alice Shelton Gray, had founded the Human Betterment League, the North Carolina branch of the national eugenically oriented sterilization movement. Alice Gray supervised the experiments and Dr. Clarence Gamble, heir to the Proctor and Gamble fortune, was the sterilizers' national field operations chief.

The experiments tested school age children and identified any of them who should be considered for sterilization. Three percent of the children were determined to be either insane or feebleminded based on IQ scores below 70. Sterilizations were then performed on the children as they reached the age of eight to ten years old. All of this was done in conjunction with North Carolina law, the state Eugenics board and the local news media. Gordon Gray owned the Winston-Salem Journal, the Twin City Sentinel and radio station WSJS.

BUSH, NIXON AND WATERGATE

In 1968, former Eisenhower Vice President, Richard Nixon, was elected President of the United States. Nixon, who had campaigned for George Bush in 1964 and 1966, was also supportive of the Bush population control efforts. Nixon made

Henry Kissinger the most powerful man in his administration, through his role as National Security Advisor and later, Secretary of State. In 1971, Nixon appointed George Bush as ambassador to the United Nations and Bush worked closely with Kissinger, who essentially became his mentor. Later, George Bush was also selected as Chairman of the Republican National Committee.

In 1971, Kissinger convinced Nixon that a covert operation was needed to combat repeated unauthorized divulgence of classified material. The problem had surfaced in early 1971, when author, Daniel Ellsberg, produced a publication entitled the Pentagon Papers. John Paisley assumed responsibility for overall leak analysis that included the classification, severity and frequency of leaks associated with certain journalists. On August 9, 1971 at CIA headquarters in Langley, Va., Paisley met with Howard Osborne of the Office of Security, Kissinger confidant, David Young, and the covert operations team that eventually became known as the "plumbers".

On June 17, 1972 the plumbers were caught after breaking into the Democrat National Committee in the Watergate office building and then seeming to bungle the operation. Nixon was forced to resign on August 8, 1974 from the fallout of trying to obstruct an investigation into that break-in. A subsequent Senate investigation led by Sam Erwin uncovered information that would have likely resulted in Nixon being impeached by a House Judiciary Committee led by Peter Rodino since the plumbers were believed to be White House operatives who broke in to uncover documents and plant bugs. Upon request of Miami Station Chief Jake Esterline, Langley's Cord Meyer had replied to Deputy Director of Plans, Thomas Karamessines, that organizer E. Howard Hunt was on domestic White House business of an unknown nature.

But the unreported story of the Watergate scandal reveals the plumbers were almost all CIA operatives who may have had other loyalties. The plumbers and those who supported them included:

- E. Howard Hunt retired CIA staff officer believed by many to be involved in the Kennedy assassination;
- James McCord, CIA Office of Security official who was responsible for securing all CIA offices in the U.S.;

- G. Gordon Liddy, who worked for both the FBI and Treasury Dept.
- John Paisley, CIA liaison to the White House investigative unit and future George Bush CIA appointee;
- Frank Sturgis, CIA agent famous for helping Fidel Castro to power in Cuba and then trying to remove him;
- Bernard Barker, long-time CIA operative who handled funding for the Watergate operation;
- CIA Miami station anti-Castro Cubans including;
- Eugenio Martinez, Felipe de Diego, Virgilio Gonzalez, and Renaldo Pico.

Hunt and Frank Sturgis had worked on many related CIA operations from the Miami station although they claimed they did not know each other at the time. They helped bring Castro to power in Cuba, were involved in the Bay of Pigs invasion and worked on Operation Mongoose to eliminate Castro from power. Hunt, who assembled the team, recruited anti-Castro Cubans for Watergate from these operations. His close friend, Howard Osborne from the Office of Security was the immediate superior of James McCord who provided security for all CIA installations and personnel in the United States. McCord, who organized the break-in, was also a close friend of CIA Counterintelligence Director James Jesus Angleton, now suspected of being a double agent for the Isreali Mossad. It is almost inconceivable that a man with the credentials and resources of McCord would be accidentally caught in the most rudimentary of all break-ins.

Even the reporting of the break-in and subsequent cover-up had CIA fingerprints. The journalists who led the charge and broke new information were Bob Woodward and Carl Bernstein of the *Washington Post*. The publisher of the Washington Post was Philip Graham, a graduate of Army Intelligence School in Harrisburg Pa. Graham directed CIA Operation Mockingbird, under Frank Wisner for the Office of Policy Coordination. The program was designed to infiltrate the national news media, establish hundreds of cooperative media assets, provide supplemental compensation to the assets and even takeover news outlets as necessary.

George H.W. Bush had numerous connections to the Watergate plumbers. Wright Patman, chairman of the U.S. House of Representatives Banking and Currency Committee, confirmed that the largest single amount of funds going into the Miami bank account of plumber Bernard Barker was the $100,000 sent by Penzoil President William Liedtke. Liedtke, who appeared to be involved in funding as much as $700,000 towards the operation, was a longtime business partner of George H.W. Bush. As explained earlier, Bush was involved covertly in the CIA anti-Castro Cuban operations through his role as head of Zapata Oil, which had oil-drilling rigs in the Caribbean. CIA officer Fletcher Prouty delivered ships for the failed Bay of Pigs invasion to Bush, who had them painted as civilian and then named *Barbara and Houston*. Almost all of the Watergate plumbers were a part of those operations. The involvement by Paisley in Watergate did not deter Bush from employing him when Bush became CIA director in 1976. Bush appointed Paisley to coordinate three subdivisions of a team responsible for determining Soviet capabilities and intentions. In September of 1978, Paisley disappeared while sailing on the Chesapeake Bay.

On August 5, 1974, the White House released the "smoking gun" transcript of a June 23, 1972 conversation where Nixon discussed ways to subvert the investigation into the Watergate break-ins. In these tapes, his conversations with H.R. Haldeman make several things clear:

Nixon was obviously unaware of the original break-in until Haldeman informed him;

- Nixon was also unaware of the Texans and others who funded the break-in until Haldeman informed him;
- Nixon tried to obstruct justice to by agreeing with Haldeman to have the CIA stop an FBI probe;
- Nixon believed the break-in was an operation of the CIA who would have a vested interest in covering it up;
- Nixon told Haldeman Hunt's involvement would open a scab to a lot of other things;
- Nixon told Haldeman the investigation would specifically open up the whole Bay of Pigs things again;

Nixon's referral to Hunt and the "Bay of Pigs thing" is believed by many to be a knowledgeable reference to the assassination of John F. Kennedy. Nixon was in Dallas on November 22, 1963, the day of the Kennedy assassination and had addressed Pepsi-Cola distributors the previous day. Nixon, Hunt, Sturgis, Jack Ruby and some anti-Castro Cubans met at the Cabana Motel in suburban Dallas on the eve of the assassination according to Marita Lorenz, a former Castro mistress and CIA operative. Later that evening, Nixon, Lyndon Baines Johnson (LBJ), FBI director J. Edgar Hoover, Carlos Marcello, Jack Ruby and Dallas Mayor Earle Cabell were at a party and private meeting in the home of Clint Murchison according to several authors and Madeleine Duncan Brown, mother of LBJ's only son, Steven, who died after filing a claim against the LBJ estate.

Earle Cabell is the brother of Gen. Charles Cabell, who was fired by JFK for his role in the Bay of Pigs. As mentioned earlier, those associated with the Bay of Pigs considered JFK a traitor for reselecting the invasion site and withdrawing air support when the covert operation was underway. These actions sabotaged the attempt to remove Castro from power and resulted in 1500 anti-Castro Cubans being killed or captured. Consequently, elements of the anti-Castro Cuban movement have been directly connected to the Kennedy assassination by numerous authors throughout the world. Although their relatives have provided alibis, Hunt and Sturgis even appear to be in a famous photo of "tramps" near the railroad tracks at the site of the Kennedy assassination. Some have speculated they broke into DNC headquarters to retrieve the pictures but that is not likely since they would have no guarantee other copies did not exist elsewhere.

Specific anti-Casto Cubans along with Sturgis, Felix Rodriguez, Barry Seal and William Seymour, who is widely believed to have served as a double for Lee Harvey Oswald, were all members of the Operation 40 team. They and others appear in a group picture used by Daniel Hopsicker for the cover of his book, *Barry and the Boys.* Hopsicker determined Operation 40 was a special assassination team assigned to invade Cuba and kill Fidel among other dastardly tasks. Richard Nixon is believed to have founded Operation 40 during his 1959 presidential campaign in response to Castro nationalizing American interests in Cuba. Several authors have stated

Nixon delegated general oversight of Operation 40 to Bush while Hopsicker determined Howard Hunt had detail operational control. All of this knowledge would certainly account for Nixon's well-known paranoia.

The Nixon "smoking gun" tape shows that although Nixon attempted to obstruct the investigation, he appeared to be unaware of the original DNC break-in and seemed to take a while to figure out what hit him. Another taped conversation with John Ehrlichman days before Nixon's November 1972 re-election confirms he was furious such a break-in could accomplish nothing. Liddy is on record as stating his participation was ordered by John Dean but Dean clearly never informed Nixon.

Liddy, the only non-CIA participant served well over four years of prison time after being convicted for his role in the break-in. McCord and other CIA participants got off lightly after cooperating with authorities. Hunt was linked to the operation through a phone number carried by the plumbers. He too, was eventually convicted and served 33 months in prison after being unable to get Nixon to commute his sentence. Had Nixon ordered the break-in he surely would have arranged some form of clemency for Hunt

The participants, their background and the facts illustrate the original break-in was a CIA operation but it is still unclear what in DNC headquarters would be of any value to the CIA. Haldeman contends: "the overwhelming evidence leads to the conclusion that the break-in was deliberately sabotaged." It is certainly true the operation was conducted by very powerful, skilled and resourceful people who could have easily covered up any mistake. Haldeman also stated: "the CIA was an agency hostile to Nixon, who returned the hostility with fervor", much like Kennedy. All of the facts give the operation ear markings of an effort designed deliberately to remove Nixon from the White House. George H.W. Bush, who had worked as a CIA operative and would soon become its director, was actually the first Nixon loyalist who wrote a letter telling him to resign.

Perhaps Nixon could have remained in office longer had it not been for a mysterious plane crash six months after the famous "smoking gun" conversation. On December 8, 1972,

Dorothy Hunt, wife of Howard Hunt, and other Watergate figures died when United Airlines Flight 533 crashed near Midway airport on route from Washington D.C. to Chicago and a final destination of Omaha. The NTSB ruled "pilot error" was the cause but Sherman Skolnick obtained government crash investigation documents and had NTSB hearings reopened during June 13-14, 1973. Although the NTSB did not really change its conclusion, testimony, recordings and documents identified multiple acts of sabotage and showed that Mrs. Hunt had as much as two million dollars in money orders and travelers checks. When the plane crashed over 100 federal agents were on the scene before police and emergency vehicles could get there. Skolnick believes that Nixon had ordered them there to arrest Dorothy Hunt and others for bribery against the president. Nixon's attempt to save his presidency may have crashed with the sabotaged plane.

This leaves the question of what did Nixon do to so alienate himself from the CIA power structure in the same manner as John F. Kennedy? In January of 1972, Nixon used a plan from G. Gordon Liddy to set up the Office for Drug Abuse Law Enforcement, forerunner to the Drug Enforcement Administration (DEA). In July of 1972, after the break-in, Nixon issued Executive Order 11676 to establish the Office of National Narcotics Intelligence. Nixon was well on his way to wresting control of drug trafficking operations away from the CIA power structure and placing them under the control of the President where he could use them for his own political purposes. Although the DEA was eventually established, it has been in a decades long battle with the CIA from its inception. Ever since then, the CIA has frequently thwarted key DEA drug trafficking investigations under the guise of national security.

SATANIC CONNECTIONS

So far this book has detailed links of George H.W. Bush to drug trafficking, two presidential assassination attempts, funding activities for the rise of Hitler, profiting from the buildup of the Nazi war machine and racist eugenics efforts to create "superior" human beings. That should be enough to keep almost any American citizen from supporting him or anyone in his family. But his long documented association with satanic rituals related to these activities is still another aspect of the Bush legacy.

The Bush association with satanic rituals erupted at Yale with his initiation into the morbid Skull and Bones society and it continued throughout the century as he ushered in the new millennium at the Pyramids in Egypt. Skull and Bones is head-quartered in a stone building resembling a mausoleum known as "the Tomb". It conducts macabre initiation rights often associated with various aspects of death. Its alarming racist and drug related historical origins are documented earlier in this chapter.

George H.W. Bush is also member of the Bohemian Club and an attendee of the heavily guarded, male only, Bohemian Grove summer gatherings in Northern California. The annual occult gatherings have attracted U.S. leaders for over a century and feature bizarre Babylonian style worship ceremonies. Bohemians who assemble from around the world are "reverent" before a 40' stone owl, "the prince of mortal wisdom", in his "leafy temple". The Bohemian "shrine", with its "holy" pillars, is the site of the "Cremation of Care" ceremony where the effigy of a human being representing care is burned alive against the will of God. Worshippers rejoice that "midsummer sets us free" to continue their activities without concern for the impact on other people in the world. The ceremony, which was filmed when talk show host, Alex Jones, infiltrated the group one evening, is almost beyond belief.

Perhaps even more disturbing is the satanic origin of the re-pulsive child prostitution ring described in *The Franklin Cover-Up* by John DeCamp, a former Nebraska Republican State Senator who also headed Operation Baby Lift in Vietnam. That book explains how some of the children were brought to a party where George H.W. Bush was present and that the sus-pected prostitution ring organizer sung the anthem at the 1984 Republican National Convention.

All of this information combined is too overwhelming for a truly informed individual to refute. Despite what may be written about Bill Clinton, George H. W. Bush has participated in the most inherently evil activities of any U.S. president in our time. Ironically, Bush has gotten significant support from many Christians who are uniformed about his family history, continuing activities and future tendencies. With that support,

Bush has now groomed his two sons, Jeb and George W., another Bonesman and Bohemian Grove attendee, to carry on his devastating legacy.

REFERENCES

Alex Jones, *Dark Secrets Inside the Bohemian Grove* (video), Alex Jones Productions

Drugs Law Enforcement and Foreign Policy Vol 1-2, Hearings Part 1-4, 5/2787, 7/15/87, 2/8-2/10/88, and 4/4-4/7/88, Subcommittee on Narcotics, Terrorism and International Operations for Senate Foreign Relations Committee.

Inspector General's Report of Investigation, Vol.1 The California Story, Central Intelligence Agency.

Inspector General's Report of Investigation, Vol.2 The Cortra Story, Central Intelligence Agency.

L.D. Brown, *Crossfire*, Black Forest Press.

Alexander Cockburn & Jeffrey St. Clair, *White Out*, Verso.

Celerino Castillo III & Dave Harmon, *Powderburns*, Mosaic Press.

Col. James "Bo" Gritz, *Called to Serve*, Lazarus Publishing.

Mark Lane, *Plausible Denial*, Thunder Mouth's Press.

Joesph McBride, *The Nation*, columns by July 16-23, 1988, August 13-20, 1988.

Terry Reed & John Cummings, *Compromised*, Shapolsky Publishers.

Rodney Stich, *Drugging America*, Diablo Western Press.

Webster Tarpley and Anton Chaiktin, *George Bush: The Unauthorized Biography*.

Gary Webb, *Dark Alliance*, Seven Stories Press.

Michael Ruppert, From the Wilderness newsletters, *From the Wilderness*.

Dan Hopsicker,*Barry and the Boys*, publisher to be announced

Dan Hopsicker, *In Search of the American Drug Lords* (video), Mad Cow Productions.

Michael Ruppert, *50 Years of CIA Drug Dealing* (video), Justice Vision.

Mena, Arkansas: Under Investigation (video), American Investigator, Free Congress Research and Education Foundation.

POW/MIA: You are Not Forgotten (video), Col. James "Bo" Gritz and Bobby Steward, Dandridge, Tennessee.

John Decamp, *The Franklin Coverup*, AWT Inc.

Sherman Skolnick, *The Secret History of Airline Sabotage - Parts 1-4*, www.skolnicksreport.com

Anthony Sutton, America's Secret Establishment, An Introduction to the Order of Skull and Bones, Trineday

BUSH / CIA DRUG AND ASSASSINATION CONNECTIONS

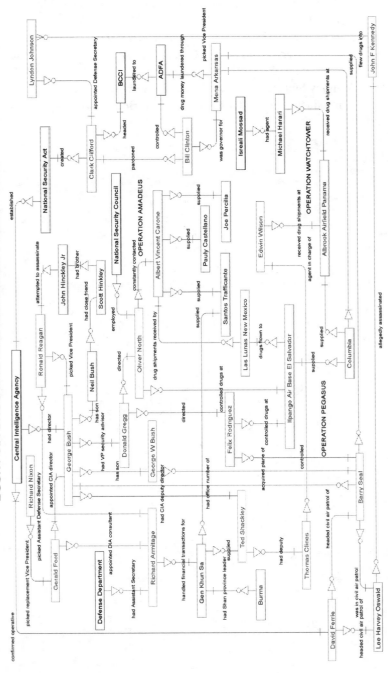

III
The Real
America

CHAPTER ELEVEN
AMERICA IMPEACHED

THE NEED FOR ACCOUNTABILITY

During the 1980s, President George H.W. Bush was the beneficiary of a total media blackout for his illicit activities. He was afforded a far greater degree of protection than even Bill Clinton. While some conservative leaning news agencies would report various corrupt activities involving Bill Clinton during the 90s, virtually no national news organization would report on CIA drug trafficking operations during the 80s or even now. The black out leads some liberals to conclude that the media was "right wing" while nearly all conservatives believe that the media is "left wing". This chapter will show how globalists gained control of the news media and suppress corruption on all sides of the political spectrum so that the controllers can implement their own agenda.

The major media organizations falsely portrayed the impeachment movement as consisting of people who hated Bill Clinton. I never hated Bill Clinton. I love America and want to help save it. America cannot survive as a free nation if we let a President or any other elected official live above the law and desecrate the Constitution. America has an intricate system of checks and balances to protect its citizens from corrupted individuals operating within the government. Therefore, the corruption of one individual, regardless of who it is, does not really bother me. What bothers me are the individuals and organizations who cover up the activity. These are the people who subvert the American system of justice and pose an equally serious threat to our freedom as the offending individual.

Bill Clinton thrives because he appoints people who are willingly corrupted, he obtains compromising information on his adversaries and he takes orders from the globalists who drive his agenda. George H.W. Bush, a CFR member and trilateralist like Clinton, receives media protection because he is also implementing a globalist agenda he calls the New World Order.

Bill Clinton developed a stream of organizations and individuals willing to protect him at almost all costs. These include his fellow Democrat party members, the major media outlets, the U.S. Attorney General who he appointed to head the Justice Department, two independent counsels and even a substantial portion of the opposing political party. All of these individuals and organizations must be exposed to prevent repititions and protect the future of America.

THE DEMOCRAT PARTY

During the 90s, the Democrat Party became morally bankrupt. Most Democrats are now perfectly willing to set up an unprecedented double standard of justice in America to protect a President just because he shares their political views. Based on the passed Articles of Impeachment, these separate standards of justice would absolve:

- A President vs. a judge who would be impeached;
- The commander in chief vs. a military officer or soldier who would be court-martialed;
- A government executive vs. a corporate executive who would be fired;
- An elected official vs. a private citizen who would be jailed.

The Declaration of Independence states "We hold these truths to be self-evident that all men are created equal." The Pledge of Allegiance states we are "one nation under God, indivisible, with liberty and justice for all." The Democrat Party has already destroyed these principles which most Americans hold dear.

Not only are the Democrats advocates of a double standard of justice, they are perfectly content to let the President set up a tyranny and engage in the fascist use of government agencies like the FBI, IRS and Treasury to persecute political adversaries. In fact, many Democrats now participate in the tyranny either directly or by helping to cover it up.

Worse yet, Democrats have even sold our souls to our enemies. The Clinton / Gore campaigns and the Democrat National Committee (DNC) had seven sources of revenue traceable through 11 streams to Communist Chinese government agencies and individuals connected with the People's Liberation Army. Even before receiving much of this money, the Clinton administration transferred export decisions to the Commerce Department by Executive Order and gave the Communists many dual use and military technologies, despite the objections of government agencies. Four separate transfers occurred over separate objections of the National Security Administration, Department of Defense, Department of State and Department of Justice. Never before in American history had any President given military technology to a Communist controlled military government over the objections of his own security and defense departments. This is as clear a case of treason as can be defined.

THE REPUBLICAN PARTY

When Republicans took control of Congress, they authorized roughly a dozen investigations into various aspects of the Clinton administration. These investigations uncovered astounding, irrefutable evidence of criminal activity in Arkansas, treason and bribery with the Communist Chinese military, abusive use of government agencies to persecute political adversaries and a whole host of obstructions of justice that even involve drug trafficking and organized crime.

All of this evidence, which would have easily established a national consensus for impeachment, was left out of the Articles of Impeachment by House Republican leaders, even though they have a majority in both the House and the Judiciary Committee. Instead, the Judiciary Committee and House Republican leadership deliberately protected Bill Clinton by going forward with only evidence from the Starr report and throwing America into national sex soap opera.

When Articles of Impeachment based on the Starr report evidence passed the House, House managers tried to do the best they could with what they had been given. They requested only two weeks to present all of their evidence, including a brief presentation and cross examination of about 12 witnesses they felt were essential. (The Andrew Johnson impeachment trial had 25 witnesses in just over five days). But the Republicans in the Senate used their majority vote power to sabotage the case of the House managers.

The Senate Republicans eliminated all hostile witnesses that were to be called against President Clinton, eliminated much of the evidence that the House managers thought was essential to the case, prevented the public from hearing most of the actual testimony against Bill Clinton, prevented the Chief Justice from presiding over the depositions, instituted artificial time limits and implemented delaying tactics such as making motions, debating them and re-deposing all witnesses before they testified. It is clear that the founding forefathers, who thrived on balance of power, never intended for the Senate to redefine the Constitutional concept of a trial and usurp power from the prosecution, defense, presiding judge and American public.

Republicans could have gotten 12 Senate votes to convict Bill Clinton on a two-thirds majority at any time during the impeachment process simply by conducting a REAL trial and threatening to use Congressional investigation evidence of criminal activity, abuse of power, treason and bribery in additional Articles of Impeachment. Democrat Senators would then have been forced to convict Bill Clinton on perjury and obstruction or dismiss real crimes such as treason, which would not go over well with the American public. The Democrats stuck together without worrying about that because they knew there was no real opposition party.

After Bill Clinton gave his State of the Union speech on February 20, 1999, House members, Jennifer Dunn and former football player Steve Largent, gave the Republican response. Largent specifically mentioned that part of the Republican mission statement was to protect individual liberty. At the very same time, Republicans Senators were doing everything they could to destroy it by protecting the man who was threatening the liberty of every American citizen. The Republican Senators pandered to and assisted corrupt Democrats as they were destroying the republic. Republican leaders refused repeatedly to honor their mission statement to protect the individual liberty of citizens from tyranny, treason, fascism and communism. They clearly demonstrated that they are not a viable alternative to Democrats. I believe that the Republican Party has become a black hole that sucks up the legitimate Democrat opposition into a twilight zone of uselessness.

THE JUSTICE DEPARTMENT

The Justice Department is now totally unaccountable to the American citizens. Consider the following summary of actions by Attorney General Janet Reno to illustrate that point:

- She refused to support the conclusion of a Justice Department investigation that found an FBI sniper shot, which killed Vicki Weaver at Ruby Ridge, was unconstitutional;
- She approved the internationally banned CS military gas attack at Waco that led to the deaths of over 80 men, women and children who had never committed any crime;
- She stated that she "could not find anything wrong" with FBI actions in Waco, despite the fact that aerial videos show a tank destroying a Davidian building while people were still inside, and autopsy reports indicate that six bodies found in the rubble of that building were crushed to death;
- She fired all 93 U.S. attorneys for the first time in American history;
- She fired FBI Director, William Sessions, on trumped up travel misappropriation charges the day before Vince Foster was murdered;
- She hired Louis Freeh, who mishandled cases involving FBI files, FBI lab work, Waco, Ruby Ridge, Richard Jewell, Gary Aldrich, illegal immigration checks and the Oklahoma City bombing;
- She refused a 1993 FBI recommendation to prosecute the former Arkansas U.S. attorney who was to be tried for obstruction of justice for shutting down a federal drug investigation that would have exposed the Mena drug operation and likely solved the Ives / Henry murder case;
- She terminated the investigation of union boss, Arthur Coia, who raised nearly $17,000,000 for the DNC in 1995-96, despite a Justice Department complaint that he was "associated with, influenced from and controlled by" organized crime;

In addition, Janet Reno used the Justice Department as a defense team for Bill Clinton and essentially became his accomplice. Consider these actions:

- She stalled investigations by making repeated false privilege claims for both Bill and Hillary Clinton that were unanimously rejected by the Supreme Court;
- She appointed Robert Fiske as independent Whitewater counsel even though Fiske was a lawyer for the company that sold Clinton and McDougal Whitewater land;
- She barred expansion of the Mike Espy probe so that it would not include Don Tyson, a major Clinton campaign contributor and a possible suspect in the Smaltz investigation;
- She refused seven separate requests to appoint a special prosecutor to investigate different aspects of the Clinton / Gore and DNC Chinese fundraising scandal, despite clear evidence of treason and bribery.

The actions of Janet Reno illustrate clearly that any President can set up a tyranny in America simply by appointing a corrupt Attorney General who is willing to implement the Presidential agenda and ensure that the president is above the law.

THE RENO CONFIRMATION

But much like the impeachment saga of Bill Clinton, accountability for the confirmation of Janet Reno must be laid squarely on the shoulders of the Republican Senate. Although Gary Aldrich confirmed that Bill Clinton did not have the FBI conduct pre-nomination background checks, the Republicans had clear cut, irrefutable evidence that Janet Reno was unfit to be the United States Attorney General before her confirmation by the Senate Judiciary Committee.

Jack Thompson, a Florida attorney who once ran against Janet Reno, documented nearly a dozen separate, verifiable incidents that confirmed Janet Reno is a closet lesbian. The more serious incidents include use of organized crime call girls, involvement with at least on detainee, getting caught at the Ft. Lauderdale Galleria mall in the back seat of a car with an underage teen girl and harassment of an office secretary who had to transfer out of Reno's department to avoid her.

Thompson was driven by the fact we could not risk having a U.S. Attorney General who could be compromised by organized crime or anyone else, for that matter. He cited the previous example of J. Edgar Hoover, whose closet lesbian affair caused him to deny the existence of organized crime until the late 1950s, when local police discovered a national organized crime meeting in upstate New York. Thompson gave information about Reno to two FBI agents who visited him and he faxed President Bill Clinton a letter that was delivered via his best friend in law school, Sam Johnson, a partner of Bruce Lindsey. Lindsey delivered the letter to Bill Clinton and Thompson was quickly contacted by Lanny Davis.

In addition, five Dade County police officers were prepared to testify at the confirmation hearing that they had each stopped Reno on separate occasions for driving while intoxicated. But no Judiciary committee member was willing to mention it until there were media reports about it. In a sworn affidavit, Thompson stated that John Bliss, Senate Judiciary Committee staffer reporting to Colorado Senator Hank Brown, asked him (and a witness) to mention the public drunkenness stories to the *New York Times* and *Washington Post*. Thompson refused when Bliss would not give him the names of the officers. Although others were willing to do so, the Republican Judiciary Committee members still did not mention it during the confirmation. In fact, Orrin Hatch and Hank Brown even stated to Reno during the hearing that Jack Thompson was making up stories about her.

Reno's escapades continued as Attorney General in Washington D.C. Thompson was called by David Johnston, Sr. Political Writer, Washington Bureau of *New York Times* for confirmation of the drunkenness allegations in case his editor would agree to run a new story. Johnston mentioned that Reno had slipped out from her FBI security and been found drunk in D.C. An FBI agent told Thompson to contact two private investigators who confirmed that they were also contacted by Johnston in regards to the same story. The *NewYork Times* never printed the story and Thompson discovered that Reno was eventually stopped in Florida by a sixth officer who is willing to testify.

If all of this is not enough, Jim and Ken Collier were prepared to testify at the confirmation hearing that for decades,

Janet Reno had covered-up one of the most massive, far reaching voter fraud scandals in American history, even to the point of having Jim Collier arrested when he delivered evidence to her that a candidate for mayor in Opa Locka, Florida was printing his own ballots. So what was it that froze the Republican Judiciary Committee members? It just so happens that the vote counting scandal had national implications that also involved Republicans.

VOTESCAM

The Colliers became suspicious about Florida vote counting when Ken Collier ran against incumbent Rep. Claude Pepper in a Florida Democratic primary. Collier was getting over 30% of the votes and gaining but suddenly local television stations reported that election computers were down and when reporting resumed, Collier found himself at roughly 10%. The Colliers later uncovered documents that showed election computers were never down. They also found that local news accurately predicted 40 races w/250 candidates based on results from a single voting machine. They then conducted their own remarkable investigation that exposed a media conglomerate called News Election Service, and revealed the following vote count corruption:

- In the 1970 Florida election, the Colliers found forgeries in the majority of canvass sheets that are signed by precinct captains to certify that voting machine counters are initialized to zero;
- In a 1972 Florida election, the Colliers found canvass sheets from many counties all were signed using the same handwriting with signatures that were collected in advance from precinct workers. The FBI and the Dade County Organized Crime bureau verified that the sheets were forged;
- In a 1974 Florida election, the Colliers proved that Printomatic equipped voting machines were set with pre-printed paper to falsely portray that the counters were initialized to zero. The precinct workers walked out in protest on election;

- In 1982 Florida election, the Colliers filmed a worker running previously counted non standard ballots through a BMX ballot multiplexor;
- In 1982 Florida election the Colliers filmed large quantities of duplicate seals that were used to replace broken ones on ballot boxes;
- In a 1982 Florida election, the Colliers filmed 70 League of Women Voters in piles of chad punching holes in ballots on election night before they were counted;
- In 1985 in Hamilton Country, Ohio the Colliers filmed more League of Women Voters punching holes in ballots on election night before they were counted;
- Jim Collier also seized evidence that a candidate for mayor in Opa Locka, Florida was printing his own ballots and Collier took them to state attorney, Janet Reno, who had him arrested.

The Colliers presented all of this Florida vote fraud evidence to Janet Reno while she was in various positions of power to investigate the scandals but Reno always protected the criminals. The Colliers presented evidence to Mike Wallace of *60 Minutes*, which refused to do the story. The Giraldo Rivero show, *"Now it Can Be Told"*, canceled their schedule episode about the Colliers. The Miami Herald reported the election worker walkout in protest of rigged Printomatic voting machines printouts as a 'snafu'. Even the Washington Times would not run the story after Jim Collier gave the information to top notch journalist, Jerry Seper.

The Colliers also presented some of the evidence to Frank Farenkopf, chairman of the RNC, which was offering a reward for proof of voter fraud but the RNC never paid and the Colliers were forced to sue. Farenkopf, who apparently either never expected to receive such solid evidence or never intended to pay the reward, is now the co-chair of the FEC.

In 1986, Antonin Scalia wrote an unsolicited memo to fellow Court of Appeals Circuit Judges advocating dismissal of a negligence lawsuit brought by the Colliers against Justice Dept Attorney Craig Donsato. Shortly thereafter, Scalia was nominated and confirmed to the Supreme Court.

The Republican Senate Judiciary Committee members were most likely forced to protect Janet Reno because the Colliers had uncovered a vote count scam that involved both parties and the national news through their ownership of News Election Service. News election service was established by ABC,CBS, NBC, the *New York Times* and the *Washongton Post* in early 1964, a few months after the assassination of John F. Kennedy. It was later reincarnated as Voter News Service, which played an interesting role in the false reporting of the 1996 Republican primary and the year 2000 presidential election.

NON-INDEPENDENT COUNSELS

Independent counsels are supposed to resolve corruption problems, but in reality, the counsels that are appointed are frequently not independent. As previously mentioned, in 1993, Janet Reno appointed as Whitewater prosecutor, Robert Fiske, a lawyer for International Paper, the company that sold Clinton and McDougal much of the Whitewater land. In 1994, when Fiske ruled Vince Foster's death a suicide and his background was exposed, he was replaced by Starr, who was appointed by a three-judge panel, despite being on the original Janet Reno short list.

As Chris Ruddy discovered, Starr's firm, Kirkland and Ellis, was hardly independent since it contributed 86 percent of its 1993-1994 PAC money to Democrat Party candidates. In addition, Starr was retained by Chinese Communist controlled Citisteel at the same time he confirmed the Vince Foster suicide ruling. Citisteel is controlled by China International Trust Investment Co.(CITIC) which also controls the China Ocean Shipping Company, that was caught shipping 2,000 illegal AK47s into the Oakland port after the CITIC chairman, Wang Jun, met with Bill Clinton in the White House.

Although Starr was portrayed as a biased Republican out to get the President, the history of his investigation tells another story. In 1994, Starr hired many liberals for his team such as Miguel Rodriguez, Sam Dash and Mark Tuohey, who had a party for Janet Reno in his house. In 1995, Rodriguez, who was sincerely trying to get the truth, complained to Starr that Touhey was interfering with the Foster investigation, and when Starr did nothing about it, he resigned, citing ethics problems.

In 1996, Starr confirmed the Fiske suicide ruling and attempted to resign under pressure for the obviously flawed decision. In his 1998 testimony before the House Judiciary Committee, he stated, "The controversy surrounding the death of Vince Foster has dissipated because of our thorough and accurate reporting."

Starr also testified that he could find no impeachable offenses in the FBI file scandal but never interviewed key witnesses, such as Director of Records Management, Terry Good, and Chief of Staff, Mack McLarty. When Congressman Barr asked Starr under oath whether or not his team had interviewed McLarty, Starr replied that he thought so.

Also in 1998, Starr withdrew his subpoena of Bill Clinton so that Clinton could find out what questions were to be asked before he would be forced to answer them during his grand jury testimony. When the press claimed that the Starr report would only have evidence regarding the Monica Lewinsky scandal, and they could have only found that out through a leak in Starr's office.

Replacement independent counsel, Robert Ray, a lifelong Democrat continued the trend set by Ken Starr. While wrapping up the investigation into the illegal file acquisitions by the White House, Ray indicated that he had not spoken with Linda Tripp about her sworn testimony that she observed FBI files being loaded onto White House computers. Ray also admitted that he had not spoken to Betty Lambuth and Sheryl Hall, two White House whistleblowers who revealed that the White House had suppressed up to 1,000,000 Emails containing incriminating evidence on the illegal file acquisitions and other scandals. He also confirmed that the files that were illegally obtained are still in a vault in the White House!

Independent counsels are appointed by the Attorney General or a panel of judges who have been given a predefined, carefully selected, narrow list of candidates to select from. In either case the independent counsel investigation is typically flawed because the selection process is corrupted.

Instead of fixing the independent counsel law to ensure that we have real independent counsels, the Republican-led Senate removed the law altogether by allowing it to expire in 1999. This eliminated one of the last threads that the citizens have to make government officials accountable to the same laws as citizens. It also illustrates once again the tyrannical nature of the Republican Party leadership.

MEDIA ORGANIZATIONS

Major media organizations stated repeatedly during the impeachment process that America doesn't care. I say that America doesn't know. Media organizations covered up the Arkansas criminal activity of Bill Clinton to get him elected President of the United States. They covered up his abusive use of government agencies in Washington to get him re-elected. Then they covered up the Communist Chinese infiltration of the Clinton / Gore campaigns and the Democrat National Committee in an attempt to avoid his impeachment. Perhaps we should have impeached the media.

When knowledge of Clinton administration corruption became so great that media organizations could no longer cover it up, they were forced to adopt one of their standard back-up strategies, which is to attack the person that they are defending but use more trivial charges. In the case of Bill Clinton, the spotlight was shifted from Whitewater and government abuse to sexual related matters.

This accomplished three major objectives for them. First, it diverted attention from the real crimes and redefined the impeachment movement as a matter about sex. Second, it made the media appear more unbiased since it was finally attacking Clinton on one of his shortcomings after covering up all of the criminal, treasonous and tyrannical activity that he had undergone during his Presidency and governorship. Third, it fooled most Americans into thinking that Bill Clinton simply had a personal problem and was no threat to their freedom or the American form of government.

Like many others, I believe that the major media organizations are able to distort political information consistently because they are controlled by members of the Council on Foreign Relations (CFR). CFR members hold positions of power such as chairmen, presidents, managing editors, editorial page editors, network TV news anchors, magazine editors, political columnists and many other key positions in the media world. They control all of the political news at major networks, the AP and UPI political news wires and editorial pages of many major newspapers around the country. This allows them to distort political news consistently to fulfill their political agenda.

Congressman Oscar Callaway explained how all of this was implemented in the Congressional Record of 1917:

"In March, 1915, the J.P. Morgan interests, the steel, shipbuilding and powder interests, and their subsidiary organizations, got together 12 men high up in the newspaper world and employed them to select the most influential newspapers in the United States, and sufficient number of them to control generally the policy of the daily press...They found it was only necessary to purchase control of 25 of the greatest papers...An agreement was reached, the policy of the papers was bought, to be paid for by the month; an editor was furnished for each paper to properly supervise and edit information regarding the questions of preparedness, militarism, financial policies, and other things of national and international nature considered vital to the interest of the purchasers."

The dominance of their achievement with the media was shown shortly thereafter when the passenger ship *Lusitania* was being used to ship arms to the British. The Germans took out ads in major newspapers across the country to warn American travelers not to sail on the ship. The ads were rejected by all American newspapers but the *Des Moines Register*. The Germans then sank the *Lusitania* just after its naval escort had mysteriously deserted it, and World War I ensued. The *Lusitania* just happened to have been owned by a rival shipbuilder of J.P. Morgan.

Since 1915, CFR media dominance has expanded to include key network TV positions such as CNN news President, Tom Johnson, and ABC, NBC and CBS news anchors Peter Jennings, Tom Brokaw and Dan Rather. These media organizations allowed Bill Clinton to live above the law because he implemented their global socialist agenda for a one-world government. It is time that we realize we do not have American media. We have anti-American media.

THE ONE WORLD SOCIALIST GOVERNMENT

The not-so-hidden agenda of the CFR and its worldwide sister organization, the Tri-Lateral Commission, is to improve foreign relations by implementing a one-world government, which the members would essentially control. Their planned power comes at the expense of American sovereignty. Essentially, the members of a single organization dedicated to global socialism, currently establish American political agendas, control American monetary policy and manipulate public opinion to implement their agenda. This is what George Bush really meant when he talked about the "New World Order".

CFR members dominate many government agencies, educational institutions, public policy foundations such as the Rockefeller Foundation and monetary establishments such as the Federal Reserve, which is neither federal nor has adequate reserves. All presidents since Richard Nixon, with the exception of Ronald Reagan, were CFR members, and many of their cabinet members were as well. The CFR controls the Democrat Party agenda, has many Democrat Party members and includes key Republican members such as George Bush, Newt Gingrich, Henry Hyde and Jim Leach. All of these Republicans have protected Bill Clinton in various ways either before or during his Presidency. George Bush did not mention a word about Clinton corruption during the debates. All of the Congressmen were instrumental in preventing Congressional investigation evidence such as criminal activity, treason, bribery and abusive use of government agencies from finding its way into the Articles of Impeachment.

The CFR operates primarily in America, while the Tri-Lateral Commission, founded by former Chase Manhattan Bank chairman, David Rockefeller, consists of units representing Asia, Europe and the Americas. The power of these organizations should never be underestimated. A couple thousand strategically located CFR members dominate nearly all aspects of American policy without the knowledge of the American citizens. During the height of his problems just before his impeachment, Bill Clinton reportedly met with David Rockefeller on three separate occasions. Some of us believe that he was begging to keep his job.

Americans are kept uninformed about all of this through various media strategies that are discussed in the next chapter. One example is to keep America citizens divided on issues. The strategy pits one class of Americans against another so that Americans lose sight of the fact that their freedom is being stolen. This strategy is simply known as divide and conquer. The strategy divides America into rich vs. poor, black vs. white, Christian vs. Muslim vs. Jew, homosexual vs. heterosexual, conservative vs. liberal, left wing vs. right wing and so on. In reality, we are all Americans and want the same basic things. We believe in the American Constitution to protect our American freedom. The battle to be fought is not about conservatism vs. liberalism anymore. It is about Americanism vs. anti-Americanism.

THE COMMUNIST MANIFESTO

Although America was set up to be a free republic, its leaders have implemented many anti-American laws that facilitate the principles of Communism as defined in the *Communist Manifesto*, which was written by Karl Marx. The manifesto consists of ten basic planks. The planks with information on how they are being implemented in America are shown below:

Abolition of private property

The rights of private property are being attacked via environmental laws which have been used to take the property of citizens or render it unusable because of environmental considerations. There are numerous cases where environmental protection agencies have not allowed citizens to build houses or businesses on their property for esoteric environmental reasons. Executive Order 12986 also references a grant of immunity to international agencies which confiscate the property of American citizens for conservation purposes.

A heavy progressive or graduated income tax

This plank was implemented in 1913 when a one percent income tax was established and gradually increased to today's exorbitant rates, which exceed 50 percent total on federal, state and local taxes. When Ronald Reagan took office, the federal tax rate on income over $100,000 was 88 percent.

Abolition of all rights of inheritance

This plank is being implemented through inheritance tax. Many heirs have to sell the property that has been bequeathed to them so that they can pay the estate taxes on assets that were already taxed and paid by their ancestors.

Confiscation of the property of all emigrants and rebels

This plank is being achieved by asset forfeiture laws. Drug dealers have been used as the excuse to implement these laws. However, several cases exist where private citizens have had cash confiscated and never returned, even though they were innocent of all wrongdoing.

Centralization of credit for the state through a central bank with an exclusive monopoly

This plank was implemented in 1913 with the establishment of the Federal Reserve, which is neither federal nor has adequate reserves. It is actually a private trust owned primarily by European families, who have since diversified by buying interests in the controlling N.Y. banks. The normal 10 percent reserve on deposits has gradually been reduced to under three percent today. American monetary supply is essentially controlled by foreigners, who do not necessarily share the interests of the American citizens.

Centralization of the means of communication and transport in the hands of the state

This is being achieved gradually by different organizations such as the Federal Aviation Administration and the Federal Communications Commission. You now must have an ID to board an airplane, and there has been a major attempt to standardize state drivers' licenses with fingerprints. Federally controlled organizations such as Amtrak, Pubic Broadcasting and National Public Radio have made inroads towards this goal, but automobiles and the Internet pose control problems for the Communist agenda.

Extension of factories and instruments of production owned by the state

Advances on this plan have been made through various government owned businesses throughout America, such as the Tennessee Valley Authority, which produces electricity.

Equal liability of all to labor

Advances on this plank have been made through the graduated income tax which attempts to equalize the income of all Americans. The minimum wage law is another smaller attempt to equalize income of Americans. Equalization of income facilitates equalization of labor.

Combination of industries and gradual abolition of town and country distinctions

Combining industries into larger, centralized ones can help facilitate nationalization of the industries by a central state. Abolishing territorial distinctions provides much greater emphasis on central government in lieu of state and local rights. American legislation decidedly favors big business and labor unions. Two examples that help large research-oriented businesses steal smaller business ideas are recent patent bills, HB-400, S507 and their successors, that contain clauses such as those requiring patent information to be published 18 months after an application is submitted, even if a patent has not yet been granted.

Free education for all children in public schools

This plank has already been implemented, and its purpose is to provide the children only what information the central government wants them to have. An excellent example is the Magruder's American Government textbook used in some high schools. Although the Second Amendment clearly states that

"....the right of the people to keep and bear arms shall not be in-fringed," the text book claims that the amendment is "widely misinterpreted" and that it does not guarantee a right to keep and bear arms free from restriction by government. The textbook also states that the Constitution can be changed by "informal amendment" such as "the passage of basic legis-lation, actions taken by the President, decisions of the Supreme Court, activities of political parties and custom." Clearly, the founders of America never had any such intentions. I believe that these are rather blatant attempts to "dumb down" America's children to the point that they do not understand how they were able to be born free.

AMERICA'S FIRST STEPS TOWARD COMMUNISM

Dr. Edward Griffin, in his book entitled, *The Creature from Jekyll Island*, explains how many threads of Communism have been implemented in America. Several of the Communist planks were completely implemented during the Presidency of Woodrow Wilson, a Democrat elected in 1912 through a classic example of power politics. Wilson faced William Howard Taft, the Republican incumbent who had just opposed the Aldrich plan for a central bank, not because it was Communist in nature, but because it did not give the government enough power over the bankers who wanted to control the money supply. Taft had won the Republican nomination easily and was popular with the voters since he served during a time of prosperity. Wilson's dry personality and aloof mannerisms made Taft a clear favorite for the election.

However, two executives from J.P. Morgan and Company convinced former Republican President, Teddy Roosevelt, to run for the Presidency as the "Bull Moose" candidate of the Progressive Party, which was heavily funded by J.P. Morgan and Company interests. The third party entry of a former Republican successfully split the vote so that the chosen Democrat candidate, Woodrow Wilson, a champion of the central bank, was elected President.

Wilson was nominated by Colonel Edwin Mandell House, who had close contacts with J.P. Morgan and was a founder of the Council on Foreign Relations. House went on to become

Woodrow Wilson's closest advisor and was the point of contact for the banking families who wanted to implement the federal reserve system to control privately the American money supply.

The system was conceived during a 1910 secret meeting at Jekyll Island, Georgia. Attendees included: Nelson Aldrich, Republican Senate Whip who was the father-in-law of John D. Rockefeller and chairman of the Monetary Commission; Henry Davison, Sr. Partner of J.P. Morgan and Co.; Paul Warburg, a Kuhn Loeb & Co. partner representing the Warburgs and Rothchilds in Europe; Frank Vanderlip, National City Bank of New York president representing William Rockefeller and Benjamin Strong, the head of J.P. Morgan Bankers Trust who also became the first Federal Reserve head.

Carter Glass, the Democrat Chairman of the House Banking and Currency Committee, objected to the original plan in a 1913 House report because it lacked government control, concentrated power into the hands of the larger New York banks, established a banking monopoly, increased inflation and underestimated the taxpayer cost. However, in a textbook example of coordinated politics, he and Senator Robert Owen drafted a new federal reserve plan that was nearly identical to the plan he had opposed when originally presented by Nelson Aldrich. This plan became law in 1913.

During the Woodrow Wilson Presidency, the 17th Amendment to the Constitution was passed. It allowed the Senators to be elected by popular vote instead of by the state legislative bodies. While this appeared to give the people more power, it actually was a clever move to eliminate state representation in the federal government. Since most Senators have millions of constituents and massive fundraising machines, they have little accountability to the people they represent. This was clearly and recently illustrated when the Republican controlled Senate implemented sham trial procedures to protect Bill Clinton and sabotage the House managers' case. The amendment allowed the major socialist power brokers essentially to buy one half of the United States Congress.

Also under Wilson in 1913, the burdensome federal income tax was implemented. This percentage began as an option applying only to one percent of foreign earned income and eventually grew to 88 percent of all domestic income over

$100,000. Many Americans do not realize that the American government functioned superbly for 130 years with no personal income tax.

Woodrow Wilson ran for re-election in 1916 using the slogan, "He kept us out of war." Shortly after he was re-elected and began his second term in 1917, America entered World War I. Afterwards, Wilson tried but failed to form the League of Nations, the first attempt at global government and a precursor to the United Nations.

NOTE: It is particularly important to note the fraudulent way in which the income tax was implemented as the 16th amendment to the U.S. Constitution. Article 1 Section 8 of the Constitution allows indirect taxes such as excises taxes but Article 1, Section 9 prohibits direct federal taxes that are non-apportioned to the states according to the census. During 1894, federal courts upheld this clause under challenge and required a constitutional amendment to implement federal taxation. An amendment required ratification by 36 of the 48 states at that time to achieve the still necessary 3/4 majority for the exact wording proposed.

In February of 1913, Secretary of State Philander Knox certified that 38 of the states had ratified the amendment but one of the certified states, Kentucky, actually voted against the amendment. Another, Minnesota, never voted on the amendment in both legislative houses. Still another, Oklahoma, changed the wording to mean the opposite of the proposed amendment before voting for it. Other states also changed the wording, thus voiding the ratification, or ratified the amendment in violation of their own constitution that prohibited additional federal tax collection. William Benson, a former investigator for the Illinois Department of Revenue and the author of *"The Law That Never Was"*, discovered these discrepancies when he visited the capitols of all 48 states and obtained the appropriate certified state documents. He determined that only a handful of states actually passed the 16th amendment as worded and required by law and neither the 16th nor 17th amendments were ever legally ratified.

Numerous other experts and organizations have made startling discoveries that reveal American individuals and corporations are currently under illusions about what is contained in the actual tax laws. For example, We The People

Foundation, established by Bob Schulz, published around the time of this writing that:

- Sections 1401 and 7701 of the IRS code still state the only persons required to withhold and pay income tax are under Sections 1441-1443 which pertain only to non-resident aliens and foreign entities
- Likewise, the Office of Management and Budget has only authorized for use under Section 1 of the Internal Revenue Code, Form 2555, entitled, "Foreign Earned Income"
- Furthermore, Section 3402 imposes withholding only upon wages defined in Section 3401(a) and (a) (8) (A), which exempt citizens living and working in the U.S. from the definition of wages subject to withholding

Other portions in the Internal Revenue Code, IRS internal manuals and even several agents themselves have confirmed these findings. We the People Foundation has invited the IRS, Congressional members and U.S Justice department officials to participate in panel discussions to explain the discrepancies but they have always declined or reneged on their commitments.

One can only imagine the difficulty corrupt federal politicians had with citizens, state legislatures and some fellow congressional members while attempting to implement this key platform of the Communist Manifesto in America. Although lawmakers could never legally pass the desired laws, the newly controlled news media began playing a critical role in conditioning America to pay their fare share and accept a more severely graduated communist based, income tax. Within five years, the new money that began to enter the U.S. Treasury and the freshly controlled media quickly led us to the First World War in 1917.

AMERICA'S DICTATORSHIP BEGINS

Franklin Delano Roosevelt (FDR) was the next President who moved America deeper into a Communist dictatorship. Immediately after being elected in 1932, he used the 1933 gold crisis to extract more power from the citizens. In March of 1933, Franklin Roosevelt issued Presidential Proclamations 2039 and 2040 to declare an ongoing national emergency that only another President could remove. He also got Congress to amend the Trading with the Enemies Act to give the President absolute war powers in a general state of emergency and automatic approval of all Executive Orders at all times. This was a major step in establishing unconstitutional dictatorial powers that could easily be implemented by a President during any perceived crisis.

Roosevelt also implemented a dramatic further extension of income tax by creating the Social Security system in 1935. Although it was unconstitutional in its forced savings, it was originally created as a legitimate retirement system. However, in 1939, Congress quietly transformed the system from a personal savings vehicle into another tax, when they began using the money to spend on other programs. This trend has continued through today where all social security revenue is included in the federal budget and the difference between revenue and expenses continues to be spent as soon as it is collected. Any announced budget surplus still includes the amount of social security revenue that exceeds expenses and, therefore, is not a surplus at all. Thus, our federal government robs from the citizens daily and then plans to rob our children to repay us.

Under Roosevelt, America entered World War II when Japan bombed Pearl Harbor. German intelligence reports describing decoded British-American communications reveal that Roosevelt was warned by Churchill about the pending Japanese invasion on November 26, 1941 but Roosevelt sent a multi-day cable to warn the naval base at Pearl Harbor rather than using standard military intelligence communications. He also seemed to prolong the war until the second nuclear bomb was dropped on Japan while it was already prepared to surrender. Roosevelt was re-elected President three times, serving for 13 years until he died in 1945, the longest term in American history. After his death and the end of World War II, the United Nations was formed. Under the auspices of peacekeeping, it has become a vehicle to implement global government.

AMERICA MOVES TO TYRANNY AND FASCISM

The first and perhaps, most important, sentence of the Constitution states that "... all legislative power granted herein is vested in Congress...". This clause was obviously given such prominence to prevent tyranny and fascism in America. However, during his presidency, Bill Clinton, implemented thousands of now automatic Executive Orders, many of which are unconstitutional because they exceed the authority of the executive branch and attempt to legislate to the American citizens.

Some of these orders have been described in this book, but perhaps, the most dangerous of all orders implemented by Bill Clinton is EO 12919. This order allows the federal government to take over our private property under any emergency that the President defines. Specifically mentioned are food, water, health resources, energy, transportation, materials and supplies. Therefore, if any emergency occurs, these orders could be selectively put into place. Given the track record of Bill Clinton for using government agencies like the FBI, IRS, INS and Treasury Dept. to persecute political adversaries, anytime could be a perfect opportunity for him, or a successor, to implement further tyranny.

Republican leaders are insincere in their attempts to resist these unconstitutional Executive Orders and offer half-hearted opposition while refusing to take them off the books. Although Republican leaders occasionally denounce Bill Clinton and Janet Reno, this book describes how the leaders have consistently protected them while they controlled Congress. The leaders have allowed Clinton, with protection from Janet Reno, to persecute political adversaries by constantly using government agencies. This is a dangerous form of fascism. During his presidency, Bill Clinton and the Republican leaders removed nearly all-remaining forms of accountability in government. Their actions have plunged America deeper into a hole of potential tyranny from which it may not be able to recover.

THE ELIAN GONZALEZ SAGA

The tyranny was once again illustrated by the recent siege on the home of Elian Gonzalez. While the Communist Chinese infiltration of the American government impacts the freedom of all 280+ million Americans, the "American" news media successfully diverted attention for months to the freedom of this lone Cuban boy. The Cuban media also focused heavily on this story in what almost appears to be a coordinated multi-national effort. Cuban citizens were even pumped up with rallies by Fidel Castro, who seemed to know about the raid or the success of the custody battle well in advance.

Elian Gonzalez survived an escape from Cuba when his mother and the others in the boat, in which he was traveling, drowned after the boat capsized. He was rescued by a fisherman and his cousin, the now famous Donato Dalrymple, and taken to a Florida hospital. After he recovered, the INS granted temporary custody of the boy to his uncle, Lazaro Gonzalez and his family. Juan Miguel Gonzalez, Elian's natural father who was divorced from his mother before the birth of Elian, was not allowed to travel from Cuba to the United States for months after Elian was rescued. Eventually Juan Miguel requested custody and the Clinton administration said they would let state courts decide the matter. About five months later in April of 2000, Juan Miguel entered America and the Clinton administration had the case transferred to a federal court that ruled in favor of the father. The Gonzalez family then made an asylum appeal and the 11th Circuit Court of Appeals at Atlanta agreed in April to hear the case on May 11.

Just days after the Atlanta appellate court ruling that also specifically denied a request by Janet Reno to transfer custody to the father, Reno took the law into her own hands. She ordered dozens of heavily armed agents to storm the house without presenting any search warrant or court order and without evidence of any crime being committed. Videos and family statements show they broke down the front door without knocking or identifying themselves, pointed their automatic weapons at everyone in the house, including two other children, cursed and threatened to shoot the people inside. A dramatic photo, by an AP photographer, who was invited to stay at the house captured the terror on Elian's face as the armed agent pointed his MP5 sub machine gun at Donato Dalrymple and Elian after they hid in a closet. A female agent took him from the house as he screamed "what's happening" and "help me". She rushed him to a white mini-van with a masked driver. When asked at her Saturday morning press conference about the incredible photos, Reno made the ludicrous excuse that the gun was not pointed directly at Elian and the agent did not have his finger on the trigger, as if that would make any difference to those inside. Reno stated that this level force was necessary "to uphold the rule of law".

To help resolve the custody dispute before the legal issues were settled during the next few weeks, the Gonzalez family asked to meet Juan Miguel and his family somewhere in the Miami area with "no pre-conditions, no government and no lawyers". Juan Miguel was apparently never allowed to do so by Castro and Reno did not agree to those terms of the meeting. Several community leaders who were helping in the negoti- ations sent Reno a signed fax at five PM on Good Friday, April 21 agreeing to the terms she outlined for the meeting. Family lawyer, Roger Bernstein, and others stated that between four and five AM just before the break-in, Reno changed the con- ditions and gave them 5 minutes to decide whether the new conditions were acceptable. Before they could respond Reno ordered the attack. Reno then claimed in her press conference that the Gonzalez family "moved the goalposts".

Reno had also told the Gonzalez family said she would not use marshals or come at midnight to take Elian away. Instead she used INS and border patrol agents who attacked at five AM. Reno stated in her press conference that eight INS agents participated in the raid even though videos clearly showed dozens of INS and border patrol agents were involved.

A day earlier, Greg Craig, a Clinton attorney who helped Juan Miguel, sent a two-page letter to TV network presidents requesting that they not cover this obvious breech of 4th amendment rights about to occur. Within hours after the raid, Craig also produced photographs of a happy, well-rested Elian in the arms of his father while preventing the Gonzalez family or anyone other than propaganda specialists from seeing him. The photos caused Marisleysis Gonzalez to make a fascinating discovery that can be verified by most any American who has access to the photos of the raid, from inside the house, or the videos that were taken outside.

Marisleysis, the 21-year-old cousin who essentially became Elian's surrogate mother, during the five months he was in her care, discovered something only a mother would notice. She stated at the Gonzalez family press conference, on Easter morning, that photos of Elian with his father were doctored because she had just given Elian a haircut and the photos showed him with significantly longer hair than he had at the time of the raid. A simple examination of the photos confirms almost conclusively she is telling the truth. Elian is seen with a closely shaven head both in pictures taken in the house and the videos taken outside the house. The pictures allegedly taken when Elian was reunited with his father show he had several weeks of additional hair growth during the few hours of his incredible "hair raising" experience.

Immediately after the press conference CNN, in its classic style, repeated Marisleysis claim the photos were doctored but deliberately did not mention the hair discrepancy. They made the irrelevant point that his half brother, who was shown in some photographs, appeared to be the correct age and then asked the audience to make their own decision after failing to properly inform them. CNN was much more skillful and subtle than Fox News, who used a more blatant distortion later in the afternoon, when they said Marisleysis Gonzalez claimed it was not Elian in the photographs. Thus, once again when it came to real government corruption the national news media duped both sides of the political spectrum with fascist propaganda to cover up federal tyranny and deceit.

DEATH BY GOVERNMENT

Janet Reno said in this case her interest was the child. She made the same claim about the children in Waco. While the Gonzalez family was fortunate to have independent photographers and news coverage, the federal agents were much more prepared at Waco. They confiscated and destroyed most film and kept photographers so far away they could not really see all of the details that forensic evidence, infrared film and debris have revealed. We are left with government-selected videos, pictures of charred bodies in autopsy reports and many provably false excuses for what happened there. The children at Waco were in a concrete bunker where there was a horrible fire that can be seen on the videos. Sources such as the video *Waco: A New Revelation* illustrate convincing forensic and debris evidence that some form of military explosives were placed on top of the bunker. Many of the women and children died from the explosion that created the horrific fire.

Regardless of whether you believe Elian should stay in America or return to Cuba with his natural father, I hope every American citizen can see the severe threat posed by continual federal sieges against innocent American citizens in violation of the 4th amendment of the Constitution. Fascists selectively apply and break laws while using the power of government to achieve political tyranny and totalitarianism. I believe the Clinton / Reno Justice administration exemplifies a near true Fascist state that lacks only in total government control of commercial enterprises. Reno's actions at Waco, her extensive cover-up in the Communist Chinese military infiltration of the American government and a dozen other examples detailed earlier in this chapter must surely qualify her as the leading candidate for the most corrupt Attorney General in American history.

The threat posed to American citizens by the corruption of the American government is perhaps best illustrated by R.J. Rummel in his book, *Death by Government*. Rummel documents nearly 170 million murders that have occurred in the 20th century alone, all at the hands of the victims own "peace time" government. Most of these murders were conducted by Communist, Fascist or tyrannical governments who committed acts of genocide against their own people to fulfill their political motives. These figures do not include deaths of soldiers or other individuals in wars between countries. Thus, the most dangerous threat to any individual, exceeding any type of disease and all wars combined, is simply, government.

Politicians we have elected, primarily in the 20th century, have gradually shifted the American government to a similar type of pro-Communist, pro-Fascist tyranny as those governments who have committed these murderous atrocities against their own citizens. Those Americans who do not believe such atrocities can happen here need only to consider that, on one day, April 19, 1993, our government added more than 80 innocent men, women and children to this count when it attacked the Branch Davidian Church with military tanks, internationally banned CS tear gas and automatic weapons fire in violation of the Posse Comitatus act and their 4th amendment rights.

REFERENCES

G. Edward Griffin, *The Creature From Jekyll Island*,
    American Opinion Book Services.
Karl Marx, *The Communist Manifesto*, (reprinted by) The John
    Birch Society.
Jack Thompson, *The Truth about Janet Reno* (video),
    American Forum
James and Kenneth Collier, *Votescam*, Victoria House Press
John McManus,*The Insiders*, The John Birch Society.
Daniel New and Cliff Kincaid, *Michael New: Mercenary or
    American Soldier.*
R. J. Rummel, *Death by Government*, Transactio.
Dr. Gene Schroder, *War and Emergency Powers*, American
    Agriculture Movement.
The New American magazine, "Special report, Conspiracy for
    Global Control."
Harry Browne,*Why Government Doesn't Work,* St. Martin's
    Press.
Waco: a New Revelation (video), MGA Films.

CHAPTER TWELVE
SAVING AMERICA

REPUBLICAN FRAUDULENCE

Political parties and candidates can easily get people to vote for them, simply by telling Americans what they want to hear. The media makes it difficult for citizens to have any kind of detail knowledge about the legislation activity, voting records or backgrounds of most candidates. Therefore, there is no easy way for a citizen to verify whether or not candidates are fit for office or have kept their promises. The two major political parties are then free to operate fraudulently in regards to political issues.

This book has already mentioned several issues where the Republican Party has been fraudulent. This book also illustrates details of how during the impeachment process Republican leaders actually protected Bill Clinton while impeaching him. Although House Republicans voted to impeach Bill Clinton, House Republican leaders prevented the Articles of Impeachment from including any evidence of treason, bribery, Arkansas criminal activity and abuse of the FBI and IRS. Although Senate Republicans voted to convict Bill Clinton Senate Republican leaders sabotaged the House Managers' case by implementing unprecedented trial procedures to ensure that no damaging evidence or hostile witnesses would be presented to corroborate the charges against him. These tactics allowed both Democrats and Republicans to dupe their constituents into believing that there were real conflicts and differences between the two colluding parties.

One example involved their subsequent efforts to pass a balanced budget amendment that failed to gain the required two-thirds majority by a single Senate vote in 1995. After the 1996 elections, when amendment supporters were elected to replace the lone Republican dissenter, Mark Hatfield of Oregon, and some Democrat Senators, Republican initiatives to pass the amendment suddenly ceased. Likewise, when Republicans launched and implemented the contract with

America in 1994, it was so successful that it resulted in a complete change of power to Republican Congressional control for the first time in 40 years. But by 1996, Republican leaders abandoned the contract, did not even mention it and had no desire to duplicate its success. That should indicate the insincerity and fraudulent nature of Republican leaders.

One of the most fraudulent issues of all for the Republican Party is its advocacy of the phony drug war. Republican support for a law and order society has allowed its leaders to dramatically decrease the rights and freedoms of the American citizens under the guise of fighting drug distribution. If the Republican leaders were serious about fighting drugs they would have started by getting the CIA out of the drug business. But they cannot do that because of the involvement by George Bush in several worldwide operations previously described in this book. Even if some of the allegations raised against George Bush are proven false, it is inconceivable that he could be innocent on all counts. Thus, Republican leaders continue fighting the drug war and spending billions of taxpayer dollars to protect our children from drugs, all the while they knowingly run the drugs in through the back door of America for various profit motives. I cannot think of a bigger scam being played on the American people.

Another issue that illustrates the fraudulent nature of the Republican Party is the divisive issue of abortion. Many Republicans claim to want a constitutional ban against abortion. However, the party has never done anything to decrease abortion in America other than pass the partial birth abortion ban that they knew Bill Clinton would veto.

When Republicans took control of Congress in 1995 they could have quickly re-directed some Planned Parenthood funds into a nationwide "Just Say No" campaign against abortion and facilitated the development of an inexpensive web based adoption system. The adoption system that might also contain pro-life statements and articles could have been available in high schools, colleges, clinics or any home that has web access. Anyone could then go to the web site, enter a query and get pictures and background information on adoptive parent candidates. Therefore, almost any young girl unable to raise a child could choose prospective parents for her child as early as the first day that realized she was pregnant.

I am convinced if these approaches were correctly implemented, abortion in America would have been cut in half by now without passing a single law that infringes upon American freedom. Although Bill Clinton vetoed the ban on grotesque partial birth abortions, his support for a more sophisticated adoption system may actually do more to reduce abortion in America than anything Republicans have done in five years of controlling Congress.

The Republican actions on abortion perfectly implement the divide and conquer strategy of the media by giving it a divisive issue for the population. It appears that Republican leaders actually prefer to be viewed as divisive so they can return to minority status and not have to confront the media with the agenda of their constituents.

One of the more amazing aspects of the Republican Party is how it can be involved in drug trafficking operations and still retain support from Christian leaders. I know that God gave these Christian leaders a brain so I have to wonder whether some of them are sincere or whether they have their own agendas.

DEMOCRAT FRAUDULENCE

The Democrat party has the same type of stranglehold over the American Black community that Republicans have over the Christian community. Although Democrats convinced America's Black leaders that they represent their interests, history tell us a completely different story.

In 1860, pro-slavery Democrats were defeated by Republican President, Abraham Lincoln, who is credited by nearly everyone for his key role in abolishing slavery. During 1964, 100 years later, Democrats filibustered in the Senate to prevent passage of the Civil Rights Act, but the filibuster was broken by Republican Senate minority leader, Everett Dirksen. In 1968, although Blacks were accepted in Republican state parties, they were not allowed in the Mississippi Democrat party and were forced to form their own Freedom party in an attempt to be seated at the 1968 Democrat Party convention in Chicago.

Democrats have over emphasized racism and used a fraudulent commitment toward race issues to divert attention from the evidence of their anti-Black American history. The American Black community continues to support them, in many cases at the request of Black leaders. The same question must be asked of these leaders as of some Christian leaders. Are they sincere or do they have their own agenda for personal power and wealth?

Another fraudulent issue for the Democrat Party is their concern for what seems like every cause under the sun. For example, environmentalism was the excuse when President Clinton repaid his illegal contributions conduit, as he helped Indonesia maintain a monopoly on clean burning coal by declaring 1.7 million acres around competing mines in Utah as a national monument. Likewise, curbing teen smokers was the excuse when the Democrat Party received a $400,000 contribution from the head of the Communist Chinese Pagoda Red Mountain Cigarette Company and initiated major anti-tobacco legislation against American companies.

These examples involve apparent pay-backs for illegal foreign contributions but others simply increase their power. If you analyze legislation and proposals by Democrat congress members and administrations, almost all of them involve better protection for the citizens by spending more federal money to increase the size and power of a central government. This theme is so consistent it cannot be an accident. I am convinced the Democrat Party is not truly concerned about these causes but support them only to implement their own agenda.

Both major political parties are anti-freedom. Democrats generally attack economic freedom while Republicans assault personal freedom, usually under the guise of law and order. If you find this had to believe, try to remember when the last law was passed that gave Americans more freedom. For hundreds of years, both parties have consistently implemented new laws taking away freedoms by offering more security from a larger, more powerful, more centralized government. Their legislation strategy to obtain ultimate power has imposed increased risks of tyranny on American citizens.

THE ANTI-AMERICAN MEDIA

I believe that increasing government power over American citizens, while subordinating American law to international law, is actually the agenda of those who control the national news media. While individual media organization ownership changes hands from time to time, new owners always maintain Council on Foreign Relations control of the editorial process dating back to its inception, as explained in the previous chapter.

Many Americans are easily susceptible to exchanging their freedoms for more security. The highest editorial levels of the national news media successfully program the American public by using a simple theme: Freedom for Security. Take some time to seriously consider the many news, political and trash talk programs conforming to the theme of having some form of government or law which protect Americans from dangerous, crazed, immoral or unethical individuals.

We are a trusting kind of people. We trust our elected officials to represent our interests. We trust the news media to keep us informed about what is happening. However, they have their own interests and power desires. Many federal elected officials use our trust to further their own power or the power of those who financially control them. In many cases, their controllers also control major media organizations.

Major media organizations are managed in a way so their political stories manipulate public opinion to support the agenda of their owners, associates and advertisers. Many of these same media organizations report non-political news fairly and therefore, are able to fool us into thinking they report political news fairly as well. Most conservative talk show hosts falsely claim that new media organizations are biased. As you can see from this book, the news media organizations are way beyond bias. They have established a tightly coordinated socialist propaganda machine that has driven an anti-American agenda for decades.

To discover the tight control of political news by the major media outlets get a copy of the *Washington Times* and *Washington Post*. Read the political news each day. After a few days you should be wondering whether or not these papers were produced in the same country, much less the same city. *Washington Post* reporting is relatively consistent with other major newspapers and networks. But during the impeachment, it was the *Washington Times* that broke one unreported story after another, which were proven factually correct by subsequent congressional investigations.

If you cannot get reasonably easy access to these news-papers, and have a satellite dish or expanded cable TV system, there is another test you can perform. Try watching politically oriented programs on the Fox News Channel during weekday evenings and compare them to the political content on CNN or the other network news programs. After a week or two you should find that you are being informed with significantly different information about the same events depending upon what channel you are watching. These experiments should produce a desire within you to seek the political truth. If so, you may be ready to subscribe to the Spotlight newspaper, for perhaps, the most unfiltered, yet disturbing political news in America. (The owners and employees now publish the *American Free Press* newspaper)

In this chapter I identify techniques that media organizations use to misinform their audiences. To counter them, we must identify trusted news sources and become properly informed rather than depend on civic leaders to point the way. We must watch or listen to entire political events rather than rely on filtered news summaries. We must also be willing to communicate and distribute information as best as we can to all we know who show the slightest interest. Only then will Americans be able to judge politicians by what they do, not what they say.

I believe that media editors deliberately misinform their audiences so that the controllers of major media organizations can compromise both sides of the political spectrum and force conformance to their global new world order goals. They are attempting to convert America from a Republic based on the rule of law to a democracy based on public opinion derived from polls that they conduct. The conversion will allow them to control America by reporting news in a manner that manipulates public opinion to support their agenda.

REPUBLICAN AND DEMOCRAT COLLUSION

Libertarians, Reformers and Constitution (formerly U.S. Taxpayer) Party members have said for years that Democrats and Republicans are essentially two sides of the same party. I found this impossible to believe during the period when

Republicans launched and implemented the contract with America. At that time, there appeared to be significant differences between the two parties over the strategic direction of our country. But in 1998 and 1999, the impeachment movement subtly illustrated massive collusion between the two major parties.

The key to understanding the extent of collusion is to acquire basic knowledge of the depth and breadth of Clinton administration corruption. Then it is possible realize the magnitude of cover-up that Republican leaders instituted during the impeachment movement to protect Bill Clinton.

Democrats had already performed the same favor for Republicans in the 1980s by focusing on the arms for hostage Iran-Contra minutia and covering up Bush related CIA drug trafficking operations. The idea that Republicans and Democrats may collude to protect each other could be foreign to some readers, but whenever there are only two controlling entities of any kind they can very easily achieve collusion.

Sometimes the collusion is very deceptive as demonstrated in a recent Email scandal example. The White House failed to record and search, under subpoena requests, more than 1 million e-mails and attached documents sent to at least 526 staff members during a period from August 1996 to May 1999. In addition, nearly all Email to and from Vice President Al Gore and at least 24 of his staff members has been omitted from archives. Most of the five Northrop Grumman computer contractors who testified in 2000 before Congress swore that high-level White House staff members threatened them in various ways including jail if they revealed the problem.

While Republicans have held few in the Clinton administration accountable for any serious wrongdoing including these threats, the House Government Reform and Oversight Committee was quick to refer perjury charges against White House computer specialist Daniel "Tony" Barry to the Justice Department. Barry had issued a sworn statement that said, "Since July 14, 1994, Email with the EOP (Executive Office of the President) system administered by the Office of Administration has been archived in the EOP Automated Records Management System (ARMS)." His statement cleverly omits the problems that resulted in the lost Email but is defensible as being technically true.

Although the House Committee appeared to be taking aggressive action against the culprit, WorldNetDaily investigative reporter, Paul Sperry, uncovered a completely different story. The former reporter for Investor's Business Daily found numerous White House internal memos and trouble reports, dated from August 13, 1998 to May 5, 1999, where Barry had alerted several of his superiors and associates to the problem as he attempted to seek corrective action. The memos are filled repeatedly with quotes expressing the frustration that Barry was having in attempting to get help to remedy the problem. Thus the "opposition" Republican Party, led by Chairman Dan Burton, actually became another Clinton "scorched earth" policy facilitator. Burton was also responsible for the firing of David Bossie, one of the most serious investigators on the committee.

Sometimes the collusion is not by agreement but by force. This book illustrates how only one hour after the House Judiciary Committee voted to begin the impeachment inquiry of Bill Clinton on October 8, 1998, the Clinton controlled CIA publicly released the Inspector General report Volume II on CIA drug trafficking. That report, while still essentially denying CIA involvement, confirmed many of the allegations against the CIA, particularly those regarding Contra related drug running managed by individuals under the control of George Bush.

We are programmed by the national news media to believe Democrats and Republicans are diametrically opposed to each other, and in less important instances, there are real differences. But when it comes to serious corruption, both parties help each other through compromise and cover-up to gain concessions. Before the impeachment, L.D. Brown, the former Clinton bodyguard, Arkansas State Police Association president and CIA recruit, summed up the collusion about Bill Clinton for me in three words: Mutually Assured Destruction.

OBSTRUCTION OF JUSTICE

Perhaps no better or more serious example of this Mutually Assured Destruction policy exists than the case of the "train deaths" murders of Kevin Ives, Don Henry and subsequently seven other individuals who had knowledge about the Ives / Henry murders. Linda Ives has undergone a 13-year struggle to seek justice for the murder of her son and his friend but has been met at every turn with another facet of the most massive corruption and cover-up by federal, state and local officials since the political assassinations of the 60s. I became motivated to fight for issues of honest government after seeing this story told in a riveting documentary, entitled *Obstruction of Justice.* The story has also been published in a book entitled *The Boys on the Tracks*. The video is something that every American should see. The following brief summary only begins to scratch the surface of the compelling drama shown on the video.

Early in the morning on August 23, 1987, a train ran over the bodies of Kevin Ives and Don Henry while they were lying across railroad tracks at Alexander in Saline County, Arkansas. Fahmy Malak, the Arkansas State medical examiner, ruled that the deaths were accidental because the boys were under the influence of drugs and had fallen asleep on the tracks. The parents did not believe the examiner and spent over a year trying to get a second opinion while Malak refused to comply with court orders for information. During a second autopsy, Atlantan Joe Burton and six forensic pathologists or homicide detectives determined that Don Henry had been stabbed in the back and Kevin Ives skull was crushed, before Malak mutilated it during the initial autopsy. A grand jury changed the official death ruling to murder. The L.A. Times documented nearly 20 suspicious or inaccurate death rulings by Malak, including ones that favored Clinton's mother, a nurse anesthetist. Other examples include a suicide ruling for Raymond Albright who was shot in the chest 5 times; also an ulcer as the cause for James Milam, who was decapitated. During the controversy, Bill Clinton introduced legislation to give an incredible 40 percent raise in pay to Malak, who reported directly to Jocelyn Elders. When citizens held protest demonstrations to force his resignation in 1992, Clinton created a new position in the state health department for Malak and told reporters that Malak was 'stressed out'. Elders stated, "Arkansas owes Dr. Malak a great debt and a real apology."

The video meticulously documents an incredible series of systematic cover-ups by local police, prosecutors, courts and federal agencies that did everything within their power to avoid solving the case. From 1988 to 1995, 7 people with knowledge of the Ives / Henry murders, including grand jury witnesses and people who were on the tracks that night, have also been murdered. Only one person has been convicted in any of the murders and only one other person has ever been charged with one murder.

Several drug traffic investigations revealed that Ives and Henry had likely stumbled across a drug drop point known as A12 by the pilots who had flown for Barry Seal. The drugs were dropped regularly out of planes flying from Columbia to Mena, Arkansas. Ground crews that picked up the drugs typically included local government officials and police. The investigations uncovered compromised local judges and prosecutors, drug operations at Mena, possible money laundering, suppression and distortion of information by the media and additional details about the murder of Kevin Ives and Don Henry, as well as the other subsequent deaths.

However, the federal drug investigation was shut down by then U.S. Attorney Chuck Banks, a Reagan / Bush appointee who dismissed a grand jury after the conclusions implicated a number of people within the state and local governments. Banks, was expected to be tried for obstruction of justice, as recommended by a 1993 FBI investigation, however, the FBI recommendation was ignored by the Clinton/Reno Justice Dept. Assistant U.S. Attorney Bob Govar, resigned as head of a federal drug task force in protest of the shutdown. He assembled a substantial amount of the federal information from Jean Duffey, head of a drug task force investigation that was shut down by Judge John Cole.

The persecution of Duffey, during her investigation, is astounding in itself. She was attacked with 200 false press articles, pressured to turn over evidence to the people she was investigating and threatened with imprisonment on an illegal warrant issued by the same judge who shut down her investigation. She was even forced to temporarily flee the state when her mother received a tip from a dispatcher that she would be killed if imprisoned. After nearly a decade of deceit, Dan Harmon, a prosecutor who she initially implicated, was tried and convicted in June of 1997 on 5 drug related felony counts. Harmon was one of the two prosecutors named in the video that was instrumental in creating public pressure for his arrest and trial.

THE $14,000,000 LAWSUIT TRIAL

Clinton apologists have attempted to discredit the video and write this story off as a fairy tale because of a recent verdict in a $14,000,000 defamation lawsuit brought by two officers. The video implicates Arkansas police officers, Jay Campbell and Kirk Lane among others, for further questioning in regards to the Ives / Henry murders. On August 9, 1999 a federal jury awarded them $598,000 in their suit against Pat Matrisciana and his related organizations. The award was made despite the fact that Linda Ives, and drug task force investigator, Jean Duffey, testified for the defense. Both stated emphatically that they are convinced the officers were the "hands-on killers" of the boys.

The trial was a classic textbook example of how a judge can make a single ruling to control the outcome of a case even if it requires a unanimous jury verdict. Before the trial, Judge Warren Urbom somewhat mysteriously replaced another judge who was already assigned to the case. Urbom had previously been selected to hear a complaint against independent counsel Kenneth Starr but withdrew citing conflicts of interest.

The plaintiff's defamation claim was based solely on a single word, "eyewitnesses" used once in a statement that asserted, "eyewitnesses had implicated several people in the murders and subsequent cover-up". Three police officers, a sheriff and two prosecutors were named. The plaintiffs challenged no other facts presented in the shocking, one-hour video.

One potential eyewitness named Ronnie, who may be the only one who has survived, was subpoenaed to testify by the plaintiffs and then released during a lunch break, on the second day of the trial, while the defense was not present. The witness fled the court as well as the state, and could not be relocated by the defense even though they hired a detective to find him.

Duffey explained to me that his eyewitness information was contained in a damaging police report as well as a police report that documented another witness. However, Judge Urbom ruled that information in many police reports and some corroborating affidavits were "prejudicial" so they were not admitted into evidence. Thus, without the police reports and corroborating affidavits the defense had no defense.

The "prejudicial" ruling was particularly unusual since the case of the plaintiffs was based almost exclusively on their own character witnesses. Over one-dozen of them testified for the plaintiffs, including some fellow police officers, two FBI agents and a sheriff. Their testimony was reminiscent of 1990 when a string of character witnesses including former Attorney General and U.S. Senatorial candidate, Winston Bryant, testified to have the license of prosecutor Dan Harmon reinstated after he was convicted on a tax evasion charge. Harmon was eventually fined $150,000 and convicted in 1997 on 5 drug related felony counts, each carrying a 20-year maximum jail sentence.

The defamation trial appears to have ushered in an incredible, complete, new round of cover-ups in the Ives / Henry murders involving still another policeman. Former Alexander Police Chief, John Brown, who appeared in the video, claimed during depositions, "...portions of the video containing statements from me were edited and spliced to give the appearance that I made a statement that was never made by me". This claim is particularly fascinating since Brown was satisfied, and even proud of, the video, until the lawsuit was filed. Brown had gone on radio across the country promoting the video, obtained 350 copies of his own, and displayed them proudly during his unsuccessful campaign for county sheriff.

After the lawsuit was filed, Brown claimed to disapprove of the statements about the officers and stated that he told Pat Matrisciana not to use their names. His testimony was contradicted by Ives, Duffey, Matrisciana and Pat's editor, who provided the jury with his notes and an unused film clip where Brown names the suspects himself. Brown also stated in the video that "we know who killed them" but claimed during the trial he was referring to Sharline Wilson, who was never mentioned in the video as a suspect.

In perhaps the most sensational testimony of the trial, Brown stated he had a signed confession to the stabbing of Don Henry from Sharline Wilson. Wilson was sentenced to 30 years in prison, on a minor drug possession charge, after being near the tracks the night that Ives and Henry were killed. Brown's testimony left the burning question as to why Brown, who had championed Wilson's release for years, would want to discharge someone from prison who he claimed to be a murderer.

Sharline Wilson has stated that, while in prison, Brown took her to another location for a polygraph regarding what she knew about the murders. Before the polygraph, there was an initial interrogation that included another sheriff. Afterwards, she stated that Brown interrogated her alone, roughed her up, "busted her lip", put her in a straight jacket and left her in a padded room for more than a day. When he returned, she agreed to sign a confession that he dictated to her. She also agreed to confess during the polygraph but she was found to be untruthful. When the polygraph administrator asked her why, she stated she was saying what they wanted to hear. The administrator then found those statements to be true. Later, John Brown returned, took her out to dinner and said he would help her, since the polygraph showed that she did not kill the boys. Brown, who was eventually found to be working closely with the FBI, had evidently gotten what he wanted: a polygraph is not admissible in a court of law while a signed confession is admissible.

But the cover-up didn't stop at the local level. The testimony of Bob Govar, was limited by an authorization letter that prevented him from discussing any details of the Ives / Henry murders. U.S. Attorney, Paula Casey, the Clinton appointee who replaced Chuck Banks, attended court during his testimony apparently to ensure that the letter was enforced. Likewise, FBI agent, Phyliss Cournan, testified under a similar authorization letter from the FBI and could not discuss any details of the murder case.

The jury reached its verdict after experiencing firsthand the lack of respect for the Constitution that has become commonplace in today's courtrooms, when they requested a copy of the First Amendment for deliberations and were denied access to it. After the trial, the defense filed a motion to strike the verdict as a matter of law, since a single questionable word, in an hour long video, should not qualify as "reckless disregard" for the truth. Judge Urbom denied the motion as expected, however, the content of his denial was stunning to most of us familiar with the trial facts. After less than a page of some related case analysis, the judge provided one paragraph about trial specific evidence to justify his ruling. It is loaded with so many statements I believe to be patently false that it requires the following sentence-by-sentence rebuttal:

"There is evidence in the record that the defendant Matrisciana had obvious reasons to doubt the truth of the statement before it was published, but he decided to do nothing."

Pat was aware of the police reports and still firmly believes, along with Linda Ives and Jean Duffey, that the statement about eyewitnesses was true.

"In particular, the defendant Matrisciana had been told by John Brown that there was no documentation that justified the statement. This is significant. Mr. Brown was a major source of information for the video that contained the statement. In fact, Mr. Brown had complete editorial control over one-third of the video. Mr. Brown was relied on by the defendant Matrisciana. His research was trusted for a major portion of the video."

Here the judge admits that John Brown had editorial control over his portion of the video while essentially supporting Brown's contradicting claim that the video was edited without his consent. The judge accepted John Brown's testimony over Pat's testimony even though Brown was contradicted by Linda Ives, Jean Duffey, Pat and Pat's editor, who even showed an unused video clip of John Brown naming both the officers as suspects.

"In addition, the defendant Matrisciana had knowledge of a signed confession from a Sharline Wilson, who claimed she was on the tracks with the boys that night and that she stabbed one of them. The confession did not mention (the plaintiffs) and thus it lends support to the doubts of Mr. Brown."

The Sharline Wilson confession was so coerced that most knowledgeable individuals believe it is phony. That is why she has never been charged with the crime. The fact the judge would even mention it as true is a very disturbing indicator that he may be a part of the corruption.

"This evidence demonstrates there was reason for the defendant Matrisciana to question the truth of the statement. Yet he did not interrogate his other sources or editors who had knowledge of the same facts."

Pat discussed the video content in detail with Linda, Jean, John Brown and his own editor.

"He avoided objective, independent sources such as the police file."

This is one of the most amazing and apparently false statements in the ruling since not only did Pat, Linda and Jean use the police files, but Judge Urbom specifically refused to allow information in important police files into trial evidence.

"He failed to follow-up with Ms. Wilson."

Pat was in frequent contact with Ms. Wilson and knew her confession was coerced.

"He made no effort to contact the alleged eyewitnesses."

Pat relied on Jean, Linda and John Brown to contact the eye-witnesses so there is no reason he would duplicate their efforts.

"In short, he made no attempt to confirm the truth of the statement. Instead he decided to turn the other cheek."

Pat confirmed the truth of the eyewitness statement through the police reports.

"He wanted to avoid the truth because he wanted to sell more videos. That is reckless disregard".

This appears to be the most blatant lie of the ruling since the word "eyewitness", buried one time in the film, certainly did not sell any more videos because buyers never even knew it was there.

I fail to see how the judge could find that a single word mentioned once in an hour long video could be construed as "reckless disregard" for the truth. (The verdict in the case was unanimously overturned by the 8th Circuit U.S. Court of Appeals that even included a Clinton appointed judge.)

Testimony indicated the officers were advised to sue, by FBI Agent, Mike Smith, who was also present in a meeting when Ives and Duffey asked the FBI to investigate the officers. Despite repeated pleas from Linda Ives to many law enforcement agencies, the officers have never been investigated for the murders and no other individuals have ever been charged. In short, Linda Ives has found that federal, state and local officials have deliberately impeded any serious effort to solve any of the murders.

MUTUALLY ASSURED DESTRUCTION

The Ives / Henry murder cover-up has persisted for so long because the related drug trail has compromised the highest levels on both sides of the political spectrum. In Mississippi, the federal government intervened to solve the 1964 slaying of three civil rights workers. However, that will not happen in this case, because members and agencies of local, state and federal governments would be implicated.

Former Arkansas Development Finance Authority (ADFA) director, Larry Nichols, explained that ADFA was established with Act 1072, which was originally drafted by Webster Hubbell. Former governor, Bill Clinton, totally controlled ADFA by appointing all members. Nichols statements indicate that Mena drug money was laundered through ADFA, which was also used to payoff Clinton campaign contributors. Mena drug trafficking was part of a longtime CIA operation. Many researchers discovered CIA involvement in American drug traffic sources from Burma, Laos, Columbia, Panama, Nicaragua, and El Salvador. Control of these operations has been traced back to various direct reports of former President George Bush, ever since he was appointed CIA director in 1976.

Thus, with both former opposing Presidents involved in one of America's darkest secrets, each side will do everything they can to protect drug sources and the public officials involved in local ground distribution crews. The Ives/Henry murders illustrate how powerful people in the federal government have instituted a criminal enterprise that is actually more authoritative and threatening to American citizens than organized crime.

ELECTION 2000: COMMUNISM vs. DRUG TRAFFICKING?

The Democrat and Republican front runners, who have been promoted by the national news media for President in the Year 2000, are Vice President Al Gore and Texas Governor George W. Bush, respectively. Both are handsome, attractive candidates who are perfectly positioned to continue the détente of existing corruption.

The main contenders to the Gore and Bush 2000 nominations were former Senator Bill Bradley, a member of the Council of Foreign Relations, and Senator John McCain, a member of the CFR and the notorious Keating Five savings and loan scandal. All are insiders who have been anointed and were promoted by the national news media. McCain, a former POW who adamantly supported the NATO bombing of Yugoslavian citizens, still denies the U.S. left POW/MIA troops in Southeast Asia after the Vietnam War. Some POW / MIA families have expressed concern about the special treatment McCain received in prison, the warm hug he recently gave his former Communist prison commander and the possibility of psychological programming he may have received while he was removed from other prisoners. These concerns appear justified and may make John McCain the most dangerous presidential candidate in American history.

Only one picture is needed to understand why Vice President Al Gore should not become President. That picture shows Al Gore sitting at a table during an April 1996 fundraiser in the Hsi Lai temple in Southern California. It can be found In the book entitled, *Year of the Rat*, written by congressional investigators Bill Triplett and Ed Timperlake. Congressional investigation evidence indicated the temple laundered illegal foreign campaign contributions for the DNC and that it had a relationship with Al Gore dating to 1988. The picture shows Gore sitting with Maria Hsia, Ted Sioeng and a Buddhist monk, who is sworn to poverty.

Maria Hsia is a known Communist Chinese agent, who organized the fund raiser, supported three other fund raisers for Al Gore and formed the Pacific Leadership Council with John Huang to raise money for the DNC. Ted Sioeng is the head of the Chinese Communist controlled Pagoda Red Mountain Cigarette Co., which donated $400,000 to DNC. Immediately afterwards, the Democrats helped Sioeng get a foothold in the American market by introducing a significant amount of anti-tobacco legislation against American companies under the guise of concern about teen smoking.

Maria Hsia, who was convicted on all five counts of campaign finance violations brought against her, is apparently not the only Communist agent who has been supporting the Gore family. Others have documented how Al Gore has several Communist connections through his father, Al Gore Sr., former American Communist party leader, Armand Hammer, and Gore's son-in-law, Andrew Schiff, descendant of Jacob Schiff, who helped finance Trotski, and Lenin. The details of these connections are outside the scope of this book.

Meanwhile, the Republican alternative, George W. Bush, has been harassed repeatedly by the media to answer the question of whether or not he used cocaine. Republicans believe he has been harassed unfairly, considering the media suppression of cocaine use by Bill Clinton. But the media has actually protected Bush by suppressing a specific cocaine allegation that has been raised against him. The specific allegation is that in 1985, George W. and his brother, Jeb, were caught on video at the Tiamiami airport in a DEA sting operation picking up two kilos of cocaine for personal use from a plane owned by CIA operative Barry Seal. This book explains how the ownership of that plane was traced by serial number and FAA registration number from Seal through several individuals and organizations connected to various government officials and agencies. Its current owner is non other than the state of Texas, where it frequently was used by George W. Bush personally, as Governor.

The media has focused most of its attention on the cocaine allegation from the book entitled, *Fortunate Son*. The book states that George W. Bush was busted for cocaine around the same time frame as the drug drop and his father had to pull strings to turn a jail sentence into a year of community service for a project called Operation P.U.L.L.. The publisher, St. Martin's Press, eventually stopped distribution of the book, even though they reviewed it carefully before publishing. When questioned about the charges, Bush simply stated that the author, who still stands behind the charge, is a convicted felon. Bush refuses to talk about cocaine use or charges during that time and has never offered an explanation as to why he would want to perform a year of community service in a ghetto during the prime of his party life when he was frequently intoxicated, according to his own family.

The most disturbing point, however, is that cocaine allegations are nothing new for the Bush family. This book describes three CIA run drug operations that have been traced to direct reports of former president George Bush since he was appointed director of the CIA, in 1976, by Gerald Ford. They include support of the Contras, operations in Southeast Asia during the Vietnam War, and control of special flights between Columbia and Panama that also involved Manuel Noriega.

Bill Clinton had knowledge of Bush involvement in CIA drug operations since evidence indicated that he and Web Hubbell set up the Arkansas Development Finance Authority, ADFA, which was used as a money laundering agency for the Mena, Arkansas drug operation, according to ADFA director, Larry Nichols. Bill Clinton attempted to spread some of this knowledge (exactly when his impeachment began) by releasing a CIA Inspector General drug trafficking report. I believe he successfully compromised the Republican party leadership, which was forced to protect the year 2000 candidacy of the former President's son, George W. Bush.

This makes the potential Bush / Gore election match-up in the Year 2000 one of compromise and corruption. If either is elected no one in the Clinton administration will ever be held accountable for their wrongdoing and America will continue to be desecrated by drug trafficking and closet communists determined to implement a new world order at the expense of American sovereignty. America is quickly running out of time to correct these problems. It is essential, for the citizens of America, to elect a third party Presidential candidate just to begin breaking the détente of mutually assured destruction that has strangled the integrity of our government.

MEDIA MISINFORMATION TECHNIQUES

In the future, Americans must not only develop trusted sources for news, but must also learn to distinguish and disregard false reporting. Many people are led to believe that misinformation reported by the media is a result of media bias. However, it should be clear to those who have read this book that media misinformation is not accidental but part of a carefully crafted plan to deceive the public and implement the agenda of those who control the media.

To help distinguish deceitful reporting, I have identified 25 misinformation techniques that are frequently used by many media organizations. To further illustrate these points, I have selected one chapter of a new book to use as an example. The book I have chosen is entitled, *The Hunting of the President* by Joe Conason and Gene Lyons. It describes "The ten-year campaign to destroy Bill and Hillary Clinton". I have chosen Chapter Nine, of this particular book, because I have some personal knowledge of the information it reports and have already written about that information in this book. Therefore, the readers should get a clear illustration of these misinformation techniques. Many of the examples could actually apply to multiple techniques even though they are listed under only one. The techniques and examples are:

Suppression of Major News

Media organizations frequently suppress entire stories or large segments of news they do not want audiences to hear because it might interfere with their agenda. For example, the sample book I selected purports to discuss the major

Clinton related scandals in Arkansas but it completely avoids any details of the 13-year federal, state and local cover-up of the Ives / Henry murders and the direct connections that illustrate Bill Clinton participated in the cover-up.

Attacking Adversarial Motives

Media organizations frequently divert attention from allegations of corruption by attacking motives of those raising the allegations. On page 137 of the sample book, the authors refer to Citizens for Honest Government (CHG). They say, "In practice, the new organization had two main purposes; to propagate political and religious nostrums of the extreme religious right with which its founder and sole proprietor, Pat Matrisciana, was closely allied; and to promote and distribute videotapes produced by Jeremiah Films and Integrity Films, two 'for profit corporate entities' he owned".

First of all, the bulk of focus by CHG was on the murders of Kevin Ives and Don Henry, the murder of Vince Foster and drug trafficking through Mena, Arkansas. These have nothing to do with politics or religion since any sincere American citizen would be against murder and government sponsored drug trafficking. Periphery connections that involved Bill Clinton in money laundering and murder cover-up were not obvious until after the facts were investigated. Secondly, the film companies have not made any significant profit that has offset the cost of the videos. In fact, Jeremiah Films, which operated smoothly as a Christian film production company, was on the verge of bankruptcy after it produced the videos.

Selective Reporting

Media types frequently report only information supporting their agenda or a conclusion they want their audience to reach. On page 140 of the sample book, the authors report a few of the mysterious deaths that have various connections to the Clinton administration. However, all information about their suspicious circum-

stances and most of the connections to the Clinton administration were left out, even though this information was
freely available to them on the web site that they researched.

Intentional Misleading

Media types frequently mislead their audiences by using a
portion of the truth without explaining the entire subject
matter. This is a particularly clever technique sure to fool
most people. On page 143 of the sample book, the authors
refer to information in The Clinton Chronicles video. They
state: "One of the video's silliest charges was that the
ADFA had laundered $100 million per month (or $1.2
billion per year) in illicit cash. In the agency's nine-year existence it made loans totaling only $1.7 billion". In the
video, ADFA director Larry Nichols specifically states that
funds he believed to be drug money went in and out during
the month, were balanced before the end of the month, and
not recorded on the books by month end. Therefore, no
loans were ever made to launder the money. I believe the
authors were fully aware of this and deliberately deceived
their readers.

Misquoting of Adversaries

Media types frequently misquote allegations made by adversaries and change the type of allegation so they can
truthfully deny it. On page 146 of the sample book, the
authors refer to the president's reaction to the videos. They
state, " The president's complaints caused a flurry of front
page stories in newspapers like the *Times* and *Philadelphia
Inquirer* that inevitably focused on the more sensational accusations and observed that the videos offered no proof
Clinton was a drug smuggling murderer". Many Clinton
apologists have used the terms "drug smuggling" and
"murderer" because they know there is no evidence to
support those allegations. In fact, these exact terms were
used directly by Hillary Clinton in an NBC interview. The
videos have never accused the president of drug smuggling
and murder. At the worst case, they have accused the

president of involvement in money laundering and murder cover-up. The evidence to support these allegations is very precise and convincing.

False Implication

Media types will frequently report generic information that is essentially true in a manner to imply detail facts that are not true. On page 155 of the sample book, the authors refer to "an Arkansas lawyer named Jean Duffey who promoted a conspiratorial view of The Henry / Ives case". This is basically a true statement with a false implication that Jean Duffey is a little unbalanced. First of all, Duffey is not just a lawyer but was the head of the drug task force investigation that uncovered much of the corruption documented in this book. Secondly, she does believe there was a conspiracy to cover-up the murders of Kevin Ives and Don Henry, but that is not unusual since any truth seeking individual, who is familiar with the evidence, can clearly see there was without question, a government conspiracy to cover-up the murders. Third, I know Jean Duffey personally and she is an incredibly detailed and thorough investigator who is totally non-partisan and has detailed knowledge of drug corruption in Arkansas. This makes her a threat to corrupted government officials who hold positions of power in Arkansas.

False Insanity Implications

Media types typically attempt to portray adversaries as slightly crazy. To do this, they frequently use the word "conspiracy" as though anyone who believes in a conspiracy (such as organized crime) must be somewhat deranged. On page 145 of the sample book, the authors call Indiana Congressman Dan Burton "a Foster conspiracy buff." The implication is that anyone who does not believe Foster committed suicide is a nutty conspiracy advocate. The simple fact remains, Vince Foster's prints were not even on the gun that was used to kill him. This book only scrapes the surface of hundred of pieces of evidence confirming Vince Foster was murdered.

Inadequate Detail

Media types frequently leave out key details to keep their audiences uninformed about events where public opinion may conflict with media agenda. On page 142 of the sample book, the authors refer to allegations against Bill Clinton as made in The Clinton Chronicles. They state, "Had he, as the video alleged, issued a full pardon to a political supporter named Dan Lasater, who was convicted of giving cocaine to his acquaintances? Impossible because Lasater had pleaded guilty to a federal crime". First of all, Lasater was charged with a federal crime but it was dropped when he pled guilty to a state crime. Bill Clinton then had full control of the case and got Lasater released after he served about five months of his sentence. The authors also did not mention that the acquaintances of Lasater were teenage girls.

Unsupported Conclusions

Many media types are notorious for making conclusions that have no basis in fact, in order to support their agenda. On pages 141 and 142 of the sample book, the authors refer to many other individuals such as reporters who have disproved various allegations made in CHG videos; however, they never explain precisely what evidence disproved a single allegation.

Attacking Adversarial Sources

When media types cannot factually refute adversarial sources, they frequently resort to attacking their perspectives. On page 155 of the sample book, the authors refer to Lt. Col. Tom McKenney as a " military intelligence figure with extreme right wing views". I know Tom McKenney personally. He is the kindest, gentlest, most sincere man I have ever met in my life. Honest individuals would never consider Tom to be "extreme" regardless of their political views.

Distortion of Facts

Media types frequently distort facts to the brink of falsehoods in order to support their agenda. On page 157 of the sample book, the authors refer to Kathy Ferguson: another mysterious death. They state, "Despondent over a failed love affair, she had called 911 and then turned a gun on herself". The authors mention that Chris Ruddy investigated her death and felt it was suspicious but they conveniently left out what Ruddy discovered.

Kathy was the ex-wife of Danny Ferguson, the trooper who brought Paula Jones to Bill Clinton at the hotel where he allegedly made improper advances. She was also a nurse who found shot to death on May 11, 1994 after packing her bags to leave town. Her autopsy report that indicated suicide, was contradicted by six of her nurse friends and a doctor who stated she had a gunshot wound in the back of her head. Women rarely commit suicide with a gun and it is equally unusual for someone to shoot themselves in the BACK of the head.

The claim that she was "despondent over a failed love affair" is also unsupported and easily contradicted. Her fiance, Bill Shelton, was an Arkansas police officer highly critical of the suicide ruling. One month later, on June 12, 1994, he was found dead at her grave site. His death was also ruled a suicide and he, too, had a gunshot wound in the BACK of his head.

Credentialism

Many media types attempt to substitute credentials for facts they cannot refute. The implication is that large media organizations or famous media individuals cannot be wrong because of their established credentials. This helps media controllers implement their agenda. In many cases, media organizations idolize their own people by propagating awards and organizations to recognize them. On the jacket of the sample book, the author's awards are mentioned as an indication that they have the proper credentials to write the book regardless of how distorted its content may be.

Divisive Demonization

Media types frequently use divisive words such as "left wing" or "right wing" to demonize an adversary that they cannot factually dispute. The intent is to get the audience to classify the adversary negatively so they do not have to think about the actual facts being discussed. The audience is left with the assumption that the position of the adversary is not worth considering since he or she is of a different political persuasion. In the sample book, the authors use the term "right wing" several times in Chapter Nine to describe individuals such as Lt. Col. Tom McKenney.

Change of Subject

When faced with irrefutable facts contradicting their agenda, media types will frequently change the subject. All 400 pages of the sample book I selected, attempted to change the subject from the evidence of Clinton administration corruption to the background of the individuals who have presented the evidence.

Authoritative Confirmation

When media organizations want to impose their viewpoint upon their audiences, they frequently use experts who they know will provide a professional opinion to confirm the direction of the media agenda. For example, they may interview a general to confirm the need to bomb a country or tout a Congressman who is sponsoring a piece of legislation they are seeking to pass. For five pages of the sample book, beginning with page 153, the authors refer to former Saline County Sheriff John Brown as an authoritative source. As previously described, Brown's testimony in the defamation suit was refuted by four witnesses and Brown even went so far as to tout the coerced confession of Sharline Wilson during his testimony and make the ludicrous claim that she killed Don Henry.

Partial Quotation

Media types frequently pick selected words out of an adversarial quote to distort the original intent of the quote.

This allows them to tell their audiences the adversary said something offensive or incorrect even though it never really happened. On page 372, in the Afterword of the sample book, the authors reference Congressman Barr. They state, "Barr did not serve his cause well when he characterized the effort to remove the president as a 'civil war' nor when he lectured a distinguished Black federal judge (testifying before the House Judiciary Committee) that 'real Americans' favored impeachment". The authors raise the classic racial implication so often used to divert attention from corruption.

First of all, although a Black federal judge did testify before the House Judiciary Committee, Barr made the remark during testimony by Alan Derschowitz, who appeared shortly thereafter and is neither black, nor a federal judge. The reference to "real Americans" refers to the citizens who are constituents of Congressmen and Congresswomen, not paid legal experts who frequently appear on talk shows to furnish propaganda in support of the media agenda.

Poll Manipulation

After adequately misinforming their audience, media organizations conduct polls intended to produce results supporting their agenda. The questions are frequently twisted so the answers yield the desired result. For example, during the height of the impeachment, one news organization actually conducted a poll that asked the question, "Should Bill Clinton NOT be impeached?" On page 370, in the Afterword of the sample book, the authors refer to Bill Clinton. They state, " A poll commissioned by CNN and the Wall Street Journal in early February 1998, recorded an astonishing 79 percent of respondents favoring him". I am by no means astonished that a CNN poll would claim a 79 percent favorable rating for Bill Clinton. However, I do not believe Bill Clinton, who never even gained 50% of a presidential election vote, has ever had a 79 percent favorable rating, particularly during a peak in one of his many scandals.

Corrupted Sources

Media types sometimes use corrupted sources to support their agenda when the facts do not support it. On pages 140 and 153 of the sample book, the authors reference CHG financial records and ledgers without explaining how they got them. The references state, "The authors also obtained CFHG internal documents, fund-raising letters and correspondence from confidential sources". The sources are not confidential to me or to Pat Matrisciana who told me about two employees I know who broke into the files. When the employees were terminated, they attempted to mis-appropriate computer equipment and take over the web site. After CHG filed legal action against them, Pat discovered they were under FBI protection from the Clinton / Reno Justice Department. Stolen copies of records, including false information about a multi-million dollar bank account, were eventually leaked to the Salon web magazine, and picked up again by Geraldo on CNBC, immediately before the National Impeachment Town Hall.

Mixing Lies w/ Truth

Media types will frequently mix a lie in with the truth to keep their audiences misinformed about facts that, if known, could damage the media agenda. This technique makes it almost impossible for the audience to distinguish fact from fiction. On Page 154 of the sample book, the authors refer to the Ives / Henry murders. They correctly state the Obstruction of Justice video had claimed, "Eyewitnesses have implicated several people in the murders and subsequent cover-up". But the authors immediately state, "It then proceeded to list Prosecutor Dan Harmon and the two officers as the killers". The video never listed anyone as the killers. It only "implicated several people in the murders and subsequent cover-up". It suggested these people should be questioned and possibly investigated for their potential roles.

Blatant Lie

The final desperate attempt by media types, when they have completely failed to refute the facts is to blatantly lie. On page 153 and 154 of the sample book, the authors make their only significant reference to the Ives / Henry murders. They say, "The case first drew notice due to a foolish error by the state medical examiner." They continue with a run-on sentence. It states, "Whether the overworked medical examiner – deemed overly solicitous of law enforcement by some observers, incapable of admitting error by almost everybody – had simply misplaced a decimal point was hard to say". It is easy for almost anyone to understand an honest, competent medical examiner cannot mistake a stab wound and a crushed skull for marijuana intoxication. In addition, the medical examiner had many other bogus death rulings which were documented by the *L. A. Times*. To imply the medical examiner may have "simply misplaced a decimal point" is not only a terrible affront to Linda Ives, but one of the biggest insults to the intelligence of the American people I have ever seen.

I have illustrated 25 media misinformation techniques in a single chapter and Afterword of one sample book. In addition, the authors of the book attempt to discredit many people I know personally. A few them are Jean Duffey, Linda Ives, Pat Matrisciana and Lt. Col. Tom McKenney. I can truthfully say these people are my friends who I know well enough to trust them with my life. All of them have an uncompromising integrity that appears to be totally lacking in the authors of the sample book.

The back cover of the sample book references the sum of allegations against Bill Clinton. The cover states, "It is also the story of the most successful and long-running "dirty tricks" campaign in recent American history, fomented by a handful of professional Republican operatives and corporate lawyers and funded by a network of wealthy conservatives". This is the classic concept the Democrat Party uses to dupe their own members. When Republicans expose real Democrat corruption, Democrat apologists simply say they are up to their "dirty tricks".

I was deeply involved in the impeachment movement but I am not wealthy. I am not a lawyer but a computer consultant who has a typical analytical mind like many of those in my profession. I am not a professional Republican operative since the Republican Party disgusts me. I am not a conservative since conservatives would never talk about Bush drug trafficking allegations and the need to decriminalize drugs. I simply want honest government. I am convinced that most of the allegations against Bill Clinton are true and that is why I wanted him impeached.

GETTING INVOLVED

Because of the many corrupted media organizations who suppress critical information about inner government workings, most of us either do not realize our freedom is being threatened or do not realize the severity of the threat. We are caught up with our personal lives, our families, our friends and the overall fun of enjoying life in the world's most prosperous country. We have been successfully programmed into a state of complacency and lack of knowledge. Even many of us who realize the freedom of our children is in jeopardy, have been programmed to think we are helpless to do anything about it. Therefore, this is a fatal situation for America.

To counter this fatalistic complacency, we must get involved in our government. Voting is simply not enough. We must get to know our Senators and Representatives on a personal basis and should financially support those who we trust to do the right thing. Representatives still listen to their supporters, and can be effective in establishing an American agenda from the bottom up. We must avoid any financial contributions to national committees because they use the money in an attempt to get Congressmen to support a pre-established top down agenda that is invariably always corrupt.

During the impeachment, thousands of American citizens got involved in their government. They spent their personal time and money by:

- writing, calling, faxing and visiting their Congressmen,
- signing and collecting impeachment petitions,:
- participating in town halls and talk shows,

- explaining the facts to their friends, and
- pressuring the media organizations to tell the truth.

Protecting our freedom requires a commitment of some time and money. Freedom is not free. It was a key factor that damaged my marriage. If we want to preserve our freedom we must be willing to devote at least a small portion of our income and spare time to protecting it. We are in a battle for control of America being fought by two groups. One group is the citizens who simply want honest government. The other is the global socialist controlled media. They want to subordinate American sovereignty to a one-world government plan being implemented by compromised politicians who they control.

A PLATFORM FOR FREEDOM

To save America we must completely redirect our country away from the Communist mentality of our elected leaders and force them to implement a pro-American platform by systematically removing legislation that they have already adopted in support of *Communist Manifesto* planks. Ten points for a platform of freedom are:

1. Protect American sovereignty

All laws that subordinate American government regulations to global organizations should be eliminated. The Committee on anti-American activities should be restored and manned by independent citizens. Bills must pass Congress by a full majority of total members, not a majority of those present. Any bill submitted in either body of Congress should have at least three days of lead time to allow the members to review it before voting on it.

2. Stop unconstitutional executive orders

The first sentence of the U.S. Constitution says, "all power granted herein is vested in a Congress of the United States…" Therefore, Congress can stop executive orders at any time it chooses. The House Constitutional Subcommittee should review the books for all unconstitutional orders, list them and remove them in a single bill. All war powers acts currently in place should be terminated and the capabilities for automatic executive orders removed. Any rights given to the federal government, during the gold crisis in 1933, should also be reclaimed by the states.

3. Reform the election process

The election process must be reformed to ensure that :

- money does not play an overwhelming part in who is elected,
- only eligible voters are allowed to vote,
- the results of the voting can be certified for accuracy,
- existing election and finance laws are enforced, and
- no American taxpayer money should be used to fund any candidates whatsoever.

Taxpayer funding of political candidates should be terminated. Democrat and Republican presidential candidates currently get upwards of $60 million in taxpayer funds that give them an insurmountable advantage in the presidential elections.

The "soft" money donated to political parties should be eliminated since it helps to drive corrupted, top-down agendas. Only donations from individuals to candidates should be allowed. All corporate, union and non-local political action committee donations should be eliminated. Representatives should get their funds only from their respective districts, and Senators should get funds only from their respective states.

Any Presidential candidate on the ballot, in all 50 states, should be allowed to participate in debates. Debate questions should be asked not by media representatives, but only by American citizens who are selected randomly from the debate attendees.

The composition of the Federal Election Commission (FEC) should be changed to disallow political party members from serving. Political party independence could help achieve fairness for third parties since all current FEC members are either Democrat or Republican. The FEC must also be held accountable for proving to the American citizens that election results are valid.

Citizens must show some form of identification to cast their votes and prevent duplicate voting. Votes must be tallied and verified, at the precinct level, to prevent massive, centralized voter fraud. When procedures are violated at a precinct, an independent audit should be conducted to certify the results. If the results cannot be certified and the election hangs in the balance, then the voters at that precinct should be required to vote again. Manual vote counting should be filmed to ensure accuracy. Software must be impounded and readily available to verify there are no software irregularities that can be used to falsify election results. Election machine vendors unwilling to abide by the rules should be replaced with the new vendors.

4. Ensure Justice Department accountability

Justice Department agencies must be held accountable to the basic laws of the land and not serve as a defense agency for a President. The appointment of the Attorney General should be made by Congress, to help protect the citizens against a tyrannical dictatorship. All law enforcement should be consolidated under the Justice Department to ensure no rogue law enforcement outfits, such as previous IRS and ATF units, are allowed to operate outside the bounds of the law. ATF and IRS law enforcement agencies should be abolished in conjunction with eliminating the income tax. Each law enforcement agency must have public, Congressional accountability for its actions to ensure there will be no future events such as the FBI actions at Waco or CIA drug trafficking. A citizens' review panel must be established to ensure the Justice Department does not adopt a double standard of justice for government official vs. citizens. No individual or organization should be allowed to operate above the law for national security reasons.

5. Decriminalize drugs

The CIA has become so deeply involved in drug trafficking it is unwilling and unable to eliminate its entanglement with organized crime. The temptation of using the profits from drug running to fund covert operations, has made the CIA a willing partner to drug traffickers throughout the world for decades. Other military units have been involved as well. Congress is simply too intimidated by the CIA to make it accountable. The CIA essentially has a license to live above American law under the guise of national security. This concept is unconstitutional and a threat to every American citizen, regardless of what agency may happen to have such a privilege.

The phony drug war has been used as an illegal excuse to confiscate the property of honest Americans; destroy our Fourth Amendment rights to unreasonable search and seizure, and even kill innocent American citizens, such as those at Waco where the ATF used the false excuse of a non-existent drug lab to gain military training and equipment in violation of the Posse Comitatus laws.

The only viable solution is to decriminalize drugs to remove the profit in drug running. The illegality of drugs has caused prices to escalate to as much as 100 times their actual cost to manufacture. The removal of the profit motive will also spur a dramatic drop in crime and return America to a law and order society like we had during the 50s when drugs, such as cocaine, were legal but never used. Dramatic reductions would occur in drug-related crimes such as drive by shootings, gang-related murders and robberies to support drug habits. In addition, no pimps would find it worthwhile to hang around high schools and try to hook our children on drugs.

6. Eliminate asset forfeiture laws

There is no condition under which our government should be allowed to steal the property of its citizens against their will, even if they are suspected to have committed crimes. Federal, state and local governments should have no more rights over and above the victims of the crimes. Once an individual has been convicted of a crime where assets were acquired illegally, government should be allowed to file a grievance in the courts to recover incarceration costs, legal fees or other expenses incurred. Automatic forfeiture of property should not be allowed.

7. Balance the budget

Despite the claim of the politicians, the federal budget is not balanced. The difference between social security revenue and expenses must currently be added to the budget as income to balance it with the excessive spending that still exists. The budget must be balanced after social security funds are taken completely off line. All off budget projects must be eliminated or included in the normal federal budget. A balanced budget amendment must also be passed to force politicians into doing their duty.

8. Eliminate social security

Since the social security money we give our government is spent as soon as it is received, social security is simply another income tax that should be eliminated. Americans should be free to invest for their retirement wherever they choose, using their own personal accounts which would give them dramatically improved returns. Under no condition should money be taken from the citizens under false pretenses and spent against their will by legislators.

9. Eliminate the inheritance tax

Our government does not have a Constitutional right to seize property from citizens at the time of their death. Any taxes that apply to the transfer of assets to family heirs is an income tax that should be eliminated. This will help preserve the right of each American to a full inheritance undaunted by government interference at the time of their ancestor's death.

10. Eliminate income tax

The federal income tax must be removed, despite the complexity that may be involved. A flat tax would not resolve any of the IRS abuse cases where there were disagreements over the amount of income that was earned by the taxpayer. Therefore, if the government needs tax revenue, it should be collected at the time of consumption as a national sales tax. The advantages of a national sales tax over an income tax are:

PROMOTES FREEDOM
Citizens decide when and how much tax to pay through their purchases.

ABOLISHES COMPLEXITY
No personal time is required from citizens to pay taxes.

ELIMINATES INTRUSIONS
The IRS cannot be used to persecute citizens for political purposes.

REDUCES TAX BURDEN
The IRS cuts costs by dealing only with businesses and state agencies.

REDUCES LOBBYING
Tax breaks that account for about 65 percent of all lobbying would be eliminated.

TAXES UNDERGROUND
Criminals, drug dealers and illegal aliens must pay sales taxes just like honest folks.

IMPROVES TRADE DEFICIT
Reduced cost of producing goods with no employee income tax will increase exports.

STIMULATES ECONOMY
Potential for more personal savings will increase business investment and lower interest rates.

PROMOTES EQUALITY
No one receives arbitrary tax breaks or special privileges.

HELPS DISADVANTAGED
Lower income citizens benefit the most from the proposed credit on social security tax up to poverty level.

If a sales tax is ever implemented in place of the income tax, Americans must ensure Congress does not quietly allocate part of the money to global causes such as the United Nations or International Monetary Fund. American sales tax collected from American citizens should not be used to fund the "New World Order."

SAVING AMERICA

These suggestions are just a starting point on the road back to true, honest government. We are running out of time. If we Americans do not act now, we will almost assuredly lose the gift we have been given in the next few years. Then what will we say to our children or grandchildren when they ask us what happened?

Although these platform planks would be desirable to most any American, neither Democrats nor Republicans are seriously trying to implement them, regardless of their rhetoric. That is why the battle today is not about conservative vs. liberal, left wing vs. right wing, rich vs. poor, Black vs. White or Christian vs. Muslim vs. Jews. The battle that must be fought in the new millennium is about Americanism vs. anti-Americanism. The majority of all Americans must unite in the new millennium to preserve the American freedoms to which we have grown accustom.

The time has come to get the closet Communists out of the American government, to get the government out of the drug trafficking business and to force our elected officials to implement a platform to restore the freedom of American citizens so that the government once again runs on the principles of the United States Constitution. It is my sincerest desire that every reader will join the battle by picking an issue and getting involved. Together, we can save America.

REFERENCES

Harry Browne, *Why Government Doesn't Work*, St. Martin's Press.
Joe Conason and Gene Lyons, *The Hunting of the President*,
    St Martin's Press.
Paul Sperry, *Did House panel fry good guy?*, WorldNetDaily
Ed Timperlake & Bill Triplett, *Year of the Rat*, Regnery Publishing.
The New American magazine, "Al Gore's Red Connections,"
    3/31/97, American Opinion Book Services.
Michael Ruppert From the Wilderness newsletters, various issues.
Mara Leveritt,*The Boys on the Tracks*, St Martin's Press.
Obstruction of Justice (video), Integrity Films

CHAPTER THIRTEEN

VOTER NEWS SCAM 2000 and the "OPPOSITON" PRESIDENT

BUSH PROTECTS CLINTON

The previously published chapter contends that regardless of whether Al Gore or George W. Bush was elected President in the year 2000, the Clinton Administration would not be held accountable for the actions defined in the book. For some Americans, this may seem to be a somewhat outlandish prediction regarding George W. Bush of the "opposition" party, but during 2001, the predication was more than just proven correct. In his first year, newly elected president, George W. Bush, and his "opposition" party administration actually took several steps to protect Bill Clinton and the previous administration. Specifically:

- In December 2001, George W. Bush invoked executive privilege to prevent the House Government Reform and Oversight Committee from viewing prosecutorial documents involving campaign finance abuses and other criminal matters by citing the grounds that it "would be contrary to the national interest";
- In September, 2001, the Ashcroft Justice Department refused to allow the House Government and Reform Committee to view documents concerning decisions by three Clinton-era federal prosecutors not to prosecute officials in various scandals;
- In November, 2001 George W. Bush signed Executive Order 13233 which allows the records of a former president to be withheld indefinitely by a sitting president, former president or his family;
- The Bush Administration refused to turn over to the Government Accounting Office investigation any information collected about White House vandalism performed by the Clinton administration in January 2001 when Bill Clinton left office

- George W. Bush and John Ashcroft did not remove any of the U.S. Attorneys appointed by Clinton administration after Janet Reno fired all 93 previous U.S. attorneys upon taking office, a move unprecedented in American history;
- In February 2001, the Ashcroft Justice Department allowed Mary Jo White, the U.S. Attorney for Southern District of New York, a Clinton appointee, to investigate evidence that pardons were given by Bill Clinton in exchange for cash and other favors;
- In February of 2001, George W. Bush chose not to withhold any of the 138 Clinton pardons even though 44 of them were illegal since no requests were pending for them and no charges had been filed;
- In March 2001, the Ashcroft Justice Department lawyer, Dan O'Brien, supported the plea agreement James Riady negotiated with the Reno Justice Department to do community service in Indonesia for funneling millions of dollars in illegal cash to the Clinton / Gore campaigns
- In January 2002, the Ashcroft Justice Department terminated its criminal investigation of the illegal transfer of missile technology by Loral Corp. and CEO Bernard Schwartz, a large Clinton campaign contributor, in exchange for a $14 million judgment
- In 2001, the Ashcroft Justice Department denied repeated requests from federal magistrate judge, John Facciola to grant John Huang and Charlie Trie immunity to testify in federal court in the same manner they were granted immunity to testify for Congress;
- In 2001, the Ashcroft Justice Department continued the Clinton administration assertion that the Privacy Act does not apply to the White House in cases involving Billy Dale and Juanita Broaddrick even though federal Judge, Royce Lambeth already ruled that it does in the FBI file case
- In 2001, the the Ashcroft Justice Department appealed the ruling of the U.S. Southern District Court that Janet Reno was not immune from damage claims filed by victims in the Elian Gonzalez raid;
- In 2001, a Bush appointed interim U.S. Attorney indicted Peter Paul on stock fraud charges after he went public about a $2,000,0000 direct, in kind contribution he made to the Hillary Clinton Senate campaign, which she never reported;

- In January 2001, the Bush administration requested the resignation of Linda Tripp while retaining all Clinton
  appointed U.S. attorneys and opposing her Privacy Act suit
  against Clinton Pentagon officials who released her confidential government files;
- Throughout 2001, the Bush Administration refused to hire
  Linda Shenwick, the former State Department official who
  uncovered waste fraud and abuse of authority at the United
  Nations and Clinton State Department headed by Madelyn
  Albright
- In 2001, the Ashcroft Justice Department intervened in the
  civil suit filed by Notra Trulock, the Director of Intelligence
  for the Dept of Energy, against Wen Ho Lee and issued an
  opinion to recommend the rejection of deposition requests
  for Janet Reno, Louis Freeh and Randy Bellows, the Justice
  Dept special investigator whose report exonerated Notra
  Trulock from false claims of racism made by Wen Ho Lee.

While the merits of any one or two of these points could be
debated, together they provide a clear, unmistakable pattern of
protection that the Bush administration has provided for Clinton
officials. It should be obvious to even the most ardent major political party supporter from these actions that the two parties are
not actually opposites, but they are on the same team.

In each of these cases and more, the George W. Bush administration took carefully crafted action to protect Bill Clinton or
conceal various corrupt activities that involved his administration.
In fact, Bush has almost never even mentioned the past, unresolved
scandals much less taken steps to ensure that justice was served.

Furthermore, Bush cabinet member selections and other appointments indicate his intent to continue and maintain
cover-ups involving drug trafficking, money laundering and the
Communist Chinese infiltration of the American government.
Some of his more intriguing appointments and cabinet
members include:

Elaine Chao, Secretary of Labor

Elaine Chao was a board member of Protective Life Corp.,
which co-owns CRC Protective Life Insurance with the Lippo
Group and China Resources. China Resources is " AN AGENT
OF MILITARY, POLITICAL AND ECONOMIC ES-

PIONAGE " according to Senate Governmental Affairs and Defense Intelligence Agency reports. Chao and her father have regular and deep contact with communist China's President, Jiang Zemin, according to WorldNetDaily sources. Mrs. Chao's father, James S. C. Chao, attended college with the Chinese president until he fled to Taiwan in 1949, before the communist government takeover. In regards to the findings of the May 1999 report on Chinese espionage, released by the select committee chaired by Rep. Christopher Cox (R-CA), Chao characterized them as "racist". John Huang has already admitted to at least one illegal donation to the campaign of Chao's husband, Sen. Mitch McConnell (R-KY). In a Nov. 6, 2000, deposition taken by Judicial Watch, John Huang admitted to funneling $2,000 to McConnell's Senate campaign at a 1990 Los Angeles fund-raiser. Huang acknowledged being reimbursed for the McConnell donation and other contributions by his employer at the time, the Lippo Group. The Lippo group, is the conglomerate founded by Indonesian billionaire and Clinton backer Mochtar Riady, who has a joint partnership with China Resources and other business dealings with Communist controlled companies as explained in previous chapter 5.

Nancy Dorn, White House Office of Management and Budget Deputy Director

While she was a law firm partner, Nancy Dorn was a registered agent for Hutchinson Port Holdings, the subsidiary of Hutchinson Whampoa, which was in the process of taking over the Panama Canal. Several sources have reported her relationship including the Conservative Caucus and New American magazine.

Hutchinson Whampoa is owned by Li Kashing, a Hong Kong billionaire who has three major connections with the Communist Chinese government. First, he is a partner in CITIC, owner of COSCO, which was caught shipping 2000 illegal AK 47s into the Oakland port. CITIC is chaired by Wang Jun, son of Wang Zhen, a PLA general involved in the Tiananmen Square massacre. Second, Li was also a principal in Beijing Enterprises, which collapsed and profited the Lippo group. Third, Li partners with Lippo and China Resources to own the Hong Kong Chinese Bank. CITIC, Beijing Enterprises and China Resources have always been controlled by the

Communist Chinese Government. In addition, China Resources is "AN AGENT OF MILITARY, POLITICAL AND ECONOMIC ESPIONAGE" according to Defense Intelligence Agency and Senate Governmental Affairs reports.

After Dennis Hastert succeeded Newt Gingrich as Speaker of the House, he appointed Nancy Dorn, as his top national security aide in 2000 despite her lobbying activities as a foreign agent. As Hastert received a continual growing number of complaints about her appointment from House Republicans, and other concerned citizens, she was offered a new position by Vice President Dick Cheney in 2001 as his legislative affairs assistant for matters involving the State Department. In December 2001, George W. Bush appointed her to a more powerful position in his office.

Richard Armitage, Deputy Secretary of State

Richard Armitage was originally appointed to a Tehran post for the DIA by Gerald Ford. Upon assuming the presidency, Ronald Reagan appointed him as Deputy Assistant Secretary of Defense and then, two years later, as Assistant Secretary of Defense. Armitage was in charge of the failed POW/MIA recovery efforts as Assistant Secretary of Defense for International Security Affairs during the Reagan administration. As a result, the Pentagon has continually denied the authenticity of evidence and disputed any testimony confirming live POWs, despite estimates that over 2,000 POW/MIAs were left in Southeast Asia after the Vietnam War. Contrary to their denials, POW/MIA existence has been confirmed by refugee reports, intelligence documents, numerous individuals in the intelligence community, DIA satellite photography and a famous picture taken on May 25, 1990 of three live prisoners of war still held in captivity.

Richard Armitage was investigated for gambling and prostitution by President Reagan's Commission on Organized Crime in 1984, exposed for drug money laundering in 1986 and personally protected by George H.W Bush after Ross Perot confronted him with money laundering evidence as explained in Chapter 11. In 1989 George H.W. Bush then nominated Armitage for Assistant Secretary of State and appointment that the U.S. Senate denied for obvious reasons. Armitage was implicated in Southeast Asian money laundering for drug trafficking operations originating in Burma and running through Laos while he was Assistant Secretary of Defense.

On March 23, 2001, without a publicly aired hearing, Richard Armitage was unanimously confirmed as Deputy Secretary of State reporting to one of his best friends, General Colin Powell. Senate Democrats, who made a ridiculous attempt to deny the nomination of Attorney General John Ashcroft solely on ideological grounds, were stone silent when presented with a candidate who has an extensive background of international crime.

Robert Mueller, FBI Director

As director of the Justice Department's criminal division under former President Bush, Robert Mueller oversaw high-profile cases like the prosecution of ousted Panamanian leader Gen. Manuel Noriega on drug charges and the investigation into the 1991 collapse of the Bank of Credit and Commerce International (BCCI). Both of these major prosecutions involved a cover-up of drug trafficking and money laundering activities connected to U.S. Government officials. Chapter 10 of this book provides evidence that Gen. Manuel Noriega was involved in Operation Watchtower, a U.S. military controlled operation that established beacons to support low flying planes carrying drugs from Columbia into Panama. BCCI, perhaps the most scandalous financial institution of all times, was established by Clark Clifford, the Secretary of Defense for Lyndon Johnson. Clifford was instrumental in establishing the 1947 National Security Act that created the CIA, which now operates above the law. Chapter 10 also summarizes evidence of CIA involvement in several worldwide drug trafficking operations.

Asa Hutchinson, DEA Director

Asa Hutchinson is the former Congressman and House Impeachment manager who spoke eloquently to remove Bill Clinton on grounds of lying about sex and related obstruction of justice. He was also reluctant to go forward with evidence of the more serious charges of treason, bribery, abuse of the FBI and IRS or criminal activity in Arkansas. The background of Asa Hutchinson is perhaps best explained by Mara Leveritt, author of the book, *"The Boys on the Tracks"*, which documents the murders of Kevin Ives and Don Henry.

In 1982, when Asa took office as U.S. attorney for the Western district of Arkansas, Barry Seal moved his drug operation from Louisiana into that district at the city of Mena. Federal officials were already aware that Seal controlled an extremely well organized and extensive international smuggling organization. Immediately upon arrival, Seal was under surveillance by agents of the DEA, FBI, U.S. Customs, IRS and Arkansas State Police, much of which was coordinated by Hutchinson. By the end of 1982, U.S. Treasury agent Bill Duncan and an Arkansas State Police investigator brought Hutchinson evidence that Seal was involved in narcotics trafficking and the laundering of funds derived from such trafficking. They requested 20 subpoenas for a federal grand jury but Hutchinson allowed only three. Two of those three who testified, a banker and a secretary for one of Seal's partners, Rich Mountain Aviation, complained that Hutchinson did not ask them the appropriate questions and they could not provide the grand jury with the evidence that they had accumulated. Hutchinson continued to protect Seal, the most notorious drug smuggler in American history, for the entire time Hutchinson was the U.S. Attorney.

John Magaw, Undersecretary of Transportation Security Administration

In 1992, George Bush appointed John McGaw as director of the Secret Service. He was then selected by Lloyd Bentzen to head the BATF in 1993 after the attack on the Branch Davidian church complex near Waco. Magaw was instrumental in continuing the BATF cover-up of their role in the Davidian massacre. In February of 1994, after the Davidians were acquitted of murder charges and convicted on lesser charges such as weapons violations and voluntary manslaughter, Magaw stated that: " ...mistakes do not justify the mass murder that David Koresh ordered on Feb. 28 and concluded on April 19."

The evidence collected to date indicates rather clearly that Magaw was lying about Koresh. Videotapes, debris, the FLIR tape and testimony from survivors corroborate how the FBI started the fire that killed most of the Davidians on April 19.

Videotapes of the February 28 raid that would prove Davidian claims about the ATF attack have been permanently withheld by the ATF while under the direction of Magaw.

Magaw also covered-up information about ATF prior knowledge of the Oklahoma City bombing. In a May 24, 1995 CNN interview, Magaw told Charles Bierbauer the ATF, which suffered no fatalities, was not forewarned of the bomb threat. However, three witnesses saw a bomb squad near the building just before the bomb went off and three other witnesses interviewed by KFOR TV stated that ATF agents told them they were warned not to come into work that day. Magaw also repeated false information from the ATF May 23, 1995 press release claiming two ATF agents were in an elevator that had free fallen five stories and they then finally escaped, taking 10 - 15 people with them. The service technician and his employer, the President of Midwestern elevator, stated the elevators could not have free fallen since they are counterbalanced and all cables were found in normal working condition. If an elevator had free fallen, the passengers inside would have suffered serious injuries.

In spite of some disregard for truth, Magaw did slip once when he was caught with a surprise question and identified who burned down the Davidian church complex. After being asked by Sanja Hilligram at a September 25, 1995 National Press Club meeting about whether the ATF should be folded into the FBI, Magraw replied: "had we been left in charge of the Waco incident we would not have burned that building".

John Danforth, Special Ambassador to Sudan

John Danforth, a former three-term Missouri Senator, was selected in 1999 by Janet Reno as a special prosecutor to investigate the attack on the Branch Davidian church complex near Waco. The Justice Department investigation was needed because the 1995 U.S. House investigation could not quell the uproar about government wrongdoing in the attack on the Branch Davidians. Videos such as the award-winning Waco: a New Revelation had precisely defined how the fire started, how agents shot at the Davidians when they tried to escape and how the military was used illegally. But Danforth concluded:

(Government agents) "did not start or spread the tragic fire of April 19, 1993";

(Government agents) "did not direct gunfire at the Branch Davidians";

(Government agents) "did not unlawfully employ the armed forces of the United States";

Danforth also stated that:

"He had "100 percent certainty" there was no government wrongdoing";

"The blame rest squarely on the shoulders of David Koresh. This is not a close call."

"Sensational films construct dark theories out of little evidence and gain ready audiences for their message".

Despite Danforth's claims, videotapes, debris, the FLIR tape and testimony from survivors corroborate the FBI started the fire that killed most of the Davidians on April 19. The FLIR tape showed automatic weapons fire so conclusively that "nothing in nature could duplicate the thermal signature" according to FLIR creator Edward Allerd, a former Defense Department Night Vision Lab Manager. Evidence has also shown the ATF falsely stated the Davidians were manufacturing drugs so the ATF could receive military training that would normally violate the Posse Comitatus Act. The expertise used by Danforth to cover up the Davidian murders may now be applied to his appointment in Sudan where millions of predominately Christian southern Sudanese have been murdered.

The appearance by Danforth at the July 21, 2000 press conference to announce his findings was particularly chilling. I concluded I had never seen anyone issue so many rapid-fire back-to-back lies in such a short time frame and with such smoothness. Unlike Clinton or George W. Bush, it was impossible to determine whether or not Danforth was telling the truth without having predefined knowledge of what he was discussing. The style and delivery of the former Episcopalian minister make him the epitome of deception and good enough to fool most of the Christian community who has supported him.

BUSH CFR LINKS

From the beginning of his run for the presidency, George W. Bush surrounded himself with members of the Council on Foreign Relations. This same powerful organization to which his two predecessors, including his father belonged, assured his selection over Al Gore. Many of these CFR members were involved in the administration of his father and work behind the scenes to make the key decisions in the Bush presidency. The CFR members involved in the George W. Bush presidential candidacy or administration include George Schultz, James Baker, Dick Cheney, Colin Powell, Donald Rumsfield, Paul Wolfowitz, Elaine Chao and Condolessa Rice.

These advisors and appointments of George W. Bush propagate the corruption of both of his two immediate predecessors, one of which is his own father. They establish a trend showing that George W. Bush is not likely making his own decisions but actually operating under control of his father.

VOTER NEWS SERVICE AND ELECTION NIGHT

But George W. Bush was only able to gain the presidency after one of the most controversial elections in American history. Vice President Al Gore actually won the popular vote by five hundred thousand votes but narrowly lost the electoral vote. The outcome hinged on the results from the State of Florida where Jeb Bush, the brother of George W. Bush was governor. However, on election night, Tuesday, November 7, 2000 an historic event occurred that may become even more significant than the closeness of the Presidential election.

At about 7:40 PM, Voter News Service (VNS) falsely projected that Al Gore had won Florida. VNS is a New York based company owned by major national news organizations including ABC, NBC, CBS, CNN, FOX, and the Associated Press. It is essentially a recreation of News Election Service (NES), which was established by ABC, CBS, NBC, the New York Times and the Washington Post in 1964 shortly after the Kennedy assassination. VNS made the false Florida projection despite the facts that:

- No Florida county results had been announced.
- The polls were still open in many western Florida precincts that are in the Central time zone.
- The Florida presidential race was much tighter than races in other eastern states where VNS had not projected Bush as a winner.
- The Florida Secretary of State specifically requested not to prematurely project the state while polls were open.

Roughly two hours later, VNS finally retracted their projection and that was when I was, once again, convinced that George W. Bush would become President. About 2:15 AM, VNS prematurely projected that George W. Bush had won Florida. Roughly two hours later VNS retracted that projection, also. The VNS projections for election night 2000 make a great case study in election manipulation and are described later in this chapter.

The actual Florida vote count completed the next day, gave Bush a 1,784-vote lead. On Thursday, Nov. 7th, at 5 PM, the Florida Secretary of State, Katherine Harris held a press conference as Bush still held a 1,700-vote lead with 53 of 64 counties certified. On Friday afternoon, results indicated that the Bush lead was reduced to 960 votes with 66 of 67 counties certified. However, the national news media outlets reported throughout the weekend that the lead was 327 votes. This number that nearly all media outlets used was an AP projection. AP gets its voting result information from VNS, which was projecting a 331-vote difference according to Fox News. Thus, the deceptive information being portrayed over the weekend came from the same source that falsely projected Al Gore had won Florida.

When Palm Beach, the last county to certify vote counts, reported their totals, the Bush lead was reduced by 682 votes to 288. By contrast, the other counties had no more than a 30-vote differential and an average of only 15 votes per county. The Palm Beach numbers were out of proportion to the rest of the Florida counties by a factor of 20 times, thus indicating a significant potential for fraud. AP and VNS must have had advanced notice of this heavily skewed county results since they had already projected the large decrease in the Bush lead.

By Friday, the Gore campaign got Democrat led canvassing boards in Democrat stronghold counties like Palm Beach, Broward and Dade to begin manually recounting votes the machines could not read to try and give Gore the election. When the Bush campaign attempted to block the selective manual recount in court, the news media outlets falsely reported that: "Bush sues to block recount". In reality, the Bush campaign fully supported the recount but attempted only to block the selective manual counting.

On Tuesday, November 14, Terry Lewis, although a Lawton Childs appointed judge, confirmed the discretion of the Secretary of State. He denied an injunction sought by the Gore campaign to include more selective manually counted votes in the total after the 5 PM deadline that was mandated by Florida law. At 6:30 PM, Florida Secretary of State, Katherine Harris, announced that the certified vote total showed George Bush winning by exactly 300 votes with only overseas absentee ballots left to count on the following Saturday. These ballots are primarily military and tend to favor Republican candidates. The following afternoon the Secretary of State used her discretion to confirm that she considered the certified vote count as the final count from each county with the exception of the overseas ballots. In spite of this, the media frenzy continued to focus on manual ballot counting even through they knew the ballots would not be included in the official certified count unless a Gore campaign lawsuit succeeded in the Florida Supreme Court.

At no time after initial Florida count was completed, did media outlets announce that Bush had won Florida pending a recount and credit him with the electoral votes. At no time after the certified totals were completed, did media outlets announce that Bush had won the certified recount pending the overseas absentee ballots. Other than claiming that they have won, Bush representatives, including James Baker, did little to explain the details of the fraud perpetrated by the national news media outlets and nothing to expose VNS, which has a track record documented in this chapter of attempting to manipulate elections. On Friday, the Florida Supreme Court, issued a stay of the certification results against the Secretary of State despite the fact that their action was unsolicited by any party and therefore, an unconstitutional attempt to run the executive branch of the Florida state government and overturn Florida election law. On Monday, at the Supreme Court hearings, the lead Bush attorney, Michael Carvin, presented a relatively weak case for Bush despite having a position of strength clearly articulated by Joe Klock representing the Florida Secretary of State's office. In fact, the Carvin case was so weak that it appeared as though the Bush administration was complicit in creating and prolonging the election fiasco.

THE FLORIDA SUPREMES
MAKE UP THEIR OWN LAW

On Tuesday night, November 21, 2000 the Supreme Court of Florida entered the fray again by issuing one of the most historic decisions of any state Supreme Court in America. The Court ordered that the Florida Secretary of State must accept amended returns after the deadline imposed by Florida law. The order conflicted with federal law, was in direct contradiction with Florida law and even overturned two Florida Court rulings. The state and federal laws are specifically intended to avoid voter fraud.

To issue such an order the court first had to intercede in pending cases to take jurisdiction away from the First District Court of Appeal. The appeals by the Gore campaign and the Volusia County Canvassing Board challenged the Secretary of State's discretion as to whether or not to accept amended returns from the counties after the 7-day deadline from the November 7 election date as imposed by Florida law.

Judge, Terry Lewis, the Democrat appointee for the Second Judicial Circuit Court in Leon County, upheld the discretion of Secretary of State, Katherine Harris, according to Florida law. U.S. District Court judge, Donald Middlebrooks, confirmed much of the Lewis decision in a related court case. The Lewis order is quite clear as shown by the following excerpts:

"...the statute by its plain meaning, mandates the filing of returns from the canvassing boards by 5:00 PM on November 14, 2000". "It is then up to the Secretary of State, as the Chief Election Officer to determine whether any such corrective or supplemental returns filed after 5:00 PM are to be ignored." "... the Secretary of State has the authority to exercise her discretion in reviewing that decision, considering all attendant facts and circumstances and decide whether to include or to ignore the late filed returns in certifying the election results and declaring the winner". The Court specifically ruled that it cannot "rewrite the Statue".

The first issue of discretion involved the legality of performing manual recounts. The Secretary of State contended that manual recounts authorized by Florida Statute section 102.166, are limited to "errors in vote tabulation". The county canvassing boards found no such errors. Therefore, the

Supreme Court had to rule that errors in vote tabulation include actions that require interpreting the intent of the voter, which is actually a felony under federal election law, if done by anyone other than a canvassing board member.

The filing deadline and discretion is clearly articulated in the Florida Statutes for both the Secretary of State and the state Elections Canvassing Commission. Section 102.111 addresses the Elections Canvassing Commission and states: "If the county returns are not received by the Department of State by 5 PM of the seventh day following an election, all missing counties shall be ignored." Section 102.112 addresses the Secretary of State as follows: "If the returns are not received by the department by the time specified, such returns may be ignored".

Although these statutes address different organizations and clearly intend to exclude late returns, the Florida Supreme Court claimed that these two statutes conflict and then issued an order in direct contradiction with these laws. Their order stated: "The Secretary of State and the Elections Canvassing Commission shall accept any such amended certifications..." Their order also conflicts with federal law, specifically 3 USC Section 7, that does not allow a court to change election vote tabulation rules while an election still in progress.

The court imposed an artificial deadline for the remaining 3 counties to provide their returns by 5 PM on November 26, 2000. The unprecedented Supreme Court order was handed down at the unusual time of 9:30 PM EST, too late to air on the evening news even on the West Coast. Television network reporting on the illegality of the court order was almost totally bypassed when Vice President elect Dick Cheney made a remarkably timed visit to the hospital, later that same night. Network news on the following morning focused almost exclusively on the Cheney hospital visit, thus allowing the Supreme Court Justices to avoid scrutiny in making perhaps, the most historically corrupted state Supreme Court ruling in American history.

THE ELECTION CONTEST AND
THE SUPREMES STRIKE AGAIN

On November 27, the Gore/Lieberman campaign contested the certified Florida election results that showed the Bush/Cheney ticket winning by 537 votes. The contest was heard in the Leon County Second Judicial District Court of Judge Sanders Sauls. The contest trial put Gore in the incredible position of not only opposing the Bush campaign and the Florida Secretary of State, but also the Democrat controlled canvassing boards of Palm Beach and Miami-Dade counties, as well as numerous Florida citizens who filed their own briefs contending that selective manual recounts of certain ballots conflicted with their right of equal protection under the Constitution. Specifically, the Gore campaign wanted the court to:

- Include 215 net votes for Gore from a partial manual recount of machine rejected votes in Palm Beach county.
- Include 168 net votes for Gore from a partial manual recount of machine rejected in Miami-Dade county.
- Overturn a Nassau County decision to certify its election night results instead of an incomplete machine recount.
- Challenge the method used by Palm Beach county to identify voter intent for machine rejected in its manual recount.
- Challenge the decision by Miami-Dade county not to review 9,000 machine rejected votes due to time constraints.

Sauls ruled on December 4, 2000 that the Gore campaign did not meet the required burden of proof. Specifically, he stated that:

- Sec. 102.168 requires a contestant to prove that new statewide election results would be different than the certified count.
- Voter error cannot support or effect any recounting in Dade County without the evidence required by Section 102.168.
- There is no authority under Florida law to certify incomplete manual recounts or returns submitted past the deadline.
- Palm Beach county properly exercised its discretion in compliance with a previous Circuit Court order and a Florida Attorney General opinion.

- Nassau county acted within the proper exercise of its discretion upon adequate and reasonable public notice.
- Sec 102.168 requires the plaintiff to seek as a remedy, a review and recount of all ballots and all counties in the state with respect to the particular irregularities or inaccuracies alleged to have occurred.

The Gore campaign appealed to the First District Court of Appeal, which certified it to the Florida Supreme Court, thus setting the stage for another landmark historic decision. The Supreme Court ruled 4-3 on December 8, 2000 that the "trial court erred as a matter of law" in regards to manually recounting the 9,000 machine rejected ballots in Miami-Dade. They stated that these 9,000 rejected ballots met the definition of legal votes that must be counted according to Section 102.168.

To justify their ruling they used Sec. 101.5614, which states: "no vote shall be declared invalid or void if there is a clear indication of the intent of the voter as determined by the canvassing board". A stinging dissent from Chief Justice Wells pointed out that "Section 101.5614 (5) however, is a statute that authorizes the creation of a duplicate ballot". Specifically, the statue applies where a ballot card "is damaged or defective so that it cannot properly be counted by the automatic tabulating equipment".

In his dissent of the Florida Supreme Court ruling that also advocated a new statewide recount, Wells summarized: "My succinct conclusion is that the majority's decision to return this case to the circuit court for a count of the undervotes from either Miami-Dade county or all counties has no foundation in Florida law as it existed on November 7, 2000, or at any time until the issuance of this opinion".

In a near equally remarkable portion of the ruling, the Florida Supreme Court reinstated the 215 and 168 net votes for Al Gore in Palm Beach and Miami-Dade counties, respectively. This was in defiance of a U.S. Supreme Court order to vacate the Florida Supreme Court decision that extended the certification deadline for the selective manual recounts to November 26 in violation of Florida Statues. That previous Florida Supreme Court decision violated three Florida statues, two lower court decisions, federal election law and the U.S. Constitution. The U.S. Supreme Court unanimously stated "that there is considerable uncertainty as to the precise grounds for the decision" and that "The judgment of the Supreme Court of Florida is vacated and the case is remanded for further proceedings not inconsistent with this opinion". This clear decision on December 4, 2000 was portrayed by the national news media as though the U.S. Supreme Court only sent the case back to the Florida Supreme Court to "clarify" its "incomplete" opinion.

A SUPREME BATTLE

On December 9, 2000, the U.S. Supreme Court once again stepped in to issue a stay of further manual recounts. On December 12, 2000, they ruled that Article II, Sec. 1 of the U.S. Constitution provides that elector procedures "Having once granted the right to vote on equal terms, the state may not by later arbitrary and disparate treatment, value one person's vote over that of another" and that "The want of those rules here has led to an unequal evaluation of ballots".

Since Florida code Sec. 97.012 authorizes discretion to the Secretary Of State and Sec. 102.668 authorizes discretion to the state circuit court, the U.S Supreme Court stated that: "the general coherence of legislative scheme may not be altered by Judicial interpretation so as to change the statutorily provided apportionment of responsibility among these various bodies". The justices also concluded that "Florida statutory law cannot reasonably be thought to require the counting of improperly marked ballots" because each precinct provides instruction on how to properly cast a vote, each polling place contains a working model of the voting machine it uses, each voting booth contains a sample ballot and in precincts using punch card ballots, voters are instructed to punch out the ballot cleanly and clearly with no chips left hanging on the back of the card.

The U.S. Supreme Court issued strong conclusions such as "Because it is evident that any recount seeking to meet the Dec. 12 deadline will be unconstitutional, we reverse the judgment of the Supreme Court of Florida ordering a recount to proceed" and "the judgment of the Supreme Court of Florida is reversed and the case is remanded for further proceedings not inconsistent with this opinion". The national news media outlets generally used only that last phrase and rarely if ever, fully reported the firmness of the U.S. Supreme Court or its rational.

Justices Rehnquist, Thomas, Scalia, O'Connor and Kennedy formed the base of the 5-4 majority opinion. Justices Souter and Breyer admitted that Constitutional problems existed with the Florida Supreme Court decision but disagreed on the remedy. In dissent, Justice John Paul Stevens, with Justices Ruth Bader Ginsburg and Stephen Breyer joining, concluded that "The majority orders the termination of counting before all such votes have been tabulated" even though all votes were tabulated as "undervotes" (no hole punched for president) or "overvotes" (more than one punch) two separate times.

But the dissenters also made some enlightening observations about their perspectives on this case and the U.S. Constitution. They stated that the Florida Supreme Court can intercede because "The Constitution assigns to the states the primary responsibility for determining the manner of selecting presidential electors" and " Section 5, like Article II, assumes involvement of state Judiciary in interpreting state election laws and resolving disputes under those laws." They specifically ignored the clause in Article II that designates authority to the Legislature. It reads: "Each State shall appoint, in such manner as the Legislature thereof may direct, a number of electors, equal to the whole number of Senators and Representatives to which the State may be entitled in the Congress".

The dissenters helped to justify their opinion with this fascinating statement that may ultimately explain what is wrong with American government officials: "the interpretation of constitutional principles must not be too literal". Remarkably, they also concluded: "The federal questions that ultimately emerged in this case are not substantial". Stevens included in the dissent closing: "If we assume -as I do- that the members of that court and the judges who would have carried out its mandate are impartial, its decision does not raise a colorable federal question". Based on the previous track record of the Florida Supreme Court, this is obviously a false assumption.

U.S. Title 3 Section 5 states: "Laws enacted prior to the day fixed for appointment of electors... shall govern the counting of electoral votes". Appointments of the electors shall have been made at least six days prior to said time of meeting of the electors" (scheduled for Dec. 18). The Florida House acted on December 12 to ensure the electors but the Senate did not vote to provide Florida voters with the safe harbor even though they had a significant Republican majority. On December 13, after the U.S. Supreme Court vacated Florida Supreme Court orders for the second time, Al Gore conceded. If he had not, and any Florida electors were challenged, the case could have been forced into the U.S. Congress to resolve the presidency. The inaction of the Florida Senate once again illustrates the unwillingness of elected Republican officials to stand up for what they supposedly believe in, even if it could have cost them the Presidency.

THE REAL PALM BEACH COUNTY ELECTION FRAUD?

While much of the controversy about the Florida election focused on Palm Beach County, the wrong topics were promoted and discussed by the national news media. As the media focused on manual recounts and a confusing "butterfly" ballot, the real question that must be answered is whether or not voter fraud occurred on election night in that county. Robert Cook, a Marietta, Ga. Quality Assurance manager, nuclear engineer and software testing specialist who also has an MS in statistical quality control, provided the following significant evidence of ballot tampering:

- The national error rate of double-punching ballots is less than .5%, however, Palm Beach county had 19,120 double punched ballots out of 425,000, a number that is almost ten times the national average.
- Palm Beach County also had 15,000 double punched ballots in the 1996 presidential election even though a "butterfly ballot" was not used.
- In Palm Beach County, Al Gore gained at least 682 votes in a recount while the 63 Florida counties that previously filed their recounts reported a net difference of less than 30 votes

between various candidates, 50 of these were less than 8 votes.

- In Palm Beach County, the statistical error rate in favor of Al Gore, was 100-200 times that of all but two other Florida counties.
- In Palm Beach County, George W. Bush received less than 65% of the registered Republican vote (152,954 out of 231,626) while in all other Florida counties on the average, Bush received more votes than the number of registered Republican voters.
- In every Palm Beach precinct where Gore got more votes than there are registered Democrats, Bush received less than 60% of the registered Republican votes.
- Palm Beach County was the only one of 10 counties with over 100,000 votes for Al Gore where Gore drew more votes than Senator elect Nelson.

The most rational explanation that would account for these anomalies is that about 17,000 non-Gore punched ballots were invalidated with a punch for Al Gore after the voters submitted them. This could be accomplished simply by having the right person with the right tools in the right place at the right time for about a half an hour. Even more disturbing is a revelation that the national Democrat party hired a Texas telemarketing firm to call voters in Palm Beach County late Tuesday night and prompt them to complain that they were confused about the ballot. The calls indicate that Democrat party operatives knew about the double-punching before the Palm Beach results were released.

Despite the implications, the Bush campaign did not mention any of this detailed evidence of potential voter fraud. Their public comments were limited to vague references that the process is "flawed" and their testimony before the Florida Supreme Court did not mention any of these details nor how they could impact the current certified returns or manual recounts.

CONGRESS AND THE MEDIA HOLD A VALENTINES DAY LOVE FEST

On Valentine's Day, Wednesday, February, 14, 2001, A House Telecommunications, Trade and Consumer Protection Subcommittee, chaired by Billy Tauzin (R-La.), heard testimony from network news executives who tried to explain their Election Night 2000 coverage fiasco. On that historic night, not only was former Vice President Al Gore falsely projected to win Florida before all state polls closed, but a slew of other states were immediately projected for Gore as polls closed while projections for states where George W. Bush won by similar margins, were delayed for hours.

Testifying before the committee were ABC President, David Westin, CBS President, Andrew Hayward, NBC President, Andrew Lack, CNN CEO, Tom Johnson, Fox News President, Roger AIles, Associated Press CEO, Louis Boccardi, new Voter News Service (VNS) Executive Director, Ted Saviglio and VNS Editorial Director, Murray Edelman. They admitted that all of these major news networks receive election data (and prospective projections) from VNS, the New York based consortium that the networks co-own. All pointed toward VNS for releasing erroneous data and all except Ailes stated that their coverage had "mistakes". Their solution was to change their procedures and spend more resources on fixing VNS.

But missing from the hearings was any probe into the deliberate attempt by VNS to manipulate the election results. The hearing was successfully diverted to topics like exit polling and uniform poll closings. No Congressman, including Tauzin, seriously challenged VNS about the evidence that Tauzin previously presented on CNN's Spin Room and other talk shows when he initially called for the investigation. That real evidence indicates:

- VNS falsely projected that Al Gore would win Florida at 7:40 PM before any Florida county results had been announced, before western Florida polls had closed and in defiance of a request by Florida Secretary of State not to prematurely project the state while polls were open.
- VNS prematurely projected all closely contested states for Al Gore including New Mexico, Wisconsin, Iowa and later, even Oregon, although the winner could not be assured until absentee ballots were counted a week later.
- VNS projected all 4 states that Al Gore won with a victory margin of 6-14% immediately when their polls closed but none of the 9 states that George W. Bush won with the same margin were projected when their polls closed.

- VNS time of projection from poll closing on states with 6-
  14% victory margins were instantaneous for Al Gore but
  over 2 hours per state for George W. Bush.

The following table illustrates some nationwide aberrations
of VNS projections based on CNN projection times compiled
by Congressman Tauzin:

STATE	BUSH%	GORE%	WINNING%		POLL CLOSE	PROJECT TIME	MINUTE WAIT
Arizona	51	45	Bush	6	9:00pm	11:51pm	171
Arkansas	52	46	Bush	6	6:30pm	12:15am	345
West Virginia	52	46	Bush	6	7:30pm	10:46pm	196
Missouri	54	47	Bush	7	8:00pm	10:15pm	135
Virginia	52	45	Bush	7	7:00pm	7:33pm	33
Louisiana	53	45	Bush	8	9:00pm	9:21pm	21
Colorado	51	42	Bush	9	9:00pm	11:00pm	120
Vermont	41	51	Gore	10	7:00pm	7:00pm	0
California	42	54	Gore	12	11:00pm	11:00pm	0
Georgia	55	43	Bush	12	7:00pm	7:59pm	59
Illinois	43	55	Gore	12	8:00pm	8:00pm	0
Delaware	42	55	Gore	13	8:00pm	8:00pm	0
North Carolina	56	43	Bush	13	7:30pm	8:09pm	39

The odds that all of these medium range margin projections
could be skewed in a single direction by accident are mathematically implausible. Therefore, these knowledgeable news
executives must have lied under oath when they testified that
their election coverage simply had some "mistakes". Of particular interest is the statement of Fox News Chairman, Ailes,
who was irritated at being sworn in and claimed "We will tell
the truth whether we are under oath or not".

Despite the evidence, subcommittee investigators quickly determined that there was no deliberate attempt to manipulate the
presentation of election results. Therefore, the results of this
Republican led investigation appear to similar to those during impeachment when Republican leaders avoided evidence of treason,
bribery, tyranny and fascism against former President Clinton and
instead turned the impeachment into a sex soap opera.

The Year 2000 Presidential election is not the first election
that VNS has attempted to manipulate. VNS was much more
successful in the 1996 Iowa Republican primary. Dubuque
county election monitors, Jim Condit Jr. and Chris Schaper,
found that their totals reported to Voter News Service were
changed dramatically by the service before being reported to
the national media. In that case, Pat Buchanan, who had an
overwhelming 42% certified vote share in the nine candidate
race ended up second to Bob Dole in Iowa by a margin of 26%

to 23% after VNS subtracted many of Buchanan's votes and distributed them to other candidates. VNS never produced final corrected totals and their unofficial totals became the official totals since no other government organization is charged with tabulating and certifying cross-county election results.

THE ULTIMATE VOTING SCANDAL

During the recount fiasco that was primarily generated by the Florida Supreme Court, news media outlets saturated the airwaves for months with many hours of coverage on the air showing election workers arguing about already defined procedures or holding up paper ballots while looking for dangling or indented chad. Knowing that the national news media always operates with a political agenda, the question is what was their agenda this time. I believe that the national news media overemphasized this coverage to focus attention on a need for electronic voting machines that will ultimately give them more precise control of election results.

News media voting result control and vote count corruption by candidates and election workers as documented in Chapter 11 and the book *Votescam* by Ken and Jim Collier, are not new. In 1964, Ron Keller and William "Joe" Cooper, a former assistant to New Orleans District Attorney, Jim Garrison, demonstrated for many television network crews how to rig votes. They showed how initial vote counts could be preset without detection in the widely used Shoup voting machines, whose inventor was indicted on vote fraud charges in New York and Pennsylvania. In a 1968 South Dakota Senate race, Dick Murphy consistently received 30-40% of manually cast votes but only about 10% of the electronic votes. Nationally known speaker, Devvy Kidd, who experienced potential vote fraud in her California races during the 1990s, discovered that the suspicious voting results were always skewed in favor of candidates who support global policies such as NAFTA and GAAT. She also determined that the ABC poll results accidentally posted BEFORE the 1996 elections were miraculously accurate to roughly .1%.

In addition to the previously mentioned VNS initiated voting distortions of the 1996 Iowa Republican primary, Dan

Gutenkauf reported other types of voter fraud in the 1996 Arizona Republican primary. There 60,000 duplicate voter ID cards were issued, the ID's were not checked at any precinct, voters could vote in any precinct and the identity of personnel used for verification was never disclosed. These anomalies resulted in a situation similar to Iowa where Bob Dole edged Pat Buchanan in another questionable state primary. While Buchanan has made some general statements regarding his experiences with these fraudulent elections he has never specifically emphasized any of the details. However, his 2000 presidential campaign manager and former Vice Presidential candidate, Pat Choate, called the 1996 Republican primary ' one of the most corrupt elections in American history".

Simple steps could have been taken to prevent many of these anomalies and ensure free and clean elections. For example:

- Votes should be cast by paper ballot only to reduce risk of electronic rigging.
- Votes should be counted and posted at the precinct where they are taken to reduce risk of tampering while in transport.
- Vote counts should always be open to the public to prevent the repeated occurrences of fraud by election workers.

When normal procedures are so severely violated, serious consideration must be given to the question of whether it is accidental or intentional.

As a computer consultant with over 30 years of experience, I know that electronic voting machines can easily be programmed to distort voting results and still go undetected in pre-election test sampling. For example, voting machines can be programmed to:

- Distort vote counting after a certain number of ballots are counted.
- Distort vote counting on certain days.
- Distort vote counting after a certain combination of candidates are selected by a vote.
- Distort vote counting after receiving a signal via their modems that are used to communicate results.
- Electronically transfer results to a central machine that distorts vote counting.

Nearly all of the electronic voting machine vendors consider their counting software to be proprietary and will not agree to procedures that make the software available for verification at the time it is used. Furthermore, nearly all plan to transfer their results via modem to a central computer controlled by an organization such as VNS for final tabulation. Therefore, the outcome of future elections will likely be determined by unverifiable software provided through a very small number of election machine vendors with final tabulations under the control of the national news media as they have been in key cases during the past. This scenario is quickly becoming a reality without the American people even realizing what is happening.

Voting machine vendors and elections division procurement officials could prevent the types of distortions or fraud previously described by implementing basic external audit trail procedures. For example, corruptible elections could be prevented with the following four steps:

- The voting machine should assign a unique sequentially generated number to each electronically recorded ballot;
- As a ballot is completed, the number can be displayed or printed for voters to write the number down, memorize it or take a receipt showing the number with them;
- When polls close, the machines should print the vote details of all ballots ordered by the unique ballot identification number and totaled for public posting at the precinct;
- After poll workers publicly post precinct detail and totals, voters could match their number against the detail to verify the machine correctly recorded the vote.

In this manner, the identity of the voter is still private, no one knows how any individual voted and the voter has the assurance the vote was recorded correctly. But despite its simplicity, no such external audit trail or equivalent procedure exists in FEC voting system standards, Congressional bills or the majority of electronic voting machines on the market. The closest language currently offered is in Senate bill, S565, Title III, Section 301, Paragraph A4 which states: "The voting system shall produce a record with an audit capacity for each ballot cast." At the time of this writing, only one machine, called Vote Trakker, by Avante International Technology Inc. in

Princeton Junction, New Jersey has just such an audit trail but it has not been certified by the FEC.

Regardless of the machine, vendor or particular audit trail, the principal of a verifiable vote count must be upheld for each citizen if America is to have legitimate, open, free and verifiable elections in the future. While most readers expect almost every citizen and election official would concur they want verifiable voting, states are planning and implementing unverifiable voting machines nationwide, thanks to the anticipation of a $5,400 per precinct allotment of new Congressional funding generated after the Election 2000 fiasco.

On Friday December 13, 2001, while America focused on a provably phony videotape of Osama Bin Laden released by the Pentagon, the U.S. House passed H.R. 3295 to allocate millions of dollars for just such a setup. The Republican led House voted to spend the money despite the fact that the new war on terror had left no budget for it. Their actions represent a giant step to negate the most precious right of the American citizens, the right to vote. A quote attributed to Joseph Stalin is most appropriate for the new American age of electronic voting: "Those who cast the votes control nothing. Those who count the votes control everything".

REFERENCES

Palm Beach County Canvassing Board, Petitioner, vs. Katherine Harris, atc., et al., Respondents, Supreme Court of Florida, Nos. SC00-2346, SC00-2348, SC00-2349

Albert Gore and Joesph Lieberman, Appellants vs. Katherine Harris as Secretary, etc., et al., Supreme Court of Florida, No. SC00-2431, December 8, 2000

Clay Roberts, Statement of the Division of Elections, Florida Division of Elections, November 7, 2000

Statement of Katherine Harris, Secretary of State, Florida Division of Elections, November 13, 2000

James and Kenneth Collier, Votescam, Victoria House Press Robert Cook, Explicit statistical evidence of massive ballot tampering in Palm Beach, Fl, Regan Information Interchange November 9, 2000

Michael Ruppert, From the Wilderness Newsletter and www.copvcia.com (numerous articles about Richard Armitage)

Mara Leveritt, Asa and Me, Arkansas Times 05/25/01

Paul Sperry, Chao has biz ties to Lippo, www.worldnetdaily.com January 17, 2001

Paul Sperry, Elaine Chao's ties to Chinese Leader, world netdaily.com January 13, 2001

Paul Sperry, McConnell's Belated Dirty-Money Discovery, January 26, 2001

Bush Invokes Executive Privilege, The New American Magazine, October 8, 2001

Hastert advisor's past is an issue, K.C. Star (from the Washington Post) July 16, 2000

Matt McLaughlin, Nancy Dorn nominated to replace O'Keefe at OMB, Government Computer News December 28, 2001

2002 State of the Union Report - Bush Administration Ethics Enforcement, Judicial Watch, February 1, 2002

www.worldnetdaily.com, various other articles published from November 2000 through January, 2001

www.newsmax.com, various other articles published from November 2000 through January, 2001

www.votescam.com, various articles

CHAPTER FOURTEEN
THE ULTIMATE BETRAYAL

SEPTEMBER 11, 2001

On the morning of September 11, 2001 I arrived at work early. My co-worker, Heather, arrived shortly after I did and asked me if I had looked up to see what was in the sky. I told her no and she suggested I take a minute and go outside to look. I walked out, glanced up into the skies of South Kansas City, Kansas and noticed an absolutely perfect circle of jet exhaust that formed another one in a series of more unusual "chemtrails". I considered this and some of the other sightings, such as "knitting" patterns and concluded these could not be simple exhausts of jet planes traveling in one direction. While many potential "chemtrail" sightings are quickly written off as simple jet exhaust, this one had a clear and deliberate pattern that could not be discredited quite so quickly. In fact, it was so unique that a photograph of it appeared in the Kansas City Star the next day. But in another classic case of media deception, the photo contained a completely false caption. The caption stated the exhaust trail indicated a "U-turn" "after" the FAA had recalled planes. Actually it was a perfect circle but not from a commercial flight, it had been there before any planes were recalled.

A few minutes later, I was back inside the building and concentrating on work again when our department received an E-mail alert from another co-worker. He reported a plane had crashed into the north World Trade Center tower and that pictures from TV were almost unbelievable. We assumed this was an accident but as I walked into the lobby to see it on TV, another plane crashed into the south World Trade Center tower. We later watched in amazement, as another report indicated a third plane had struck the Pentagon and a fourth went down in Pennsylvania after being hijacked and diverted towards Washington.

During that time, I saw a live report near the scene at New York City with one of the World Trade Center (WTC) survivors who insisted there was an explosion near the base of one tower after a plane had struck it. Much later I learned Louie Cacchioli, a noble 51-year-old firefighter who nearly died fighting the blaze, corroborated for *People* magazine the survivor's account by confirming that the group of firefighters he was with, also heard an explosion after the second plane crash. They believed there were bombs set in the building. At about 5:20 pm, the 44-story Seven World Trade Center building collapsed with a puff of smoke in a manner that is still a mystery to structural engineers and fire engineers.

Subsequent reports released before the end of the month, revealed four planes had been hijacked. American Flight 11 from Boston to Los Angeles was diverted into the north World Trade Center tower by suspected hijackers, Mohammed Atta, Qail Alshehri, Waleed Alshehri, Satam Al Suqami and Abdulaziz Aloman; United Flight 175 from Boston to Los Angeles was diverted into the south World Trade Center tower by suspected hijackers Marwan Al-Shehhi, Mohand Alshehri, Ahmed Alghamdi, Hamza Alghamdi and Fayez Rashid Ahmed Hassan Al Qadi Banihammad. American Flight 77 from Washington Dulles to Los Angeles was diverted into the Pentagon by suspected hijackers Hani Hanjour, Salern Alhazmi, Nawaf Alhazmi, Majed Moqed and Khalid Almihdhar. United Flight 93 from Newark to San Fransisco, which crashed southeast of Pittsburgh, was diverted by suspected hijackers Ziad Samir Jarrah, Saeed Alghamdi, Ahmed Alnami and Ahmed Ibrahim Ak Al Haznawi. About 14 of the 19 hijackers were nationals of Saudi Arabia. The Saudi government stated later that the FBI had misidentified 6 or 7 of them, some who are still alive and were victims of stolen passports or other forged documentation produced by the real hijackers.

Thousands of innocent Americans lost their lives in these coordinated attacks, which certainly could be considered acts of war much like the December 7, 1941 bombing of Pearl Harbor where approximately 2,800 Americans died. Most of the horrific 9/11 deaths, including those of many brave New York police, fire and rescue workers occurred at the WTC. News reporting of these tragic deaths was handled exactly opposite, as most previous catastrophic events where deaths are conservatively reported with unrealistically low preliminary counts. Many WTC news reports began with estimates such as 15,000 later decreasing to 10,000 and then 7,500. "Official" estimates of confirmed deaths went from 5,000 to 3,400 to 3,000 and then to 2,600 where the count stands at the time of this writing. Although some feeble references have been made to duplicate identity lists, no rational explanation has ever been given by New York authorities as to how official confirmed death counts could actually decrease so dramatically.

Like the death toll, reporting of potential suspects behind the attack was also handled in the exact opposite manner as most previous types of terror attacks. In most cases, news government officials and media outlets are painfully slow to identify official responsibility in such a horrific event for fear of falsely implicating an innocent individual and facing numerous lawsuits and perpetual ridicule. But reporting on the 9/11 attack suspects was handled differently from the norm. Before many dedicated American firefighters could put the fires out at the Pentagon, numerous government officials and the controlled national news media had implicated Osama bin Laden as the "mastermind" and main culprit behind the plane hijacking attacks. Immediately, I knew something was seriously rotten since I had briefly researched his connections as part of the original version of my book. I knew bin Laden was a long time CIA operative who was working with multiple Western intelligence sources as recently as 1999.

Bin Laden, a wealthy Saudi Arabian, was reported to be living in Afghanistan and in control of the Al Qaeda terrorist network based there. Taliban leaders who controlled 90% of the Afghan territory were portrayed as highly oppressive religious extremists harboring bin Laden and the terrorists. Thus, the stage was quickly set to invade Afghanistan in response to the WTC attacks and to prevent future terrorist attacks throughout the world. The operation, originally named "Infinite Justice", was later renamed to the more palatable "Enduring Freedom", apparently after someone at DOD recognized the difference between God and government.

General Colin Powell quickly traveled to Pakistan to obtain support from President Musharraf and Afghan warlord groups known as the Northern Alliance, who controlled the remaining 10% of Afghan territory. On Sunday, October 07, 2001, U.S. and British led forces began a bombing campaign and covert force deployment against Afghanistan and their Taliban leadership in retribution for the WTC attacks. Although Congress never declared war, President George W. Bush stated that this was only the first step in a new "War on Terror" that will be conducted against all nations who harbor terrorists.

The horrific nature of the WTC and Pentagon attacks brought a new, remarkable spirit upon the American people. They provided overwhelming support for victims of the attacks through letters, donations and many different types of remembrances. The citizens also adopted a new sense of patriotism by displaying flags and bumper stickers and other shows of support for the president's new war on terror. But there are many disturbing discrepancies between suppressed facts of these events and what we have been told by the national news media. Based on these discrepancies, I have identified the following 10 myths that most Americans think are true about the 9/11 attacks and the ensuing war on terror.

Myth 1: Osama bin Laden is a major enemy of the United States

The national news media portrayed Osama bin Laden as Public Enemy No. 1 almost hourly after the 9/11 attacks, primarily because of his previous antagonistic comments towards the U.S. However, this alleged enemy of the United States has a 20-year working relationship as a covert operative for our own Central Intelligence Agency (CIA). Shortly after the 1979 Soviet invasion of Afghanistan, bin Laden left Saudi Arabia with some of his brothers to assist the Afghan Mujahideen guerillas in repelling the Soviets. At the same time, the CIA began pumping roughly three billion dollars into the Afghan battle against the Soviets through Pakistani Inter Services Intelligence and reportedly, the bin Laden family themselves. Funding was also obtained through opium poppy production as explained later in this chapter. By the time the successful resistance forced the Soviet Union to withdraw in 1989, the CIA had essentially established a religiously oriented power base for bin Laden.

Shortly after the 9/11 attacks, Senator Kerry of Massachusetts stated that during 1980, the Kerry Committee determined that bin Laden received funds from the notoriously corrupt Bank of Credit and Commerce (BCCI). BCCI was established by Clark Clifford, an ex-Wall Street banker who was the former Secretary of Defense for Lyndon Johnson. Clifford also established the National Security Act of 1947, which created the CIA and allowed it to operate above the law. Some of the funds were used to buy stinger missiles and establish the same system of tunnels that Al Qaeda terrorists subsequently hid in during the bombing of Afghanistan.

Although some in the national news media claimed that bin Laden turned on America after the bombing of Iraq in 1991, facts indicate the contrary. According to Yosef Bodansky, director of the U.S. Congress Task Force on Terrorism and Unconventional Warfare, bin Laden attended at least one secret Chechnyan war-planning summit with Iranian and Pakistani intelligence officers in Somalia during 1996. One of the leaders of that war, Al Khattab, was actually a Mujahideen commander who fought with bin Laden against the Soviets in Afghanistan. Both Khattab and Shamil Basayev, the other war leader, were trained and indoctrinated in the CIA sponsored Amir Muawia camp in Afghanistan. Basayev also received training in the Markaz-i-Dawar camp in Pakistan where he established relationships with the very highest Pakistani military and intelligence officers.

Before bin Laden was expelled from Sudan on May 18, 1996, Sudan offered to arrest him and hand him over to either Saudi Arabia or the U.S. government. Former National Security Advisor, Sandy Berger, confirmed that the Clinton administration declined the offer.

On August 7, 1998, American embassies in Kenya and Tanzania were bombed. To investigate the bombings, Bill Clinton established Accountability Review Boards chaired by Admiral William Crowe, a former chairman of the Joint Chiefs of Staff under Ronald Reagan, who was appointed by Bill Clinton as chairman of his Foreign Intelligence Advisory

Board. Crowe had just acquired a significant ownership stake in BioPort the notorious anthrax vaccine maker described in the next chapter.

But on August 20, 1998, before Crowe had even begin his new assignment, Bill Clinton retaliated by bombing bin Laden training camps in Afghanistan. He initiated the assault without consulting a single member of his joint chiefs of staff in planning the attack. The bombing was ordered three days after the President testified in his "lying about sex scandal" and attempted to redefine the word "is" to avoid perjury charges. Estimates contended that 70 cruise missiles were launched at a cost of 750,000 a piece and 35 individuals, who may or may not have been terrorists, were killed. The Al Queda terrorists were likely hiding in the same caves that were built with money from the CIA during the 1980s. The attack was so ineffective, ill conceived and excessively costly that it is difficult to believe Bill Clinton was seriously attempting to kill bin Laden or destroy the terrorists.

In 1999 Crowe eventually concluded bin Laden sponsored the attacks. But when the African embassy bombers were tried and convicted in 2001, as explained in the next chapter, no direct evidence was entered that tied bin Laden to the planning or execution of the bombing. After 9/11 a former CIA / FBI informant under arrest for terrorism suddenly claimed he planned the bombings with bin Laden.

In 1997-1998, according to Russia's Federal Security Service, "Chechnyan warlords started buying up real estate in Kosovo . . . through several real estate firms registered as a cover in Yugoslavia." Some of these same Chechnyan and Afghan warlords were connected to Osama bin Laden joined and supported the KLA through 1999 in a successful effort to destabilize and overthrow the Yugoslavian government.

In 1998, while bin Laden was accused of the bombings, State Department FBI and military intelligence reports all confirmed bin Laden was helping to arm, train and equip the Kosovo Liberation Army (KLA). In this operation, bin Laden worked not only with the CIA, but many other Western intelligence sources. *The London Telegraph, Jane's Defense Weekly*, a German PDS Party report and the *PBS News Hour* explained the KLA was also trained by British special force SAS units,

Canadian soldiers, the German Secret Service and specially selected American Vietnam war veterans, respectively. The German report also revealed that the CIA founded the KLA by funneling funds through European drug smuggling operations.

Le Figaro and *Radio France International* reported that the CIA / bin Laden relationship was still in place during July of 2001 when bin Laden entered the American hospital in Dubai where he received kidney treatments from Dr. Terry Callaway of the Urology Department, from July 4th to July 14th. There he was supposedly accompanied by his personal physician, bodyguards and an Algerian nurse. Visiting him during his stay, were family members and a CIA official who was immediately recalled to Washington on the 15th. Radio France later said the hospital denied the report although Dr. Callaway has repeatedly refused to comment on the visit. A CIA spokeswoman issued an intriguing denial despite all of the background information just stated about bin Laden and the CIA. She was quoted as saying: "For the record, you should know the CIA never employed, paid or maintained any relationship whatsoever with bin Laden". The denial was reminiscent of the one issued for Barry Seal, who Daniel Hopsicker eventually proved to be a long time CIA operative and member of Operation 40 as explained in Chapter 10.

Even if the *Le Figaro* report is completely false, the facts are clear that Osama bin Laden has become the latest in a list of American adversaries who have been empowered, nourished and protected by the CIA and other U.S. government agencies. Perhaps this explains why the CIA, which had extensive information about bin Laden and received authorization from Bill Clinton to assassinate him in 1998 did not do so. It would explain why the CIA and American military could gain control of the entire Afghan country where he allegedly lived, yet not be able to locate him. It would also explain why they cannot seem to locate any of his four wives or his several dozen children. The relationship between bin Laden and the CIA is so deep that even a report of his death could not be trusted.

Myth 2: Osama bin Laden masterminded the September 11 attacks

While Osama bin Laden was touted by the national news media almost hourly as the culprit behind the 9/11 attacks, tremendous pressure was generated on the federal government for evidence. Some of the people began to question how a religious figurehead living in a relatively primitive country could coordinate the most devastating attack in the history of the United States without state support. Nearly every expert on terrorism agrees that any spectacular terrorist activity must be sponsored by some government to achieve a political purpose. A typical assessment of the 9/11 attacks appeared in a *Barnes Review* editorial:

"This meticulously orchestrated attack does not have the characteristics of a normal terrorist operation. At present, there is no terrorist organization operating anywhere, that anyone knows of, that has the capability, sophistication and manpower to pull off such an operation, which was done evidently without the slightest difficulty and with hardly a hitch."

Nevertheless, the formal document touted to define the precise links between Osama bin Laden, Afghanistan and the 9/11 attacks was released on Thursday, October 4, 2001 by the British government, which was not even directly attacked. The 70-point document contained virtually no points linking Afghanistan to the attacks and only 9 points (61-70) that actually attempted to link bin Laden to them. Here is the original document text for these points:

61. Nineteen men have been identified as the hijackers from the passenger lists of the four planes hijacked on 11 September 2001. At least three of them have already been positively identified as associates of Al Qaeda. One has been identified as playing key roles in both the East African embassy attacks and the USS Cole attack. Investigations continue into the backgrounds of all the hijackers.

62. From intelligence sources, the following facts have been established subsequent to 11 September; for intelligence reasons, the names of associates, though known, are not given.

- In the run-up to 11 September, bin Laden was mounting a concerted propaganda campaign amongst like-minded groups of people including videos and documentation justifying attacks on Jewish and American targets; and claiming that those who died in the course of them were carrying out God's work.
- We have learned, subsequent to 11 September, that bin Laden himself asserted shortly before 11 September that he was preparing a major attack on America.
- In August and early September close associates of bin Laden were warned to return to Afghanistan from other parts of the world by 10 September.
- Immediately prior to 11 September some known associates of bin Laden were naming the date for action as on or around 11 September.
- Since 11 September we have learned that one of bin Laden's closest and most senior associates was responsible for the detailed planning of the attacks.
- There is evidence of a very specific nature relating to the guilt of bin Laden and his associates that is too sensitive to release.

63. Osama bin Laden remains in charge, and the mastermind, of Al Qaeda. In Al Qaeda, an operation on the scale of the 11 September attacks would have been approved by Osama bin Laden himself.

64. The modus operandi of 11 September was entirely consistent with previous attacks. Al Qaeda's record of atrocities is characterized by meticulous long term planning, a desire to inflict mass casualties, suicide bombers, and multiple simultaneous attacks.

65. The attacks of 11 September 2001 are entirely consistent with the scale and sophistication of the planning which went into the attacks on the East African Embassies and the USS Cole. No warnings were given for these three attacks, just as there was none on 11 September.

66. Al Qaeda operatives, in evidence given in the East African Embassy bomb trials, have described how the group spends years preparing for an attack. They conduct repeated surveillance, patiently gather materials, and identify and vet

operatives, who have the skills to participate in the attack and the willingness to die for their cause.

67. The operatives involved in the 11 September atrocities attended flight schools, used flight simulators to study the controls of larger aircraft and placed potential airports and routes under surveillance.

68. Al Qaeda's attacks are characterized by total disregard for innocent lives, including Muslims. In an interview after the East African bombings, Osama bin Laden insisted that the need to attack the United States excused the killing of other innocent civilians, Muslim and non-Muslim alike.

69. No other organization has both the motivation and the capability to carry out attacks like those of the 11 September only the Al Qaeda network under Osama bin Laden.

Of these 9 points, three are irrelevant to the 9/11 attacks (66, 67, 68), two are unverifiable opinions (61, 62), two are circumstantial evidence (63, 65) and two are false statements (64, 69). (The modus operandi of 11 September was unlike any other event in world history and other groups such as the Isreali Mossad have the motivation and the capability to carry out such an attack). Perhaps even more amazing is the fact that the document contained no new information and appears to be compiled and written as a general news article rather than a specific finding of facts.

Some American citizens believed at the time of the initial bombing that evidence could not be revealed because it would give away our intelligence capability for tracking communications. However, this argument collapsed when Mohammed Atef was killed early during the Afghan bombing. Military intelligence immediately announced that he was dead and explained how they had determined his location by tracking specific phone calls.

As an evidence summary, if you ask most Americans what is the precise connection between any of the hijackers and Osama bin Laden or Afghanistan, few, if any, could actually define one. That is because no such precise evidence link was established before Afghanistan was bombed just as the Arabs have repeatedly claimed. In spite of this, 200+ million Americans overwhelming favored the bombing campaign against Afghanistan. This is perhaps, the greatest modern day example of the classic psychological programming power possessed by our national news media.

Myth 3: Osama bin Laden admitted involvement in the 9/11 attacks

When pressed on the issue of evidence, most Americans justify their support for bombing Afghanistan because they believe Osama bin Laden confessed to the 9/11 attacks. However, all of the alleged confessions were produced by Western media outlets during the bombing campaign. The "confessions" conveniently supplement the previously released British document of evidence and help offset criticism about its lack of substance. Each of these "confessions" contradicts previous assertions by Osama bin Laden and they contain illogical or probable false content.

Contrary to western media reports, Osama bin Laden consistently denied involvement in the 9/11 attacks through Middle Eastern media sources such as *Al Jazeera* and the *Pakastani Unmat*. Actual quotes by bin Laden from these sources tell a completely different story than those from Western media. For example, these are his quotes from a September 28, 2000 *UnMat* interview suppressed in the United States until after the bombing started:

- "I have already said that I am not involved in the 11 September attacks in the United States. As a Muslim, I try my best to avoid telling a lie. I had no knowledge of these attacks, nor do I consider the killing of innocent women, children and other humans as an appreciable act. Islam strictly forbids causing harm to innocent women, children and other people. Such a practice is forbidden even in the course of a battle."
- "I have already said that we are against the American system, not against its people, whereas in these attacks, the common American people have been killed."
- "I have already said that we are not hostile to the United States. We are against the [U.S. Government] system, which makes other nations slaves of the United States, or forces them to mortgage their political and economic freedom."

His comments were further corroborated in other *Al Jazeera* interviews after the Afghan bombing campaign begun such as this one from November 4, 2001":

- "All the West, with rare exceptions, supports this oppressive campaign, for which no evidence links what happened in the United States to the people of Afghanistan, who have nothing to do with this matter, but the campaign continues annihilating villagers, women and children, without right."

Although *Al Jazeera* is portrayed by Western media sources as biased toward the Arab perspective, media monitors, when pressed, are forced to admit the *Al Jazeera* repeatedly covered President Bush, Secretary of Defense Rumsfield and other government officials uncut and unedited. The entire American public was denied similar access to bin Laden comments under the grounds that he may be sending coded messages to operatives. Ironically, Arabs had true freedom of the press, while Americans received suppressed news.

Our controlled news media began releasing confessions on Sunday, November 11, 2001. Then, the *London Telegraph* reported that an interview video with Pakastani journalist, Hamid Mir documented a confession that would be publicly released. Despite their claim, the video was never released. The report essentially claimed that the video showed bin Laden doing a little "internal" bragging about 9/11 to fellow terrorists. But rather than use his standard media outlet, *Al Jazeera*, he supposedly risked getting captured or killed during the bombing, by answering unfriendly questions from a Pakastani journalist who could have easily been set up with a homing device chip. The journalist claimed he met bin Laden after a couple of hours drive from Kabul, but later Western journalists reported bin Laden was actually near Tora Bora. News outlets released a picture of bin Laden wearing a camouflage jacket in a classic pose with a rifle between him and the journalist. He then gave the journalist a highly inflammatory video message that contradicted nearly everything he has ever said about 9/11 through Arab sources. The video never seen through normal Arab channels happened to fall into the hands of the *London Telegraph* and was distributed through the controlled AP wire. Of course, none of the hundreds of worldwide CIA media assets from Operation Mockingbird could be involved in producing or distributing the illogical content of this video.

The other major "confession" occurred on December 13, 2001 when American government officials released the highly touted "smoking gun" video of bin Laden discussing the 9/11 attacks with a cleric and a few other Muslims who cannot be positively identified. The video appears to show bin Laden visiting a cleric during the bombing campaign at the site where an American helicopter was damaged or downed on November 3. But the events are clearly recorded out of sequence since the entry of bin Laden appears near the end of the video and the latter part of his conversation appears near the beginning. A video tour of American helicopter parts and children outside singing are in the middle of the recording. The Pentagon offered no explanation as to who recovered the tape, why bin Laden would want to record such a tape, why the actual vehicles being used would be recorded or why the tape is recorded out of sequence

Comments on the video show prior knowledge by bin laden of the 9/11 attacks and contradict his denials of involvement released through Arab media outlets. But the video comes with a selective translation lacking in impartiality. For example, the word, '*figh*', is not translated into the English word, 'faith', and therefore, looks more like the inflammatory word, 'fight'. In other commentary, translators insert names like the World Trade Center, Pentagon, bin Laden and Atta in parenthesis when they are never actually spoken. Bin Laden spoke only for a few minutes in the hour-long video. Almost all of bin Laden's talk was barely audible except for a brief excerpt where he recites a poem. Although clear shots of bin Laden exist on the video, the national news media avoided any simple pictorial comparisons by electing to print very blurred images, such as those on the front cover of the December 14-16 weekend edition of the *USA Today*.

The "smoking gun" video showed that war must have been good to Osama bin Laden; it appeared he gained over 40 pounds during the previous month of battle in Afghanistan when the last *Al Jazeera* video was released. Apparently, the Al Qaeda network had stores of gourmet Middle Eastern food in the caves where bin Laden had supposedly hidden. Bin Laden, whose FBI profile lists him as 160 pounds, always appears as a frail looking man in all photographs and on videos, even as recently as one or two months previous to the "smoking gun" tape. But on the video released on December 13, 2001 and filmed sometime just after November 3, 2001 bin Laden appeared to weigh in at well over 200 pounds.

Even more interesting is that bin Laden, who on previous videos had a long neck, an oblong face, inverted cheeks, rounded eyebrows and thin hands with long fingers, suddenly possessed a short neck, square face, protruding cheeks, straight eyebrows and fat hands with short fingers. While one or two discrepancies could be explained, the extent of these discrepancies seriously illustrates the December 13, 2001 "smoking gun" video is NOT authentic.

Within a month, *Al Jazeera* released another bin Laden interview that was recorded sometime after the November 16 "errant" bombing of a mosque in Khost. This was roughly about three to four weeks after the "smoking gun" video was recorded. The interview showed bin Laden had been "restored" with his normal size and facial features. Despite the obvious impersonation, the "smoking gun" video was good enough for the British government, which updated its preposterous document of evidence with new information from the video.

Myth 4: Osama bin Laden and George W. Bush are isolated adversaries

Although the national news media outlets portray George W. Bush and Osama bin Laden as enemies, George W. Bush has taken steps to protect the bin Laden family, which has had several business dealings with the Bush family, including George W. Bush. Just days after the 9/11 attacks, bin Laden family members from Boston were allowed to fly out of the country on a special charter under the assumption that Osama is the "black sheep" of the bin Laden family, which itself, is above reproach.

On November 6, 2001, BBC reported the Bush administration has tightened restraints on the FBI which was prohibited from continuing its investigation into The World Assembly of Muslim Youth, (WAMY), whose U.S. president and treasurer was Abdullah Bin Laden. WAMY was not investigated even though Pakistan expelled WAMY operatives, India claimed that WAMY was funding an organization linked to bombings in Kashmir. The Philippines military accused WAMY of funding Muslim insurgency. The WAMY office in Leesburg, Virginia is just a few blocks away from where four of the suspected 9/11 hijackers are listed as once having lived.

On November 14, 2001, Chicago FBI Special Agent, Robert Wright, filed a 118 page complaint of retaliation with the Justice Department Office of Inspector General (IG) and the Office of Professional Responsibility (OPR). Wright, an 11-year FBI veteran, conducted a successful terrorist money-laundering investigation of a Saudi businessman, who he believed was linked to Osama bin Laden. At a May 30, 2002 press conference, with his lawyers, David Schippers and Judicial Watch, he stated his subsequent investigations were "thwarted" and "obstructed" to the extent they became an "intentional failure". Wright was also denied approval to fulfill an interview request from the *New York Times* and to release a manuscript for a book had written about some of his investigative work BEFORE 9/11. He was eventually demoted while another agent who was uncooperative in the investigation received no disciplinary action.

The book, *Osama bin Laden: the Forbidden Truth*, claims FBI Deputy Director, John O'Neill resigned in July 2001 for similar reasons. He was prevented by the U.S. State Department from fully investigating Al-Queda while the U.S. attempted to negotiate a national unity government for Afghanistan that was in the best interests of U.S. oil and Saudi Arabia. Dasquie is publisher of *Intelligence Online*. Brisard worked for French secret services and wrote the first Western report on the Al Qaeda in 1997.

Bush business dealings with the bin Laden's date to 1978 when Osama's oldest brother, Salem, hired James Bath, a close friend of George W. Bush, to make investments. Bath, who served with Bush in the Texas Air National Guard, acquired the Houston Gulf Airport for bin Laden and also invested $50,000 in George W. Bush's Arbusto Energy, which profited extraordinarily. Bush was fresh from Harvard Business School, the same University that received two million dollars in endowments from the bin Ladens for the study of Islamic law. Salem bin Laden died in a strange microlight plane crash in Texas during 1988.

In 1995, the bin Laden family also invested at least $2 million in the Carlyle Partners II fund, part of the Carlyle Group, whose senior advisor is former President, George H.W. Bush. The Carlyle Group was founded by David Rubenstein, a lawyer who worked as an aide in the Carter White House, Bill Conway, a former CFO at MCI and Dan D'Aniello a former finance executive for Marriott. The group now includes former U.S. Defense Secretary Frank Carlucci, former Secretary of State, Jim Baker and former White House budget director, Dick Darman. Bush, who makes speeches for the Carlyle Group at about $100,000 a piece, is a senior advisor for the Asian Partners fund. Baker is senior counselor and Carlucci is the group chairman. All have visited bin Laden family head-quarters in Jeddah, Saudi Arabia and Bush has met the bin Laden family twice apparently to secure investments for the Carlyle fund.

The Carlyle group has major interests in some of the largest U.S. defense and aerospace contractors like Lockheed Martin and General Dynamics. Its overall private equity stake equates to the nation's 14th leading defense contractor and it is listed in Pentagon documents as a Defense Department contractor.

The bin Ladens liquidated their publicly known Carlyle investments when they were exposed as benefiting from the terrorist acts for which Osama bin Laden was accused. The bin Ladens received roughly $1.3 million in completed investments and made a profit equating to nearly 40 per cent per year. The family's Saudi Binladin Group also received a contract to build replacement military barracks and airfields for U.S. troops after the 1996 Khobar Towers truck bombing in Dhahran, Saudi Arabia, that killed 19 U.S. servicemen. The approval was granted even though Osama bin Laden, was highly critical about U.S. presence in Saudi Arabia. The Saudi Binladin Group is a major contractor for the Saudi royal family and the U.S. government in the Middle East. Charles Freeman, president of the non-profit Middle East Policy Council, may have summed this irony up best when he remarked: "If there were ever any company closely connected to the U.S. and its presence in Saudi Arabia it's the Saudi BinLadin Group".

Like his father, George W. Bush also served the Carlyle group. In 1990, George W. Bush was appointed to the board of a Carlyle airline food business subsidiary called Caterair. He left that board in 1992 and became Governor of Texas where he was responsible for appointing several members of the board that controlled the investment of Texas teachers' pension funds. A few years later, the board decided to invest $100 million dollars of public money in the Carlyle Group.

Any doubt about the Carlyle Group influence in the U.S. Defense Department should be removed by documents uncovered by Judicial Watch through Freedom of Information Act requests. A February 15, 2001 letter, on Carlyle Group letterhead from former Defense Secretaries Frank Carlucci and William Perry, was sent directly to Defense Secretary Donald Rumsfield, who replied directly to them on April 3, 2001. The correspondence initiated by the Carlyle group appears to discuss a restructure of the Defense Department.

Myth 5: Osama bin Laden declared war against the United States

Books, videos and hundreds of media reports all touted as fact that Osama bin Laden literally declared war against the United States and its citizens, even to the extent of advocating mass slaughter of innocent Americans such as those attacked on 9/11/01. These claims were based on some of his comments that were highly antagonistic to America but exaggerated by the national news media. Many of the exaggerations stem from his use of the word "jihad". The Western media consistently misinterprets this word as "holy war". The Arabic word "jihad" is much more accurately interpreted as "struggle", which may or may not be violent. All holy wars are struggles but not all struggles are holy wars. A search of Arabic transcripts will reveal that "jihad" is frequently used in its non-violent context. The media interpretation of this word as "holy war" has incited hatred against Muslims and fanned flames of war by the West against Arabs.

Myth 6: The Taliban harbored terrorists in Afghanistan before September 11

President Bush, his cabinet members and nearly all of the national news media insisted the bombing and invasion of

Afghanistan was because the Taliban leadership harbored terrorists such as Osama bin Laden and the Al Qaeda network. On the contrary, Afghanistan and the Taliban have never been included on the State Department list of countries and leaders that sponsor terrorism before the 9/11/01.

Myth 7: Pakistani General Musharraf is an ally of freedom and opponent of terrorism

President Pervez Musharraf was a military general who instigated a coup in 1999 when Prime Minister Nawaz Sharif attempted to fire him. Musharraf declared himself president, suspended elections in Pakistan, and had Sharif jailed and subsequently exiled to Saudi Arabia. There are also reports of Sharif supporters being killed in the coup. Many from India suspect that Musharraf backed terrorist attacks in Kashmir and sent Pakastani troops into the Indian sector in 1998 although Sharif ordered a withdrawal and was attempting to reach diplomatic resolutions.

Since his takeover, Musharraf has refused to deliver on numerous promises to re-institute free elections in Pakistan. In 2002, he allowed the Pakistanis to vote on a "Yes" or "No" referendum for him only and that vote was completely controlled by the Musharraf government. Musharraf representatives claimed that he got a "Yes" vote on 97.7 percent of all votes cast and that the turnout was over 50%, far exceeding the 38% turnout for the 1997 parliamentary election. The Human Rights Commission of Pakistan and other Islamic groups quickly condemned the referendum as an obvious fraud.

Myth 8: Taliban prohibited women from work or education while requiring them to wear burquas

The national news media constantly reported that Taliban leaders were fundamental Muslim extremists who require Afghan women to wear burquas and prohibit them from working or receiving an education. First lady, Laura Bush, methodically echoed these assertions when she gave the first ever-presidential radio address by a first lady on November 17, 2001. But the few Americans fortunate enough to know an

Afghan who has no government connection may realize these allegations are not quite true.

The wearing of burquas and the intent for women to be mothers instead of workers are Muslim religious customs, not necessarily laws imposed by the Taliban. These cultural trends are followed more closely in smaller Afghan cities and tribes than in larger ones. The national news media cleverly avoided any video footage from larger cities such as Kabul that would have shown women still going to and from work without burquas. If the Taliban had immediately removed every Afghan woman from the workforce they would have significantly impacted an already depressed economy.

The Taliban did attempt to limit where women could work to certain sectors such as health care. But claims made by Laura Bush and the media can be easily disproved with a single event which she is probably aware of that happened in her state. In December of 1997, the Taliban visited Sugarland, Texas to talk about building an oil pipeline across Afghanistan with Unocal, who was competing for the job with an Argentinian firm named Bridas. Unocal commissioned the University of Nebraska to teach 140 Afghan men pipe construction in Kandahar and planned training for Afghan women in administrative skills. Training organizers confirmed the Taliban raised no objections to the women being trained to work. Women wearing burquas obviously could not perform most health care and pipeline administration jobs.

Leaders of many countries in the Central Asian region are very oppressive to women and the Taliban was no exception. Dayna Curry and Heather Mercer who were imprisoned in Afghanistan for spreading the gospel of Jesus Christ too aggressively, confirmed they saw instances of women being beaten in prison during the bombing. But Heather also stated that: "Considering the circumstances the Taliban always treated us well. There were Taliban who treated us as sisters". Even in jail they were allowed to pray and sing. Their captors also prepared special meals for them during the bombing campaign.

The Taliban received millions of dollars in U.S. government subsidies and was on the verge of becoming the U.S. recognized Afghan government after they gained control of 90% of Afghan territory. Although oppressive, they had gained trust with the Afghan people because they did not steal or loot from them. The U.S. still believed the Taliban offered stability as late as July 2001, while they were still negotiating for a united Afghan government. U.S. attitude changed when the Taliban refused overtures to build the Unocal oil pipeline described by Congressional testimony later in this chapter. The U.S. then threatened overt action in July 2001, according to Niaz Naik, the former foreign minister of Pakistan, as confirmed by Lee Coldren of the State Department. The news media portrayed this threat as being related to demanding the turnover of Osama bin Laden instead of building the oil pipeline. But the Clinton administration had already refused to accept bin Laden a few years earlier and George W. Bush certainly would want no part of prosecuting a family member of his father's business partners.

The Taliban clearly imposed strict or severe enforcement of laws that are archaic compared to those in western countries. However, in October 2001, Human Rights Watch actually cited the opposition Northern Alliance warlords for severe human rights violations that affect all Afghans, not only women. Unlike the Taliban, who imposed punishment for violations of law, the Northern Alliance warlords were cited for gross abuses that were politically motivated. The Human Rights Watch report cited "summary executions, burning of houses and looting, principally targeting ethnic Pashtuns and others suspected of supporting the Taliban". Warlords such as Uzbek general Rashid Dotsom and Tajik Ismail Khan actually fought on the side of the Soviet Communists. Dotsom, who is noted for committing atrocities even against his own soldiers, seized 89 tons of food from U.N. warehouses during his 2001 victory at Mazar-E-Sharif.

U.S. officials were aware these types of atrocities and looting would occur as the warlords overtook Kabul against U.S. will. Just hours before the warlords entered the city on November 13, missiles hit the *Al Jazeera* television studio as well as offices of the Associated Press and British Broadcasting Co. Lt. Col. David Kaplan was quoted as saying they "had no information that it was the *Al Jazeera* office" even though two of the strikes hit very selective targets in residential areas. The missiles prevented graphic images of warlord deeds from being transmitted around the world. Although the Taliban had retreated and there was no resistance, hundreds of Afghans were killed according to a Red Cross spokeswoman. The warlords looted banks and assaulted the *Al Jazeera* staff that was eventually saved by other Afghan tribesmen. Syrian *Al Jazeera* reporter, Tayseer Allouni, stated that he was in "deep psychological shock" from "scenes that, I'm sorry, I couldn't describe to anybody". The executive director of the National Defense Council Foundation, retired Major Andrew Messsing, summed up our Northern Alliance partners with this quote: "We always end up with the scum".

Myth 9: Muslims hate Americans and our freedom

To generate American support for the war, the national news media had to portray many Muslims as fundamental extremists who justify the 9/11 attacks religiously and hate America so much they want to kill even its innocent citizens. George W. Bush referred to them in several speeches as those who "hate freedom" and he exhorted Americans to "defend freedom" from those who hate us.

But while Muslims certainly have a different lifestyle and worship a different God than those of us who are Christians, their objections are not against American citizens but American foreign policy set by American leaders. Specifically, they object to the U.S. occupying forces in Middle East countries, our unconditional support for Israel regardless of circumstances and the sanctions the U.S. imposes against Iraq, which they claim are killing thousands of children monthly.

Whether Americans agree or disagree with these claims, it is important for every citizen to understand how a foreign viewpoint has been completely distorted to fulfill a domestic political agenda. One famous example was a frequently repeated TV clip showing Arab children cheering after they allegedly heard about the 9/11 attacks. This clip was eventually found to be contrived by an Israeli reporter who gave candy to young children so far removed from America that they could not have even known what the WTC was. I know of no broadcasted retraction by the many TV stations that ran the inciting clip.

Myth 10: The Taliban funded terrorism with drugs

Afghanistan has long produced 70% of the world's opium that is refined into heroin. This accounts for 80% of the gross domestic product of the country. The national news media has logically parlayed this into a by-product of the Taliban regime. But the Taliban is a strictly religious sect that prohibits the growth and use of drugs. They imposed a ban on cultivating opium poppies that carried a three-month jail sentence. That ban produced a 96% drop in opium production from a million pounds in 1999 to 40,600 pounds in 2001 according to the U.N. Drug Control Program. Afghanistan even accepted $43 million dollars from the U.S. government in conjunction with this eradication. The annual U.N. report on opium poppy production released in October of 2001 revealed that the majority of Afghan opium exports actually originated in the 10% of the territory controlled by the Northern Alliance.

WHAT S WRONG WITH THIS PICTURE?

The purpose of defining these myths is not to defend bin Laden. He and his family may actually be funding terror attacks but if so, are doing it as assigned roles, which have profited the Bushes, the bin Ladens and other former defense industry officials. These myths expose the following ridiculous scenario we have been told to believe:

- A bunch of guys living in caves in an incredibly remote mountainous portion of the world orchestrated the most vicious act of war ever against the United States without any state support;
- Osama bin Laden masterminded the 9/11 attacks even though the British government could not define any direct, concrete evidence against him after spending a month trying to do so;
- Osama bin Laden is a major enemy of the United States even though he is a long-term CIA operative who worked with several Western intelligence groups as recently as 1999;
- Osama bin Laden is an adversary of the President G.W. Bush even though his family and the president's family have had multiple business deals with each other;

- Osama bin Laden's family cannot be located even though he has four wives and dozens of children;
- Osama bin Laden has been living in Afghanistan even though the U.S. and British forces gained complete control of the country and could not find him;
- Within a month, Osama bin Laden gained 40 pounds and changed facial features for his appearance in the "smoking gun" video only to lose the weight and revert to his original features a month later;
- The Taliban and Afghanistan have been harboring terrorists even though they were never listed on the State Department list of countries and leaders that sponsor terrorism;
- Pakistan General Musharraf is our ally in freedom fighting even though he declared himself president, suspended elections in Pakistan, and had the former prime minister jailed and exiled;
- Northern Alliance warlords are our allies even though they control the Afghan territory where most opium is produced and they were cited by Human Rights Watch for gross human rights violations;

This list could go on and on but by now any reader should have a clue that there is something wrong with this picture. Most Americans feel they should be able to rely on the media to accurately report facts. They should also be able trust their own government officials to make the right decisions. But the performances of the media and government officials in major events have proven untrustworthy. The millions of Americans who believe that our own government agencies and media outlets would never deceive us about such a horrendous attack such as the one on 9/11 should consider these historical examples:

- In the 1993 attack on the Branch Davidians, three investigations concluded that the Branch Davidians set themselves on fire even through debris, videos, the FLIR tape and surviving witness testimony all corroborated the fire started immediately after a tank inserted internationally banned CS military tear gas into the church complex;

- In the 1995 Oklahoma City bombing case, the FBI and national news media protected other potential Middle Eastern accomplices who were involved with McVeigh and Nichols and were seen with McVeigh by numerous witnesses up to and including the day of the bombing;

- After the 1996 crash of TWA 800, the CIA released a simulation video that showed the front fuselage of TWA 800 climbing 3,200 feet after the plane exploded in mid air. The video was a ridiculous attempt to counter statements from over 100 witnesses who had seen a streak that looked like a missile traveling upwards toward the plane just before it exploded;

- In the 1993 death of Vince Foster, two independent counsels emphatically claimed the Vince Foster committed suicide by shooting himself in Fort Marcy park even though his fingerprints were not on the gun, there were no dirt or grass stains on his shoes, his clothing was covered with carpet fibers, there was almost no blood at the scene and the powder burns on both his forefingers were consistent with defending against armed attack;

- In the 1999 Yugoslavia bombing, the Clinton administration and news media falsely portrayed a civil war as genocide even though no such evidence was ever produced and almost all of the alleged "war crimes" against Slobodan Milosevic occurred after the bombing and were attributable to para-military groups that could not be controlled during the bombing;

- In May of 2000, dozens of INS and border patrol agents broke into the Gonzalez home in Miami to remove a terrified Elian Gonzalez at gunpoint. In the photographs of Elian being carried from the house, he clearly had a closely shaved haircut. But just hours later, former Clinton attorney, Greg Craig, released a photo of Elian's father holding a happy Elian, who suddenly had several weeks of hair growth. The national news media propagated the picture throughout the country while cleverly diverting attention from his "hair raising" experience;

- In 1963, government officials released a picture of the head of Lee Harvey Oswald pasted on the body of a man carrying a rifle and a pistol in a holster. The head showed a short, vertical mid-day nose shadow while the body cast a long, sharp angled shadow. That picture appeared everywhere in the media including the February 21, 1964 front cover of *Life* magazine with the title of "OSWALD ARMED FOR MURDER". The actual body more likely belonged to either CIA operative, Roscoe White or CIA agent, William Seymour. Anyone who has seen the Zapruder film can tell that the fatal bullet that killed John Kennedy came from the grassy knoll and everyone agrees, no matter what they believe about the Kennedy assassination, that Oswald was not on the grassy knoll. But that picture was used to temporarily dupe the American public into believing Oswald was a lone, crazed gunman.

Can any government agency or national news media outlet be trusted to tell the truth when we have been deceived about so many events. The propaganda from these events should make it clear to any informed American that our own government agencies and national news media have no more credibility than Osama bin Laden. Therefore, it is time for informed, rational thinking Americans to begin asking the following questions about the 9/11 attacks:

- Why did U.S. government officials begin a bombing campaign against Afghanistan and Osama bin Laden without being able to provide evidence of their involvement in the 9/11 attacks?

- Why did the national news media begin a major campaign to convince Americans Osama bin Laden was responsible for the attacks even before valiant firefighters could put the fires out on the first day?

- How could a single individual supposedly living in an incredibly remote mountainous portion of the world orchestrate the most vicious, multi-faceted surprise attack ever conducted on the most powerful country in the world without any state support?

- Why would a long time CIA operative, who worked with the CIA as recently as 1999, conduct terrorist attacks against the U.S. so closely before and after his involvement with the CIA?

- Why would multiple family members of America's foremost public enemy be involved in multiple business deals with the President of the United States and his father, the former President of the United States?

To answer these questions about the 9/11 attacks and the invasion of Afghanistan there must be a consistent understanding of unreported facts concerning several key points in modern American history. They are:

- The last American invasion of a foreign country, (Yugoslavia), as explained in Chapter 7;
- The last major act of terrorism committed on American soil, (Oklahoma City bombing) as explained Chapter 15;
- The history of CIA involvement in drug trafficking operations related to military conflicts as explained in Chapter 10;
- The history of Bush family involvement in profiteering from war as explained in Chapter 10;
- The deception imposed on us by the national news media as explained throughout this book.

Once these facts are clearly understood some more rational explanations can be discovered for the motivations of attacking Afghanistan.

THE OIL MOTIVATOR

Perhaps one of the real motives for the bombing and control of Afghanistan can be found in the second session of a February 12, 1998 hearing conducted by the Committee on International Relations. The hearing took place before the Subcommittee On Asia And The Pacific and was entitled *U.S. Interests In The Central Asian Republics.*

Hear is the opening statement from Mr. John J. Maresca, vice president of international relations, Unocal Corporation:

"Mr. Chairman, the Caspian region contains tremendous untapped hydrocarbon reserves. Just to give an idea of the scale, proven natural gas reserves equal more than 236 trillion cubic feet. The region's total oil reserves may well reach more than 60 billion barrels of oil. Some estimates are as high as 200 billion barrels. In 1995, the region was producing only 870,000 barrels per day. By 2010, western companies could increase production to about 4.5 million barrels a day, an increase of more than 500 percent in only 15 years. If this occurs, the region would represent about 5 percent of the world's total oil production.

One major problem has yet to be resolved: how to get the region's vast energy resources to the markets where they are needed. Central Asia is isolated.

The only other possible route is across Afghanistan, which has of course its own unique challenges. The country has been involved in bitter warfare for almost two decades, and is still divided by civil war. From the outset, we have made it clear that construction of the pipeline we have proposed across Afghanistan could not begin until a recognized government is in place that has the confidence of governments, lenders, and our company.

The Central Asia and Caspian region is blessed with abundant oil and gas that can enhance the lives of the region's residents, and provide energy for growth in both Europe and Asia. The impact of these resources on U.S. commercial interests and U.S. foreign policy is also significant. Without peaceful settlement of the conflicts in the region, cross-border oil and gas pipelines are not likely to be built. We urge the Administration and the Congress to give strong support to the U.N.-led peace process in Afghanistan. The U.S. Government should use its influence to help find solutions to all of the region's conflicts. U.S. assistance in developing these new economies will be crucial to business success."

Mr. Maresca further stressed the need for a single Afghan government recognized by other governments, lenders, and his company during questioning by Congressman Doug Bereuter of Nevada:

Mr. BEREUTER: Mr. Maresca, if I could just interrupt here. Why wouldn't you have the situation whereby whoever is in power drawing resources from that pipeline would find that their adversaries would decide to damage their resource base and stop the flow?

Mr. MARESCA: It's not going to be built until there is a single Afghan Government. That's the simple answer. We would not want to be in the situation where we became the target of the other faction. In any case, because of the financing situation, credits are not going to be available until there is a recognized government of Afghanistan.

His testimony and answers produced the following intriguing exchange when Congressman Dana Rohrabacher followed during his questioning period:

Mr. ROHRABACHER: I am reminded of a joke where God is asked when peace will come to the Middle East. He says, "not in my lifetime." I am afraid that this may well be true of Afghanistan as well. In fact, I am more hopeful right now, having just returned from one trip to the Middle East and another trip to Central Asia that there is a greater chance for peace between Israel and its neighbors than there is for peace in Afghanistan. And I know Afghanistan probably better than anyone else in the Congress. I hate to tell you that.

But let me ask a few questions. So there will be no pipeline until there is an internationally recognized government and a government that is recognized by the people of Afghanistan too, I would imagine that you wanted to put that caveat on it. Right? It's not just internationally recognized, but it has to be accepted by the people of the country. Right?

Mr. MARESCA: It depends on who you mean by the people. I assume that no matter what government is put in place, there will be some people who are opposed to it.

As Congressman Rohrabacher, who is decidedly anti-Taliban, expressed additional hesitations and the need for a peaceful resolution, the exchange continued with these remarks:

Mr. MARESCA: We are hesitant too, Mr. Congressman. I appreciate the fact that you are a person well-read into these issues. I think you would agree with us that the international community needs to pay a lot more attention to this problem. We would like to see the international community focused hard on this problem and pushing for that kind of a peaceful resolution that you described.

Mr. ROHRABACHER: If I could just say just a couple more words. During the break, I did manage to take a swing through Central Asia that took me to Turkey and Azerbaijan and Uzbekistan, Turkmenistan, Kazakhstan. I, Mr. Chairman, agree with the witness. The most important thing we can do now is to try to get this region that's been isolated for so long into the global economy. There is so much potential there, wealth as well as the people there, are fine. They are the traders of ancient times. They could do very well in the global economy.

Congressman Bereuter concluded the questioning by addressing Robert W. Gee, Assistant Secretary for Policy, U.S. Department of Energy as follows:

Mr. BEREUTER. Switching geography slightly, what is the status of proposals by Unocal and others to build a gas pipeline through Afghanistan to Pakistan.

Mr. GEE. Perhaps the Unocal witness can give you more detail. I do understand that they do have an agreement with the government of Turkmenistan. They have also been in discussions with the various factions within Afghanistan through which that proposed pipeline would be routed.

The U.S. Government's position is that we support multiple pipelines with the exception of the southern pipeline that would transit Iran. The Unocal pipeline is among those pipelines that would receive our support under that policy.

I would caution that while we do support the project, the U.S. Government has not at this point recognized any governing regime of the transit country, one of the transit countries, Afghanistan, through which that pipeline would be routed. But we do support the project.

This 1998 Congressional testimony should speak for itself regarding the motivation for oil transportation profits by U.S. politicians and their donors. The pipeline is the reason the Bush administration was willing to block terrorist investigations as described earlier and to continue negotiating with the Taliban for a unified government through July of 2001. If there is still any doubt the bombing of Afghanistan was largely triggered by the desire for oil pipelines, consider that Hamid Karzai, the new Afghan leader picked by Western powers to replace Mullah Omar of the Taliban, once worked as a consultant for Unocal.

THE OPIUM MOTIVATOR

As mentioned previously, no concrete, direct evidence connecting any of the 19 suspected hijackers in the 9/11 attacks to Afghanistan, the Taliban or even Osama bin Laden was developed prior to the Afghan invasion. In spite of this, U.S. and British military forces invaded and gained complete control of Afghanistan only to find that, despite their repeated claims, Osama bin Laden was not even there.

To understand why these forces would invade Afghanistan it might be useful to consider why the Soviet Union may have. The Soviet invasion and attempts to control the Afghan government are sometimes attributed to concern for access to Persian Gulf oil. Geographically this does not make much sense because a successful invasion of centrally located Afghanistan would not necessarily produce the desired result. In December of 1973, the *Wall Street Journal* ran a front-page story entitled "*Do the Soviets Covet Afghanistan? If so, It's Hard to Figure Why*" by journalist, Peter Kann, went on to become chairman and publisher. This mystery that baffled even the *Wall Street Journal* publisher and chairman is most likely explained by Soviet lust for control of Afghan opium. Those lucrative profits would have helped offset serious economic problems. Opium accounts for 80% of the gross domestic product of Afghanistan. To understand the value of this product, consider what happened to the Soviet Union after their invasion of Afghanistan failed. The Soviet Union collapsed.

Is it just a coincidence that the country the George W. Bush administration picked to invade produced 70% of the world's opium that is refined into heroin. Is it just a coincidence British and U.S. forces sought assistance of Afghan warlords who control most of the Afghan territory that produces opium, according to the October 2001 U.N. report? Is it just a coincidence the next country expected to require U.S. troops is Columbia, the world's leading producer of cocaine? Perhaps the Afghan invasion could be written off as circumstantial if not for the history of CIA involvement in worldwide drug trafficking operations connected to military action.

As explained in Chapter 7, British and American forces aligned with the KLA to overthrow the Yugoslavian government and confiscate the Trepca mining complex. The KLA, was a drug funded Arab terrorist group armed trained and equipped by Osama bin Laden along with British, German, Canadian and American intelligence support. Several news sources have reported how the KLA eventually ended up in control of European drug trafficking routes.

As explained in Chapter 10, during and after the war in Vietnam, high-ranking CIA and Defense Department officials were involved in money laundering and drug trafficking operations that originated in Burma and were routed through Laos. In addition, Chapter 10 explains how drug trafficking was used to support the Contras during the Nicaraguan conflict. It also explains how the invasion of Panama was linked to Operation Watchtower where military intelligence had installed beacons so that low flying planes could transport drug cargo undetected from Columbia into Panama where they were met by the Noriegas.

The previous CIA track record in Afghanistan continues the same theme. During the 1980s, within two years of initial CIA involvement in Afghanistan, the area known as the Golden Crescent began producing heroin. A study by Alfred McCoy confirmed that: "the Pakistan-Afghanistan borderlands became the world's top heroin producers, supplying 60 percent of U.S. demand. In Pakistan, the heroin addict population went from near zero in 1979 to 1.2 million by 1985..."

The previous Afghanistan experiences, the drug related CIA military track record and the inability to develop direct,

concrete evidence linking Afghans to the 9/11 attacks should
offer an obvious conclusion to most informed Americans:
Afghanistan is just another in the long line of military action
taken to support worldwide drug trafficking operations for the
profit of those who control Western politicians.

ISRAELI COMUNICATIONS ESPIONAGE

This chapter has made the case that Afghanistan, Osama bin
Laden and the Taliban are very unlikely perpetrators of the 9/11
attacks. If so, then who are the real culprits? The Arabs claim
the Israelis, specifically the Mossad intelligence service, may
be behind the 9/11 attacks. Israel benefits tremendously from
the 9/11 tragedies by having a superpower conduct war against
her enemies while the Arabs receive little or no benefit from
being attacked. But is there any solid evidence to support the
Arab perspective?

In December 2001, the Justice Department announced 60
Israelis had been arrested or detained since the 9/11 attacks,
either under the new anti-terrorism law or for immigration violations.

Of the 60 detained or arrested Israeli suspects believed to
have prior knowledge of 9/11, a half dozen worked for Amdocs
Ltd., an Israeli communication support services company with
a U.S. headquarters in St. Louis. In court cases involving some
of these individuals, INS officials have testified they are of
special interest to the government. In 1997, Amdocs reportedly
helped install the new $30 million communications system for
the White House. Afterwards, Monica Lewinsky provided
details to the Office of the Independent Counsel that Bill
Clinton believed a foreign government had tapped his phone
lines. In fact, the Starr Report specifically states: "He suspected
a foreign embassy was tapping his telephone lines and he
proposed cover stories". Both the FBI and CIA denied the
claims of Lewinsky and told Congressional investigators no
such investigation of phone tapping was ongoing.

In a series beginning on December 13, 2001, *Fox News* re-
ported that: "In 1999, the super secret National Security
Agency, headquartered in northern Maryland issued a Top
Secret sensitive compartmentalized information report

(TS/SCI) warning that records of calls in the U.S. were getting onto foreign hands, Israel in particular". Carl Cameron mentioned "Investigators don't believe calls are being listened to, but the data about who is calling whom and when is plenty valuable in itself". *Fox* also stated: "The NSA has held numerous classified conferences to warn the FBI and CIA how Amdocs records could be used."

How could Amdocs do this? *Fox News* explained that: "Most directory assistance calls and virtually all call records and billing in the U.S. are done for the phone companies by Amdocs Ltd. Amdocs has contracts with the 25 biggest phone companies in America and more worldwide. The White House and other secure government phone lines are protected, but it is virtually impossible to make a call on normal phone lines without generating an Amdocs record of it." Although these comments about Amdocs penetration scope are overstated, the implication about the danger of the Israeli Mossad having access to most American call detail records is certainly valid and quickly falling into place.

During 2000, more than two-dozen U.S. intelligence, counterintelligence, law enforcement and other officials told *Insight* magazine the FBI believes Israel intercepted telephone and modern communications on some of the most sensitive lines in the U.S. government. Included are suspected tapped lines in the White House, National Security Council and the Departments of State, Defense and Justice. When the FBI searched the work area of an Israeli businessman whose wife is believed to be a Mossad officer, they found a remarkable phone number list. These included the FBI "black" lines used for wiretapping and FBI counterintelligence lines used to keep track of the suspected Israeli spy operation. Ironically it turned out that Israel was actually monitoring the lines the FBI used to monitor Israel.

Officials believe the interceptions were coordinated with telephone support service software designs for technical billing records and support equipment required for interfacing with local telephone company software. In the May 29, 2000 *Insight* magazine study, authors Michael Waller and Paul Rodriguez quoted a U.S. official with this remarkable observation: "The (FBI) uncovered what appears to be sophisticated means to listen in on conversations from remote telephone sites with capabilities of providing real time audio feeds to Tel Aviv."

Insight was shown a separate D.C. area telephone site that plugs into the White House communications system. It operated for years with an open "back door" allowing control by remote access. The White House system has 5800 fax, voice and modem lines with systems designed to electronically mask routes and generate secure connections. A U.S. Intelligence source confirmed that: "The access had to be done in such a way as to evade our counter measures. That's what is most disconcerting."

Another part of the *Fox* series by Carl Cameron dealt with Comverse Infosys, a subsidiary of an Israeli-run private telecommunications firm that has many U.S. offices. It provides wiretapping equipment for law enforcement and has raised security concerns best stated by the exact *Fox News* transcript:

"Every time you make a call, it passes through the nation's elaborate network of switchers and routers run by the phone companies. Custom computers and software, made by companies like Comverse, are tied into that network to intercept, record and store the wiretapped calls, and at the same time transmit them to investigators."

"...the complaint about this system is that the wiretap computer programs made by Comverse have, in effect, a back door through which wiretaps themselves can be intercepted by unauthorized parties. Adding to the suspicions is in Israel, Comverse works closely with the Israeli government, and under special programs, gets reimbursed for up to 50 percent of its research and development costs by the Israeli Ministry of Industry and Trade."

And what troubles investigators most, particularly in New York, in the counterterrorism investigation of the World Trade Center attack, is on a number of cases, suspects they had sought to wiretap and surveil immediately changed their telecommunications processes. They started acting much differently as soon as those supposedly secret wiretaps went into place"

"But investigators within the DEA, INS and FBI have all told *Fox News* to pursue or even suggest Israeli spying through Comverse is considered career suicide. And sources say while various F.B.I. inquiries into Comverse have been conducted over the years, they've been halted before the actual equipment has ever been thoroughly tested for leaks."

When federal investigators believe it is career suicide to investigate a foreign power spying on the U.S. something is rotten in America.

The DEA agents took matters into their own hands by leaking a DEA draft report that was obtained and published by American Free Press. The report detailed how the DEA had questioned, detained or arrested 125 Israelis posing as art students. Several used false names, had false driver licenses or gave false information when questioned. All had served in the Israeli army and many had experience in military intelligence, electronic surveillance interception or explosive ordinance units. The Israelis specifically targeted DEA offices in 15 different divisions nationwide as well as personal residences of DEA agents. Several times they were caught diagramming the offices they had targeted. They also penetrated 3 laboratories, two military bases and several other government operations centers. The El Paso Division received a teletype stating the they were part of a terrorist organization.

THE INSLAW PROMIS SOFTWARE

Israel has previously conducted massive spy operations within and against the United States. Once such example, during the mid 1980s, involves Jonathan Pollard who turned over 500,000 documents to his Israeli handlers. Some of them were eventually routed from Israel to the Soviet Union for the benefit of Israel. U.S. intelligence officers are still puzzled as to how he knew which documents to search, how he constantly searched them without detection and how he obtained the appropriate security clearances. Pollard's handler was Rafel Eitan, a Mossad operative who headed an Israeli Defense Force Intelligence Unit known as LEKEM.

In early 1983, Eitan posed as a "Dr. Ben Orr" of the Israeli Ministry of Justice to get a demonstration of the famous Prosecutor Management Information System, PROMIS, software developed by Bill and Nancy Hamilton of INSLAW Co. The Ed Meese Justice Department arranged the demonstration and Eitan was most impressed but, to the surprise of the Hamiltons, never bought the software. The Justice Department had already signed a contract in 1982 for the software and began to install one of its two different versions in the offices of all 94 U.S. attorneys.

Meanwhile, Dr. Earl Brian, a long time associate of Meese, offered to buy Inslaw from the Hamiltons but was refused. Afterwards, Justice withheld $7 million in payments, canceled the contract in 1984 and forced Inslaw to seek Chapter 11 bankruptcy protection in 1985 as Brian began hostile takeover attempts. During this time Justice continued to use PROMIS and the software was even found by Charles Hayes on surplus government computer hard drives in 1990.

The Hamiltons obtained representation from former Attorney General Elliott Richardson who Richard Nixon had replaced with Judge Robert Bork after Richardson refused to fire special Watergate prosecutor, Archibald Cox. The Hamiltons sued Justice and won a $10 million dollar judgment in 1988. Judge George Bason concluded Justice had used "trickery, fraud and deceit" to deliberately bankrupt Inslaw and get control of the software without paying for it. Although U.S. District Court judge William B. Bryant, upheld his decision, Bason was denied reappointment and replaced with Martin Teel, the key Justice attorney who defended against the INSLAW charges.

On June 27, 2001, Teel issued an order to shutdown the *Spotlight* newspaper, a leader in reporting on the theft of the PROMIS software. In May of 1990 Justice got the U.S. Court of Appeals to rule the bankruptcy venue was not the right venue for the case. In 1992, the Supreme Court upheld that decision. In 1991, William Barr appointed ex-federal judge Nicholas Bua as special counsel to investigate Justice actions in the INSLAW matter and in March 1993 Bua issued a report clearing the Justice Department. In August 1997, the Court of Federal Claims found that Justice was not guilty of any wrongdoing.

PROMIS was developed to track individuals being pursued or prosecuted by government agencies. It had a vital capability that allowed it to interface with other remote databases without reprogramming. The remote capabilities, frequently referred to as a "back door", were quite advanced for the time and of great interest to the Israeli government. The Hamiltons later learned through sworn affidavits from Michael Riconosciuto, Ari-Ben-Menashe and Richard Babayan that Brian had obtained an illegal copy of the software source code, provided Eitan a copy for use by the Israel Defense Forces and arranged to modify it for installation in law enforcement and intelligence agencies worldwide. Riconosciuto also swore in his affidavit that Justice representative, Peter Videnieks, threatened him with specific prosecution if he cooperated with a House Judiciary Committee investigation.

On September 10, 1992 the House Judiciary Committee issued a report entitled *The Inslaw Affair* that identified a dozen separate sections of 18 USC and charged that: "the following criminal statues may have been violated by certain high level Justice Department officials and private individuals during the course of the Inslaw affair". Included were statues of fraud, wire fraud, obstruction, witness tampering, witness retaliation, perjury, racketeering, transportation of stolen goods, receiving stolen goods, conspiracy, threatening violence to interfere with commerce and illegal conversion of property by a U.S. official.

The report did not address links to over a dozen people having connections to the case who mysteriously died. In a February 14, 1994 brief, Elliott Richardson stated that: "The Justice Department's secret intelligence agency also has its own 'proprietary' company that employs scores of agents of diverse nationalities as well as individuals who appear to be regular employees of various departments and agencies of the U.S. government or members of the U.S. Armed Forces..." He specifically identified "The Nazi war criminal program" as "a front for the Justice Department's own covert intelligence service." That program is run by the Office of Special Investigations (OSI), which the Hamiltons suspect was the unit within Justice that stole their software.

Much of this story is told in a book called *Octopus* about INSLAW investigative reporter, Danny Casolaro who was murdered on August 10, 1991 and embalmed immediately without permission of the family. Richardson's brief suggests evidence indicating Casolaro was murdered by the secret unit operating inside of Justice. Author Michael Colllins Piper once again identifies the unit as the OSI. The OSI's Nazi war criminal program has a long standing working relationship with the Israeli Mossad. Would elements of a U.S. Government agency or the Mossad be involved in the killing of innocent Americans? As mentioned in Chapter 10, the Mossad was a likely suspect in the murder of five Special Forces colonels who were probing a South American drug operation involving the CIA and Mossad. Even if they were uninvolved, it is clear Israel and the Mossad are not nearly the allies the news media would have us believe.

ISRAELI FOREKNOWLEDGE OF 9/11 ATTACKS

As mentioned earlier, many U.S. officials believe the Israelis had precise, specific information about the 9/11 attacks they collected from communications interceptions and spying they were conducting on Arabs within the U.S. Another example of precise foreknowledge, confirmed by worldtradeaftermath.com, involves the Zim American Israeli Shipping Co., which moved out of the WTC during the first week in September although still listed as a WTC tenant. Zim broke its lease for offices on the 16th and 17th floors of the north tower before the normal year-end renewal at a loss of $50,000. Its parent company, Zim Israel Navigation Co. is owned by Israel Corp. and the State of Israel.

Another example of foreknowledge involves Israelis who photographed and celebrated the WTC collapse. Just after the 9/11 attacks, Dan Rather appeared on the David Letterman show and mentioned that a cell of America hating Arabs has been spotted across the river videotaping the World Trade Center tragedy and celebrating on the roof of a building. This was another case of classic media deception since the "Arabs" were actually known to be Israelis from the very instant they were taken into custody.

An Israel Embassy spokesmen confirmed at least 13 Israelis were taken into custody in connection with the 9/11 attacks.

There were three different groups all related to Urban Moving Systems, which has offices in New York and New Jersey. Police stopped an Urban Moving Systems van they believed contained the same individuals eyewitnesses saw celebrating the WTC disaster in Liberty State Park at Jersey City. Another group was on the roof of Urban Moving Systems in Weekawken filming the WTC disaster and shouting "cries of joy and mockery" according to Israeli Ha'aertz news. Both sites have unique vantage points of the WTC.

Five of the suspects were officially listed Oded Ellner, Omer Marmari,Yaon Shmuel and brothers Paul and Sivan Kurzburg. On September 12, 2001, The *Bergen Record* stated some men had maps with certain places highlighted, bomb sniffing dogs reacted as if they had detected explosives and there was other evidence linking them to the bombing plot.

Immediately afterwards, the moving company owner, Dominic Otto Suter, fled to Israel after questioning by the FBI. The moving company, which had no discernible assets, closed up and was later determined to be a front for the Israeli Mossad. The American Jewish newspaper, *Forward*, confirmed the Israelis were connected to the Mossad. The Sept. 28-30 issue of the *USA Today* made the typical U.S. news media claim that there was nothing more than "unsubstantiated rumors that implicate Israel".

So what did the Ashcroft Justice Department do with the five Israelis who celebrated the deaths of 2,600 Americans in the WTC and were suspected by investigators of being involved in the WTC plot? Did they remain under a detailed investigation since they may be the only ones in America with foreknowledge of the WTC attacks? Were they prosecuted for their possible involvement in the WTC plot? No, they were simply deported at the end of November 2001 for Visa violations.

ISRAELI INFLUENCE OF OUR NEWS MEDIA

So why do we never hear about Israeli involvement in 9/11? The answer is: Israelis strongly influence our national news media. A publication, entitled *Who Rules America?*, by

National Vanguard Books explained some remarkable ownership details of major media conglomerates starting with recent history including a snapshot of current status as we entered the new millennium in January of 2000:

Leonard Goldenson originally owned ABC. David Sarnoff and subsequently, his son, Robert owned NBC. William Paley was Chairman of CBS until 1985 when Laurence Tisch became Chairman and CEO from 1986 to 1995 after a friendly takeover. Murray Rothstein, who now goes by the name Sumner Redstone, bought CBS in December 1999. He also heads Viacom, the conglomerate that produces TV programs and owns Showtime, MTV, Nickelodeon, Simon and Schuester publishing, 13 TV stations, 12 radio stations, Free Press, Pocket Books. It distributes videos through Blockbuster stores and owns Paramount Pictures, which is headed by Sherry Lansing.

Michael Eisner took over as Chief Executive Officer of the Walt Disney Company in 1984. Joseph Roth is head of the Walt Disney Motion pictures group, which also includes Touchstone, Hollywood and Caravan Pictures. In August of 1995, Eisner acquired Capital Cities/ABC. ABC owns 10 large TV stations, 7 newspapers, an ESPN cable subsidiary, ABC Radio Network and it has 225 affiliates. ABC Radio Network has 26 AM and FM stations and it has 3,400 affiliates. Steven Bornstein heads the ESPN cable subsidiary that controls Lifetime and A&E TV cable networks.

Gerald Levin has been the Chief Executive Officer of Time Warner, which includes HBO, all of the Turner Broadcasting Systems cable channels, 50 labels of Warner Music, Warner Brothers Studio, Castle Rock Entertainment, New Line Cinema, America On Line and Time Warner Publishing, the largest U.S. magazine publisher Editor-in-chief, Norman Pearlstine, is responsible for *Time, Sports Illustrated, People* and *Fortune* among others.

Edgar Bronfman Sr. owns MCA and Universal Pictures, now merged into Universal Studios. He also acquired PolyGram records, the largest record company in America. Universal, Disney, Paramount and Warner Brothers account for roughly 2/3 of total annual box office receipts.

Peter Chernin is president and CEO of Fox Group, which controls all of News Corporation's U.S. news, film, TV and publishing operations. This also includes the *New York Post* and *TV Guide*. Peter Roth is president of Fox Entertainment while Laura Ziskin is president of 20th Century Fox.

Paul Friedman produces ABC World News Tonight with Peter Jennings. Neal Shapiro produces NBC Nightly News with Tom Brokaw. Al Ortiz produced CBS Evening News with Dan Rather. Rick Kaplan was brought over from ABC to head CNN.

Adolph Ochs purchased the *New York Times* in 1896. His great, great, grandson, Arthur Sulzberger, is the publisher of the *New York Times* and chairman of the New York Times Co., which owns 33 other newspapers, 12 major magazines, 7 radio and TV broadcasting stations, a cable TV system and three book publishing companies. The *New York Times* news service also supplies stories, features and photographs to over 500 other newspapers, magazines and news agencies.

Eugene Meyer bought the Washington Post in 1933. His daughter, Katherine Meyer Graham became the board chairman of the *Washington Post Co.* She appointed her son, Donald, as publisher and he is also the president and CEO of the company, which controls 11 military publications, 6 TV stations, Cable One and *Newsweek* magazine.

Peter Kann is CEO and chairman of Dow Jones as well as the publisher of the *Wall Street Journal*. Dow Jones publishes Barron's and 24 other daily newspapers. Mortimer Zuckerman bought the *New York Daily News* in 1993. He also owns and publishes the *U.S. News & World Report*.

Samuel Newhouse bequeathed his media empire, Advance Publications, to his sons, Samuel and Donald, upon his death in 1979. They own 26 newspapers, 12

TV stations, 87 cable TV systems and about 24 major magazines.

Joe Farah founded the top web site World Net Daily. David Geffen, Jeffrey Katzenberg and Steven Speilberg founded the much-ballyhooed Dreamworks SKG. Leonard Stern owns the Village Voice.

What do all of these people have in common? The publication *Who Rules America* points out that they are all of Jewish descent. The ownership and management picture listed will change frequently over time but the point will likely remain the same. Jewish Americans have a high degree of control over American public opinion and many feel that they have a higher allegiance to Israel than to America. Is it any wonder why we so frequently get a pro-Israel, anti-Arab news slant throughout much of our news reporting? Someone may want to raise the bogus "anti-Semite" claim when facts like these are revealed. The issue is not prejudice but that the priority for all Americans, regardless of background, should be to do what is best for America, not what is best for Israel or some other foreign country.

U.S. FOREKNOWLEDGE FROM ITS AGENCIES AND ALLIES

Although Israel had specific foreknowledge of the 9/11 attacks they did not fully inform the American government of what was about to take place. Israeli officials simply warned their counterparts in Washington that: "large-scale terrorist attacks on highly visible targets on the American mainland were imminent." according to the *Jerusalem Post*. They offered no specific information about targets nor did they reveal the date of the attack. The glee of the former Israeli soldiers who watched the WTC being destroyed illustrates the lack of concern they have for American lives.

Similar types of generic warnings were issued to the U.S. from French, German, Russian and Egyptian intelligence sources according to a variety of reports from around the world. Russian President Vladmir Putin and Egyptian President Hosni Mubarak are quoted as confirming these intelligence warnings personally. Most foreign warnings did not define the type of attack although a German warning referred to the use of airliners and a Russian warning mentioned suicide pilots, which had already been documented in an unclassified September 1999 CIA report entitled. "*Sociology and Psychology of Terrorism: Who Becomes a Terrorist and Why?*"

America was first alerted about a plot to blow up airliners in January of 1995. Philippine authorities said they found computer disks containing detailed plans of the operations in a Manila apartment that had caught on fire from explosive chemicals left in a sink. The project, called Bojinka involved leaving bombs under airline seats. It was likely tested in December 1994, on a Philippine Airlines flight where a Japanese tourist was killed. Ramzi Yousef, Abdul Hakim Murad and Wali Khan Amin Shah were arrested and tried in New York for the airline bomb plot after Murad had returned to the apartment. Phillipine authorities also found information on his computer about a suicide hijacking plan to crash into CIA headquarters according to the warning mentioned in the *Sociology and Psychology of Terrorism* report.

In a July 10, 2001 memo, Arizona FBI agent, Kenneth Williams, warned FBI headquarters to be wary of Middle Eastern men training at American flight schools. After an un-related investigation revealed several nonresident Arab men sought training at a commercial aeronautical school in Prescott, Arizona, the agent supervisor wrote a memo to Washington stating that:

"Phoenix believes the FBI should accumulate a listing of civil aviation universities/colleges around the country. FBI field offices with these types of schools in their area should establish appropriate liaison. FBIHQ should discuss this matter with other elements of the U.S. intelligence community and task the community for any information that supports Phoenix's suspicions. FBIHQ should consider seeking the necessary authority to obtain visa information from the USDOS [State Department] on individuals obtaining visas for attending these types of schools and notify the appropriate field office when these individuals are scheduled to arrive in their area of responsibility."

Early in 2001, the Phoenix office of Pan Am International Flight Academy called the FAA about Hani Hanjour, a student who was later believed to be the pilot of the plane that flew into the Pentagon. The Pan Am instructor questioned how Hanjour got a flight certificate with such inadequate English. Since English is a universal language of aviation, the instructor did not want to continue training. The FAA inspector suggested that he could help find an Arabic-speaking person who could assist him.

On August 15, 2001, two program managers at the Pan Am International Flight Academy in Eagan, Minneapolis alerted Special Agent Dave Rapp of the Minneapolis FBI office they had concerns about a student named Zacarias Moussaoui. Moussaoui lacked a pilot's license, seemed inept in basic flying procedures, paid a $6,300 deposit in cash and wanted to take a few lessons in a Boeing 747 flight simulator as an "ego thing." He also drew suspicion because he claimed to be from France but then did not seem to understand French and subsequently said he was from the Middle East.

Moussaoui, a Moroccan French citizen, was arrested in Minnesota for an immigration violation on August 16, 2001. When the FBI checked his name with foreign intelligence agencies, they were warned by French intelligence that he might have terrorist connections. The information was so sketchy though, that the Minneapolis agents were unable to persuade FBI lawyers in Washington, D.C., to seek a search warrant under the Foreign Intelligence Surveillance Act, which requires evidence that the suspect is an agent of a foreign power or terrorist group. Colleen Rowley, general counsel for the Minnesota office and a 20-year FBI employee, filed a complaint to Director Mueller that headquarters actually thwarted their investigation.

Moussaoui is believed to be the missing 20th hijacker and a possible replacement for Ramzi Binalshibh, a Yemeni citizen who was denied a visa to enter the United States three times. Moussaoui is alleged to have made many telephone calls to known associates of the 9/11 hijackers who were then living in Hamburg, Germany. Between 8/1 and 8/3, Moussaoui is also alleged to have received a $14,000 wire transfer from a Hamburg resident who may have funded the hijackers. The

Justice Department decided to seek the death penalty for Moussaoui in murder and conspiracy related charges for the 9/11 attacks even though he was in jail at the time and is not believed to have been involved in planning the attacks.

After the attacks, a Hamburg man later identified as Mounir El Motassadeq, was arrested by German authorities when they determined he was one of several who signed the will of Mohammed Atta and had power of attorney over the account of Marwan Al-Shehhi. Spokesman Frank Woesthoff of the German Lower Saxony Justice Ministry confirmed an Iranian man phoned U.S. police from his deportation cell in Langenhagen prison to warn of a planned attack during the week of September 9.

Finally on May 15, 2002, the Bush administration admitted they were warned about possible hijackers in early August, however, Ari Fleischer stated: "The president was also provided information about bin Laden wanting to engage in hijacking in the traditional pre-9/11 sense, not for the use of suicide bombing, not for the use of an airplane as a missile". If the President was not provided that information then he was deliberately kept uninformed by his closest advisors. The FBI had full knowledge the hijackers were going to attempt to fly the planes not just hijack them in the traditional sense. The unclassified September 1999 Sociology and Psychology of Terrorism report stated:

- "Suicide bombers belonging to Al Qaeda's martyrdom battalion could crash-land an aircraft packed with high explosives into the Pentagon, CIA Headquarters, or the White House."

Thus the Bush administration, even by their own documents had several warnings of the exact type of operation that would take place. But the Bush administration also seems to have received information from the German ambassador to the U.S. stating the exact potential days of the attack. An April 5, 2002 German intelligence document presented by Gregory Douglas at the Barnes Review conference on June 14 begins with these paragraphs:

"On Monday August 6. August, 2001, at 17:50 (German) Ambassador Ischinger personally notified the

President of the United States that information developed by the Bundesamt fur Verfassungsschutz [German domestic secret service] as well as the BND (Bundesnachrichten-dienst, German foreign secret service) indicated clearly that an attack by a radical Arab group partially based in Germany was to occur on 10-11 September, 2001. The President was at that time in residence at his farm in Texas. Our Ambassador was acting in direct response to instructions from Foreign Minister Fisher.

This information was developed from official surveillance of Arab extremist groups operating in the Federal Republic as well as from intercepted communications between the Embassy of Israel and the Israeli Foreign Ministry in Tel Aviv concerning this matter.

The information was 'gratefully received' by the U.S. President who stated at the time that he was also aware of the same pending assaults.

Subsequent to these attacks, the office of the U.S. President through the U.S. Department of State, made an urgent request to the government of the Federal Republic of Germany that no reference whatsoever should be made to the official warnings given by Ambassador Ischinger."

This document also confirms precise Israeli foreknowledge of the 9/11 attacks. The documents previously mentioned combine to show that the Bush administration knew the type of attack, the originating source of the attack (major commercial airports) and the potential dates of the attack. To prevent the attack, it is not necessary to know the exact targets or perpetrators in advance since existing federal resources could have been used to monitor suspected passengers and stop the attackers at the originating airports. In spite of having access to all of this information, the Bush administration took no significant preventive action.

But the letter from Colleen Rowley to FBI director Mueller goes beyond the concept of U.S. government foreknowledge. Here are a few excerpts from the 13-page document:

"Also intertwined with my reluctance in this case to accept the "20-20 hindsight" rationale is first-hand knowledge that I have of statements made on September 11th, after the first attacks on the World Trade Center had already occurred, made telephonically by the FBI Supervisory Special Agent (SSA) who was the one most involved in the Moussaoui matter and who, up to that point, seemed to have been consistently, almost deliberately thwarting the Minneapolis FBI agents' efforts (see number 5). Even after the attacks had begun, the SSA in question was still attempting to block the search of Moussaoui's computer, characterizing the World Trade Center attacks as a mere coincidence with Misseapolis' prior suspicions about Moussaoui."

"Although the last thing the FBI or the country needs now is a witch hunt, I do find it odd that (to my knowledge) no inquiry whatsoever was launched of the relevant FBIHQ personnel's actions a long time ago. Despite FBI leaders' full knowledge of all the items mentioned herein (and probably more that I'm unaware of), the SSA, his unit chief, and other involved HQ personnel were allowed to stay in their positions and, what's worse, occupy critical positions in the FBI's SIOC Command Center post September 11th. (The SSA in question actually received a promotion some months afterward!)"

"The fact is that key FBIHQ personnel whose jobs it was to assist and coordinate with field division agents on terrorism investigations and the obtaining and use of FISA searches (and who theoretically were privy to many more sources of intelligence information than field division agents), continued to, almost inexplicably, throw up roadblocks and undermine Minneapolis' by-now desperate efforts to obtain a FISA search warrant, long after the French intelligence service provided its information and probable cause became clear. HQ personnel brought up almost ridiculous questions in their apparent efforts to undermine the probable cause.6 In all of their conversations and correspondence, HQ personnel never disclosed to the Minneapolis agents that the Phoenix Division had, only approximately three weeks earlier, warned of Al Qaeda operatives in flight schools seeking flight training for terrorist purposes!"

"My only comment is that the process of allowing the FBI supervisors to make changes in affidavits is itself fundamentally wrong, just as, in the follow-up to FBI Laboratory Whistleblower Frederic Whitehurst's allegations, this process was revealed to be wrong in the context of writing up laboratory results. With the Whitehurst allegations, this process of allowing supervisors to re-write portions of laboratory reports, was found to provide opportunities for over-zealous supervisors to skew the results in favor of the prosecution. In the Moussaoui case, it was the opposite -- the process allowed the Headquarters Supervisor to downplay the significance of the information thus far collected in order to get out of the work of having to see the FISA application through or possibly to avoid taking what he may have perceived as an unnecessary career risk.7 I understand that the failures of the FBIHQ personnel involved in the Moussaoui matter are also being officially excused because they were too busy with other investigations, the Cole bombing and other important terrorism matters, but the Supervisor's taking of the time to read each word of the information submitted by Minneapolis and then substitute his own choice of wording belies to some extent the notion that he was too busy."

"Mr. Director, I hope my observations can be taken in a constructive vein. They are from the heart and intended to be completely apolitical. Hopefully, with our nation's security on the line, you and our nation's other elected and appointed officials can rise above the petty politics that often plague other discussions and do the right thing. You do have some good ideas for change in the FBI but I think you have also not been completely honest about some of the true reasons for the FBI's pre-September 11th failures. Until we come clean and deal with the root causes, the Department of Justice will continue to experience problems fighting terrorism and fighting crime in general."

"And both of the violations originally cited in vain by the Minneapolis agents disputing the issue with FBIHQ personnel are among those on which Moussaoui is currently indicted."

"During the early aftermath of September 11th, when I happened to be recounting the pre-September 11th events concerning the Moussaoui investigation to other FBI personnel in other divisions or in FBIHQ, almost everyone's first question was "Why?--Why would an FBI agent(s) deliberately sabotage a case? (I know I shouldn't be flippant about this, but jokes were actually made that the key FBIHQ personnel had to be spies or moles, like Robert Hansen, who were actually working for Osama Bin Laden."

Rowley specifically states:
- An "FBI Supervisory Special Agent was consistently, almost deliberately thwarting the Minneapolis FBI agents' efforts";
- "The SSA in question actually received a promotion" some months after all of the problems were known to FBI leaders;
- Headquarters personnel never disclosed to the Minneapolis agents that the Phoenix Division warnings about Al Queda operatives seeking flight training for terrorist purposes;
- When she recounted the events to other FBI personnel they asked "Why would an FBI agent(s) deliberately sabotage a case?";
- FBI Supervisors are allowed to alter FBI affidavits and lab report results;
- In regards to Director Mueller: "I think you have also not been completely honest".

The conclusion is inescapable. The highest levels of FBI headquarters were consistently thwarting the investigation of a key terrorist suspect in the 9/11 hijackings. On May 29, 2002, two days after her letter was made public, John Ashcroft and Robert Mueller held a press conference to announce a cosmetic reorganization for the FBI. Mueller publicly thanked her for her letter, said he was grateful for her coming forward and welcomed criticism of the bureau and even himself. That same afternoon John Collingwood, assistant director of public affairs, sent Judicial Watch a letter threatening termination, criminal proceedings and a revoked security clearance if Special Agent Robert Wright revealed specifics about his complaints at his press conference the next day.

U.S. FOREKNOWLEDGE FROM ENCRYPTED COMMUNICATIONS

Another compelling point of foreknowledge involves Osama bin Laden phone calls. Records of over 500 calls were entered as evidence in the Manhattan trial of 4 African embassy bombers from January to May of 2001. Prosecutors said that the calls were between bin Laden, the defendants and another accomplice in London named Khalid Al Fawwaz. The NSA supposedly broke the encrypted communications and intercepted the calls by using the infamous Echelon system. The intercept capability would have to be revealed in February of 2001 when the evidence was introduced. Although only seven months before the 9/11 attacks, officials claimed there was no forewarning of 9/11 on any of the calls. Item 66 of the British document specifically states such an operation takes years of planning:

"Al Qaeda operatives, in evidence given in the East African Embassy bomb trials, have described how the group spends years preparing for an attack. They conduct repeated surveillance, patiently gather materials, and identify and vet operatives, who have the skills to participate in the attack and the willingness to die for their cause."

On September 9, two days before the attack, NBC claimed in a widespread report that intelligence intercepted a call by bin Laden to his mother where he said: "In two days you're going to hear big news, and you're not going to hear from me for a while". In addition, immediately after the 9/11 attacks, Senator Orrin Hatch told the AP that U.S. intelligence had intercepted calls between bin Laden and two other associates discussing the aftermath of the attacks. Congressman Barr told me after Hatch made his comments, the U.S. was no longer able to intercept bin Laden phone calls.

The Bush administration was furious with Hatch for revealing the supposed intercept capability. But were they furious because bin Laden would change communications or were they furious because he accidentally revealed what could be proven later that Bush had foreknowledge of the attacks? It is reasonably clear from all of these facts the NSA had a constant capability to intercept the communications of bin Laden all along, regardless of what he was saying. If Hatch was telling the truth and bin Laden was the real perpetrator of 9/11, it is virtually impossible for the Bush administration NSA not to have known the complete details of the 9/11 attacks. If the reports were falsely generated from the CIA or NSA, as I personally suspect, then they are just two more pieces in a mountain of evidence that Osama bin Laden is a CIA designated operative who helped government insiders gain the riches of Afghan oil flow and opium.

After Vice President Dick Cheney and others placed significant pressure on Congress not to investigate the 9/11 attacks, Congresswomen Cynthia McKinney (D-GA, 4) released a bold public statement calling for an investigation on April 12, 2002.. She questioned: "...what role does the close relationship between the Bush Administration and the oil and defense industries play, if any, in the policies that are currently being pursued by this Administration?". She mentioned many news accounts that "...indicate that many different warnings were received by the Administration". She also stated: "...what is undeniable is that corporations close to the Administration, have directly benefited from the increased defense spending arising from the aftermath of September 11".

Although she made no actual accusations, she was immediately attacked from all sides for accusing George W. Bush of allowing the 9/11 attacks to happen while profiting from them. But her comments were actually the opposite. She stated: "I am not aware of any evidence showing President Bush or members of his administration have personally profited from the attacks of 9-11. A complete investigation might reveal that to be the case." Nevertheless, her own fellow Georgia Democrat, Senator Zell Miller, called her comments "loony", "dangerous" and "irresponsible". The attacks on McKinney were even stronger than ones on those who were early advocates for the impeachment of Bill Clinton

On that same day, White House Press Secretary, Ari Fleischer, responded to a question about her call for an investigation with a false reference to the Kennedy assassination: "All I can tell you is the congresswoman must be running for the hall of fame of the Grassy Knoll Society." Despite the Warren Commission report, anyone who has seen the Zapruder film should know the fatal bullet that killed Kennedy struck him in the right front temple and pushed his head (and brain matter) backwards; therefore, it had to have been fired from the Grassy Knoll area. His reply was particularly galling since he was working for the man whose father has multiple connections to the Kennedy assassination as documented in Chapter 10 and many other highly credible reference books.

REFERENCES:

Hearing on U.S. Interests in the Central Asian Republics, House Subcommittee on Asia and the Pacific, February 12, 1998

Responsibilities for the Terrorist Atrocities in the United States-11 September 2001, British government, October 4, 2001

Daniel Golden James Bandler Marcus Walker, *Bin Laden Family Has Intricate Ties with Washington*, Wall Street Journal, Sept.28-29 2001

Frank Connolly, U.S. President's father was in Business with bin Laden's Family, Sunday Business Post, September 30, 2001

Roger Miller, *Bush and Bin Laden*, American Free Press, October 15, 2001

Peter Allen, *Bin Laden's Family Link to Bush*, The Daily Mail, September 27, 2001

Robert Novak, With Friends Like These, Who Needs the Taliban, Washington Times National Weekly,

Craig Nelson, With Taliban Gone, Poppy Cultivation Surges; Atlanta Journal Constitution, December 26, 2001

Christopher J. Petherick, Still Alive? *FBI Mixed up on True Identities of Hijackers,* American Free Press, October 21, 2001

Jennifer Bryson, *Al Jazeera Reporters defend Afghan Coverage*, NewsMax.com, November 16, 2001

Jennifer Bryson, *Is Rumsfield Criticism of Al Jazeera Justified?*, Newsmax.com, October 30, 2001

Pakasani Unmat Newspaper, September 28, 2001 pages 1-7, BBC Monitoring and American Free Press, October 29, 2001

Christopher Bollyn, *Free Speech Bombed*, American Free Press, November 26, 2001

Christopher Bollyn, *Bin Laden Tape Dupes Public Say Experts*, American Free Press, January 7-14, 2001

Steve Bonta, Meet the Real Northern Alliance, The New American magazine, December 17, 2001

Larry Kaplow, Taliban Isn't the Only Ruthless Militia Feared by Afghans, Atlanta Journal Constitution. December 5, 2001

Taliban in Texas for Talks in Gas Pipeline, BBC, December 4, 1997

The Inslaw Affair, House Judiciary Committee, Sept 10, 1992

Paul Rodriguez and Michael Waller, (special report on Israeli espionage), Insight Magazine, May 29, 2000

Carl Cameron, Brit Hume Special Report (Part 1 and 2), Fox News, December 13, 2001

Christopher Bollyn, *Did Isrealis Have Foreknowledge*, American Free Press, October 1, 2001

Michael Collins Piper, *Confirmed Exclusive: Mossad Front Companies Operating in and Around City on 9-11*, American Free Press, April 8, 2002

Paulo Lima, Five Men Detained as Suspected Conspirators, Bergen Record, September 12, 2001

Yossi Melman, 5 Israelis Detained for "Puzzling Behavior" after WTC tragedy, Ha'aertz, September 19,2001

Did Israel Have Advance Knowledge of the September 11, Terrorist Attacks? (Special DEA Report), American Free Press

Kenn Thomas and Jim Keith, Octopus, Octopus, Feral House Final Report on the Bombing of the Alfred P. Murrah Building April 19, 1995, Oklahoma Bombing Investigation Committee

AMERICA DECEIVED BY
"SMOKING GUN CONFESSION"

The majority of Americans believe that Osama bin Laden confessed to the 9/11 attacks on a "Smoking Gun" video released by the Pentagon on 12-13-01. But side-by-side picture comparisons show that the Pentagon used an imposter who is about 40 lbs. heavier and has a significantly different facial structure. All publicly released pictures of the imposter were blurry so Americans could not notice these differences.

Released by Al-Jazeera on
10-08-01

Released by Al-Jazeera on
11-03-01

Released by Pentagon on
12-13-01

Released by Al-Jazeera on
12-26-01

The real bin Laden has a long nose, inverted cheeks, oblong face, tall neck, rounded eyebrows and thin hands with long fingers, while the imposter has a wide nose, protruding cheeks, square face, short neck, straight eyebrows and fat hands with short fingers. Also notice how the health and happiness of the imposter is inconsistent with the deteriorating condition of bin Laden as shown in the Al-Jazeera pictures.

CHAPTER FIFTEEN
THE INFINITE WAR ON TERROR

THE PATRIOT ACT FOR A POLICE STATE

Immediately after the 9/11 attacks, Congress passed massive anti-terrorist legislation that infringes on the rights of American citizens. It was a déjà vu performance of their actions after the Oklahoma City bombing. Whenever Congress attempts to destroy Constitutional rights it is always in the form of a bill that is crammed through by the Executive branch under a voting schedule established by the Majority Leader so that the Congressional members do not get time to read it. The Patriot Act, initiated by H.R.3162 was no exception. Nat Hentoff described how the bill was passed.

The Ashcroft Justice Department gave the House Judiciary Committee an atrocious draft bill that even included the suspension of habeus corpus, which was removed by James Sensenbrenner. The committee, bitterly divided since the impeachment of Bill Clinton, unanimously agreed to remove the most draconian measures and passed a version of the bill by a 36-0 vote. Afterwards, House Speaker Dennis Hastert, dropped that legislation and created a new H.R. 3162 bill with other Republican leaders and White House operatives. Hastert was ultimately responsible for the bill presentation where no amendments could be offered and inadequate time was available for members to read it before a vote was scheduled. Only two copies were available to the entire minority side according to John Conyers, ranking minority Judiciary Committee member. Barney Frank of all people may have summed it up best when he said: "This was the least democratic process for debating questions fundamental to democracy I have ever seen. A bill drafted by a handful of people in secret, subject to no committee process, comes before us immune from amendment."

A similar process took place in the Senate where an even harsher 243-page version of the bill was passed on October 11 by a 96-1 vote, with only Russ Feingold dissenting. On October 12, the House voted, 337 to 79, for a 175-page bill now blatantly misnamed as the Patriot Act. Although the legislation is typically vague and subject to interpretation in many places here is a brief overview of some of the infringements identified primarily by the Electronic Frontier Foundation:

- Section 213 legalizes secret searches on demand without properly obtained warrants prior to the search. It is a clear violation of the 4th amendment;

- Section 215 authorizes the FBI to acquire any business records whatsoever by order of a secret U.S. court. The recipient of such a search order is forbidden from telling any person that he has received such a request;

- Section 203 allows information gathered in criminal proceedings to be shared with intelligence agencies such as the CIA, (which is already unaccountable to the American people);

- Section 216 allows investigators to obtain "dialing, routing and signaling information" for any citizen without probable cause of a crime or judicial review if they certify that it is relevant to an ongoing criminal investigation;

- Section 216 also gives law enforcement unbridled access to Internet communications and allows the FBI to have access to entire Emails before they supposedly separate the content from the addresses;

- Section 217 allows federal agents to intercept messages that they suspect are being sent through computers without authorization. Suspected messages are identified by those intercepting them;

- Section 218 Relaxes restrictions for foreign intelligence gathering on Americans by accommodating any significant purpose as long as certifications are not clearly erroneous;

- Section 219 allows a search warrant issued in one district to apply to property or person outside the district even though the person or property was not identified in the original warrant;

- Section 220 allows an order to be served on any telecommunications company or service provider nationwide without any need that the particular service provider be identified in the warrant;

- Section 207 allows for roving wiretaps that are not specific to a given phone identification number but rather to an individual regardless of where that individual may be;
- Section 211 overrides protections provided by the Cable act for customer records related to telecommunications services;
- Section 210 expands records that can be sought without a court order to include: session times and durations, temporary network addresses; means and source of payments, including any credit card or bank account number;
- Section 802 defines the definition of terrorist so loosely that it could be applied to almost anyone who may have broken a law and therefore subject them to the provisions of the bill;

The Patriot Act also contains many provisions that are not necessarily related to terrorism. They involve government spying on computer trespasses as well as expanded scope and penalties for computer fraud. It also has some sunset provisions with new powers that expire in December 31, 2005, unless Congress renews them. But there is no reporting mechanism for Congress to judge the effectiveness of how these new powers are implemented. Therefore, the sunset provisions are basically irrelevant. Chapter 11 provides the federal income tax as one example of how Congress almost never restores freedom after confiscating it.

Morton Halperin, explained the problem with the terrorist premise of the Patriot Act: "Historically, the government has often believed anyone who is protesting government policy is doing it at the behest of a foreign government and opened counterintelligence investigations of them." The Patriot Act inhibits legitimate political activism that a citizen truly believes is conducted in the best interests of the United States government. Perhaps that was part of its intent.

On November 13, 2001 George W. Bush signed an Executive Order to establish military tribunals for prosecuting terrorists outside of the justice system. The new procedures will allow for two out of three military commissioners to impose the sentences including the death penalty based on a preponderance of evidence. This is in start contrast to the current justice system that requires a unanimous decision by a jury based on evidence "beyond a reasonable doubt". There are also no judicial appeals but reviews only by the Secretary of Defense or the President. These two individuals will have the power to create tribunals, appoint the officers to sit on them, define regulations for how they operate and preside over appeals. Thus they will acquire executive, legislative and judicial powers that reside in all three separate branches of the American government.

One defender of the military tribunals is Judge Robert Bork, who fired Watergate prosecutor Archibald Cox for Richard Nixon, after Attorney General, Elliot Richardson, refused to and resigned. Bork wrote in an article for National Review: "If there is a problem with Bush's order it is the exemption of U.S. citizens from trials before tribunals". Most citizens do not realize they do. Anyone who may not happen to have a driver's license or other form of ID available when confronted could be whisked away as a terrorist never to be seen again.

The Patriot Act and military tribunals were designed to apply to terrorists but the definition of a terrorist is not what Americans might think. The Joint Terrorism Task Force identifies "defenders of the U.S. Constitution against the government and U.N." as terrorists. The Alex Jones 911 video illustrates the problem best with a 7/19/2001 tape he received from Missouri. The video clearly shows a belligerent Federal Emergency Management Agency (FEMA) representative is making an obnoxious presentation to local police and firefighters. He asks them: "Who were the first terrorists in America? The answer: "The founding fathers" (because they fought against British rule when they won our freedom). The Bush administration representative also uses an apparent reference to the Roman Catholic Church of the 1500s to identify more of today's terrorists. He states when Christians asked people, "Do you believe that Jesus Christ is your Lord and Savior?" and you said, "No", what happened? He answered" "They took your head off". His chilling conclusion is: "They are the terrorists."

ILLEGAL IMMIGRATION FOR TERRORISTS

The 9/11 attacks have generated a renewed push to have a National ID card for citizens even though no citizens were involved in the attacks. If an ID card is implemented it should be required for immigrants, not citizens. While Congress and the Bush administration have taken drastic measures to implement a police state, little has been done to address illegal immigration a root cause of 9/11. In fact, the immigration problem had been largely ignored until the INS erroneously issued visa extensions for Mohammed Atta and Marwan Al-Shehhi months after they were identified as suspected hijackers in the 9/11 attack. Michelle Malkin explained how investigations determined that of 19 suspected hijackers, two were illegal aliens, three illegally overstayed their visa, at least two tried to cross illegally through our borders and seven obtained fraudulent ID cards with the help of illegal alien day laborers in Virginia.

Border Patrol agents from the Canadian border provided more insight at a Senate Sub-Committee hearing for U.S. Policy on Illegal Aliens. At that November 13, 2001 hearing chaired by Carl Levin they explained many disturbing policies. For example, when aliens are caught trying to enter the country illegally, most of them are released **INTO** the country after being detained. The INS schedules them for a removal hearing and since they simply never show up, the INS has no way to track them down. Many illegal aliens know that this is the policy and are not even worried when the Border Patrol catches them.

Border Patrol agents, Mark Hall and Robert Lindemann, the president and vice president of the local Border Patrol agents union, explained to the Detroit Free Press that the Michigan Canadian border lacked adequate resources to protect against terrorism. A total of 28 field agents guarded 804 miles of shoreline border with one working boat, several damaged electronic sensors and a broken remote camera. Senior INS officials initially sought to terminate them and later recommended them for suspensions and demotions after they made this information public.

Iowa Senator Charles Grassley wrote a letter on March 28, 2002 to INS Commissioner James Ziglar, a Bush appointee, stating the INS retaliatory actions were in violation of the 1989 Whistleblower Act. He expressed concern they were "more worried about suppressing embarrassing information than enforcing immigration laws and protecting the nation's security". He also stated: "It is especially galling that INS and Border Patrol managers initially sought to terminate the employment of these two agents..." No such comparable disciplinary actions were issued to the INS officials responsible for extending the visas of Mohammed Atta and Marwan Al-Shehhhi after the 9/11 attacks.

What are our governments doing to correct this root cause problem of 9/11? . In Georgia, a state representative attempted to pass a bill to grant drivers licenses for all current illegal aliens. On March 12, 2002 the House passed H.R. 1885 by a vote of 275 to 137, including Section 245(i), amnesty for illegal aliens. And on April 25, 2002, rather than to correct the problems at the INS, the House voted to abolish it altogether just as they did with the independent counsel law.

INSIDER TRADING ON 9/11

The Israelis have made their own case as to how America can determine who might be behind the 9/11 attacks. One key is to identify who profited from insider trading just days before the attacks. During the week before, an abnormally high number of put options were placed to short the stocks of United Airlines, American Airlines and major WTC tenants, Merrill Lynch & Co. and Morgan Stanley Dean Whitter & Co. On September 21, 2001 The Israeli Herzliyya International Policy Institute for Counter Terrorism provided a fascinating financial trail as explained by Michael Ruppert in some of his *From the Wilderness* bulletins.

During September 6 and 7, 2001 the Chicago Board Options Exchange had 4,744 put options placed on United Airlines and only 396 call options. On September 10, 2001 the Chicago exchange saw 4,518 put options placed on American Airlines and only 748 call options. This level is considered to be more than six times higher than normal. No other similarly abnormal trading is known to have occurred on other airlines.

Morgan Stanley Dean Whitter, had 2,157 of its October put options bought on the three trading days prior to the attacks (September 6, 7, &10) compared with just 27 put option contracts per day before September 6. Merrill Lynch had 12,215 October put options on its stock in the four trading days before the attacks compared with 252 put option contracts per day before September 5. During the week before the 9/11 attacks, the put options for those stocks were over 50 times the normal numbers.

The *Wall Street Journal, San Francisco Chronicle* and *Baron's* confirmed that 2,000 put option contracts for United Airlines were purchased through the Alex Brown, the American investment banking arm of the German Deutsche bank. The *Chronicle* also mentioned that investors have not claimed about 2.5 million dollars in profits from their put option contracts. Der Spiegel, a German news source reported that Deutsche bank also handles accounts valued at around 100 million dollars for the bin Laden family. These were part of 10 accounts that Deutsche bank identified for German authorities as possibly being used for terrorist activities, according to the Guardian, an English news source.

The Chairman of Alex Brown until 1998, was A.B. "Buzzy" Krongard. At the time of the 9/11 attacks, he was Executive Director of the CIA, one of the highest three positions. The CIA has long been intertwined with stock trading since its inception in 1947 under the National Security Act. William Casey was chairman of the SEC. David Doherty, Vice President of Enforcement for the New York Stock Exchange is the retired General Counsel of the CIA. "Buzzy" Krongard was also a former General Counsel of the CIA until he was appointed as Executive Director on March 26 by George .W. Bush.

Clark Clifford, a Wall Street bank lawyer, wrote the act that created the CIA, which can essentially operate above the law under the grounds of national security. Clifford became the Secretary of Defense under Lyndon Johnson in the 1960s. During the 1980s, as chairman of First American Bankshares, he claimed he was unaware it was illegally owned by the same Arab shareholders who owned the scandalous BCCI. In 1992, he was indicted on charges of fraud, lying to bank regulators about the illegal ownership and accepting $40 million in bribes from BCCI. The charges were dropped during the Clinton administration because of fear he would have a heart attack if tried.

On September 19, 2001 SEC enforcement director Stephen Cutler, released a public statement that in cooperation with other agencies, it is investigating whether terrorists profited from the acts of 9/11. It said: "We are vigorously pursuing all leads..." and "This is obviously a matter of utmost importance". But the SEC has gone stone silent for many months. After several calls to a public affairs spokesman he confirmed "Yes, that is correct. I appreciate your dedication to accuracy". Although SEC representatives testify before Congressional Committees several times a month, no one is known to have testified in open or closed session about this matter, nor has Congress or anyone in the Bush administration demanded it.

THE ANTHRAX ATTACK ON AMERICA

Exactly a week after the 9/11 attacks America was attacked by what may eventually prove to be an even bigger threat. On September 18, the first known letter in a series laced with anthrax was postmarked. The letters initiated a nationwide anthrax scare beginning on October 4, 2001 when the first case was actually reported. The letters eventually caused five deaths and the infection of as many as 18 others. The deadly letters were postmarked from Trenton, New Jersey and sent to the New York Post, NBC and the offices of Senators Tom Daschle, and Patrick Leahy. Hoax letters sent to other news agencies originated from St Petersburg, Florida or other locations unknown.

The anthrax letters were dated 9-11-01 and contained phrases such as "death to America", "death to Israel" "Allah is great", "we have this anthrax", and "you can not stop us now". The phrases implied they were sent from an Arab terrorist with an Islamic background. But use of western format dates, right slanting letters and phrasing of "Allah is great" are not consistent with Arabic writing style or Islamic phrasing. Investigators eventually concluded Arabs were not involved in the letters.

Perhaps, the best-detailed analysis of the anthrax attacks is produced by Barbara Hatch Rosenberg, director of the Chemical and Biological Weapons Program for the Federation of American Scientists. Many aspects of her analysis have been confirmed by the FBI and confidential sources of various news agencies. Her analysis explains how investigators determined that some of the anthrax was "weaponized" by a secret U.S. military process to prepare the anthrax so it would float in air without clumping. Its characteristics include:

- An unmilled variety of a concentration and purity consistent only with U.S. process;
- Use of silica and not bentonite, which is used by foreign laboratories such as those in Iraq;
- A special coating indicative of the secret U.S. process

Lab workers suggest it is unlikely someone could have stolen all 10 grams of anthrax used in the letters therefore a portion of the strain was probably stolen and cultivated by the perpetrator. In addition, the attacker must have had:

- Experience in preparing and handling anthrax without leaving personal traces,
- Vaccinations, annual booster shots and knowledge of procedures for self-protection;
- Clearance to access classified CIA information written about anthrax distribution through mail.

Those types of prerequisites immediately rule out nearly everyone in the pharmaceutical industry. They even rule out many in the defense industry since the perpetrator must have had access to a classified February, 1999 document about distribution of anthrax through the mail as written by U.S. weaponization process inventor, William Patrick.

In a January 29, 2002 letter to American Society for Microbiology Members, Van Harp, FBI Assistant Director of the Washington Field Office confirmed that the anthrax strain used in the letters was the Ames strain of Bacillus anthracis. This strain has been maintained by the U.S. Army since 1980 and is controlled by the Medical Research Institute of Infectious Diseases (MRIID) at Fort Detrick, Md. Fort Detrick had distributed that particular strain under tight controls only to Dugway Proving Ground in Utah, Batelle Memorial Institute in

Columbus, Ohio, Porton in England, Suffield in Canada and three U.S. universities. The military installations that would be involved in the U.S. weaponized process are Fort Detrick, Dugway and Batelle, a CIA contractor. Security has historically been lax at the Fort Detrick site and there are no known safety or security breaches at the other locations.

Thus the profile of the attacker would likely be a former U.S. lab worker, probably from Fort Detrick, who now works in a similar capacity for the CIA and has access to the classified documentation from William Patrick. The profile should narrow the field of suspects from 280+ million in the U.S. to less than a couple of dozen and simplify identifying the perpetrator. But Dr. Len Horowitz of Tetrahedron expressed concern that the FBI may be under pressure not to solve the case because it would expose a weaponization project developed by the CIA and Batelle called "Clearvision", which violates the International Geneva Accord.

Fort Dertick is also the site where Dr. Ayaad Assaad, a naturalized U.S. citizen from Egypt, worked until 1997 when he was dismissed by Col. David R. Franz. Assaad had complained to Col. Franz in 1991 about a series of racially oriented incidents denigrating Assaad and other Arab American scientists, two of which were also dismissed by Col. Franz.

On October 2, 2001 the FBI called Dr. Assaad in for an interview because they had received an unsigned letter accusing him of being responsible for mailing the anthrax tainted letters. The letter was forwarded by the Quantico Marine police BEFORE the first anthrax case was reported. It stated, among other things, "Dr. Assaad is a potential biological terrorist,". It also said: "I have worked with Dr. Assaad, and I heard him say that he has a vendetta against the U.S. government and that if anything happens to him, he told his sons to carry on." His lawyer Rosemary A. McDermott, said: "The person who wrote that letter knew intimate details of my client's life and his professional history, and about the Fort Detrick operation".

Eventually, FBI spokesman, Chris Murray, announced: "We have investigated the allegations against Dr. Assaad and found them to be baseless." Assad turned out to be the victim of a sophisticated framing attempt conducted by someone who knew him at Fort Detrick, the originating source of the Ames anthrax strain. But McDermott, Rosenberg and others suggest the likelihood the person who attempted to frame Dr. Assaad may be the person who sent the anthrax letters and attempted to frame other Arabs.

But how could the anthrax strain have fallen into the wrong hands? Hector Carreon of La Voz de Aztlan states lab specimens of anthrax spores, Ebola virus and other pathogens disappeared from Fort Detrick in the early 1990s during the same time when Dr. Assaad was being harassed. A 1992 inquiry into the disappearance of the deadly pathogens found evidence someone was secretly entering the laboratory late at night to conduct unauthorized research involving anthrax. Documents from the inquiry show one unauthorized person who was observed entering the laboratory at night was Lt. Col. Philip Zack who at the time no longer worked at Fort Detrick. A surveillance camera recorded Lt. Col. Zack being let in at 8:40 P.M. on January 23, 1992, by Dr. Marian Rippy, according to Carreon.

Carreon cited Dr. Philip M. Zack as a potential mailer of the anthrax letters. He indicated that Zack, a Jewish American microbiologist, may have the motive, knowledge and means to frame Assaad during the 1990s and the Arab Americans during 2001. But even if Zack is not the one responsible, the anthrax letters seem to represent another attempt by elements inside our own U.S. military to frame Arabs for a terrorist act committed by someone else. Does this sound familiar?

All indications are that the perpetrator of the anthrax attack had the knowledge, capability, and access to infect far more people than the number actually infected. It is unlikely the perpetrator anticipated postal workers would be infected by seepage of anthrax spores through the envelope. Some letters even identified the substance as anthrax and warned the recipient to take antibiotics. Therefore, Ms. Rosenberg concluded the perpetrator of the anthrax attacks did not aim to kill large numbers of people but to instill fear in the population. So who profits from fear generated by the anthrax scare?

Dr. Len Horowitz of Tetrahedron Inc., identified one possible beneficiary as the anthrax antidote maker, Bayer Corp., which was formed from portions of I.G. Farben, the Nazi company deeply involved in the rise of Adolph Hitler. On

October 24, 2001, Tommy Thompson, Secretary of Health and Human Services and Helge Wehmeier, President and CEO of Bayer, announced an agreement for a significant new federal purchase of the antibiotic Cipro. Under the contract, valued at $95 million, Health and Human Services will pay 95 cents per tablet, for a total initial order of 100 million tablets.

Horowitz and Rosenberg also identified BioPort as another primary beneficiary because its lab has been the only U.S. anthrax vaccine source since the 1970s, when it operated as Michigan Biological Products Institute (MBPI) of Lansing. The anthrax vaccine has been identified in Congressional testimony as a likely source of Gulf War Syndrome encountered by our soldiers during the 1991 Gulf War. Since then, quite a few military personnel have become seriously ill or died. Others who had taken the vaccine contracted Gulf War Syndrome without ever being in the war theatre. Many refuse to take the vaccine and have left the military. In 1997 after an inspection failure, the FDA threatened to revoke the MBPI's license. In September of 1998, a newly formed company called BioPort took over the MBPI lab in an auction.

BioPort was founded by Fuad El-Hibri, a Lebanese German who was a director of Porton Products International, a British anthrax vaccine maker. El-Hibri brought in former Joint Chiefs of Staff Chairman, Admiral William J. Crowe, as a co-owner who had little or no actual investment. Crowe was one of the few officers to back the presidency of Bill Clinton. Despite the sordid history of the lab, BioPort received a DOD contract within a month of the takeover "to manufacture, test, bottle and store the anthrax vaccine" at an increased cost from $3.50 to over $10 per dose. Since 1998, BioPort has been unable to ship the vaccine to its only customer, the U.S. military, because it could not meet FDA regulations. On October 19, 2001 BioPort was sued for negligence on behalf of one deceased and one injured soldier.

The fact that the first biological attack on the U.S. would happen to be conducted with anthrax is particularly intriguing. Public pressure from the anthrax attack could force the FDA to prematurely approve the BioPort vaccine even if it did not fully meet FDA regulations. A huge demand for the vaccine would also be generated in the private sector thus giving BioPort a vast new customer base. Sherman Skolnick, a Chicago investigative reporter with superb, proven government connections, contends one of the companies having indirect investments in BioPort is the Carlyle group.

Another interesting report of foreknowledge was revealed in an October 24, 2001 AP report by Sandra Sobieraj. It concerned the anthrax attacks and the antidote Cipro. She reported that although White House officials refuse to discuss it, personnel including Vice President Dick Cheney began taking Cipro on the evening of September 11, a week before the first known Anthrax laced letter was mailed.

FEDERAL SECRECY

The Bush family investments such as those in the Carlyle group are secret just as they were when George H.W. Bush was running for President. It is inconceivable the family of a U.S. President would be allowed to have secret investments that could conflict with national security but Congress has never taken action to force their exposure. When George H.W. Bush ran for president, the financial dealings of his oil company, Zapata Corp. and interaction with the CIA from 25 years prior were also kept secret. A similar situation occurred during World War II with Prescott Bush, the father of George H.W Bush. If the American people had known that Prescott made most of his money by funding, and profiting from, the Nazi rise to power, George H.W. Bush would have never been elected as President.

The truth about 9/11 is also secret since George W. Bush has resisted any attempt at inquiries and Vice President Dick Cheney has pressured at least six different Congressional committees not to conduct probes. The courageous call for an investigation by Cynthia McKinney actually put more pressure on Democrat Congressional leaders than the administration. The "opposition" party leaders are faced with the prospect of exposing real corruption, a task that Republican leaders shunned during impeachment. Americans are psychologically programmed to believe these parties are opposite and one is good while the other is bad. This book has explained that under pressure, they always cover each other's corruption.

The Bush administration, like many others, also has an uncanny ability to pressure Congress into voting for bad bills like the Patriot Act. I would like to be a flower on the wall in closed-door sessions to see how this is done. A recent example is that of Bob Barr who has been held up as a hero in much of this book despite his support for the phony drug war. Barr is a steadfast Constitutionalist who was forced into a 2002 primary against another solid Republican, John Linder, after Georgia Democrats redistricted the state. Barr, has been consistently against fast track trade agreement authority for a President because Article I Section 8 of the Constitution requires all trade agreements to be negotiated by Congress. Yet on December 6, 2001, after several Congressional members met at the White House he essentially cast the deciding vote on a 215-214 margin to pass the H.R. 3005 Trade Promotion Authority bill through the House.

Some Bush administration officials, such as Deputy Defense Secretary Paul Wolfowitz, also clamored for an attack on Iraq even though both Dick Cheney and Colin Powell confirmed that Iraq was not involved in the 9/11 attacks. U.N. inspector Scott Ritter, who has been critical of both the Clinton and Bush administrations, stated flatly: "Most of Iraq's biological agents and production facilities have been destroyed." The tunnels and documents that a U.S. informant claimed existed were never found and the U.N. no longer considers him credible because he has "tenuous sources and dubious motives". Ritter pointed out, "But the Bush administration has shown little interest in sending the inspectors back". The alternative is another war against Iraq. Would this one also be for profit?

In addition to the horrendous loss of life on September 11, most Americans have been impacted by financial setbacks from the attacks and the subsequent war on terror that may not even be fighting the real enemy. Although Republicans consistently blame Democrats for excessive spending, the Bush administration and Congress have reached new spending heights during the first year of the George W Bush presidency. Secretary of the Treasury, Paul O'Neill, revealed the real year-end results that are historically reported in October on the U.S. Treasury web site:

"Accrual based financial reporting is critical to gaining a comprehensive understanding of the U.S. Government's operations. For fiscal 2001, our results were an accrual-based deficit of $515 billion in contrast to a $127 billion budget surplus reported last fall,"

That's right, while politicians from both sides claimed to have a $127 billion surplus, the actual financial results for fiscal 2001 showed a $515 billion deficit. These numbers do not even reflect the full brunt that the 9/11 attacks had on the U.S. economy or the bulk of the cost of the war on terror, which by definition, is infinite.

THE 1993 WTC BOMBING

On February 26, 1993 at 12:18 pm, the WTC was first attacked when a truck bomb exploded in the parking garage killing six people, injuring over 1000 and causing $500 million in damage. On March 4, 1994, Muhammad Amin Salameh, Nidal Ayyad, Mahmud Abouhalima, and Ahmed Ajaj were convicted for their roles in the bombing. U.S. Attorney Mary Jo White led the prosecution in Manhattan at the U.S. District Court of Southern New York. On November 12, 1997, after fleeing to Pakistan and Jordan, respectively, Ramzi Yousef and Eyad Ismoil were convicted on murder and conspiracy charges for their roles. Yousef is believed to be the ringleader of the bombing while Ismoil delivered the bomb in a Ford Econoline van and claimed he thought the truck contained commercial cleaning fluids.

Muhammad Amin Salameh, a follower of Sheikh Abdel Rahman, had rented the van in his name from a Ryder rental exchange in Jersey City. The FBI suspected the van was the most likely bomb carrier based on the positioning of the vehicles and debris in the garage. They claimed they found an axle containing fragments of the VIN and were able to identify the vehicle accordingly. Salameh was arrested when he returned to the Ryder rental exchange to collect a $400 deposit on the Ford Econoline. Salameh reported the van stolen on the day of the bombing after police would not accept his report the day before because he did not have the license number. These facts raise the question that if Salameh was a knowing participant in the bombing why would he rent the van in his own name, report it stolen to the police and then attempt to collect a deposit afterwards? Federal law enforcement officers have no answer for this.

When Salameh rented the van, he used a telephone number that was traced to the Jersey City apartment of Josie Hadas according to the FBI complaint. Police reported they had uncovered other incriminating evidence of bomb making there and that a bomb-sniffing dog responded positively to one of the apartment closets, according to the *Washington Post*. But Hadas was never charged in conjunction with the crime and apparently fled the country. When a reporter asked the State Department of her whereabouts in a March 19, 1993 press briefing, the State Department refused comment. Hadas was later reported to be an operative of the Israeli Mossad.

Worse yet, the involvement of the FBI in the 1993 WTC bombing has seriously been called into question after the role of their paid informant was exposed. In 1991, the FBI hired Ahmad Salem a former Egyptian military officer, to infiltrate a suspected Arab terrorist group. They claim that Salem was dismissed in 1992 and then rehired after the 1993 WTC bombing.

Salem was having some problems with his FBI handlers and decided to secretly tape his conversations with them. Over the two-year period of his engagement he secretly recorded 70 tapes, which were released to the Assistant U.S. Attorney and defense teams. Here are some portions of transcripts that appeared October 27 and 28, 1993 *New York Times* to document conversations between Salem and FBI agents John Anticev and Nancy Floyd after the 1993 WTC bombing:

Salem: "You were informed. Everything is ready. The day and the time. Boom. Lock them up and that's that. That's why I feel so bad."

Salem: "Guys, now you saw this bomb went off and you both know that we could avoid that." "You get paid, guys, to prevent problems like this from happening."

Salem reiterated his disgust with the New York Field Office supervisor several times and agent Nancy Floyd made several attempts to console:

Salem: "Since the bomb went off I feel terrible I feel bad. I feel here is people who don't listen."

Floyd: "Hey, I mean it wasn't like you didn't try and I didn't try."

Salem: "Do you deny that your supervisor is the main reason of bombing the World Trade Center?" "We was handling the case perfectly well until the supervisor came and messed it up, upside down."

Floyd: "You can't force people to do the right thing."

The supervisor is most likely to be New York Field Office Director, William Garvin who would have such approval authority. Salem was so upset with him that he wanted to take his complaint to Washington but was dissuaded by the agents:

Anticev: "I don't think that the New York people would like the things out of the New York office to go to Washington D.C.."

Floyd: "Well, of course not, they don't want to get their butts chewed."

Salem explained his disgust he was actually redirected by the New York FBI Field Office Director to use real explosives to prepare the WTC bomb:

Salem: "He requested to make me testify and if he didn't push for that, we'll be building the bomb with a phony powder and grabbing the people who was involved in it."

The transcripts clearly point out that Salem was frustrated because the New York FBI Field Office had the power to stop the WTC bombing but did nothing to prevent it. The FBI agents even confirm and acknowledge his comments. Most astounding is that the New York FBI office was actually directing him on how to assemble the bomb and then forced him to build it with real explosive materials instead of fake ones.

THE NEW YORK BOMBING
CONSPIRACY TRIAL

Emad Salem was a key witness in the October 1, 1995 convictions of ten individuals, including Sheikh Abdel Rahman, on various offenses, including seditious conspiracy in connection with a plot to bomb the United Nations and tunnels in New York City. One of their defense lawyers and many news sources state that Salem was paid about a million dollars by the FBI for his work. While it would normally be wonderful to arrest and convict potential terrorists before they strike, this case also has some inexplicable twists.

The sedition trial was also held at U.S. District Court of Southern New York in Manhattan and prosecuted with a team led by U.S. Attorney Mary Jo White. Defense attorneys William Kunstler and Ron Kuby were removed from the case, leaving only government lawyers for the defendants. No evidence linked any of the 10 defendants to the WTC bombing or any previous terrorist attack. Each defendant received a 20-year jail term for conspiracy because they were found to be assembling bomb material in a Queens garage. In a classic case of double jeopardy, one defendant, El Sayyid Nosair, was somehow found guilty during the group trial of killing Rabbi Meir Kahane even though state court had already been acquitted of those charges in 1991. The obvious major target of the trial was the blind Muslim cleric, Sheikh Abdel Rahman, who prosecutors admitted was not involved in the details of daily operations. The government case against Rahman consisted primarily of his political leanings, antagonistic comments about both U.S. and Egyptian governments and his conversations with other co-conspirators as defined in court documents. Rahman claims he is not the first person to go to prison for political beliefs.

Abdel Rahman received his visa in Khartoum, Sudan and came to America in 1990 even though he was on a watch list from the State Department, which was warned by the American and Egyptian embassies about his political activities. The Embassy official responsible for issuing visas in Khartoum was a CIA agent, according to the December 4, 1993 *London Times*. Salameh, Rahman and several other defendants appear to have no known criminal record in any country. Prosecutors even admitted when asked by the FBI informant about blowing up the United Nations, Rahman said: "It would be bad for Muslims" although he may have suggested some other military target would be more acceptable. Defendants argued they did not have the actual explosives background necessary to carry out such acts and the primary individual who did was the FBI informant himself, Amhad Salem. The FBI seems to have paid Salem a huge sum to instigate a case of entrapment that conveniently diverted attention from embarrassing public knowledge that the FBI may have actually been directing in the WTC bombing.

THE 1998 AFRICAN EMBASSY BOMBINGS

On the morning of August 7, 1998, a truck bomb exploded at the American embassy in East Nairobi, Kenya killing 213 people. Ten minutes later another truck bomb exploded at Dar es Salaam, Tanzania, killed an additional 11 people. Over 4,500 people were injured. Each of the truck drivers died instantly.

Four men were arrested: Khalfan Khamis Mohamed, a 27-year-old from Tanzania, who purchased the Tanzania bomb delivery vehicle; Mohamed Rashed Daoud Al-'Owhali, the 23-year-old from Saudi Arabian who was a truck passenger at Nairobi and apparently rejected martyrdom by running away from the scene; Sadeek Odeh, a 35-year-old Jordanian accused of helping prepare the Nairobi attack; and Wadih El-Hage, a 40-year-old naturalized American citizen born in Lebanon, who was a member of Al Qaeda.

Although the crimes were committed in Africa, the defendants went to trial in February 2001 at the U.S. District Court of Southern New York in lower Manhattan. U.S. Attorney Mary Jo White once again led the prosecutors in the same scene and scenario as the peculiar sedition trial. Each was convicted in May 2001 for their roles in the bombings and sentenced in October of 2001 to life without parole.

Al Owhali was convicted of murdering 213 people, including 12 Americans, in Kenya. Mohamed was convicted of murdering 11 people at Tanzania. Odeh, was convicted of the 213 murders in Kenya. Odeh, who said he had no role in the bombings, did admit membership in Al Qaeda, which he believed to be an "organization to change oppressive circumstances", according to his attorney. El Hage, 41, a Lebanese American citizen, was convicted of conspiracy and perjury. Although he was not convicted of any violent act, U.S. District Judge Leonard Sand gave him the same life without parole sentence.

On May 5, 2000 indictments were issued for 13 additional conspirators. Three were arrested in England where they have been fighting extradition. Two detainees, Abdul Bary and Eidarous, were Islamic Jihad members while Khalid Al-Fawwaz is believed to be an Al Queda member with communication connections to Osama bin Laden. As part of the indictment, prosecutors claimed that the Egyptian Islamic Jihad led by Ayman Al Zawahiri And Muhammad Atef merged with Al Queda led by Osama bin Laden.

Although the trial was touted to some degree as proving that bin Laden was behind the bombings, no direct evidence was presented to indicate that he was involved in the execution or planning of them, which the FBI said started in the spring of 1998. The prosecution established Al Owhali had previous associations to bin Laden before he came to Kenya. They also entered into evidence over 500 phone call records and some wire-tap transcripts which were used primarily as evidence against El Hage. These established four calls between El Hage and Khalid Al-Fawwaz who had many contacts to a satellite phone they said belonged to bin Laden. Prosecutors contended that bin Laden used Khalid Al Fawal to issue public "fatwa" statements that could be interpreted as supportive of the operation. But the actual bin Laden link to the bombings was indirect and based primarily on four phone calls between Al-Fawwaz and El Hage, who was not convicted of either terrorist act.

Ten families of the 12 U.S. citizens killed in the Nairobi bombings joined together in an administrative claim against the State Department. Attorney Stuart Newberger said the government failed to beef up security at the embassy even though there were warnings of a threat.

THE USS COLE BOMBING

On Oct. 12, 2000, two men in a small boat pulled along side of the Navy warship USS Cole refueling at a commercially run, water-borne platform known as a dolphin about 600 meters off shore from Aden harbor in Yemen. The men waved at the crew just before the boat exploded. The explosion killed 17 sailors, injured 39 others and caused about $240 million in damages, roughly a quarter of the original cost to build the ship.

An investigation determined the boat contained 400-700 pounds of C-4 explosives probably made in the United States. Yemen authorities eventually arrested 9 other individuals who they believed had varying roles in the crime. U.S. and Yemen officials cooperated well in the beginning of the investigation but relations became strained as the investigation proceeded.

President Ali Abdullah Salih refused to allow the extradition of Yemeni suspects for trial in the United States, because it is forbidden by the Yemeni constitution. In January 2001, Yemen authorities were prepared to begin trial for the suspects in custody but the U.S. requested they take time for a more thorough investigation.

Yemen authorities determined a couple of the suspects may have come from Afghanistan but did not establish any evidence that Osama bin Laden planned or ordered the bombing. On January 30, 2001 ABC News announced Mohamed Al Owhali, who was arrested 2 1/2 years earlier for the Kenyan Embassy bombing, provided the FBI details of a plan to attack an American warship in Yemen. Since Al Owhali was connected to bin Laden in Afghanistan the implication was that bin Laden planned the Cole attack.

But ABC didn't mention there was a problem with the admission by Al Owhali. The FBI's own executive summary dated November 18, 1998, stated the embassy bombers began to locate to Kenya in 1993 to early 1994. Had Al Owhali and bin Laden actually been involved in the planning of the USS Cole bombing it would have taken place 7 years before it occurred. By contrast, the same FBI document stated the more complex embassy bombings were planned about four months in advance.

THE 1995 OKLAHOMA CITY BOMBING

On April 19, 1995 a truck bomb exploded at the Alfred P. Murrah federal building in Oklahoma City killing 168 innocent Americans. Government officials and most of the national news media claim: Timothy McVeigh drove to the building by himself in a Ryder truck containing a fertilizer bomb he created with some assistance from Terry Nichols, that bomb was the sole cause of all destruction and no other people assisted McVeigh. Overwhelming evidence has been collected by numerous sources that illustrate the standard government and media reporting of this bombing is utterly false. Some of the sources have been mentioned earlier in this book but for the sake of quick recap I will refer to facts primarily contained within the Final Report produced by the Oklahoma Bombing Investigation Committee, which includes former Oklahoma state representative, Charles Key, and survivor, V. Z. Lawton. A few of the key points that directly contradict the standard media and government contentions are:

- The three local news channels in Oklahoma City reported different federal authorities told them at least one additional bomb was found in the building during the first hour after the bombing;
- The ATF later claimed the additional bomb was actually an inert device they used in training exercises but never explained why such a device was in an office building;
- Seismic evidence from the Oklahoma City and the University of Oklahoma indicated two mismatched sound wave patterns;
- Many witnesses at the scene stated there were two explosions;
- Several qualified explosive experts have seriously questioned how a fertilizer truck bomb could have blown out concrete support posts after dissipating in the air between the truck and the posts;
- Experts also question how a concrete post near the back of the building was blown out even though the sheet rock on the posts nearer the truck was not even damaged;

- Two witnesses stated ATF agents told them the ATF had received advance warning of the bomb and most of their agents were not in the building;
- 70+ witnesses saw McVeigh with other people, 20 of them saw Middle Eastern individuals;

The Final Report contains an interesting affidavit from 26-year FBI veteran, Henry Gibbons concerning a man named Abraham Abdallah Amhad. According to the affidavit, Ahmad left Oklahoma City on April 19, 1995, at 10:43 am, aboard an American Airlines flight to Chicago, where he was to catch another plane to Rome and then another to his final destination in Jordan. American Airlines personnel in Oklahoma City noticed he looked nervous and called their Dallas national security office, which in turn, notified the FBI in Chicago. Ahmad was detained in Chicago while his bag went to Rome where Italian officials were alerted and searched it. In his luggage they found multi-car radios, shielded and unshielded wire, a tool kit and tools "consistent with use for both explosive devices and normal electric repair or installations". Also found was a set of blue jogging pants consistent with ones seen on one of two men running from the vicinity of the Murrah Building toward a brown Chevrolet pickup truck. Ahmad was released, secured passage to England, found to be ineligible to enter the country and returned to the United States.

KFOR-TV INVESTIGATION

An astounding court order about the bombing was filed on Nov. 17, 1999 for Case 97-1535-L in the U.S. District Court of Western Oklahoma. The order defines court accepted facts collected by KFOR-TV reporters Jayna Davis and Brad Edwards indicating Middle Eastern accomplices likely assisted McVeigh in bombing the building. The U.S. District Court order resulted from a defamation suit filed by Hussain Al Hussaini against Palmer Communications, KFOR-TV, Davis, Edwards and news director Melissa Klinzing.

The order resulted when the court denied an additional discovery request by Al Hussaini because he failed to show how specific depositions would create a genuine issue of fact as to whether defendant statements were defamatory. But worse yet for Al Hussaini, the order publicly documented long suppressed, devastating facts collected by KFOR-TV reporters implicating him in the April 19, 1995 bombing. Here are some key excerpts by fact number that are so conclusive they are taken verbatim from the court order without commentary:

"...the court accepts as undisputed the following facts as stated by defendants:

- 3. A witness reported to the FBI two Middle-Eastern looking men were seen running from the vicinity of the Murrah Building toward a brown Chevrolet truck. A third person was believed to be in the truck.

- 4. On April 19, the FBI issued an all points bulletin for authorities to be on the look-out for a late-model Brown Chevrolet pickup truck with tinted windows and a smoke-colored bug deflector.

- 6. On April 20, 1995, the federal government issued an arrest warrant for "John Doe #2," who was described as of medium build 5'9"-5'10" tall, about 175-180 pounds, with brown hair and a tattoo on his left arm.

- 9. On April 20, 1995 federal authorities detained Abraham Abdallah Ahmad, a Jordanian-American resident of Oklahoma City, in London, England as a possible witness in the bombing. Ahmad was reported to have duffel bags containing electrical tape, silicone, a hammer, tweezers and a photo album with pictures of missiles and other weapons. Ahmad was reported to have left his home in northwest Oklahoma City approximately a half hour after the bombing and flown to Chicago, then London en route to Jordan.

- 11. About the same time, as her interview with Ahmad, Davis interviewed Ernie Cranfield, who knew Ahmad. Cranfield told Davis that Ahmad had been to Cranfield's place of employment with unusual frequency in the days just before the bombing. Cranfield said several of his co-workers were Iraqis who had been hired by his employer, Samir Khalil, in about November 1994.

- 13. Cranfield said one of his Iraqi co-workers, Al Hussaini, had a tattoo on his left arm.

- 14. Cranfield also told Davis he had seen a brown pickup truck with tinted windows and bug shield at Khalil's place of business prior to the bombing.
- 16. Davis also interviewed Samir Khalil's secretary. The secretary confirmed Cranfield's statements Ahmad had visited Khalil's office several times a day in the weeks before the bombing, which was far more often than usual; and she had also seen a brown pickup truck with tinted windows and a bug shield at Khalil's office. She confirmed Cranfield's statements about the arrival of the Iraqi employees, including Al Hussaini about November 1994. She told Davis Khalil had become unusually secretive after that.
- 18. KFOR took surveillance photographs and videotape of Khalil and his Iraqi employees including Al Hussaini. The photos were taken from a public street while the subjects of the photo were in public places.
- 19. On April 25, 1995 federal authorities issued an enhanced composite photo of John Doe #2 the full face sketch shows the suspect wearing a ball cap.
- 20. On May 1, 1995 federal authorities released a third sketch of John Doe #2; a profile view of the suspect wearing a ball cap.
- 21. After comparing videotape and still photos of Khalil's Iraqi workers with the composite sketches of John Doe #2 and talking with law enforcement persons, Davis formed the opinion Al Hussaini bore a strong resemblance to the composite photo of John Doe #2. Law enforcement persons expressed their opinions to Davis that Al Hussaini looked like the sketches of John Doe #2.
- 22. Al-Hussaini approximated the physical description of John Doe #2 and bears a strong resemblance to the composite sketch of John Doe #2. He has a tattoo of an anchor and a snake on his left arm.
- 23. In their investigation of the bombing, Davis, defendant Brad Edwards, and other reporters for KFOR discovered several witnesses who believed they had seen John Doe #2 in the company of Timothy McVeigh a few days before the bombing in a bar along N.W. 10th street, or speeding away from downtown Oklahoma City moments after the bombing

in a brown pickup truck with tinted windows and a bug shield. Each of these witnesses gave videotaped interview in which they described what they saw, picked Al Hussaini out of a photo line up as the person they saw, and assured Davis on camera they believed their observations enough to testify to them under oath before a grand jury.

- 28. The plaintiff claims, that at the time of the bombing, he was painting a house for his employer in Oklahoma City.
- 29. The plaintiff's co-workers dispute his alibi.
- 30. The person who prepared a timesheet which the plaintiff showed to the other media to substantiate his alibi later admitted she fabricated it."

The above findings of fact, from the U.S. District Court, order document more direct evidence incriminating Al Hussaini than the sum of evidence used to convict Timothy McVeigh and Terry Nichols. McVeigh had no witness testify that they saw him at the crime scene and Nichols was not even at the scene of the crime. Based on the court accepted facts and affidavit of Henry Gibbons the following details are clear:

- Middle eastern men were seen running from the bombing sight toward a brown Chevy pickup truck with tinted windows and a smoke colored bug shield. The FBI issued an all points bulletin that was broadcast on police radio for the description of that getaway vehicle but they later retracted it.
- The court found Iraqi Hussain Al Hussaini, who was employed by Khalil, fit the physical description of, and bears a strong resemblance to, John Doe 2 down to the tattoo on his arm. Several witnesses who had seen John Doe 2 with McVeigh, independently picked Al Hussaini as the John Doe 2 they had seen from public photos taken of him by KFOR-TV;
- One of the witnesses saw Al Hussaini speeding away from downtown Oklahoma City moments after the bombing in a brown pickup truck with tinted windows and a bug shield;
- The FBI detained Abraham Abdallah Ahmad as a potential "material witness" in the bombing as he was trying to leave the country. He was seen frequently by two witnesses at a

property management company owned by Samir Khalil just prior to the bombing;

- Al Hussaini, was employed at the same property management company owned by Samir Khalil (a former immigrant from Israel who is believed to be from a Palestinian territory);

- A truck matching the exact detailed description of the getaway vehicle, including the tinted windows and smoke colored bug shield, was seen by two witnesses at the same property management company owned by Samir Khalil; Several witnesses have seen Al Hussaini and McVeigh together before the bombing;

- Al Hussaini claims, at the time of the bombing, he was painting a house for his employer, Khalil, but his co-workers dispute his alibi. In addition, the person who prepared the timesheet that the Al Hussaini showed to the other media to substantiate his alibi later admitted she fabricated it.

In September 1997, Jayna Davis approached the FBI with all of this absolutely critical information and the agency refused to sign for and accept it. The Department of Justice told her attorney they did not want any more documents that would have to be turned over to the McVeigh and Nichols defense team as part of the discovery process. In 1999, Jayna Davis approached the FBI again with an attorney and, at that time, the bureau finally took receipt of the evidence. On October 29, 2001, FBI agent, Dan Vogel, was prevented by the DOJ from testifying in the Oklahoma State preliminary hearing of Terry Nichols. Agent Vogel was prepared to tell the court he received 22 witness affidavits from Jayna Davis who turned them over to the FBI Legal Department but the materials were withheld from the defense.

In 1996, the *New York Times* bought KFOR-TV from Palmer Communications but their purchase agreement did not include liability for the Al Hussaini lawsuit. Jayna also risked legal liability if any of her confidential videotaped witness interviews were released without express written consent of the witnesses. By March 1997, Jayna resigned her position and wrote letters explaining she took the interviews with her to protect the identities of her sources. The *New York Times* wanted those interviews and she agreed to turn them over if they signed a waiver to take legal liability and responsibility. They refused and Jayna subsequently turned the interviews over to the Congressional Task Force on Terrorist and Unconventional Warfare headed by Yosef Bodansky. In July 1997, the *New York Times* filed a misdemeanor theft lawsuit against her demanding the immediate return of the tapes. On March 23, 1999, a judge ruled the physical tapes belonged to the *Times* but were subject to the conditions of the confidentiality agreement between Jayna Davis and her witnesses. This was a landmark ruling because it is the first known case upheld by law for a reporter to protect confidentiality of sources from an employer. Congress still has the interviews and only Jayna Davis knows the actual identities of the witnesses in those interviews. Since then the *New York Times* has done almost nothing to bring attention to this high profile case and solve it.

Although aware of these Middle Eastern connections to the Oklahoma bombing, the corrupted Reno Justice Department did not act on it. They implied only right wing militia types were behind the bombing and allowed then President Bill Clinton to salvage his career after the 1994 Republican Revolution. But, since that time, the Ashcroft led Justice Department also has not acted on the same information. So what has paralyzed the Justice Departments of two opposing administrations from even questioning Al Hussaini? Al Hussaini admitted to Oklahoma reporter in June of 1995, he was a former member of the Iraqi army who came to America in 1994 after the Gulf War. Immigration for Iraqi soldiers was established during the Bush presidency by recommendation of the U.S. State Department. It continued during the Clinton presidency over objections of Congressmen like Rep. Elton Gallegly (R-CA, 23rd) who tried to stop it with a legislative amendment. Thus, the State Department may have imported Middle Eastern accomplices to the bombing and the Justice Department failed to act on the evidence they were involved in terrorist activities.

Based mostly on the evidence sighted above here is the apparent role of the various federal agencies and officials in regards to the Oklahoma City bombing:

The State Department almost assuredly imported the potential Middle Eastern accomplices who may have assisted McVeigh in bombing the building;

- The FBI has refused to investigate the potential Middle Eastern accomplices to the Oklahoma bombing for 7 years despite the evidence against them;
- The FBI detained Abraham Abdallah Ahmad as a potential "material witness" but released him despite the above evidence;
- The FBI refuses to make public any of the surveillance tapes that may identify the accomplice of McVeigh;

The ATF claimed an additional bomb found in the building was actually inert device they used in training exercises but have never explained why such a device was in an office building;

- The FBI has never checked the hundreds of fingerprints they have collected;
- The FBI identified a possible John Doe 2 as Todd Bunting on June 14, 1995, then retracted it and are now inconsistent in their explanations as to whether or not there was a John Doe 2;
- The FBI refused to sign for and accept the evidence that KFOR-TV investigative reporter, Jayna Davis, collected;
- An ATF agent told two witnesses the ATF had been tipped off about the bombing and paged their agents to tell them they should not come into the office;
- A federal judge removed Hoppy Heidelberg from a grand jury investigating the bombing when he requested to hear from witnesses who had seen John Doe 2 ;

KFOR-TV collected far more incriminating evidence involving these and other potential Middle Eastern accomplices as well as government agencies than the publicly available information printed in this book. America owes a great debt to reporters Jayna Davis and Brad Edwards, news director Melissa Klinzing, station manager Bill Catsafanas and the

Palmer family of Palmer Communications, all of whom committed to do what is best for America despite the risks. They have provided extensive evidence that could easily solve the Oklahoma bombing case against the will of the FBI. A simple comment from Hoppy Heidelberg has proved to be prophetic. He said: "If you can't get to the bottom of the first one there could be another one". Rather than to solve the crime, our own government agencies have become complicit in it.

THE TWA 800 PLANE CRASH

On July 17, 1996, TWA 800 crashed into the ocean off of Long Island, killing 230 people, after taking off from J.F.K. airport. Officials eventually stated the crash was caused by a center fuel tank explosion even though over 130 witnesses saw various aspects of a reddish orange missile streak, coming up from the ocean, moving towards the plane or crashing into it. Some of these witnesses were so infuriated with the phony investigation they took out an ad in the *Washington Times* to tell America what they saw.

After 9/11, there was new speculation this crash may have also been a terrorist attack instigated by the launching of a shoulder fired 'stinger' type missile. The speculation contended the government could not tell the people the truth for fear of scaring them from flying. But this explanation is disinformation. The cause would not be announced until six months after the crash and if the public had been flying safely ever since no panic would erupt. The missile also could not have been a terrorist missile because:

- The plane was flying at 13,700 feet outside the range of a shoulder fired missile;
- At least one missile was fired from sea, not from land
- The missile was too long for a 'stinger' as seen in the photo taken by Linda Kabot;
- The launching equipment would be far to big and impractical to place on a rented boat;
- The debris pattern indicates the missile was inert and there was no initial explosion;

The FAA technician who analyzed the radar concluded there were "conflicting radar tracks that indicated a missile". Reddish orange residue containing traces of elements determined to be consistent with rocket fuel, were also found to confirm it was a missile and not a bomb that brought the plane down. But the missile that brought down TWA 800 was a U.S. Navy missile, as explained in Chapter Two and James Sanders book, *The Downing of TWA 800*. Sanders, who offers the only logical and credible explanation for the plane crash, shows how TWA 800 was brought down by a missile after a target adjustment failure, during missile defense system testing, that is documented in a communiqué from the Navy to the FAA. If a terrorist organization had brought down TWA 800, there would be no need for a massive cover-up to hide missile evidence from the American public.

WOULD OUR GOVERNMENT ALLOW ITS OWN CITIZENS TO BE KILLED?

The actions of U.S. government agencies documented in this book raise the ugly question of whether or not our own government would knowingly allow its citizens to be killed and then cover it up. Chapter 11 already explained the leading cause of death in this century is simply, government. The book, *Death by Government,* documents how governments have killed well over 100 million of their own people in "peacetime" during the 20th century. Many of those were political enemies living in Communist countries. What about citizens who may not be political enemies in less oppressive governments? Such historical precedents may have begun as early as A.D. 64.

Almost everyone has heard the phrase "Nero fiddled while Rome burned" referring to the fire that started in bleachers at Circus Maximus in AD 64. Nero was emperor of Rome from 54 A.D. until his death in 68 A.D. Some historians believe the lack of concern Nero showed for Rome, at that time, was because he actually had the fire set. His objective was to embark on a new building campaign to replace the city he considered ugly, with a more artistic city to honor him. When many of the citizens began to believe Nero had set the fire, Nero blamed the fire on Christians and instigated a time period when many Christians, including the apostle Peter were slaughtered by being crucified, burned to death or thrown into an arena where they were killed by lions. While it is difficult to verify events that occurred 2000 years ago, similar, more recent examples are available.

On February 27, 1933, less than one month after President Paul von Hindenburg appointed Adolph Hitler as chancellor, the Berlin Reichstag, site of the German parliament, was burned down. A Dutch communist named Marinus van der Lubbe was at the scene, charged with arson, found guilty and executed as a classic lone crazed terrorist. More evidence has surfaced in recent years indicating the fire was set by Nazi storm troopers, who immediately arrested 4,000 Communists that very night and over 40,000 opposition members shortly thereafter. The fire allowed the Nazi Party, the second strongest party in Germany, after the 1930 elections, to pass the *Ermächtigungsgesetz* Enabling Act on March 24. That act allowed Hitler to essentially negate the German parliament, establish his own laws and seize total control of the country. It seems obvious that was the intent all along and the fire was the facilitating event that eventually led to World War II.

America entered World War II after the Japanese attack at Pearl Harbor on December 7, 1941. Recently released German intelligence documents reveal they had intercepted communications from British Prime Minister Winston Churchill to President Franklin D. Roosevelt. Churchill had actually informed Roosevelt of the attack on November 26 after the British intercepted a Japanese communiqué from Admiral Yamamoto. The exact communiqué stated: "The task force, keeping its movements strictly secret and maintaining close guard against submarines and aircraft, shall advance into Hawaiian waters and upon the very opening of hostilities, shall attack the main force of the United States Fleet in Hawaii and deal it a mortal blow." The U.S. may have also intercepted this communiqué since military intelligence had broken the Japanese purple code; however, documents needed to make this determination are still being withheld as a "national secret". Roosevelt allowed Pearl Harbor to occur so America would enter World War II and save Wall Street political supporters who had too much to lose in British investments.

America entered World War I after the Germans sunk the Lusitania, a Cunard line passenger ship carrying 1,195 people on route from the U.S.A. to Liverpool, England. The ship that was built to specifications of the British Admiralty was sunk with a single torpedo when ammunition and supplies it was covertly carrying to Great Britain exploded after being hit. Before the ship sailed, the Wilson administration had ignored a complaint by the Germans about military cargo being loaded. The German embassy then issued an advertisement to dozens of major newspapers warning passengers they were at war with Great Britain. But the newspapers, many of which had just fallen under control of rival shipbuilder J.P. Morgan, suppressed the ad under some pressure from the U.S. State Department. G. Edward Griffin explains how only the *Des Moines Register* printed the warning on the correct day. Before the Lusitania neared the coast of Ireland, at reduced speed, the British Admiralty canceled her rendezvous with the British destroyer, Juno. Under direct supervision of Winston Churchill they allowed the ship to sail unescorted straight into the area where a German U-Boat had torpedoed two ships the day before. The deaths of all 1,195 passengers and crew triggered the entry of America into the war and gave the British the assistance they needed.

In 1964, Vietnam escalated into war through a false trigger when we were told that North Vietnamese fired on our ships in the Gulf of Tonkin. The reports turned out to be false but Lyndon Johnson used the incident to create the Gulf of Tonkin resolution and activate 550,000 troops 58,000 of which never returned alive. The stage was set with the removal of Vietnamese President Diem, which was triggered by a now declassified Top Secret cable sent on August 24, 1963 to Henry Cabot Lodge from the State Department (apparently by Undersecretary Averell Harriman). It stated U.S. could not support the government if Diem did not remove his brother and wife from power. Diem's brother, Ngo Dinh Nhu, had taken steps to initiate a cease-fire with the North Vietnamese in 1962. The cable instructed Lodge to tell Vietnamese military commanders they will receive support during any interim period of central government breakdown. The commanders quickly used this as an invitation to assassinate both Diem and Nhu who believed we were there allies. War ensued and the CIA eventually gained control of Southeast Asian drug trafficking as explained in Chapter 10 under the guise of fighting communism.

A similar false trigger was used on January 15, 1999, in Yugoslavia, where there was a battle in the town of Racak between the KLA and the Serbs who were accompanied by the members of the Associated Press. The next day the KLA arranged their dead to make it look like they were massacred by Serb forces in an area the Serbs never controlled during the battle. Bill Clinton quickly used this as the pretext to begin bombing sorties with NATO and take the emphasis completely off of the Cox Committee report just released. NATO eventually took over the Trepca mining complex and the KLA reportedly gained control of European drug routes from Albania through Kosovo.

The first fatal misuse of American troops may have occurred in 1898, while the Spanish controlled Cuba. President William McKinley sent the U.S.S. Maine into Havana on January 25 to protect Americans there. On the night of February 15, 1898, at around 9:40pm, the Maine exploded killing hundreds of sailors and marines. Since the Spanish were suspected of setting mine explosives to destroy the ship, McKinley responded with an embargo on Cuba. Spain reacted with a declaration of war against America and America countered similarly to initiate the Spanish American war. The U.S. won the war quickly, gained control of Cuba, and freed it from Spanish reign, which was a long time strategic American objective.

In 1976, Admiral Hyman Rickover published a book about how the Maine was destroyed and determined through more modern scientific knowledge that the damage to the ship was inconsistent with an external explosion of a mine. The recently released 1962 Top Secret document from the Joint Chiefs of Staff about Operation Northwoods went further in explaining the Maine incident in its attempt to justify military intervention in Cuba. The document shown on the next pages stated specifically: "A 'Remember the Maine' incident could be arranged in several forms". "We could blow up a U.S. ship in Guantanamo Bay and blame Cuba."

OPERATION NORTHWOODS

Operation Northwoods is defined in a declassified Top Secret document from March 13, 1962 entitled *Justification for Military Intervention in Cuba*. It was written by Admiral Lemnitzer, the Chairman of the Joint Chiefs of Staff, for the Secretary of Defense, Robert McNamara, upon request of Edward Lansdale, chief of the Cuba Project. It can be viewed at the National Security Archive of George Washington University as well as many other web sites.

The Operation Northwoods document is the most remarkable evidence of the lengths to which powerful elements of our military will go to gain support for initiating a self-serving military action. It involves potential loss of life to both Cubans and Americans as well as serious self-inflicted damage to American military equipment and supplies. Its purpose was to describe how to gain justification for an invasion of Cuba and it mentions tactics that have consistently been employed throughout the last four decades. The document is so revealing I have included, after the discussion paragraphs, all nine major points of the enclosure memorandum so readers can make their own judgments about its impact:

The document introduces the premise with these two discussion paragraphs:

"The suggested courses of action appended to Enclosure A are based on the premise that US military intervention will result from a period of heightened US-Cuban tensions which place the United States in the position of suffering justifiable grievances. World opinion, and the United Nations forum should be favorably affected by developing the international image of the Cuban government as rash and irresponsible, and as an alarming and unpredictable threat to the peace of the Western Hemisphere.

While the foregoing premise can be utilized, at the present time it will continue to hold good only as long as there can be reasonable certainty US military intervention in Cuba would not directly involve the Soviet

Union. There is as yet no bilateral mutual support agreement binding the USSR to the defense of Cuba, Cuba has not yet become a member of the Warsaw Pact, nor have the Soviets established Soviet bases in Cuba in the pattern of US bases in Western Europe. Therefore, since time appears to be an important factor in resolution of the Cuba problem, all projects are suggested within the time frame of the next few months."

Annex to Appendix to Enclosure A: Pretexts to Justify US Military Intervention in Cuba

1. Since it would seem desirable to use legitimate provocation, as the basis for US military intervention in Cuba, a cover and deception plan, to include requisite preliminary actions such as has been developed in response to Task 33 c could be executed as an initial effort to provoke Cuban reactions. Harassment plus deceptive actions to convince the Cubans of imminent invasion would be emphasized. Our military posture throughout execution of the plan will allow a rapid change from exercise to intervention if Cuban response justifies.

2. A series of well-coordinated incidents will be planned to take place in and around Guantanamo to give genuine appearance of being done by hostile Cuban forces.

   a. Incidents to establish a credible attack (not on chronological order)

      1. Start rumors (many). Use clandestine radio.

      2. Land friendly Cubans in uniform "over the fence" to stage attack on base.

      3. Capture Cuban friendly saboteurs inside the base.

      4. Start riots near the base main gate (friendly Cubans).

      5. Blow up ammunition inside the base; start fires.

      6. Burn aircraft on air base (sabotage)

      7. Lob mortar shells from outside into base. Some damage to installations.

      8. Capture assault teams approaching from the sea of vicinity of Guantanamo City

      9. Capture militia group which storms the base

  10. Sabotage ship in harbor; large fires – naphthalene
  11. Sink ship near harbor entrance. Conduct funerals
      for mock victims (may be in lieu of 10)
  b. United States would respond by executing offensive
     operations to secure water and power supplies,
     destroying artillery and mortar emplacements
     which threaten the base.
  c. Commence large scale United States military operations

3. A 'Remember the Maine' incident could be arranged in several forms:
  a. We could blow up a U.S. ship in Guantanamo Bay and
     blame Cuba.
  b. We could blow up a drone (unmanned) vessel anywhere
     in the Cuban waters. We could arrange to create such
     incident in the vicinity of Havana or Santiago as a
     spectacular result of Cuban attack from the air or sea or
     both. The presence of Cuban planes of ships merely
     investigating the intent of the vessel could be fairly
     compelling evidence the ship was taken under
     attack. The nearness of Havana or Santiago would add
     credibility especially to those people who might have
     heard the blast or seen the fire. The US could follow up
     with an air/sea rescue operation covered by US fighters
     to "evacuate" remaining members of the non-existent
     crew. Casualty lists in US newspapers would cause a
     helpful wave of national indignation.

4. We could develop a Communist Cuban terror campaign in the Miami area, in other Florida cities and even in Washington. The terror campaign could be pointed at Cuban refugees seeking haven in the United States. We could sink a boatload of Cubans enroute to Florida (real or simulated). We could foster attempts on lives of Cuban refugees in the United States even to the extent of wounding in instances to be widely publicized. Exploding a few plastic bombs in carefully chosen spots, the arrest of Cuban agents and the release of prepared documents substantiating Cuban involvement also would be helpful in projecting the idea of an irresponsible government.

5. A "Cuban-based, Castro supported" filibuster could be simulated against a neighboring Caribbean nation (in the vein of the 14th of June invasion of the Dominican Republic). We know that Castro is backing subversive efforts clandestinely against Haiti, Dominican Republic, Guatemala and Nicaragua at present and possible others. These efforts can be magnified and additional ones contrived for exposure. For example, advantage can be taken of the sensitivity of the Dominican Air Force to intrusions within their national air space. "Cuban: B-26 of C-46 type aircraft could make cane burning raids at night. Soviet block incendiaries could be found. This could be coupled with "Cuban" messages to the Communist underground in the Domican Republic and "Cuban" shipments of arms which would be found, or intercepted, on the beach.

6. Use of MIG type aircraft by US pilots could provide additional provocation. Harassment of civil air, attacks on surface shipping and destruction of US military drone aircraft by MIG type planes would be useful as complementary actions. An F-86 properly painted would convince air passengers that they saw a Cuban MIG, especially if the pilot of the transport were to announce such fact. The primary drawback to this suggestion appears to be the security risk inherent in obtaining or modifying an aircraft. However, reasonable copies of the MIG could be produced from US resources in about three months.

7. Hijacking attempts against civil air and surface craft should appear to continue as harassing measures condoned by the government of Cuba. Concurrently, genuine defections of Cuban civil and military air and surface craft should be encouraged.

8. It is possible to create an incident which will demonstrate convincingly that a Cuban aircraft has attacked and shot down a chartered civil airliner en route from the United States to Jamaica, Guatemala, Panama or Venezuela. The destination would be chosen only to cause the flight plan route to cross Cuba. The passengers could be a group of college students off on a holiday or any grouping of persons with a common interest to support chartering a non-scheduled flight.

    a. An aircraft at Elgin AFB would be painted and numbered as an exact duplicate for a civil registered aircraft be longing to a CIA proprietary organization in the Miami area. At a designated time the duplicate would be

substituted for the actual civil aircraft and would be
loaded with selected passengers. All boarded under
carefully prepared aliases. The actual registered aircraft
would be converted into a drone.
b. Take off times of the drone aircraft will be scheduled to
allow a rendezvous south of Florida. From the
rendezvous point the passenger-carrying aircraft will
descend to minimum altitude and go directly into an
auxiliary field at Elgin AFB where arrangements will
have been made to evacuate passengers and return the
aircraft to its original status. The drone aircraft
meanwhile will continue to fly the filed flight plan. When
over Cuba the drone will be transmitting on the
international distress frequency a "MAY DAY" message
stating he is under attack by Cuban MIG aircraft. The
transmission will be interrupted by destruction of
the aircraft which will be triggered by radio signal. This
will allow ICAO radio stations in the Western
Hemisphere to tell the US what has happened to
the aircraft instead of the US trying to "sell" the incident.

9. It is possible to create an incident which will make it appear
that Communist Cuban MIGs have destroyed a USAF aircraft
over international waters in an unprovoked attack.
a. Approximately 4 or 5 F-101 aircraft will be dispatched in
trail from Homestead AFB, Florida, to the vicinity of
Cuba. Their mission will be to reverse course and
simulate fakir aircraft for an air defense exercise in
southern Florida. These aircraft would conduct
variations of these flights at frequent intervals. Crews
would be briefed to remain at least 12 miles off the
Cuban coast; however, they would be required to carry
live ammunition in the event that hostile actions were
taken by Cuban MIGs.
b. On one such flight, a pre-briefed pilot would fly tail-end
Charley at considerable interval between aircraft. While
near the Cuban Island this pilot would broadcast that he
had been jumped by MIGs and was going down. No
other calls would be made. The pilot would then fly
directly west at extremely low altitude and land at

a secure base, an Elgin auxiliary. The aircraft would be met by the proper people, quickly stored and given a new tail number. The pilot who had performed the mission under an alias, would resume his proper identify and return to his normal place of business. The pilot and aircraft would then have disappeared.

c. At precisely the same time, the aircraft was presumably shot down a submarine or small surface aircraft would disburse F-101 parts, parachute, etc. at approximately 15 to 20 miles off the Cuban coast and depart. The pilots re turning to Homestead would have a true story as far as they knew. Search ships and aircraft could be dispatched and parts of aircraft found.

Enclosure B concludes with:

"It is understood that the Department of State also is preparing suggested courses of action to develop justifi-cation for US military intervention in Cuba"

During this time period, the American military supposedly had a growing concern about a buildup of Soviet sponsored missiles that led to the Cuban missile crisis in October of 1962. However, the general discussion section of this Top Secret document from March of 1962 clearly states: "… nor have the Soviets established Soviet bases in Cuba in the pattern of US bases in Western Europe".

Another known reason for invading Cuba was to overthrow Fidel Castro because he was a Communist. However, Castro was the very man the CIA brought to power just a couple of years earlier. The 1977 House Select Committee investigation on the assassination of President John F. Kennedy shows a picture of CIA operative Frank Sturgis celebrating with Casto upon the overthrow of the Batista government in the late 50s.

The only other known reason for invading Cuba was to restore U.S. business interests nationalized by Castro when he gained power. The Cuban Project had gained well-documented support from the mafia who were also thrown out by Castro. Former Vice President, Richard Nixon, had already established initiatives to help achieve this objective such as Operation 40 but Nixon lost a very close 1960 election by 118,574 votes to

Kennedy who was a somewhat reluctant supporter of a Cuban invasion.

In April of 1961, the CIA launched the Bay of Pigs invasion that failed because Kennedy is believed to have changed the invasion site and withdrawn support for a D-Day air strike against the Castro air force. But several recently declassified documents, including the Taylor Report indicate otherwise. Kennedy, may have actually been betrayed by high-ranking "Skull and Bones" connected individuals without his knowledge. National Security Advisor, McGeorge Bundy, a Bonesman, and Director of Plans, Richard Bissell Jr. were in command and even deceived our own high-ranking military officers about aspects of the plan and invasion based on Taylor commission testimony. They are more likely to have changed the original invasion site and denied the D-Day air support without telling Kennedy. Bissell's father, Richard Bissell Sr., another Bonesman and powerful Yale alumnus, was director of the Neuro-Psychiatric Institute of the Hartford Retreat for the Insane, which evolved into the MK-Ultra mind control program of the CIA.

The Taylor Report reveals the CIA may have set up the operation to fail since it would be highly improbable that 1,500 anti-Castro Cubans could overthrow the Cuban military, particularly at the Bay of Pigs site. The bay could not be easily defended and had no capability to generate local support for an uprising. The uprising was "utterly essential" according to Secretary of State Dean Rusk. Rusk offered Bissell and Gen Charles Cabell the opportunity to speak with Kennedy directly about the D-Day air strikes but they declined. Since CIA director, Allen Dulles, could not explain how the operation would have succeeded, it is more likely he believed that a failed attempt would force Kennedy to order a full scale invasion, the real desired military objective explained later in the Lemnitzer document. Kennedy fired Bissell, Dulles, who incredibly was giving a presentation in Puerto Rico during the invasion, and Cabell, brother of Earle Cabell, the mayor of Dallas on the day Kennedy was assassinated.

The CIA connected Kennedy assassination would have been the perfect pretext to invade Cuba as desired by Operation Northwoods, had it not been for Officer J.D. Tippit who stopped Lee Harvey Oswald, when Oswald was halfway to the house of Jack Ruby. Ruby was the apparent designee to take Oswald to Red Bird airport where residents have stated a plane was waiting with engines running. Had Oswald not been arrested in the theatre, he would may have received air transportation from two of his old Louisiana Civil Air Patrol buddies, both of whom were deeply involved in transporting the anti-Castro Cubans. Author Daniel Hopsicker believes the man waiting to pick Oswald up at Red Bird was the legendary Barry Seal, of the Operation 40 team described in Chapter 10. Waiting at a Houston skating rink, was David Ferrie a CIA operative who is known to have continually called back to the headquarters of Carlos Marcello while waiting for instructions. An intermediate plane change in Houston could have easily resulted in passage to Cuba and the CIA would have the long desired excuse to achieve its overall objective. Invade Cuba to find the alleged assassin of the President of the United States.

INEVITABLE CONCLUSIONS:

The evidence presented in the last two chapters indicates the 9/11 attacks are highly suspicious terrorist acts that generated a subsequent war on terror, which has convenient financial motivations. This concept is very difficult for us as Americans to accept but consider that the Bush administration has:

- "Consistently" "thwarted" "obstructed" and "sabotaged" specific FBI investigations in Minnesota and Chicago that could have prevented the 9/11 attacks;
- Ignored precise forewarnings of the attack from the Arizona FBI, CIA documents and foreign intelligence;
- Thwarted Congressional investigations and ignored the insider trading scandal that might reveal who was behind the attacks;
- Fabricated a "confession" to implicate as the source of the attacks, a business partner family member and 20 year operative who was working with 4 Western intelligence agencies in 1999;
- Invaded Afghanistan for oil profits explained by Congressional testimony and for opium control in a manner

historically consistent with military conflicts that facilitate CIA drug trafficking;

- Initiated a war on terror that benefited the Bush and bin Laden families as well as former government defense officials;
- Protected Israelis who may have committed espionage or had precise foreknowledge of 9/11;
- Pressured Congress to create a police state in the likeness of Nazi Germany that also claims the founding fathers and Christians are terrorists.

This summary of facts represents a serious indictment of the Bush administration. Assuming the majority of information presented is largely irrefutable, it leaves us with the following state of affairs that may be unprecedented in American history for the future. Consider:

The U.S. and Israeli governments had precise foreknowledge of 9/11

The U.S. and Israeli governments knew precisely what would happen on 9/11. The Bush administration new the exact type of suicide hijacking that would take place from its own September 1999 public CIA report. The FBI was warned during 2001 of suspicious hijackers who were receiving training in Arizona and Minnesota. The Arizona office forwarded that information to FBI headquarters and the Minnesota office filed a complaint to the FBI director that headquarters thwarted their investigation. The German ambassador to the U.S. briefed the president on August 6, 2001 as to the exact potential dates of the attack. The Bush administration knew the type of attack, the originating source of the attack (major commercial airports) and the potential dates of the attack. This is enough information to stop the attacks if the administration chose to do so.

The Bush administration invaded Afghanistan for profit

No substantial evidence was ever produced by the British or American governments that linked Osama bin Laden to the 9/11 attacks. The smoking gun videotape clearly contained an imposter who was 40 pounds heavier.

The imposter has a short neck, square face, protruding cheeks, straight eyebrows and fat hands with short fingers. Bin Laden has a long neck, an oblong face, inverted cheeks, rounded eyebrows and thin hands with long fingers. The obvious profit motive for using bin Laden as the culprit was to build the oil pipeline across Afghanistan as 1998 Congressional testimony indicated. The obvious covert motive was to gain control of the world's largest source of opium, which is consistent with the decades long trend of using military conflicts to support CIA drug trafficking. Bin Laden was a willing accomplice since his family profited from the war on terror through investments in the Carlyle group and more military construction contracts in the Middle East.

The Bush administration is covering-up the truth about 9/11

The Bush administration has attempted to thwart any type of Congressional investigation into the 9/11 attacks although it is the single greatest act of war committed against our nation. The administration is not seriously investigating the insider trading scandal where individuals attempted to reap millions of dollars in profits by shorting the stocks of United and American airlines as well as major WTC tenants. The investments of George H.W. Bush such as those in the Carlyle group are conflicts of interests that profit from the war on terror but are kept secret from the American public.

The Bush administration and Congress are not trying to eliminate terrorism

If the Bush administration and Congress were seriously investigating who profited from shorting the stocks of the airlines and major WTC tenants just before 9/11 those persons would be in prison awaiting trial. The administration attempted to terminate two INS agents who publicly stated they had inadequate resources to protect the Canadian border. The administration took little action against those responsible for issuing visa extensions to two of the hijackers months after 9/11. Instead, Congress, under pressure from the Bush administration, passed legislation to implement a police state against citizens similar to the one implemented in Nazi Germany.

The Bushes are deceiving their Christian supporters

George H.W. and George W. Bush are members of the macabre "Skull and Bones" club that has alarming racist, drug related historical origins and is known to conduct initiations in coffins. They attended the Bohemian Grove summer gatherings where attendees participate in occult activities. Videotapes of the July 2000 gatherings attended by the Bushes show that the group worships a 40' owl and burns an effigy of a human being to cremate their cares away. A Bush administration FEMA member can be seen on a July 2001 videotape teaching local police and firefighters that Christians are terrorists. The Bushes have historically profited from war or drug related activity and the involvement with the Carlyle group is no exception. At least three companies run by Prescott Bush had their assets seized under the Trading with the Enemy Act in 1942 as he helped fund, and profited from, the Nazi rise to power.

Israel is not our ally

Israel has conducted massive spy operations against the U. S.. They wire tapped the White House, State Department and even the FBI lines used to monitor Israel. They acquired an unauthorized copy of Promis software. They gave classified information stolen by Jonathan Pollard to Russia. Their explosive and electronic surveillance specialists targeted DEA offices and labs nation wide. Former Israeli army members even cheered while filming the destruction of the WTC. Israel has a connection to the 1993 WTC bombing through the woman whose phone number was listed on the Ryder Truck rental form. They have a connection to Oklahoma City bombing through the employer of one of the potential accomplices. An Israeli Mossad officer is also the most likely perpetrator behind the murders of five Special Forces colonels who probed a CIA–Mossad drug operation.

Israel is protected by our media and government

Most of our news media outlets have suppressed evidence of Israel espionage, foreknowledge of the 9/11 attacks and connections to terrorist acts against America. Federal agencies have not adequately investigated Israeli connections to the 1993 WTC bombing or the 1995 Oklahoma City bombing. Although those with foreknowledge of a crime would normally be prime suspects, the Ashcroft Justice Department actually deported the former Israeli army officers who cheered while filming the WTC collapse. FBI, INS and DEA agents all told Fox News that it would be career suicide to investigate Israeli wiretapping espionage.

The Bush (and Clinton) FBI is protecting terrorists

The FBI appears to have actually directed the 1993 bombing of the WTC based on the secretly recorded conversations of the their own informant. The FBI has not investigated the potential accomplices of Timothy McVeigh despite the fact that KFOR-TV almost literally solved the case for them. The FBI has made no arrest in the anthrax attacks even though the evidence immediately limited the number of suspects to a few dozen former military scientists who are involved with the CIA. FBI headquarters even thwarted investigations in Minnesota and Chicago that could have prevented 9/11 altogether.

The Bush and Clinton State Dept has imported terrorists

The State Department imported a Sheikh who was found guilty of conspiracy to commit terrorist acts even though two embassies warned the department of his political activities. The State Department also imported the potential accomplices of Timothy McVeigh. One was seen with him before the bombing in Oklahoma City. He was seen again leaving the scene of the crime in a getaway matching a police APB. He worked at a company where a truck matching the APB was seen by two other witnesses. Identifications were made down to the tattoo on his arm as well as the tinted windows and smoke colored bug shield of the truck.

The CIA is out of control

The CIA was set up by a Wall Street lawyer and has been run in close conjunction with Wall Street power brokers ever since. It was designed to operate above the law and it is not accountable to Congress or even the president. Its media assets help make it one of the primary sources of disinformation in this country. Together with the NSA, it has the power to create deceptive information, instigate foreign policy, deceive the president, create war and lose wars intentionally, all while misinforming the American public. It has subverted legitimate governments around the world for decades while running drug trafficking operations in the same region of military conflict.

These final opinions are not intended to reflect harshly on the many honest, sincere, hardworking individuals within these agencies who are frequently restricted or diverted by their leaders. Many government agencies are corrupted at the top each time there is a new president. The political appointees frequently have their own agenda for profit, power or other motives and rarely operate the agency in the best interests of the citizens of the United States.

There appears to be three factions of elitists who constantly struggle for power within the U.S. government. These factions are:

- Communists who want to reduce American power to a level consistent with the rest of the world nations so that American sovereignty can be subordinated to an appointed global government;
- Fascists who use our military for foreign business purposes as well as domestic oppression of Americans who have differing political views;
- Israelis who want to preserve Israel at any cost and value America primarily for its ability to protect Israel.

These groups oppose, collaborate or overlap each other on individual issues as they see fit to meet their separate agendas. Although they completely dominate the Washington political landscape and the national news media, none of them represent the true interests of America.

THE INFIINTE WAR ON TERROR

The anthrax, WTC and Pentagon attacks have sparked the Bush administration to implement an infinite worldwide war on terror that allows elements in our government to identify enemies and attack them anywhere in the world without the citizens ever being able to establish whether or not the enemy is real or imagined. A more perfect script could not be written for the insiders of the most powerful nation on earth to plunder any other country in the world at the whim of a group of well-connected leaders. The enemy is no longer a nation but any individuals that are selected and branded as terrorists.

The domestic front is even scarier because the enemies can now be anywhere internal to the U.S. and the government must seek them out. The U.S. military has already conducted joint exercises with local police across the country in states like Texas, California, Maryland, North Carolina and Alabama. Some of these exercises are shown on the Alex Jones 9-11 Road to Tyranny video. You can actually watch chilling house-to-house searches by American military units reminiscent of those conducted in Nazi Germany. Many of the military personnel do not even realize the implications of what they are doing.

The Bush administration did not hesitate to implement the Orwellian thought police. On October 8, 2001, George W. Bush signed Executive Order 13228 to establish the new Homelands Security division under former Pennsylvania Governor Tom Ridge. Once established, one of its first actions was to shut down selected web sites on the grounds that they were facilitating terrorism. Some had antagonistic comments or views that were outside of the mainstream reporting. It is unclear how a public web site would facilitate terrorism since terrorists would use private Email to electronically communicate with each other.

During most of his speeches, George W. Bush is stiff, rehearsed and insincere in the same manner as Bill Clinton. When he spoke during the week after he initiated the Afghan bombing campaign, I was able to predict the exact instant when he said: "We're going to smoke 'em out". It is clear to me

George W. Bush is not running America. He is a puppet of his father's regime. He has surrounded himself with cronies of his father, many of whom are members of the CFR. These people and his father are almost certainly calling the shots behind the scenes for the profit of their secret investments in funds such as the Carlyle group. Is it a coincidence that exactly 10 years earlier on September 11, 1991 George H.W. Bush made his famous speech about the New World Order that he envisioned? I do not think that even he could have envisioned, at that time, a better scenario for implementing it.

The war on terror will be no different than the war on poverty, drugs and terrorism. In the late 60's during the war on poverty, America started to become poorer. An era of inflationary budget deficits erupted from unconstitutional social programs and pet projects of the President or a Congressional member as lenders such as the Federal Reserve reaped the benefits. In the 70's, 80's and 90's, during the war on drugs, America became more drug dependent. As politicians denounced drug use and spent billions on drug enforcement at the front door of America, CIA connected insiders ran drugs into the back door of America. Now in the new millennium during the war on terror, America will be the victim of more terrorist attacks. It seems each time politicians decide to conduct a war on something, the war is set up to facilitate its growth. Then powerful insiders operating both inside and outside of the government can subvert and profit from the new program. The Bush war on terror has the characteristics of another profit scheme.

On November 11, 2001, George W. Bush gave one of his better speeches at the United Nations. In it he said:

"Let us never tolerate outrageous conspiracy theories concerning the attacks of September 11; malicious lies that attempt to shift the blame away from the terrorists themselves and from the guilty."

The so-called public "enemy" of the United States, Osama bin Laden, may have actually given Americans a clue as to how to find the real culprits behind the attacks of 9/11. Here are his words from a September 28, 2001, Pakistani *UnMat* article that was suppressed in America until after bombing started:

"The United States should try to trace the perpetrators of these attacks within itself; the people who are a part of the U.S. system, but are dissenting against it. Or those who are working for some other system; persons who want to make the present century as a century of conflict between Islam and Christianity so that their own civilization, nation, country, or ideology could survive."

This book attempts to provide many of the unreported facts so you can decide who is telling the truth. All of the victims silently cry out for justice, not profits for those who allowed them to be killed.

REFERENCES:

Hearing on U.S. Policy on Illegal Aliens, Senate SubCommittee, November 13, 2001

Bombing of the Embassies of the USA in Nairobi, Kenya and Dares Saalem, Tanzania, FBI, November 12, 1998

Admiral L.L. Lemnitzer, Justification for Military Intervention in Cuba, GWU National Security Archive, March 13, 1962

Gen.Maxwell Taylor Adm A.G. Robert Kennedy, The Taylor Report, GWU National Security Archive, June 13, 1961

U. S. vs. Omar Ahmad Ali Abdel Rahman et al., Second Circuit U.S. Court of Appeals, August 16, 1999

Attack on the USS Cole, Yemen Gateway, www.alibab.com/yemen/cole1.htm

Tom Flocco, Profits of Death – Insider Trading and 9/11, From the Wilderness, December 6, 2001

Michael Ruppert, Criminal Insider Trading Leads Directly to CIA's Highest Levels, From the Wilderness, October 9, 2001

Christopher Bollyn, *Only U.S. Anthrax Maker Called Negligent*, American Free Press, November 5, 2001

Barbara Hatch Rosenberg, *Analysis of Anthrax Attacks*, Federation of American Scientists - www.fas.org

Peter Kornbluh (editor), Bay of Pigs Declassified, New Press

Michael D. Morrissey, Bay of Pigs Revisited (essay),
  University of Washington eserver.org, May 2, 1993

Michael Collins Piper, Corruption, Intrigue, Murder
  Characterize Infamous INSLAW Case (5 articles),
  American Free Press, February 18, 2002

Alex Jones, *911 Road to Tyranny* (video), Alex Jones
  Production

Ralph Blumenthal, Tapes Depict Proposal to Thwart Bomb
Used in Trade Center Blast, New York Times, October, 28, 1993

Ralph Blumenthal, Tapes in Bombing Plot Show Informer and
  FBI at Odds, New York Times, October 27, 1993

Sandra Sobieraj, *White House Mail Sorters Anthrax Free*,
  Associated Press,, October 24, 2001

Analysis of the Provisions of the USA Patriot Act, Electronic
  Frontier Foundation, October 31, 2001

Nat Hentoff, *Terrorizing the Bill of Rights*, Village Voice,
  November 9, 2001

Phil Hirshkorn, Trial Reveals a Conspiracy of Calls But Only
  Tidbits About bin Laden, CNN New York, April 16, 2001

Jerry Seper, *INS Whistleblowers face 'Retaliation'*, Washington
  Times, April 8-14, 2002

Scott Ritter, American Free Press, Blinkered Bush Wrong on
  Iraq, April 1, 2002

Yemen Gateway, www.al-bab.com/yemen

James Sanders, The Downing of TWA 800, Zebra

James Sanders, Silenced – Flight 800 and the Subversion of
  Justice (video)

ABBREVIATIONS

ACDA	Arms Control Disarmament Agency
ACEP	Advisory Committee on Export Policy
ACTION	Activate Congress to Improve Our Nation
ADFA	Arkansas Development Finance Authority
AP	Associated Press
ATF	Bureau of Alcohol, Tobacco and Firearms
BBC	British Broadcasting Company
BCCI	Bank of Credit and Commerce
CATIC	China Aero Technology Import/Export Corporation
CCP	Chinese Communist Party
CFR	Council on Foreign Relations
CHG	Citizens of Honest Government
CIA	Central Intelligence Agency
CIM	Chief of Implementation Mission
CITIC	China International Trust Investment Corporation
COCOM	Coordinating Committee on Multi-Lateral Exports Controls
COSCO	China Ocean Shipping Company
CS	Orthocholorbenzylidene Malonoitrile
DEA	Drug Enforcement Administration
DIA	Defense Intelligence Agency
DNC	Democrat National Committee
DOD	Department of Defense
DTSA	Defense Technology Security Administration
EDS	Electronic Data Systems
FAA	Federal Aviation Administration
FBI	Federal Bureau of Investigation
FDA	Food and Drug Administration
FDIC	Federal Deposit Insurance Corporation
FDR	Franklin Delano Roosevelt
FEC	Federal Elections Commission
FEMA	Federall Emergency Management Association
FLIR	Forward Looking Infrared
FRY	Federal Republic of Yugoslavia
GAO	General Accounting Office

IBM	International Business Machines
ICBM	Intercontinental Ballistic Missile
IG	Inspector Genera
INS	Immigration and Naturalization Service
IPI	International Paper Incorporated
IRS	Internal Revenue Service
ISA	(Army) Intelligence Support Activity
ISI	Inter-Services Intelligence (Pakistan)
KLA	Kosovo Liberation Army
LAPD	Los Angeles Police Department
MIA	Missing in Action
MIRV	Multiple Independent Re-entry Vehicle
MIT	Massachusetts Institute of Technology
MSNBC	Microsoft / National Broadcasting Company
MTOPS	Million Theoretical Operations Per Second
NATO	North Atlantic Treaty Organization
NET	National Empowerment Television
NRA	National Rifle Association
NSA	National Security Administration
NSC	National Security Council
NTSB	National Transportation and Safety Board
NYPD	New York Police Department
OSS	Office of Strategic Services
PBS	Public Broadcast Service
PLA	Peoples Liberation Army
POW	Prisoners of War
RTC	Resolution Trust Company
SEC	Securities and Exchange Commission
U.N.	United Nations
UPI	United Press International
VFR	Visual Flight Rules

Index